Praise f

MW00460501

"Who would have ever thought strands of church meeting minutes could be so compelling? The story Cindy Safronoff is writing is a tale seldom told: not only the history of Christian Science in Seattle, but of the growth of the religion outside of Boston. Safronoff uses the primary focus on church-building as a vessel to detail the momentum of that growth and both the values and the hard work—the dedication—behind it. And any church member—or member of any other kind of organization—will come away inspired to take the time to note their group's history and present-day events for future historians."

    Karla Vallance, author of the forthcoming book, *A Changed Life: The Mary Baker Eddy Story* [2021]

"Safronoff's new book *Dedication* digs deep and delves into new territory, the formation of Christian Science churches in one city. Drawing on information never before used, this fresh history overcomes stale myths and misconceptions. This is an excellent example of a new trend of bottom up history writing where the story tells itself and the reader is less subject to the writer's preconceived notions, a microhistory well done."

    Keith M. McNeil, author of *A Story Untold: A History of the Quimby-Eddy Debate*

"Part One of *Dedication* opens an ancestral treasure chest for those who wonder why their Christian Science church experience looks the way it does now, and how certain customs, certain attitudes, and certain values came about from the beginning. The distance between the Christian Science world headquarters in Boston and the branches in Seattle sheds light on the distinction between the Mother Church and the life of a Christian Scientist in the field. It's a well-told story, rich with personal anecdotes and historical details."

    Dr. Shirley Paulson, co-editor of forthcoming *An Annotated Bibliography of Academic and Other Literature on Christian Science* and Founder of Early Christian Texts: The Bible and Beyond

"*Dedication* offers a fascinating lens on the early history of Christian Science church building in Seattle. It not only illuminates the many Christian Science actors of this pivotal historical period but the broader history of the city of Seattle and the growth of Christian Science as a new American religion."

    Dr. Alexandra Prince, Mary Baker Eddy Library Fellow, 2018

"An impressive research project which shows, in detail, how each 'distinctly democratic' Seattle branch church built visible structures worthy of the cause to which they had committed. It's heartening to read about churches doing things in a new way. Thoroughly researched and well documented, with nearly 500 clarifying endnotes!"

Linda Bargmann, co-editor of forthcoming *An Annotated Bibliography of Academic and Other Literature on Christian Science*

"Few people today know what the growth of Christian Science felt like at the dawn of the 20th century. If learning from history is of any value, this book is a must read for anyone wishing to know what Spirit's divine energy can do for your community."

George Denninger, author of *Insights from the Study and Practice of Christian Science*

"A unique architectural story unfolds as Safronoff knits together the intimate details of building the first Christian Science Churches in Seattle. Through careful research and insight, Safronoff lets the story tell itself by weaving together historic records, and setting the activities in the context of world events to give perspective on the challenges they faced. This is an inspiring story of cooperation, of people rising to meet every challenge through dedication of purpose, of vision, cooperation, resilience and success told with simplicity and clarity and which stands as an inspiration to anyone committed to a great work."

Carolyn Geise, Fellow of The American Institute of Architects

"*Dedication* gives you an inside look into the dawning of a religious movement when the followers' hearts burned within them. Get to know these indefatigable pioneers who were driven by a mission to tangibly share the power and presence of the newly discovered Christian Science. Cindy Safronoff's depth of research and vivid descriptions will not leave you where it found you, inspiring with new possibilities for our times."

Sanford C. Wilder, author of *Listening to Grace: Unlearning Insights and Poems*

Podcast

Dedication is available in audio format as podcast "Dedication: A Centennial Story." It can be found in many popular podcast outlets and on the author's website:

www.CindySafronoff.com

Also by the author

Cindy Peyser Safronoff is also author of *Crossing Swords: Mary Baker Eddy vs. Victoria Claflin Woodhull and the Battle for the Soul of Marriage,* featured in the *Sunday Boston Globe* and winner of ten book awards:

Independent Publisher Silver in Women's Issues

Next Generation Indie Winner in Religious Nonfiction and Finalist in Women's Issues

Illumination Awards Enduring Light Bronze in Christian Thought

New England Book Festival Winner in Regional Literature, Runner-Up in Spiritual, Honorable Mention in Biography

USA Best Books Awards Finalist in U.S. History

National Indie Excellence Awards Finalist in U.S. History

Reader's Favorite Honorable Mention in Nonfiction Drama

"*Crossing Swords* tells the intertwined tales of Victoria Woodhull and Mary Baker Eddy — two fearless American iconoclasts whose work on sex, love, and women's rights changed the course of American culture. Cindy Peyser Safronoff does a great job of bringing these fascinating women back to life in all their brilliance and eccentricity for a new generation of readers."
   Debby Applegate, author of the Pulitzer Prize-winning biography *The Most Famous Man in America: The Biography of Henry Ward Beecher*

Dedication

Dedication

Building the Seattle Branches of
Mary Baker Eddy's Church

A Centennial Story

Part 1: 1889 to 1929

Cindy Peyser Safronoff

this one thing
SEATTLE

Dedication: Building the Seattle Branches of Mary Baker Eddy's Church, A Centennial Story – Part. 1: 1889 to 1929

Quotations from The Mary Baker Eddy Library collections and the records of Fourth Church of Christ, Scientist, Seattle, are used courtesy of The Mary Baker Eddy Library; Quotations from Longyear Museum publications and historical documents are indicated as such in the Notes, and are used with permission of Longyear Museum, Chestnut Hill, MA; Quotations from First Church of Christ, Scientist, Seattle; Third Church of Christ, Scientist, Seattle; and Christian Science Organization at University of Washington, Seattle, historical documents are indicated as such in the Notes, and are used with permission.

Opinions expressed in this work are those of the author and not necessarily approved or endorsed by The Mary Baker Eddy Collection; The Mary Baker Eddy Library; Longyear Museum; First Church of Christ, Scientist, Seattle; Third Church of Christ, Scientist, Seattle; Christian Science Organization at University of Washington; or any other organization or individual.

Historical images courtesy of Paul Dorpat collection, Museum of History and Industry (PEMCO Webster & Stevens Collection, 1983.10.345.2, 1983.10.2876.1), and University of Washington Libraries, Special Collections (UW 40939) are used with permission.

Book cover: design by Jennifer Testamarck, Make Joy Studio. Skyline photo: Pexels, Pixabay.com; First Church of Christ, Scientist, Seattle: courtesy John Cooper and Paul Dorpat; Fourth Church of Christ, Scientist, Seattle: courtesy Town Hall Seattle; Third and Seventh Churches of Christ, Scientist, Seattle: courtesy Third Church of Christ, Scientist, Seattle.

This book is a publication of:

This One Thing, LLC
Seattle, WA, USA

First edition 2020

Printed in the United States of America

ISBN 978-0-9864461-2-2 (paperback)
ISBN 978-0-9864461-3-9 (e-book)
Library of Congress Control Number: 2020920649

Dedication is also available in audio format as podcast "Dedication: A Centennial Story."

To contact the author, use website contact form:

www.CindySafronoff.com

For Jack,
who so graciously and joyfully showed me
what dedication means

dedi•ca•tion. *(from Latin dedicatio, from dedicare 'devote, consecrate')* The quality of being dedicated or committed to a task or purpose. • An inscription or form of words dedicating a building, book, etc. to a person or deity. • The action of dedicating a church or other building.

Oxford English Dictionary

God has blessed and will bless this dear band of brethren. He has laid the chief corner-stone of the temple which to-day you commemorate, to-morrow complete, and thereafter dedicate to Truth and Love. O may your temple and all who worship therein stand through all time for God and humanity!

Mary Baker Eddy

The Seattle Spirit

The Seattle spirit is the spirit of abnegation and the sinking of selfish purpose for the well being of the whole community. Seattle has long been noted for this quality....Seattle needs and must have, the co-operation and active interest of every intelligent citizen. We should invite earnestly the return of the old spirit of energy and courage and confidence.

Seattle Post-Intelligencer
March 11, 1915

Table of Contents

Foreword
i

Foreword

Reading local histories, especially local church histories, can be a painful task. They tend to be filled with isolated facts about people whose names are known but about whom nothing of importance is revealed. They repeat boiler-plate paragraphs from deeds and other equally boring legal documents. They provide much information but miss the important details of what motivated believers to create a new congregation and the life that flowed from their common endeavor to worship, serve, accomplish, and rejoice together year after year.

Thus it is a welcome surprise to encounter the tale of several local congregations of a church community that invites readers (members and non-members alike) to discover their story from its beginning, walk with its pioneers, and sit in the pews with the group of dedicated adherents to a sacred realm as they encounter the transcendent dimension of life, discover others of like faith, unite around a shared truth, and make an impact upon their community. Such is the accomplishment of Cindy Safronoff in telling the story of the emergence and development of the Christian Science movement in Seattle.

Even without knowing of Safronoff's prior experience with and knowledge of the Church of Christ, Scientist, from page one of her new book, *Dedication: Building the Seattle Branches of Mary Baker Eddy's Church, A Centennial Story*, the reader will be invited into the little known world inhabited by Christian Scientists and made to make themselves at home. She provides context for those unfamiliar with the church, highlights the often-hostile environment they encountered, and shares the healing experiences that sealed their loyalty to the fellowship. Readers who know little of religion will gain some empathy for

DEDICATION

the life of believers, while members of other churches and faiths will resonate with the substance of spirituality that drew and held members and motivated them to funnel their creative energies in building their churches.

And build they did. Drawing on architects who were often themselves Christian Scientists, they constructed monuments to their faith that became an initial proclamation to their neighbors that Christian Science was a faith of Substance, that the Mind behind it was worthy of serious scrutiny, and that the Good that flowed from those buildings was being made available to the community at large.

I am not a Christian Scientist, I do not reside in the state of Washington, but Safronoff's account of the erection of these churches even as the city of Seattle was emerging into the metropolitan giant it is today, made me at least entertain the idea that maybe I should have been. And this is just part one of the saga, from the Gilded Age to the Great Depression. I stand waiting for the rest of the story.

J. Gordon Melton
Distinguished Professor of American Religious History
Baylor University
Waco, Texas

1

The Centennial (2016)

Christian Science and Christian Scientists will, must, *have a history; and if I could write the history in poor parody on Tennyson's grand verse, it would read thus: —*

> *Traitors to right of them,*
> *M. D.'s to left of them,*
> *Priestcraft in front of them,*
> *   Volleyed and thundered!*
> *Into the jaws of hate,*
> *Out through the door of Love,*
> *On to the blest above,*
> *   Marched the one hundred.*

> *Mary Baker Eddy, 1888*

This story was patiently waiting in a box in storage at the Christian Science church in the University District. I had just moved back to Seattle after a decade in Saint Louis when Third Church of Christ, Scientist, received a congratulatory letter from the Washington Secretary of State for its centennial. Nearly 3,500 organizations incorporated in Washington in 1916. Only a small number of them exist today. Third Church is one of them. At the time of the centennial, by one measure, Third Church was only ten years old because when it merged with Seventh Church a new corporate body was created. But the state still considered December 22, 2016, to be its official centennial. The boxes of church historical records were brought out of storage and opened up. A discussion began among the members about how to celebrate the centennial.

DEDICATION

I had no thought of writing a book on this topic when I looked inside the first box. I perused the loose papers on top. I immediately came across the report that inspired me to write this story, although I did not immediately recognize its significance. It was a lengthy report for a special meeting on November 16, 1945, on the Church Building and Dedication Committee of the Churches of Christ, Scientist, Seattle. The report explained their approach. I pondered the message. I looked up some dates mentioned to see what was happening in the world. When I read the committee report again, it moved me.

With the benefit of hindsight now, I like to imagine that whoever boxed up the Third Church historical files, however many decades ago, hoped this joint effort in Seattle would be rediscovered someday. That this one report survived at all is amazing, considering all the church activities that have gone on over the past century, the immense volume of internal papers generated to support those activities, and the number of people involved in making decisions through so many decades about which papers to keep. This dedication committee must have had a quietly enduring internal legacy. But by the time of the centennial, this committee's work had been entirely forgotten.

Using several of the historical sketches in the files plus some information from the dedication committee report, I wrote a paper to give to the members of Third Church to commemorate the official centennial on December 22, 2016. The members found it interesting, but it was not worthy of publishing. It did, however, include a section called "Cornerstone," which was the very first chapter in this book I wrote.

I looked deeper into the boxes and found the old books of meeting minutes. I opened their cloth and leather covers, flipped through the marble-edged pages, and perused the notes — some typed, others written in cursive, ranging from perfect nineteenth-century penmanship to loose scribbles. I noticed random details about the earliest operations of church business. Toward the bottom of a box, I found the minutes from the original building committee.

The building committee book was unique in its comparatively spartan look, expressing a businesslike practicality. The plain cardboard cover and typing paper pages were held together in a temporary-looking homemade notebook created by looping twine through three hand-punched holes. The book was tied up tight with twine, secured with a knot and a bow in the center, like an old-fashioned gift package. It seemed to me the centennial was the perfect occasion for this gift. I accepted the gift. I loosened the bow, untied the knot, opened the book, and began reading.

What I found was the record of a thought process along with the unfolding of events. It reminded me of a laboratory notebook for a college course, documentation meticulously kept for future reference and third-party scrutiny. It seemed to me that the team that wrote this wanted their work to be seen as a scientific demonstration of great importance.

Over several months, I read through the building committee notebook along with decades of other minutes for quarterly membership meetings, special business meetings, and more frequent board meetings, as well as letters, internal notes, and reports. From my years of experience with Christian Science branch churches, I was already familiar with how things worked internally. Reverend Mary Baker Eddy, who founded The First Church of Christ, Scientist, in Boston, Massachusetts, in 1879, designed her church to be "essentially democratic" and established some basic governing rules. I knew those rules, and I was familiar with church communications. What I found in the records was familiar to me, and yet so different from my experience.[1]

There was something very special about reading from the actual documents, but for practical reasons I worked with digital images. I photographed every page and then transferred the image files to my computer. I developed a file naming convention and folder organization that allowed me to search by date, document title, key words, or source. Working with electronic files, I could quickly turn pages, magnify words to interpret the more challenging cursive handwriting, and compare documents. I often had the minutes of the building committee, board, and membership meetings all open on my computer screen together, side by side, along with correspondence, so I could read about everything happening during a particular time period.

Immersing myself in these documents, I got a sense of the rhythm and dynamic of church democracy and the unfolding of events in the development of the Christian Science movement. But more than this, I could feel the energy that animated this founding generation through their documents, and it overflowed into my own life. I got caught up in the pace of what was happening a century ago. Their irrepressible spirit was contagious. Church suddenly felt fresh and alive and urgently vital.

This story is told in honor of the church builders, who put so much effort into their edifices and did what they could to ensure continuity of their cause. They were dedicated.

CINDY PEYSER SAFRONOFF

2

U-District Society (1914)

Mollie Gerry was given the task of organizing a Christian Science church in the University District, a rapidly developing community surrounding the University of Washington college campus in northeast Seattle. On Friday, October 23, 1914, at 8:30 p.m., a meeting was convened at the Gerry residence on Sixteenth Avenue Northeast by Ravenna Park. Mrs. Gerry's husband was the Honorable Robert Gerry, a former Washington state legislator who had served three terms in the House of Representatives and continued to be active in political circles. Perhaps because of his influence, this group would follow proper democratic rules of order and take careful minutes from its very first meeting.[2]

They began by electing a chair and a secretary. The chair, Anna Columbus, took control of the meeting. Then the secretary, Mr. Rice, read aloud a letter from the board of directors of the first Christian Science church in Seattle, First Church of Christ, Scientist, Seattle, addressed to its members living in the University District, a letter that everyone in attendance had just received. The board was recommending they all withdraw their membership and form their own separate organization because it was too crowded at First Church.[3]

Most of them were relatively new to Christian Science. Mrs. Gerry had been raised Methodist. After marrying and moving to Pasco, in Southeast Washington, Mrs. Gerry experienced a life-changing healing, which she publicly shared:

> At one time I was taken very sick, and my husband insisted upon calling a doctor, who made an examination and seemed to think there was small chance for recovery. We then telegraphed to a

Christian Science practitioner, who came a distance of two hundred and fifty miles and treated me, with the result that in four or five days I was up and attending to my regular duties. For more than six months the doctor would go out of his way to meet and speak to me. He told my sister-in-law that I was the most remarkable woman he had ever seen; that any other woman would have died.[4]

She attributed her recovery not to any special strength of her own, but to the effectiveness of prayer. Much of her family became interested in Christian Science along with her. Her Methodist minister father, Reverend Jacob Giezentanner, became a full-time practitioner of Christian Science healing, advertising his services in the *Christian Science Journal* with office hours from 9 a.m. to noon daily in his home on Queen Anne Hill. On this late October evening in 1914, the Gerry home was full of Christian Scientists. The idea of forming a new church in the University District had been discussed at a meeting of all the boards of the Christian Science churches of Seattle. They agreed it was "a forward step, which would mean expansion and growth." The U-District group was perhaps an especially youthful one, some of them recent graduates of the University of Washington, some recent graduates of the Christian Science Sunday School for children. Mrs. Gerry, mother of five children ranging from seven to nineteen, would initially be their motherly guide for organizing.[5]

A few weeks later, on Tuesday, November 10, this group met again at the College Inn at the corner of 40th Street at 14th Avenue Northeast, a street that would soon be renamed through a Chamber of Commerce contest "University Way" and eventually dubbed "The Ave." With Mrs. Columbus again acting as chair, the group formally organized as The University District Christian Science Society. They elected a five-member board, including Mrs. Gerry. Their elected First Reader was Mrs. R. Ella Hensley, perhaps one of the most experienced Christian Scientists in the group. Besides having been a member at First Church Seattle for the past five years, she had previous branch church experience in Iowa. She was the only *Journal*-listed practitioner among these charter members. Mrs. Hensley lived nearby at the corner of 50th and Brooklyn with her lumber salesman husband and their eight children. Their elected Second Reader was Byron B. Renshaw, a businessman and a family man with young children. After the elections, a collection was taken, resulting in total contributions of $14.31 toward expenses, $4.50 of which was owed to the College Inn for the meeting space. It was the first act of financial support for the church they were just starting to build.[6]

They were not merely forming an organization. They were joining a revolution. Echoing the spirit of 1776, the preamble of their initial by-laws was reminiscent of the American Declaration of Independence:

We, the undersigned, . . . do hereby pledge our loyalty, our time and our money, as far as our circumstances will permit, to its support in the upholding and upbuilding of the Christian Science religion . . . not only through this organization, but by our daily lives, know[ing] that it [is] through our daily lives that we are able to demonstrate 'Immanuel, or God with us,' (*Science & Health*, p. 34). To secure these ends we further pledge ourselves to work together harmoniously and lovingly, striving to emulate and obey the life and teachings of our beloved Master and Wayshower, Jesus Christ.[7]

In their revolutionary work, they felt a need to build a visible structure worthy of the cause they had committed to, a church edifice as elegant as the one recently completed on Capitol Hill. In the meantime, they rented the University Masonic Hall on University Way for $45 a month. They decided to hold their first public church service on November 29, 1914, the Sunday after the Thanksgiving Day holiday. Members worked on publicity, including sending out personal invitations to anyone they thought might be interested. They had twenty-four placards printed and put notices in the daily papers. And they prayed steadily.[8]

The furnishings for their hall were modest. They used a homemade pulpit. The weather-beaten chairs had recently been through a fire. The 300 seats represented what they believed a very optimistic estimate of the number of people who might attend, but it was standing room only at the first service. The piano accompaniment for the hymns was less than perfect. Even so, the opening was remembered as joyously successful by the members. Next, they got to work organizing their first Sunday School session for children — and acquiring more chairs.[9]

DEDICATION

The College Inn at NE 40th Street and University Way NE
Courtesy of Seattle Municipal Archives (item 2888)

3

The New Birth (1889)

"Thy word is a lamp unto my feet, and a light unto my path."

This has been proved to me in every way. When Christian Science came to me, I was a wreck, physically, mentally, and financially; but since the reading of Science and Health *turned my thought toward the light, I have found that, as far as I am willing to receive the word and live it, all comforts are supplied me. I am especially grateful for the spiritual help. I know that things which I did and thought last year I would not do or think this year, and am satisfied. Through the careful and prayerful study of* Science and Health *I have been lifted from sickness to health, from sorrow to peace, from lack to plenty, and, the most beautiful of all, from darkness to light.*

Mrs. Hanna S. Collver, Seattle, Wash.

Christian Science Sentinel, June 13, 1903; Reprinted in "Fruitage,"
Science and Health with Key to the Scriptures by Mary Baker Eddy

When Julia Field-King arrived in Seattle, the city was being reborn. For several decades it had been a "little-known frontier city," a lumber-mill seaport in a forested wilderness in the Far West. About two months before she came, on June 6, 1889, most of the commercial district had burned to the ground in a great fire. Even the streets and sidewalks had burned, since they, like nearly everything else in the city, had been built of wood—even the water and sewer pipes. Much of the original settlement along the west-facing shores of Elliott Bay was built on sawdust over sand and clay tide flats and was vulnerable to flooding from storm surge waves and a very dysfunctional sewage system. The buildings had been infested with rats and vermin. The fire was tragic, of course. But it provided a fresh start for the residents and a boon for the local economy as disaster relief aid arrived. They would rebuild on higher ground with more solid foundation in stone and brick so that a similar disaster would never happen again. The effort launched Seattle on a new growth trajectory. Some 20,000 people arrived that year, doubling the population, making it suddenly the largest city in the region, which would soon bring a railroad line to Seattle, which then brought more people and more industries, securing regional preeminence for the city.[10]

Mrs. Field-King had traveled 2,500 miles across the American continent from Boston. Like so many others moving to Seattle, she had come for business opportunity. And, like so many others, she had come to start a new life. But she had one more reason for coming to Seattle. She had been given a mission.

While looking around for a place, she explained to the landlords that she "would not be like an ordinary boarder." She would have "many callers." The housing market was tight and rents were high, but she found affordable furnished rooms where she could live and do her work at 1111 Third Avenue, between Spring and Seneca Streets. The front of her boardinghouse was being rebuilt, and so, as she later explained,

> [T]he entrance to my rooms was through a back alley on a twelve inch plank raised about six inches above the mud, to the door of a coal and wood shed, over which the sign with my name and office hours, was hung. Passing through the coal house and across a yard on plank laid on the ground,—through the kitchen and back hall into a very pleasant front hall and up one flight of well-carpeted, wide stairs to my office and living room, a bed room—both well furnished and a bathroom all on one [floor].[11]

Even before her listing appeared in the Seattle city directory, even before her baggage was unpacked, she received her first call to help a sick woman. Field-King was a licensed medical doctor. She was a graduate of Hahnemann Medical College in Chicago. Female physicians at that time were very rare, which may have helped attract business in her new home city so quickly. Her specialty was homeopathic medicine. She had studied a variety of curative methods and had visited famous health resorts in Europe. She was "hoping to find something that would cure the sick with scientific certainty," as she explained, "for I had a sincere desire to relieve suffering and save life." In about 1884, about a year after she graduated from medical school, she looked into Mary Baker Eddy's curative system called Christian Science. This prayer-based approach to healing had only recently been introduced to Chicago. Chicago had been rapidly growing since its devastating great fire a decade earlier. It quickly became the first stronghold for Christian Science outside of Boston, and Mary Baker Eddy had just visited to teach and preach. Initially, Christian Science seemed to Field-King to be just one more alternative system, and not one that she supported. "I thought Christian Science practice was criminal, and its adherents should be severely punished," she wrote, "for <u>time</u> was such a vital factor in the treatment in the acute stage of disease." She purchased a copy of Eddy's book *Science and Health with Key to the Scriptures* and filled the margins of the book with "comments on the absurdity of its statements." Then she set the book aside.[12]

Two years later, she was suffering from a serious health problem. Because of "long-standing diseases that threatened to utterly incapacitate" her, she was uncertain whether she could continue her career as a physician. She had been "a cripple" since the age of ten. Now she faced a crisis:

> [M]y doctor told me I would probably never walk again without crutches, and it might be but a few months before my limb would have to be taken off. Then unconsciously, my heart cried out *God help me*. The next day a letter came from an invalid friend, telling me that, as a last resort, she had given up doctors and medicines, and had consented to try Christian Science; that she was really getting better, and wished I would try it.[13]

Field-King decided to look into Christian Science further. She met with a practitioner in Chicago and asked to be taught. She was not looking for a new religion. She was satisfied with hers. She had been a member of the Congregational Church since her college days at Oberlin. She only wanted to learn more about healing sickness. But while receiving this instruction in 1887, she had a change of heart. She wrote:

> In the first two lessons I saw the heavens open; I saw such wonderful Love; I saw Principle, strong and unswerving; I saw what I had been crying out for all my life; I saw freedom, rest, peace. . . . I let the light into my heart; then I shut myself away from the world, took *Science and Health* and all the articles written by its author, and read nothing else. I found the sweet Spirit of Truth, and I found rest. . . . After a while the Church thought came to me, and with it the strong desire for action. Never before had I felt a nearness to the church. But in Christian Science I learned that Christ's church is in

each heart, and that we unite with his Church only as we are 'new born of Spirit.' . . . In this church and child-thought, the physical healing came. It was not only the newness of Spirit, but with it came the renewing of the body. To-day I am a strong woman, physically, and my heart is light with joy and gladness.[14]

With this healing, she began a new life. As new as she was to Christian Science, she soon dedicated herself to it full-time. Among the articles by Mary Baker Eddy was one called "The New Birth," which read in part:

The new birth is not the work of a moment. It begins with moments, and goes on with years; moments of surrender to God, of childlike trust and joyful adoption of good; moments of self-abnegation, self-consecration, heaven-born hope, and spiritual love. . . . What a faith-lighted thought is this! That mortals can lay off the "old man," until man is found to be the image of the infinite good that we name God, and the fullness of the stature of man in Christ appears. . . . Now dear reader, pause for a moment with me to contemplate this new-born attitude of thought, for the spot whereon thou treadest is holy ground. . . . [15]

Field-King had the opportunity to meet the author and have an on-going professional relationship with her. She took class instruction from Eddy in Boston at her Massachusetts Metaphysical College in September 1888 and then the following May, again from Eddy, the Normal Class to become a teacher of Christian Science. She continued to use her medical credentials, "M.D." She simply added her new Christian Science credentials, "C.S.D." She was one of about 250 trained by Eddy by 1890 who were encouraged to go somewhere beyond Boston to establish Christian Science. Eddy "saw the possibilities of the great Northwest." Field-King had initially planned to establish her Christian Science practice in the Midwest where she had lived most of her life, but instead, she moved to Seattle.[16]

In Seattle, besides having all the patients she could handle, Field-King sold Eddy's book and began training other people to practice Christian Science. She had an impressive background in formal education at a variety of academic institutions. Besides her own experience as a college student, she had worked as a teacher as a young woman, and again after her husband died of tuberculosis. She had been on the faculty of a normal school that trained public school teachers and had even worked briefly as a school principal. But this background was not necessarily helpful to her now. She was profoundly impressed with Eddy's teaching method. This was "teaching so unlike all other teaching," she concluded. "My first class was eager, studious, earnest, but I soon saw they had not understood." She received a disapproving critique of her teaching from another Christian Science teacher who visited Seattle, resulting in her making a trip back across the country to check in with Eddy in Concord, New Hampshire. Eddy had recently retreated from the center of activity in Boston to Concord intending to retire. She gave her students control of her organization, although she still oversaw the new movement from afar and kept in close communication with her students. Correct teaching of Christian Science was always important to Eddy, and it was a concerning issue at that time because of renegade students who had their own ideas on how to heal but were still using the term Christian Science. After her meeting with Eddy, Field-King gave much thought to her teaching, recalled her students, and taught them again.[17]

With the influx of people to Seattle, the city began rapid expansion, and so did Field-King's sphere of influence. Within her first 15 months in Seattle, she had sold 100 copies of the Christian Science textbook. A community of her students began meeting at the boardinghouse where she lived. "They are learning to live the Truth as set forth in *Science and Health*," Field-King cheered in her report to readers of the *Christian Science Journal*. Her influence reached beyond Seattle to Tacoma and Portland. Field-King reported back regularly to Eddy. She wrote:

> I have taught over one hundred pupils, rich and educated, rich and ignorant, poor, foreigners,—all classes and nations it almost seems. We have our Bible class on Sunday mornings and public inquiry meeting on Sunday evening, our students meeting on Wednesday evening and a *Science and Health* class Friday noons. All the meetings well-attended. We have no organization of any kind. All is done because we love the Science.[18]

In May 1891 Field-King contributed a short article to the *Christian Science Journal* called "Wait," in which she described the Christian Science spiritual path, identifying each phase of the life and career of Christ Jesus as a stage of progress for anyone following his way. She concluded that as much as one might want to immediately leap to the triumphal stage of Christianity, each step was indispensable and might take years or even decades of preparation before one is ready. To think otherwise was a trap, the "subtlest snare," therefore humility and patience were essential.

DEDICATION

Field-King expected to stay in Seattle permanently, but after this article was published, Eddy asked her to come to Boston to serve as editor of the *Christian Science Journal*. When she was a schoolteacher, she had taught grammar, English literature, philosophy, and rhetoric, among many other things, but she had no experience with publishing magazines. She made a "vigorous protest" over Eddy's request. "I am such a babe in understanding and the responsibility is so great," she explained. But after some reflection, she agreed to take the job. "[I]f I really trusted God, I would be shown how to do it," she concluded. "I made no more protests."[19]

Julia Field-King had successfully accomplished her first mission. She had introduced Mary Baker Eddy's healing system at the foundation of a new city poised for long-term growth. Her work in Seattle ended with the conclusion of the year 1891. The call to Boston meant going away and leaving those she had so recently healed and taught—"the new-born babes" in Seattle.[20]

City of Seattle in 1878

Clarence B. Bagley

Downtown Seattle after the Great Fire of 1889

Paul Dorpat collection

Downtown Seattle after the Great Fire of 1889

Paul Dorpat collection

4

Structure of Truth and Love (1892)

When Julia Field-King cheerfully reported to her Leader in 1891 that her students in Seattle had no formal organization, it was during a brief period in the development of Mary Baker Eddy's movement when there was little formal organization even in Boston. Reverend Eddy had dissolved it. After many years of trial, Eddy unincorporated her Boston church, disorganized her student association, and closed her highly successful Massachusetts Metaphysical College, the spiritual education institution that had trained hundreds of Christian Science practitioners and teachers like Mrs. Field-King. Perhaps in trying to interpret Eddy's actions Field-King saw lack of organization as a sign of progress. But because of the informality in Seattle, unfortunately, if there were any regular activities after Field-King left the city, the organizers—or *non*-organizers—apparently did not leave any record of them.

It might have been a question among Field-King's first students and readers of the first edition of Mary Baker Eddy's book whether it was even right to form legal organizations or build church edifices. For many people associated with Christian Science, it was first and foremost a healing system. Furthermore, in the first edition of the Christian Science textbook, published in 1875, Eddy had written:

> We have no need of creeds and church organizations to sustain or explain a demonstrable platform, that defines itself in healing the sick, and casting out error. . . . The mistake the disciples of Jesus made to found religious organizations and church rites, if indeed they did this, was one the Master did not make . . . Christ's church was Truth . . . Is there any higher Christianity than this? No time

was lost by our Master in organizations, rites, and ceremonies, or in proselyting for certain forms of belief . . . [A] magnificent edifice was not the sign of Christ's Church.[21]

Eddy later removed this statement from her textbook and added a new definition of church:

CHURCH. The structure of Truth and Love; whatever rests upon and proceeds from divine Principle.

The Church is that institution, which affords proof of its utility and is found elevating the race, rousing the dormant understanding from material beliefs to the apprehension of spiritual ideas and the demonstration of divine Science, thereby casting out devils, or error, and healing the sick.[22]

Even this new way of thinking about church might lead a reader to conclude that Christian Scientists would not, or should not, create formal organizations or build church edifices. Yet, even as she was trying to get her first edition published, Eddy envisioned someday having a church of her own—with its own building. On July 4, 1876, a small group of her students formed an association. A few years later on April 12, 1879, under Eddy's leadership, the Christian Scientist Association organized The First Church of Christ, Scientist, in Boston. It was a very small group with a very big mission. First and foremost focused on the healing practice, the church was "designed to commemorate the word and works of our Master, which should reinstate primitive Christianity and its lost element of healing." The idea of building a church edifice in Boston had appeared in the *Christian Science Journal* as early as 1885:

The question is often asked, 'Is it true that the interest in Christian Science is gaining ground in the minds of the people?' The great call for the books, the magazine, and our crowded Sunday services are sufficient testimony that it *is*. Our teacher is constantly receiving letters proclaiming the good work that '*Science and Health*' is accomplishing . . . We are already obliged to have a larger hall for our Sunday services, and we hope soon to have a church-building of our own.[23]

The message from church leadership in the late 1880s was consistent. Yes, there would be Christian Science church edifices, and Reverend Eddy wanted one built in Boston. Initially, the members approached the building project fairly conventionally. They did a few fundraisers, made many appeals for donations, sometimes apparently trying to overcome a hesitancy to contribute, like this statement from an 1887 article:

> Let no one say, as an excuse for not giving, that this is a material work, and that Christian Scientists do not need a church-building. Those who offer that as an excuse for not giving, have not yet attained the understanding of their position in Mind, whereby they can do without houses, raiment, and food.[24]

Mary Baker Eddy's church was growing, the movement expanding. But Eddy's Boston church revealed organizational dysfunctions. There were factions and divisions within the ranks of her students, even rebellions resulting in scandals, lawsuits, and public disagreements that challenged Eddy's leadership. Some of these dramas made it into the newspapers across the continent in remote Seattle. All the conflict and turmoil was making it difficult to keep the organization going at all, let alone continue or even accelerate its growth. Eddy wanted to maintain a sense of unity and keep the focus on healing. She wrote to her followers:

> O Christian scientist, thou of the church of the new-born; awake to a higher and holier love for God and man; put on the whole armor of Truth, rejoice in hope, be patient in tribulation, that ye may go to the bed of anguish, and look upon this dream of life in matter, girt with a higher sense of omnipotence; and behold once again the power of divine Life and Love to heal and reinstate man in God's own image and likeness, having "one Lord, one faith, one baptism."[25]

Eddy needed a better system for authorizing teachers and practitioners, and a firmer foundation for her entire organization. By 1892, she started re-organizing. This time, she started with the church. Her reorganized church was better "designed to be built on the Rock, Christ."[26]

Previously, in 1886, while Eddy's Boston students were making their initial fundraising appeals for building funds, a small Christian Science congregation in the Midwest built and dedicated a wood-frame church in Oconto, Wisconsin—independently, quietly, and quickly. Oconto was growing in population, but compared to Boston, or even Seattle, it was a tiny town. Oconto was, however, home to a small but significant group of Christian Scientists, including several women who had taken a class taught by Eddy in 1884. They had experienced healing themselves, had been successful in healing others, and now they were dedicated to Christian Science. There was enough uncertainty surrounding the question of church buildings for Christian Science that the Oconto group felt a need to ask permission from Eddy—who gave it. The congregation built a wood-frame chapel on the corner of Main Street and Chicago Street for $1,137. The group held their first church service in their new edifice on the last Sunday in October 1886. The timing coincided with both Reformation Sunday, a holiday that long held great significance for Christianity as the anniversary of Martin Luther's movement-launching protest, and also the anniversary of the publishing of the first edition of Mary Baker Eddy's reforming book, *Science and Health with Key to the Scriptures.* A visitor to the Oconto church reported in the *Christian Science Journal*:

> The church, with its complete furnishing, stands as a monument of the unity and faithfulness of the members. It is a reminder of the fulfilment of the promises of God to those who ask in trust.[27]

Later, Eddy wrote to the Oconto church:

> Guided by the pillar and the cloud, this little church that built the first temple for Christian Science worship shall abide steadfastly in the faith of Jesus' words: "Fear not, little flock; for it is your Father's good pleasure to give you the kingdom."[28]

Science and Health readers may not have realized it at the time, but with the building of the first branch of Mary Baker Eddy's church, this movement dedicated to the practice of Christian healing was beginning an "era of church building."[29]

In February 1892 the *Christian Science Journal* published a sermon to the Christian Scientists in Boston that made clear that Eddy's "Scientific Statement of Being,"

> There is no life, truth, intelligence, nor substance in matter. All is infinite Mind and its infinite manifestation, for God is All-in-all. . . . Spirit is God, and man is His image and likeness. Therefore man is not material; he is spiritual.

set Christian Science as far apart from all other existing churches "as the north pole from the south." Adherents were heading in a different direction, which would become increasingly obvious. Of necessity, they were impelled to forward a new agenda:

> Has the time come for Christian Scientists to withdraw from the older churches, and to gather into Communions of their own? It would seem so. . . . We must either give up our Scientific doctrines, or come out and be separate. No other course is open to us.[30]

Articles about construction projects in the Christian Science periodicals began appearing with increasing frequency and with increasing meaning attached. As one author stated in an article about the March 1892 dedication of a new Christian Science Hall in Scranton, Pennsylvania, "the erection of a hall is a proclamation . . . that Christian Science has come to stay." Commenting on the new "[c]hapels and churches" that were "dotting the entire land," Eddy wrote, "The outlook is cheering."[31]

Now it was Boston's turn. With the announcement of an official Building Fund, the message to the field became more focused and serious. A proposed design with floor plans and a drawing was published in the March 1892 edition of the *Journal*. The treasurer regularly reported lists of donors and their contributions. Financial supporters were typically of very modest means, coming as they so often were from the ranks of people who had been struggling with chronic illnesses for many years. The sacrifice behind many of these contributions is exemplified by this letter to the *Journal*.[32]

> While reading the definition of "Church" in *Science and Health*, the thought occurred to me that every true Christian Scientist should add something to the Building Fund for the proposed Church in Boston. The question then arose, "Have I anything to give?" The answer came back "You can give up tea and coffee"—and some articles which seemed very necessary for winter. I accepted the proposition, and forward $5, hoping that it is sent in a spirit of Love, and will increase tenfold.— Mrs. A. D. W.[33]

Among the early donors was a contribution for $10 from "C.S. Students" from Seattle, Washington. They were starting to take action together. With the February 1893 issue of the *Journal*, for the first time the group advertised regular church services. They held one weekly meeting, a Sunday service at 11:00 a.m. at 1111 Third Avenue, the downtown boardinghouse where Julia Field-King had lived.[34]

The Seattle congregation was among the first 200 Christian Science church groups anywhere. It was one of only about a dozen in the western states. There is no record of what exactly they did at their regular Sunday services. They, like all the other new congregations, were learning along with Mary Baker Eddy how to run a Christian Science church. But the message was becoming clear. Yes, there would be a Christian Science church. In Seattle they may have already begun discussing the idea that one day they would have a church edifice of their own. Christian Science had come to stay.[35]

First Church of Christ, Scientist, Oconto, Wisconsin. Dedicated 1886

Herbert L. Dunbar

First Church of Christ, Scientist, Scranton, Pennsylvania. Dedicated 1892

Herbert L. Dunbar

Design first proposed for church edifice and publishing house The First Church of Christ, Scientist, Boston

Christian Science Journal

5

The Mother Church (1893)

The Building Fund for The Mother Church, The First Church of Christ, Scientist, in Boston, was growing. But it still had only a fraction of the $200,000 needed for the planned church edifice. The project was moving slowly, far too slowly. After many years of little progress, Reverend Mary Baker Eddy put out a grand challenge to her church officers and Christian Scientists everywhere. She publicly announced a deadline. The church edifice needed to be ready for church services by Sunday, December 30, 1894. The project needed to be completed within one year and it needed to be built without incurring any debt.

Even under normal circumstances, to complete such an ambitious project in one year would be difficult. But this was during a period of financial crisis. In 1893 a severe economic depression had begun, during which the stock markets crashed, hundreds of banks failed, thousands of businesses went bankrupt or closed, including major railroad companies, many workers were taking drastic pay cuts or were laid off, and there were national strikes and protest marches going on. Such an ambitious construction project seemed humanly impossible. That was the point. Their spiritual teacher was giving them a learning assignment that could only be accomplished through "radical reliance" on God. Eddy explained:

> No doubt must intervene between the promise and event; faith and resolve are friends to Truth, seize them, trust the Divine providence, push upward our prayer in stone and God will give the benediction.[36]

The Board of Directors for Rev. Eddy's church faced obstacles of every kind during the building project: design challenges, financial shortfalls, labor controversies, transportation issues, problems with suppliers, building site security, and weather concerns. For most of the year there was very little visible progress on the project. As board member Joseph Armstrong explained:

> November came, and found no roof on the building, the walls unfinished and snow already on the ground. There were even no suitable plans for interior finish and but two months in which to complete work that all agreed would require at least six.[37]

Yet, the church edifice was completed by the end of the year. The last finish work on the building was done on Saturday, December 29, as the clock struck twelve midnight—just in time to hold the Sunday communion service there the next morning. Armstrong declared, "It was a victory for Christian Science, a victory in which every claim of error was met and overcome." The Board of Directors had met Eddy's seemingly impossible challenge. A very high standard for church building had been set. Joseph Armstrong shared details about this example building project in his book *The Building of The Mother Church*, which would soon be read by branch church members all over the world. Above all, the Boston building project set a standard for building financing. As Eddy put it:

> Notwithstanding the perplexed condition of our nation's finances, the want and woe with millions of dollars unemployed in our money centres, the Christian Scientists, within fourteen months, responded to the call for this church with $191,012. Not a mortgage was given nor a loan solicited, and the donors all touchingly told their privileged joy at helping to build The Mother Church. There was no urging, begging, or borrowing; only the need made known, and forth came the money, or diamonds, which served to erect this "miracle in stone."[38]

For the dedication on Sunday, January 6, 1895, about six thousand people braved the cold snowy mid-winter weather to attend, including many from the far western states, who came for the event on very short notice. Had there been more advance notice, many more thousands might have attended. It was announced in Boston, and received with some disappointment, that Eddy would not attend. She was, however, with them in spirit, and she wrote a dedicatory sermon to be read at the services. The Directors printed a notice that the service would be "repeated as often as was necessary to afford ALL an opportunity to hear." They held five services that day.[39]

Those in attendance had the privilege of the first hearing of Eddy's words of blessing, which concluded:

Christian Scientists, you have planted your standard on the rock of Christ, the true, the spiritual idea,—the chief corner-stone in the house of our God. . . . Divine presence, breathe Thou Thy blessing on every heart in this house. . . . This is the new-born of Spirit, this is His redeemed; this, His beloved. May the kingdom of God within you,—with you alway,—reascending, bear you outward, upward, heavenward. . . . May all whose means, energies, and prayers helped erect The Mother Church, find within it home, and *heaven*.[40]

As to Eddy's full address, the *Christian Science Journal* described the "remarkable deliverance" this way:

There are times when human expression fails to give vent to thought and feeling. The dedication occasion of "our Prayer in stone" is surely one of such times. As well might one attempt to define the unseen quality of divine Love, or bring out in pictorial representation the glory of the Transfiguration scene, as to express in poor human language the deep emotion, the sweet sense of joy, and the peace which truly passeth all mortal understanding, which pervaded the assembly and filled the hearts of the faithful ones. Abundantly were all repaid for coming, and not one of those who made the midwinter trip across the continent but would gladly repeat it for another such benediction.[41]

In summary, the *Journal* declared:

This house of Love now stands before the world an accomplished fact, and its significance if not fully understood is at least becoming partially manifest even to non-Scientists.[42]

Mary Baker Eddy's new church in Boston was newsworthy nationally. The *Seattle Post-Intelligencer* published a lengthy article on the dedication, here in part:

Their Prayer In Stone

Dedication of the Christian Science Temple in Boston

Boston, March 11. – The mother church of Christian Science, the splendid new temple erected as a testimonial to the discoverer and founder of the denomination, at the corner of Norway and Falmouth streets, threw open its doors very recently to receive its first congregation of worshippers, and to reveal to them its wonders of interior construction and ornamentation, in which scarcely any church in the country is more unique and interesting.

A very remarkable circumstance connected with the erection of this edifice, and one which is peculiarly happy in connection with its testimonial character, is the fact that not only is there no debt upon it, but that on the contrary, the contributions continue to flow in despite the fact that there are ample funds in hand to cover its cost of nearly $200,000.

In order to stop the inflow of money from all countries where Christian Scientists are found, the treasurer, Mr. Stephen B. Chase, has been compelled to announce that no sums except those already subscribed can be received.

The occasion of the opening of the edifice for the first services was full of interest as well as of great surprise and wonderment in all. The bright Sabbath sunlight streamed through the richly colored pictoral windows upon a congregation which filled every one of the 1,200 seats in the great auditorium, and overflowed into the spaces along the walls. . . .

The large number of visitors from all parts of the country to see this most beautiful structure is almost incredible and the members of the faith are to be found in every state in the Union.[43]

Along with descriptions of pictorial windows featuring women of the Bible, the *Seattle Post-Intelligencer* devoted several paragraphs to a small "remarkably interesting feature" of the church known as "the mother's room," created with financial contributions from Christian Science children. The reporter described the room's stained-glass images based on Mary Baker Eddy's recent book, *Christ and Christmas*—one window representing the Star of Bethlehem, the second showing Mrs. Eddy searching the scriptures by the light of a candle, and above it the Christian Science seal, the cross and crown with Jesus' words, "Heal the Sick, Raise the Dead, Cleanse the Lepers, Cast Out Demons," the third illustrating a little girl reading *Science and Health* to an aged man whose Bible was closed.

The Seattle news article made note of several other things that were especially unusual about this "mother church" and its founder. Not only was Reverend Eddy not in attendance at the dedication service, but she had not even seen the church yet, nor had she indicated when she might visit it. The article also explained a significant innovation for the Sunday sermons. At the dedication service, Judge Septimus J. Hanna, who had recently been "performing the duties of pastor" at the Boston church, "announced his retirement from the pastorate, . . . and said that he gladly laid down his responsibilities to be succeeded by the grandest minister a church could have . . ." Eddy would soon explain to readers of the *Journal*:

> Humbly, and as I believe, Divinely directed—I hereby ordain, that the Bible, and *Science and Health with Key to the Scriptures*, shall hereafter be the only pastor of the Church of Christ, Scientist, throughout our land, and in other lands.
>
> From this date the Sunday services of our denomination should be conducted by Readers, in lieu of pastors. Each church or society, formed for Sunday worship, shall elect two Readers, a male, and a female.[44]

Eddy, affectionately called Mother by her close students, was starting to wean her children from dependence on personal preaching, including her own. She wanted Christian Scientists to follow principle, not person. She had begun distancing herself from her congregation and her students, encouraging her religious followers instead to look to the Bible and her writings for guidance.

A few months after the dedication, Eddy made an unexpected and unannounced first appearance at the church to deliver an impromptu sermon, described by one listener as "a deep symphony of love out breathed from an overflowing heart." A young man who was visiting the church for the first time described his experience in a letter to his mother, which was published in the *Christian Science Journal*:

> I have just returned from church, where I had the pleasure of seeing and hearing Mrs. Eddy. I think only a few of the congregation knew any more than I did that she was going to be there; and I don't know now why she came this particular day. Any way when the lesson was half through to verse 27, the readers stopped and she came into the auditorium and passed up onto the platform. The audience rose to their feet when they saw her coming in. She did not stop in the center or step to the most prominent point behind the desk, but simply to one side, and after bowing a welcome to the audience, she sat down and rested her head in silent prayer. Then a lady in the choir sang a beautiful solo, after which Mrs. Eddy arose and stepping to the desk, spoke in a quiet pleasant voice, very distinct,—for you could easily hear every word,—and yet she seemed to be talking as if she were in a small room sitting only a few feet from you instead of in that large church.
>
> Mrs. Eddy did not preach; she took no text, but I wish I could write you all she said. She must have spoken for twenty minutes,

and it meant volumes to me. It was all love—God's love, and Christ's great commandment, Love one another. She said you must learn to love God, and then you will learn to love your enemies. She said it all in such a simple, loving way that I was charmed. I don't wonder that she is loved,—she is all love. You simply feel as if she was your best friend.[45]

Afterward, the audience was instructed to remain seated while Reverend Eddy left the church. This sort of public appearance was increasingly rare. Instead, this spiritual leader focused on providing written guidance for her students, and their students, and their students' students. That year, 1895, Eddy published the first edition of her short and succinct *Church Manual* that would serve as authority for church governance for both her Boston organization and all branch churches, including those that would be built all over Seattle.

There was no question now that an "era of church building" had begun.[46]

**Auditorium of The Mother Church,
The First Church of Christ, Scientist, Boston**

Herbert L. Dunbar

27

The First Church of Christ, Scientist, Boston, November 1894

Joseph Armstrong

Dedicated January 6, 1895

Herbert L. Dunbar

6

A New Church (1895)

Contributors to the *Christian Science Journal* shared in the afterglow of the dedication services of The Mother Church throughout much of the year 1895. Then at the end of that year, the focus of attention shifted from The First Church of Christ, Scientist, in Boston, to church construction projects in other cities. Among the earliest of those following Boston's lead was Saint Louis, Missouri. If the Seattle students of Christian Science had not already heard about it through personal communications, they would have learned about the new church in Saint Louis when they read the December 1895 issue of the *Journal*. "Another Christian Science church has been erected and dedicated to the Cause of Truth," a brief article began. It was "the result, in part at least, of the labors of Julia Field-King, aided by her faithful band of students," the *Journal* reported.[47]

After about a year as editor of the *Journal*, Mrs. Field-King went back to the work of healing and teaching Christian Science, this time in the midwest region. Within three years—about the same length of time she had been in Seattle—she had taught enough classes to have 50 students to organize as First Church of Christ, Scientist, Saint Louis, and she and "her faithful band of students" had built a stone edifice on Pine Street, between 27th and 28th Street. According to the *Saint Louis Globe Democrat*, it was "a handsomely proportioned church, with interior decorations exceedingly graceful and harmonious." In total it cost $28,000, and, following the example recently set in Boston, there was no debt after construction. They held a dedication service on Sunday, November 10, at which was read a telegram from Reverend Mary Baker Eddy:

DEDICATION

I send my hearty congratulations and a Godspeed to you and your dear church.[48]

If there were any lingering doubts about where the Christian Science movement was heading under Eddy's leadership, the direction was now clear. Informal groups all over the country were incorporating as Churches of Christ, Scientist, and more building projects were in the works.

The following summer in Seattle, on August 6, 1896, Christian Scientists formed an organization. A few months later, with eighteen charter members, they officially became a legal body. This notice appeared in the *Seattle Post-Intelligencer*, on November 8, 1896, under the heading, "A New Church":

> The Christian scientists of this city have united under the name of "First Church of Christ, Scientist." Articles of incorporation have been filed with the secretary of state and certification received by the society. Services are held in Russell hall, corner of Third avenue and Cherry street, on Sunday at 11 a.m. A reading room is open at the same place every day during the week from 10 a.m. till 5 p.m. Strangers welcomed.[49]

Russell Hall was a room in the Russell House, a four-story hotel downtown near Pioneer Square. It was one of the few wood buildings that survived the 1889 Seattle fire. The church services for the small congregation were conducted by their elected readers: Mrs. Marena B. Riley, First Reader, and Mrs. Frances Carlton Baker, Second Reader. The same rented hall was used as a reading room where people could come to read or purchase Christian Science literature. Their reading room initially was staffed, somewhat irregularly, by volunteers.[50]

The Seattle church was growing, but not nearly as fast as Christian Science churches in other areas, like the Saint Louis church, which was already well on its way to outgrowing the 600-seat auditorium just built. Seattle had come to the attention of Mary Baker Eddy as an area of concern, and she communicated this to Julia Field-King in their ongoing correspondence. Field-King replied to her teacher in 1897, "Seattle has been my puzzle and a matter of much concern, ever since I left it." She was writing from London. After the completion of the edifice in Saint Louis, she took on a new mission. She crossed the Atlantic Ocean with the goal of building the first Christian Science church in England, and she had already made significant progress. With such immediate rapid growth in Saint Louis and London, the puzzle was why so little had happened in Seattle. In Field-King's opinion, they had not yet become "real Christian Scientists."[51]

People in Seattle claimed healings, sometimes from simply from reading Mary Baker Eddy's book. As one example, William Reilly began reading *Science and Health* in 1896 when friends advised him to purchase a copy. Through studying the book, he testified in the *Christian Science Journal*, he was healed of a 25-year addiction to tobacco, a 16-year problem with eczema, and other diseases, including indigestion and partial paralysis. Others in Seattle reported experiencing healing too. But Seattle lacked professional practitioners. In cities all over the United States and Canada where Christian Science had been introduced around the same time, there were already many full-time practitioners, even dozens of them, and the numbers were growing. In Washington State, there were only practitioners in cities far from Seattle: Spokane, on the far eastern side of the state; Walla Walla, in the central part of the state; Tacoma, to the south; and Everett, to the north. But at times in the 1890s, there were no practitioners in Seattle.[52]

A few Christian Science practitioners came to Seattle in the 1890s but only taught for a short time, either moving on, passing on, or choosing not to continue teaching. There were healing practitioners and teachers who used the name Christian Science but who were not affiliated with Mary Baker Eddy and had fundamental disagreements with her teaching. For a while, there had been a competing group advertising classes and regular meetings under the name "Free Thought Christian Science." Field-King told Eddy about some of these competing influences that she believed were scattering her students. She explained:

> The work there is so mixed that it can hardly be called Christian Science. . . . They need thorough, painstaking, impersonal, unselfish reteaching. Seattle is a large thriving city, and its people are energetic, intelligent refined, cultured. It is a field worthy of a strong leader.[53]

Field-King was a strong leader, sometimes to a fault. The characteristic that enabled her to travel to a new place and immediately start teaching and forming churches, could lead to too much personal control of her students. After Field-King left Saint Louis, Eddy encouraged the association of students there to turn from person to principle. It was a lesson that Christian Scientists everywhere were learning. They were becoming accustomed to following the bylaws in the *Church Manual* instead of the opinions and impulses of charismatic people. To support the goal of encouraging everyone to think for themselves through the understanding of principle, even children, one of Field-King's students in Saint Louis, Mary Kimball Morgan, in the summer of 1897, took the first steps toward starting a school, a "Christian Science School" with the blessing of Mary Baker Eddy. Inspired by the Latin word for principle, this "school which should establish thought on a right basis" would be called The Principia.[54]

To address the problem of conflicting teachings on Christian Science, Eddy asked all teachers to refrain from teaching during 1897 and instead to spend that year studying the collection of her articles in her latest book, *Miscellaneous Writings*. Then she reorganized her system for training new Christian Science teachers.

Soon after Field-King's correspondence with Eddy about Seattle's need for a teacher, they got one, although only for a brief visit: Edward A. Kimball of Chicago. In January 1898 Eddy established a Board of Lectureship with five members, led by Mr. Kimball. He had taken class instruction with Eddy in 1888 and began quietly practicing Christian Science. A few years later, when asked to serve in a more prominent role, he initially felt "unprepared and unworthy," but he quickly became a pillar of the large Chicago church. He was First Reader both during construction and at the November 14, 1897, dedication of their church, a building of Grecian classical-style architecture. It was the first Christian Science church building "in the great metropolis of the great West," and because of its "special significance," description of this first Chicago dedication was given considerable space in the *Christian Science Journal*. Reverend Eddy contributed a lengthy letter to be read at the dedication service along with addresses by both Kimball and Second Reader Ruth B. Ewing. The services were repeated four times, and all the services had overflowing audiences. Now that Christian Science was solidly established in Chicago, Kimball was assigned the role of lecturer. His job was to travel around the country and give talks on Christian Science that included the facts about Mary Baker Eddy and "a true and just reply to public topics condemning Christian Science."[55]

There had been plenty of condemning Christian Science going on in public topics in Seattle. Aside from the articles about scandals and lawsuits relating to Eddy's renegade students, the most common type of newspaper article about Christian Science prior to this had the title "Killed by Christian Science," followed by a brief story on someone somewhere in the country who had some connection to Christian Science and who had died. At times newspapers published sermons by Christian clergy condemning Christian Science, calling it anti-Christian, quackery, charlatanry, a "semi-religious craze" that demoralized women.[56]

In 1898, two years after incorporating, the Seattle church invited Kimball to give a Christian Science lecture in Seattle. It was held on Thursday, September 27, across the street from Russell Hall at the newly built 1,600-seat Seattle Theater, the city's leading venue in the 1890s for variety shows and the earliest movies. Kimball's visit got the attention of Seattle. He had a full house. Kimball began his message with this attention-getting opener:

> If you had ever sounded the depths of human misery; if you had sat, as it were, by an open grave and watched yourself dying inch by inch and then, if you had been healed and restored by Christian Science, as I have been, you could understand the impulsion which induces me to appear before you in this behalf. I stand here as one of a vast multitude of people who have been delivered from horrible depths and who, having come up out of great tribulation, are animated by the one hope of making known this gospel of healing and deliverance to all who have ears to hear.[57]

The *Seattle Times* devoted almost an entire page to the event—by far the most significant news coverage yet and the first positive publicity for Christian Science. The text of Kimball's entire lecture was published under the headline, "Explains Christian Science: Defense of the Faith of Those Who Practice Christian Science, Covering Salient Points, Listened to by Thousands of People in the Seattle Theater." Considering the "thousands" attending this first lecture, clearly interest in Christian Science had grown since 1890 when Mrs. Field-King sold the first 100 copies of Mary Baker Eddy's book in Seattle. Miss Jessie Estep, the new Reading Room librarian, who was also a new Christian Science practitioner, reported in the *Christian Science Journal* that after Kimball's lecture there was a "marked increase in demand" for copies of the book. Also, church member William Reilly reported that attendance was up at their services. "Since Mr. Kimball's lecture here in September we have added to the capacity of our hall, every seat is now taken at our Sunday services, and more chairs will be procured."[58]

The level of interest Kimball generated and the larger attendance at services must have been encouraging to the members of the new church. But they still needed stronger grounding in the practice of Christian Science. While Kimball was in town, he recommended to the members that they contact the Board of Directors of The First Church of Christ, Scientist, in Boston, and request a teacher. They followed

Kimball's advice and put in their request. It took more than a year, but Seattle would finally have a permanent teacher to support the new church.[59]

Seattle Theater on Third Avenue at Cherry Street across from Russell Hall

Paul Dorpat collection

Seattle Theater auditorium

Paul Dorpat collection

**First Church of Christ, Scientist, London, England
Dedicated 1897**

**First Church of Christ, Scientist, Chicago, Illinois
Dedicated 1897**

Herbert L. Dunbar

7

Christian Scientist (1899)

"A real Christian Scientist is a marvel, a miracle in the universe of mortal mind," Mary Baker Eddy wrote in an article included in her then-recently published *Miscellaneous Writings*. "With selfless love, he inscribes on the heart of humanity and transcribes on the page of reality the living, palpable presence—the might and majesty!—of goodness. He lives for all mankind, and honors his creator." The Seattle congregation was about to meet someone who would prove to be something like such a marvel and miracle as a real Christian Scientist.[60]

When they learned that Allen H. Armstrong was the Christian Science teacher coming to join their church in response to their request to the Board of Directors in Boston, they may have already been familiar with his name. In January 1897, Armstrong had published his personal story in the *Christian Science Journal*. In his article, "Steady Growth," he told how he seemed to be "an exception to the general experience" of transformation shared in the *Journal*. So many were quickly healed and then immediately went into the public healing practice themselves. Armstrong took a comparatively "slow pace" in learning how to practice Christian Science.

Born in Indiana and raised in rural Michigan, after graduating from the University of Michigan, Armstrong left the Midwest for the Far West. When Armstrong first learned about Christian Science, he was living in California in a small isolated town in the foothills of San Diego County and working as a rancher. His father, Charles E.B. Armstrong, was a Baptist clergyman, but young Allen had completely rejected all religious belief. He had been struggling with "a slow, wasting disease" and "a slow but certain financial disaster" for two years when a "student of *Science and Health*" came to visit. Armstrong described his introduction:

> I asked, "What is Christian Science?" The answer was brief, but they advised getting *Science and Health*. This I did at once. I read it eagerly, first, because much that I read appealed to me as self-evident; second, because it proposed to take Christianity out of the realm of blind belief and transfer it to the realm of understanding and demonstration. But aside from this satisfaction in its study no apparent result followed my reading.[61]

Armstrong wrote a letter to a Christian Science practitioner to ask for treatment, but after a few weeks he decided to do his own work through the study of *Science and Health*. Gradually he noticed "a mental change." A habit of "using very strong language when provoked dropped away." He gained the courage to throw out all his medicines, "which were many." Only after daily diligent reading for 18 months did he recognize "a single victory" that he could think of as a healing.

At this point, Armstrong took class instruction on Christian Science in Oakland with Dr. Francis J. Fluno, a well-known practitioner, teacher, and lecturer who, after reading the first edition of *Science and Health*, had given up a successful career as a medical doctor for the practice of Christian Science.[62]

For the next seven years, Armstrong continued with a serious study of *Science and Health*. "While there have been seasons of deep, quiet joy, sometimes continuing for weeks," Armstrong explained, "most of the time has been spent in persistent study and work, though relieved of much of the sense of drudgery and weariness usually implied by the word work."[63]

The humble Armstrong did not mention in his *Journal* article that one outgrowth of his steady, consistent study was a successful professional healing practice within two years after taking class instruction. By 1892 he was advertising as a Christian Science practitioner in San Jose, holding office hours at his home on Fourth Street near Saint James Park. Dr. Fluno had advised Armstrong to start his practice in San Jose because there was no Christian Science practitioner there at that time, but there had been in the mid-1880s when a young woman named Sue Ella Bradshaw, "brimming with enthusiasm" for Christian Science, had lived on Second Street. She had taken class instruction from Mary Baker Eddy in Boston and had worked as a healer and teacher in San Jose for a few years, but at Eddy's urging, Bradshaw moved to the much larger city of San Francisco. Armstrong filled the vacancy in San

Jose. It "proved to be a stepping stone" in his career. Both Allen and his wife Maud were practitioners, working together and advertising together in the *Christian Science Journal*.[64]

Another outgrowth of Armstrong's dedication was his success in establishing a Christian Science church in San Jose, with 20 charter members. What previously had been two informal groups meeting in private homes became one church with advertised meetings. As the *Christian Science Journal* later reported, this San Jose church had been started on the "sound basis" of the members having been healed and regenerated through the study of Christian Science and many of them "devot[ing] themselves entirely to the practice of this healing truth." They met one block southeast from Saint James Park at the Oddfellows Building at Third and Santa Clara Streets until they moved a block farther south to Louise Hall on Second and San Fernando Streets, where they would meet until they built their own church building.[65]

In January 1899, Allen and Maud traveled together to Boston to take advanced studies in Christian Science, the teachers' training program called the Normal Class. Edward Kimball was one of their instructors. Both Armstrongs graduated, but only Allen would be a teacher, with Maud as his assistant.[66]

Armstrong was First Reader at the San Jose church, and the congregation was getting ready to build an edifice when he "received the invitation" from the Seattle church. As a newly trained and credentialed teacher, he was a prime candidate for meeting Seattle's need. He was "exceedingly loath to leave the little band of students who loved him," but "loyal to his Leader and the teaching he had received," he agreed to make the move. At a meeting on November 10, he submitted his letter of resignation and withdrawal from the San Jose church. In response they passed resolutions "expressing regret at his intended departure," then they held a going-away party for the Armstrongs. They decorated Louise Hall with flowers and potted plants and put on "fine musical entertainment," a piano duet and vocal solos, followed by "delicious refreshments" in the dining room. Then the Armstrongs, with their two teenage children, Harry and Ottie, left for Seattle.[67]

On December 9, 1899, the Armstrongs signed the register book to become members of First Church of Christ, Scientist, Seattle. They would both be members at this branch church for the rest of their lives. But as dedicated as Allen Armstrong became to his new church in Seattle, he did not forget about the San Jose church. When his former church began construction on their planned edifice, Allen contributed the corner-stone as his personal gift. Prior to starting construction on their edifice, which cost $40,000, the San Jose church made remarkably generous contributions to The Mother Church of $24,000. In a letter of gratitude to their Leader, they wrote, "We know that all we have, we owe to your faithful love and labor for mankind. We understand that it is not words you require from your followers so much as works, and this branch has endeavored to live up to this requirement." Upon completion and dedication, the San Jose church received the rare honor of a dedicatory letter from Reverend Eddy, here in its entirety:

> *Beloved Students*:—Words are inadequate to express my deep appreciation of your labor and success in completing and dedicating your church edifice, and of the great hearts and ready hands of our far Western students, the Christian Scientists.
>
> Comparing such students with those whose words are but the substitutes for works, we learn that the translucent atmosphere of the former, must illumine the midnight of the latter, else Christian Science will disappear from among mortals.
>
> I thank divine Love for the hope set before us in the Word and in the doers thereof, "for of such is the kingdom of heaven."
>
> Gratefully, lovingly,
>
> Mary Baker Eddy[68]

For his public debut in Seattle as a practitioner of Christian Science and an esteemed teacher, in his city directory listing, it seems fitting that instead of trying to explain his professional services in a display advertisement or even adding his Christian Science educational credentials "C.S.B" after his name, he advertised simply as "Allen H. Armstrong, Christian Scientist." These two words were a perfect description for this new teacher for the far western students in Seattle.

DEDICATION

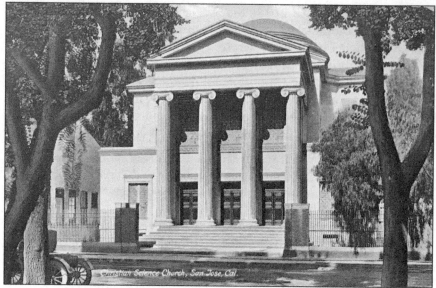

First Church of Christ, Scientist, San Jose, California

8

Christian Science Chapel (1900)

With the arrival of Allen and Maud Armstrong, the number of professional Christian Science practitioners in Seattle immediately doubled—from two to four. After the Armstrongs' first year in Seattle, the number of practitioners would double again, to eight, and after two years the number would nearly double again, to fourteen. It was the start of an exponential growth pattern for practitioners that would continue throughout Armstrong's long teaching career in Seattle. The impact of his arrival rippled out beyond the professional healing practice. Growth of church membership also accelerated.[69]

Armstrong's work as a Christian Science teacher involved interviewing prospective students, teaching a twelve-day intensive course each year, holding an annual conference with all of his students for another day of instruction, plus "patiently and persistently" supporting students individually afterward—all this besides working with patients in his own healing practice. Besides his work as a teacher, he also served in other roles in the church. He served as First Reader (with Maud as Second Reader), board chair, church president, and on the committee that interviewed applicants for church membership. For a few years, Armstrong was in the role of Committee on Publication for managing public relations and legal issues for Christian Scientists throughout the state of Washington. But as an especially significant aspect of his leadership, almost immediately upon his arrival in Seattle, Armstrong encouraged the church to undertake a building project.[70]

The church had made many moves through the 1890s, holding their services in a variety of rented rooms downtown. From Russell Hall, they moved a few blocks to the Seattle National Bank Building at Yesler Way and Second Avenue—the same intersection where the Smith Tower would later be built and one block from the totem pole at Pioneer Square. The second floor room at the bank building was the studio of music teacher John Post, one of their charter members. They moved back to Russell Hall, then back again to the bank building. For several months they met in a Unitarian church. About every year or two they moved. Sometimes they needed to move abruptly and had great difficulty finding a new location. The few halls available for rent were either on the "extreme outskirts of the city," or surrounded by taverns and brothels and other such activities that "members of other churches might hesitate about attending a service there." Besides the instability, uncertainty, and undesirability of rented spaces, the rents were high. They decided they might as well buy their own building.[71]

Armstrong, on a committee with two others, began looking for a suitable building lot. In October 1900, the membership voted to move forward with plans to build "Christian Science Hall." In November, they purchased a lot on Sixth Avenue between Columbia and Marion Streets. They soon built a wood-frame structure with a carpeted auditorium large enough to seat 500 with folding chairs. It was a dark-colored two-story building in bungalow style with a low-pitched hipped roof. It looked like a large house, and the construction cost was similar to a large house. The lot cost $3,500 and the building and furnishings about another $6,400. "The church follows the rules of Science in construction, and pays as it goes," Armstrong reported in the *Christian Science Sentinel*. They paid for construction with cash on hand, and paid off the mortgage on the lot just after the building was completed. On Easter Sunday, April 7, 1901, they held the first service in what they sometimes referred to as their "Christian Science chapel." The church service was at 11 a.m., and the Sunday School session for children followed at noon. Weekly testimony meetings were at 8 p.m. on Wednesdays. The chapel was just up the hill from their previous locations. Within two blocks was a Carnegie Library, the fire station, the new Rainier Club headquarters, and Central High School. Finally, they had a stable home base in a convenient location.[72]

One of the "first fruits" of the new church was the opening of their "first regular down-town reading rooms" in 1904. Their new reading room was on the sixth floor of the Marion Building, an office building on the corner of Second Avenue and Marion Street. It was two connecting rooms, open daily from noon to 5 p.m. Mrs. Martha E. Cliff, a Christian Science practitioner, was the volunteer librarian, a position she had held since 1898. Armstrong then moved his office from his home to the third floor of the Marion Building.[73] [74]

Having centrally-located reading rooms and active literature distribution was an important factor in the growth of Christian Science. From early on, the members of First Church looked far beyond their own congregation and their own neighborhood. They actively worked to spread Christian Science throughout the region. They sent literature 1,500 miles north to the Klondike gold rush area in the Canadian Yukon Territory to support an informal group that held occasional meetings "in halls and in cabins in town and on the creeks"—to which some reportedly traveled as far as 16 miles by dogsled to attend—and ran a little reading room that was open "all the time." Alaska and the Yukon was a focus of the Seattle church until local churches were established there. They also sponsored the first Christian Science lecture in the state capitol of Olympia, 60 miles south, and in the seaport town of Port Townsend on the Olympic Peninsula, a similar distance west.[75]

They expanded their outreach efforts with more lectures in Seattle. By 1902 they were filling Seattle's newest premier theater, the 2,200-seat Grand Opera House, to capacity with standing room on both the main floor and balcony and turning away hundreds for lack of room. Although still portrayed in the newspapers in a tone of ridicule, sarcasm, and even dismay, Christian Science was gaining respectability, in part because of the participation of prominent citizens like Judge William G. Ewing, who came to Seattle to lecture. Judge Ewing had been a close friend of President Abraham Lincoln, a law partner of Vice President Stevenson, and a US District Attorney in Illinois. Ewing left his judicial career for the public practice of Christian Science after being healed of asthma. He was introduced to the audience of nearly 3,000 people at the Grand Opera House by a Unitarian minister, Reverend W.D. Simonds, who said:

> Whether you accept this philosophy or whether you reject it, whether you believe it true in part or erroneous in part, you will all, to the last man of you, and woman too, agree with me in this,—that Christian Science has earned its right to be heard; it has earned its right to the candid and earnest attention of all sincere men. It is not possible for a rational man to dismiss this philosophy with a scornful wave of the hand, with a toss of the head, or a curl of the lip; for a faith that in a little more than a quarter of a century has won thousands of adherents in this materialistic age,—and among those, men of eminence and women of attainments, —I say, deserves the candid attention of every sincere man.[76]

43

DEDICATION

Seattle had grown tremendously from a little-known town of about 40,000 in 1890 to a city of over 80,000 people in 1900, and it was on its way to more than doubling in population again in the next decade. The seating capacity of the newest theaters was also growing, and Christian Science lectures continued to fill them. Around 3% of the entire city population was attending each of these lectures, and the lectures were being held with increasing frequency, at Seattle's largest venues— places like the Grand Opera House, the Moore Theater, the Hippodrome, and the Dreamland Dance Hall.

Attendance at church services at the Christian Science chapel was increasing too. Within five years of completing their 500-seat auditorium, First Church had outgrown it. But even as this very first edifice was being built, it was intended to be temporary. They did not lay a cornerstone, nor ever hold a dedication service. "We reverently believe that Truth will soon enable us to build a structure worthy of the city and the cause we love," Armstrong wrote. "It is the purpose of this church to go forward at once with such a work."[77]

The very idea of building a magnificent church was somewhat provocative. Around this time, Christian Scientists all over the world were building larger and more elegant buildings than ever before. They were receiving some criticism for their efforts. They were supposed to be dedicated to the fulfilment of Jesus' command: "Heal the sick, cleanse the lepers, raise the dead, cast out devils" (Matt. 10:8). To some critics, building construction was at odds with this Christian healing mission. This issue was addressed in the *Christian Science Sentinel*:

> A friend recently said to us: "It seems to me you would be more closely following Jesus, whom you profess to emulate, if you would go into the slums with your work, feeding the hungry and rescuing the perishing, instead of erecting magnificent and costly temples of worship throughout the country." . . .
>
> We voice the sentiment of hundreds of thousands in saying that they are living evidences of Christian Science fruitage from the slums of despondency, drunkenness, despair, hatred, malice, revenge, and vice. . . .
>
> Multiplied millions are expended in the construction of universities, colleges, schools, and libraries, yet the most important study which can engage the attention of man is that of Christian Science. For the proper exposition of this Science, so essential to the happiness of all, buildings are erected to meet its demands which, completed without sacrifice, free from debt, beautiful, and harmonious,—are not yet commensurate with their supreme need as focal

points for the instruction of mankind. These structures stand as evidences of the power of Truth; as lighthouses pointing the way from the rocks and shoals of material sense, to safety, reality, infinite Mind; as object-lessons to the "weary and heavy-laden," who may come and be relieved of every burden. . . . Their development marks an epoch of freedom from the world's bondage to sin and sorrow.[78]

Regardless of any perceived conflict of mission, internally or externally, First Church of Christ, Scientist, Seattle, under Allen H. Armstrong's leadership, had successfully completed a building project, a Christian Science chapel. But this was only the beginning.

Christian Science Chapel on Sixth Avenue, above vacant block, upper right
Paul Dorpat collection

Close up of Christian Science Chapel from two angles
Paul Dorpat collection

9

Mother Church Extension (1902)

At the 1902 Annual Meeting of The Mother Church in Boston, a call for financial support was put out to members. Another church building project was beginning. During the membership business meeting, held at Mechanics Hall, Edward A. Kimball offered the following motion, seconded by Judge William Ewing:

> Recognizing the necessity for providing an auditorium for the Mother Church that will seat four or five thousand persons, and acting in behalf of ourselves and the Christian Scientists of the world, we agree to contribute any portion of $2,000,000 that may be necessary for this purpose.

In support of the motion, Mr. Kimball said in part, "We need to keep pace with our own growth and progress. The necessity here indicated is beyond cavil; beyond resistance in your thought."[79]

The First Church of Christ, Scientist, in Boston, was outgrowing its stone edifice built twelve years earlier, even with three regular Sunday Services. As one writer described it,

> In larger and larger throngs they presented themselves at the doors, until not alone every seat was taken, but people stood in the rear of the auditorium, they stood at the front near the Readers' platform, they stood in the balcony, they sat on the stairs and on the wide ledges of the windows.[80]

By request of Reverend Mary Baker Eddy, branch churches were organized in Cambridge, Chelsea, and Roxbury, Massachusetts, but even with these new churches attracting some portion of the throngs, the Boston church continued to overflow. The original edifice had too much significance to be torn down and replaced with a larger building.

Instead, a new larger one would be built adjacent to the original to give more room for local regular attendance and provide a place to hold the Annual Meeting of Mother Church members in "the sacred atmosphere of church-home," as Clerk William B. Johnson described it. This extension to the Mother Church would be the largest church in Boston and one of the largest churches in the world. As for this two-million-dollar motion by Mr. Kimball, the *Boston Journal* reported:

> This astonishing motion was passed both with unanimity and assurance. It was not even talked over, beyond two brief explanations why the building was needed. Learning that a big church was required, the money to provide it was pledged with the readiness and dispatch of an ordinary mortal passing out a nickel for carfare.[81]

The Extension project in Boston meant that Christian Scientists all over the world were being asked to contribute an astronomical amount to the new Building Fund. The number of congregations throughout the country and the world had increased significantly since the original church was built. The general financial success of its members had also increased. But it was still an enormous financial commitment. Once again, Rev. Eddy required the building project to be completed without incurring any debt. During the two-year construction period, the Clerk of The Mother Church communicated the status of the Building Fund through the periodicals. "A considerable sum is still needed to complete the work," was a typical message making the need known. "[R]emittances should be prompt and liberal."[82]

Branch churches, like the one in Seattle, put their own building projects on hold to send funds to Boston. Even children collected and earned money to give to The Mother Church. The Sunday School children in Seattle made the significant contribution of $794.37. Some branch churches, like the one in San Jose, California, donated their entire building fund, an amount that may have taken years to accumulate.[83]

The architectural team, including Charles Brigham of Boston and Solon Spencer Beman of Chicago, rose to the challenge of finding a design solution for fitting the five-thousand seat auditorium into an odd-shaped lot that complemented the adjoining original church. The final design was influenced by great religious edifices in Rome, Florence, and Constantinople. It had auditorium floor space of 25,000 square feet, throughout which a "normal, unexcited, unstrained" voice from the Readers' platform could be clearly heard, without amplification.[84]

DEDICATION

The Extension was distinctly different from the original church in architectural style, in the type of stone, and in its lack of pictorial windows or any kind of symbolism. The Extension project was like the original in the number of challenges overcome to complete and pay for the edifice on schedule. Dedication services were held on Communion Sunday, June 10, 1906—almost exactly four years after the building project was initiated.

An estimated 30,000 people attended the dedication services. Among them were twelve from Seattle. A *Boston Herald* report described the impressive event:

> Five thousand people kneeling in silent communion; a stillness profound; and then, rising in unison from the vast congregation, the words of the Lord's Prayer! . . . And such was the scene repeated six times during the day. It was a sight which no one who saw it will ever be able to forget. . . . [Its] grandeur sprang from the complete unanimity of thought and purpose. There was something emanating from the thousands who worshipped under the dome of the great edifice whose formal opening they had gathered to observe, that appealed to and fired the imagination. A comparatively new religion launching upon a new era, assuming an altogether different status before the world![85]

The new church did indeed give Christian Science an "altogether different status before the world." The Boston dedication was newsworthy for newspapers across the country and beyond. In the American heartland, the *Topeka Daily Capital* reported to Kansas readers the impact the building had on one writer's view:

> Those of us who do not accept the doctrine of Christian Science are possibly too prone to approach it in a spirit of levity, too often disposed to touch upon it with the tongue of facetiousness. Too often we see only its ridiculous phases, attaching meanwhile no importance to the saneness and common sense which underlie many of the practices in its name. And many of us have missed entirely its tremendous growth and the part it has come to play in the economy of our social and religious life. . . .
>
> To those of us who have overlooked these essentials of its hold upon the public, . . . some of the evidence appears in the concrete and cannot be combated. "One cannot sneer away the two-million-dollar stone edifice or the thirty thousand worshippers who entered its portals Sunday," says the *Springfield Republican*. Neither can we overlook the steady, consistent growth of the sect in every community in which it has found a foothold.[86]

Of special interest in the national news was the unusually quiet way of the Christian Scientists in building their churches, the astonishing confidence they had in their building plans, and their even more unusual ways of paying for them. It was newsworthy how the Treasurer at The Mother Church once again asked people to stop giving money. As the *Boston Globe* paraphrased, "Please do not send us any more money—we have enough!"[87]

As with the original edifice, Eddy did not attend the opening events. Once again, she sent a dedicatory letter to be read to the congregation. This one was entitled "Choose ye." It included:

> Beloved, I am not with you in *propria persona* at this memorable Dedication and Communion season, but I am with you in spirit and in truth, lovingly thanking your generosity and fidelity, and saying virtually what the prophet said: 'Continue to choose whom ye will serve." . . . You have dexterously and wisely provided for The Mother Church of Christ, Scientist, a magnificent Temple wherein to enter and pray. Greatly impressed and encouraged thereby, deeply do I thank you for this proof of your progress, unity, and love.[88]

At Annual Meeting two days later on Tuesday, June 12, 1906, the Clerk of The Mother Church, William B. Johnson, read his letter to their "beloved Teacher and Leader," including:

> The great temple is finished! This massive pile of New Hampshire granite and Bedford stone, rising to a height of two hundred and twenty-four feet, one foot loftier than the Bunker Hill monument, stands a material type of Truth's permanence.[89]

A motion to approve the Clerk's letter was carried unanimously by a rising vote of those members attending—members who had come from all over the country and Europe.

To outside observers, as exemplified by reporter John Copley in the *Seattle Star*, The Mother Church Extension was an important architectural achievement of historical significance:

> The First Church of Christ, Scientist, in Boston, the "mother church," will probably stand for centuries as a monument to the founder of the faith. It is the most beautiful cathedral built in modern times, and beyond question the most imposing edifice in North America.[90]

DEDICATION

To Christian Scientists, the new building was an important achievement of spiritual significance. In her book about the Extension building project, Margaret Williamson wrote,

> the new church embodied a might, a majesty, and a grace far beyond the bounds ordinarily achieved by a church body seeking to erect a suitable place in which to conduct its worship. These characteristics were but the natural outward expression of an inward devotion, consecration, and development.[91]

In the *Christian Science Sentinel*, Anna Friendlich shared her insights on the topic of "Church Building in Christian Science" in her 1908 article:

> The Christian Science church rises—an exhalation out of the love, gratitude, and inspiration of hearts chastened and lives rescued by the Father in heaven. A study of the 'structure of Truth and Love,' as defined in our denominational text-book, *Science and Health* (p. 583), leads us to recognize the fact that in Christian Science building is healing. As the errors and sins, the ignorance and fears in our own consciousness are healed, the structure of Truth and Love stands revealed, the walls of salvation appear within the pure heart where the psalmist saith God is seen.[92]

With the Extension now complete and paid for, at Annual Meeting many branch church representatives announced that they would go and do likewise. They would build large elegant church edifices in their own cities. The Mother Church Extension project was the new model. A wave of Christian Science church building was about to ripple out across the globe, including in Seattle.

The Mother Church Extension under construction

Postcard

The Mother Church in Boston with completed Temple Extension

Postcard

10

Resolutions (1906)

The twelve Christian Scientists from Seattle who went to The Mother Church Extension dedication service and Annual Meeting returned ready to build a large elegant stone church inspired by the temple of New Hampshire granite and Bedford limestone just built in Boston. The Seattle congregation would soon need a new building, because they were overflowing their wood-frame chapel on Sixth Avenue completed five years earlier. To follow the examples set in Boston, however, would require a monumental financial commitment by local church members, because while The Mother Church had the financial support of branch churches all over the world, a Seattle building project could not count on outside help. The Seattle branch would, presumably, be on its own.

In November 1906, First Church of Christ, Scientist, Seattle, set their building project in motion by purchasing a building lot on credit. The 120-foot-square lot was at the corner of Sixteenth Avenue and Denny Street in the Capitol Hill District, east of downtown. This meant their new church would be in a distinctly different area from where they had been for the previous twenty years.[93]

The rationale for the move to Capitol Hill was not recorded in church meeting minutes. One reason may have been the regrade, a massive long-term municipal project to flatten the downtown streets. The regrade was a noisy, dusty, muddy mess of earth moving and construction. Buildings were being lowered, demolished, and remodeled because of the street elevation changes. In 1906 city engineers were working on Second and Third Avenues, just a few blocks from the Christian Science chapel and near their reading room. By moving to

Capitol Hill, they removed themselves from these disruptions that would continue for several years.

Capitol Hill had only recently been developing as a residential neighborhood. The district was named in hopeful expectation that Seattle would become the capital of Washington State and the hill would become a government center. But that never happened. Instead, Seattle's upper class built mansions there. The new Christian Science church would be near the homes of some of Seattle's most prominent citizens. The district was far enough away that it was then like a suburb to downtown. "Take Madison Street or Capitol Hill cars," advised the new advertisement in the *Christian Science Journal,* giving directions for taking public transit from downtown to the new location. The Christian Science church would no longer be in the center of the regional transportation system of ferries, trains, streetcars, and trolley lines where people from all the outlying areas could easily reach it. Even the members who lived downtown would have to travel a long distance uphill. The location choice was an apparently quick decision that would have a long-term impact.

It seems the members were not consulted. A committee of four men chose the building site and the board approved their choice with little discussion. The purchase was efficient, allowing the next steps in the building process to proceed immediately. But just as the building project was getting underway, the church faced a series of issues that threatened to divide the congregation. There was a controversy over church employees involving hiring criteria and salaries that triggered a round of resignations. There was also concern expressed about cliques and factions that had developed within the church.

Also around this time, they literally had to divide the congregation to fit everyone in at church services. Their chapel was designed to seat 500. Regular attendance at their Sunday morning service had grown to 600. They needed to add a second service. Members were asked to attend the evening service if possible, to allow more room for visitors at the morning service. The growing Sunday School session at noon moved to a larger space across the street into the old Rainier Hotel.[94]

The growth rate of the church was increasing. Twice each year, they were admitting twenty to thirty new members. About a third of the new members had already been members of Christian Science churches elsewhere. They had moved to Seattle from other cities in Washington State: Everett to the north, Tacoma to the south, Walla Walla to the southeast, and Spokane on the far east side of the state. Or they moved from other places in the western United States: Portland, San Francisco,

DEDICATION

San Jose, Los Angeles, Denver, Colorado Springs, Chicago, Saint Louis, Kansas City, Montana, Minnesota, and Texas. A few came from the Boston area. Some of these experienced Christian Scientists were already in the full-time public practice of Christian Science healing. Some were even Christian Science teachers. Besides Allen H. Armstrong, the teachers were Mrs. Edith Spencer Alexander, Miss Louisa C. Eaton, Mrs. Lydia Chase Glanville, and Mr. Theodore R. Hinsdale. But most of the new members were new to Christian Science. They were coming from a variety of religious backgrounds: Baptist, Congregational, Episcopalian, Greek Orthodox, Methodist, Presbyterian, Unitarian, Roman Catholic, and even a Swedenborgian. Some claimed no prior religious affiliation. Each batch of new members had to be integrated into the social aspects and operations of the church. Even newcomers were appointed or elected to important positions.[95]

With all this growth and preparation for building, by mid-1907 there was a larger stirring that needed to be addressed. At the June 7 semi-annual membership meeting, Edwin Randall Hoskins, a young stenographer from Chicago, proposed a resolution. Mr. Hoskins moved that they mail a letter to all the members with an appeal for $4,200 for the building fund and include a call for unity. No steps would be taken toward organizing any new branch churches in Seattle without the cooperation and support of "the entire church body of Christian Scientists of Seattle," and in the meantime, "this entire church body, individually and collectively" would unite in energetically supporting the construction of this first church. Once another branch church was formed, then "the entire church body of Christian Scientists in Seattle shall again unitedly cooperate in the erection" of the next church, which will be treated "in every way co-equal" to First Church, and "this accomplished, the cause of Christian Science in Seattle will have been established in such complete unity as to assure all further development being in accord with Love's plan." The motion prevailed. The unity resolution was adopted.[96]

The letter may have been intended to prevent a split of the church into two separate churches. The effort succeeded. But circumstances beyond their control were at work, resulting in a second church. Just a few days prior to the meeting, the City of Seattle had annexed the neighboring town to the north, making Ballard a new district. There was a small Christian Science church in Ballard, established several years earlier, with services and a Reading Room at the Carnegie Free Public Library. It was now officially in Seattle. First Church of Christ, Scientist, Ballard, was now Second Church of Christ, Scientist, Seattle.

Even without any split or formal agreement, the Seattle church body had just expanded. The members of First Church voted to send their greetings to Second Church.

Capitol Hill trolley car
Courtesy of Seattle Municipal Archives (item 64767)

11

Not the Old Style Church (1907)

T he members wanted a "Grecian style" building for their new church in the Capitol Hill District, sometime referred to as "Grecian temple." To oversee the construction project, First Church of Christ, Scientist, Seattle, approved the formation of an executive directorate comprised of the seven elected members of the board, the elected president, and a board-appointed building committee, initially with Allen H. Armstrong as chair. They also created a finance committee to advise the board. Mr. Armstrong explained to prospective architects that they wanted "General style, same as adopted by many of our people — not the old style church." The initial goal was a fireproof auditorium with no gallery that would seat 1,200 to 1,500 people plus a large foyer, all for less than $100,000. Later the building committee added to their list "best possible" acoustics, ample heating and ventilation, stone exterior, and "perhaps a dome with sunburst for part of the light." They wanted an organ and pews, but the committee reiterated the importance of a design that was "away from the old church style."[97]

Through a design contest by invitation in late summer 1907, the church selected Bebb & Mendel Architects, the most prominent Seattle architectural firm. As Charles H. Bebb mentioned in his statement of qualifications, the company had just been awarded the design work for the Washington State Pavilion at the upcoming 1909 international fair in Seattle, the Alaska-Yukon-Pacific Exposition (AYP). First Church chose Bebb & Mendel over two architects who were Christian Scientists: George Wesley Bullard, a prominent architect in Tacoma, and Solon Spencer Beman, the nationally known architect from Chicago who had designed The Mother Church Extension and twenty-five Christian Science branch churches (so far), and had established the neo-classical standard for Christian Science churches. The building committee's choice was quick and approved by the directorate with apparently little discussion. The church had previously worked with Bebb & Mendel for the design of their current structure, the wood-frame bungalow chapel on Sixth Avenue. The relationship with their architect was continuing, and through this building project it would develop into what felt like a partnership. Mr. Bebb's "connection with the Directors" that would extend "over a lengthy period of time" he would later describe as "one of the most interesting and pleasant experiences of my business career." Together they would explore ideas on how to "give architectural expression" to this new religious sect, "eliminating the language expressed by ecclesiastical buildings of other Christian denominations," intentionally making a "radical departure" from "precedents."[98]

Around this time, the building committee moved its meetings from Mr. Armstrong's practitioner office to Oliver C. McGilvra's law office, or occasionally the McGilvra residence just off Madison Street. Oliver McGilvra was unusually wealthy from inheriting a large portion of the 420 acres of prime Seattle real estate his father, Judge John Jay McGilvra, had acquired during the early pioneer days. Madison Street was originally a lengthy private road between the McGilvra estate on the shore of Lake Washington and the McGilvra law office downtown. John McGilvra, who would one day have a boulevard, a public school, and a park named after him, had a law partnership with Thomas Burke, a civic-minded railroad attorney and former chief justice of the Washington Supreme Court, who would one day have a museum and an urban trail named after him. Oliver, John McGilvra's only son, was following in his father's footsteps in the legal profession and in partnership with Burke, Oliver's brother-in-law. In 1907, Oliver became associated with the Christian Science Church. Even before his membership was official, McGilvra was speaking about Christian Science at public events, starting with introducing a lecture by Dr. Francis J. Fluno at the Grand Opera House. When Oliver and his wife, Maud, became members of First Church in November 1907, Oliver was immediately appointed to the building committee. He began hosting the meetings at the Burke, Shepard & McGilvra law office on the fourth floor of the Burke Building at Second and Marion. The following year, McGilvra became church president. Having such a prominent Seattle citizen take a strong leadership role in the church must have helped accelerate the momentum of the building project—and the growth of the congregation. They certainly had come a long way from the early days 15 years prior when the modest little band of beginners first started holding meetings at a downtown boardinghouse.[99]

These far-western students of Christian Science wanted to share the good news with their Leader about the expensive edifice they planned to build. On behalf of the church, Armstrong and McGilvra sent a special package to Mary Baker Eddy. They sent her a leather-bound photo album with architectural plans showing several cross sections and an artist's rendering of the design. The album also included photographs of commercial fishing in Seattle, illustrating and explaining the entire process of catching salmon and canning it. They also sent a case of canned salmon, and two fresh fish packed in ice, along with a letter of greeting. They hoped this unique Puget Sound gift package might provide a "moment of interest" and a gourmet treat for their Leader. But because of the extreme demands on Eddy's time, she may have never even known about it.[100]

As they was preparing to build—going through the design process, getting construction estimates, and looking into different types of stone and other materials—attendance at their church services overflowed, making it impossible to stay in their chapel even with two Sunday services. In the spring of 1908, they moved to a larger auditorium, Christensen Hall at Broadway and Madison Streets. According to church records, "[R]emarkable cases of healing" were "taking place daily," the members were "expanding spiritually," demand for Mary Baker Eddy's textbook was increasing, and the growth was "continuous." During the two years at Christensen Hall, attendance increased to 1,000.[101]

On the question of how to welcome strangers, handle the influx of new members from diverse backgrounds, and run their organization, the membership made a conscious choice not to rely on what they called the "old methods adopted by other churches." This church wanted to do things in a new way. All the members were on the welcoming committee. Everyone would be involved in the building project and kept informed of the progress.[102]

On December 8, 1908, the members voted unanimously to proceed at once with the building project as planned. Excavation work began in January. Under the McGilvra presidency, the membership body would make many more decisions about the building project. They decided to build with stone on all four sides rather than just a facade facing the street. They chose Bedford limestone from Indiana, the same stone used for The Mother Church Extension, instead of local Chuckanut stone. They voted to sell their chapel and put the money toward construction of the new stone temple. All these recommendations from the building committee were approved by the membership with little discussion.

But when a proposal was made to build a temporary wood structure inside the foundation for holding services while the stone walls were being built around it, it was strongly rejected. Almost two-thirds of the members present voted against it. They voted against even exploring the idea any further. So on June 9, 1909, when First Reader William K. Sheldon ended the Wednesday testimony meeting early at the request of the board and President McGilvra announced to the membership that the board thought it wise to proceed with construction of the temporary structure, it almost certainly caused a stir within the membership.

The following Tuesday, there was a special meeting of the board. After "a long informal talk," Edwin W. Craven moved to proceed with construction of a temporary structure. Frances Carlton Baker spoke strongly against the motion. She read a long statement from Mr. Sheldon that referred to the recent membership vote against this course of action. The involvement of Sheldon in the board discussion was significant because as the First Reader, although he was "not a Leader," according to Mary Baker Eddy's organizational design, he was responsible for enforcing the church bylaws and protecting the democratic process. Mrs. Baker had served as First Reader prior to Sheldon, so some members could have felt that she too held special authority.[103]

But despite the vigorous protest made by Mrs. Baker, the motion to build a temporary structure passed. All the board members voted for it, except Mrs. Baker.

Architectural rendering of First Church of Christ, Scientist, Seattle

Post card

Burke Building on Second Avenue and Marion Street

Courtesy of Seattle Municipal Archives (item 65330)

12

Letter of Withdrawal (1909)

T he board held a special meeting on Tuesday, June 29, 1909, in their usual meeting location, the Christian Science Reading Room. Several years before, First Church of Christ, Scientist, Seattle, had moved their reading room from the Marion Building to the new fourteen-story Alaska Building at the corner of Second Avenue and Cherry Street. The Alaska Building was Seattle's first steel-frame high-rise building, and it was the tallest building in Washington State. Towering over all the other buildings downtown, it was a symbol of the growth, prosperity, and innovation that had been transforming the city ever since the 1897 Klondike gold rush, for which Seattle was the gateway. The Arctic Club for businessmen involved in the Alaska trade was on the top floor, where they had a commanding view of the city and the activity of trains and ships. Even the ninth floor where the Christian Science Reading Room was located had unobstructed views of the city and Elliott Bay. The typical meeting time was eight o'clock in the evening. With the long days of summer, as the board meeting began, the setting sun would have been hanging just above the rugged snow-covered Olympic Mountains in the distance beyond Puget Sound.[104]

All of the board members were present, except Mrs. Baker. Several church members came to meet with the board. Cooper Willis, Ada Winterbourne, Alice A. Hansen, and Adela S. Hawley presented the following letter:

To the Directors of First Church of Christ, Scientist, Seattle,

Resolved. That owing to the rapid and continued growth of the Cause of Christian Science in Seattle, and to the limited capacity of our present quarters, and of the temporary structure to be erected on the new property on Sixteenth Avenue and Denny Way, and further, to meet the growing need for a downtown church, we the undersigned members of First Church of Christ, Scientist, of Seattle, hereby lovingly withdraw our membership from First Church for the purpose of organizing Fourth Church of Christ, Scientist, of Seattle, to be in a location convenient for those living in the outlying districts.

The necessity for taking this step would cause us regret did we not have the furtherance of the Cause of Christian Science at heart, and we assure you that it is taken in a spirit of love and good will.

Yours, in the bonds of Truth and Love.[105]

The letter was signed by thirty-nine members. The very first name on the list was Frances Carlton Baker. Mrs. Baker was almost certainly the one who initiated this organized withdrawal.

Mrs. Baker was neither rich nor famous. Even within the Christian Science community, she would never be widely known outside her own local church congregation. The society page of the newspaper did not report on her activities. She was typical of the early Christian Scientists of humble origins who did the hard work of healing with little fanfare. She was one of the very first Christian Scientists in Seattle, having taken the first class in 1890, and she was among the first practitioners in Seattle. She had helped build up the church from its earliest beginnings. She had consistently been one of the most dedicated members. She was the first Second Reader and had served twice as First Reader. She had been Sunday School superintendent for five years, she served two terms on the board, and on the building finance committee. She had welcomed all the newcomers, interviewing applicants and recommending them for membership. For nearly 20 years, she had supported the growth of Christian Science in Seattle. An entire generation had grown up under her nurturing care. Her name was at the top of the list of the original charter members, at the top of the list of board members that signed their Christmas greeting letter to Mary Baker Eddy in 1903, and now her name was at the top of the list of those withdrawing in protest. This pillar of the church was leading an exodus of members.[106]

The board clerk read a separate letter from Mrs. Baker: her letter of resignation from the board. But, since her letter of resignation from membership had just been accepted, the board took no action because they considered her board membership already severed. The content of this letter was not recorded in the minutes for posterity.

Another letter added three names to the list of those withdrawing, for a total of forty-two. Among them were three members of the building committee: Erika Frederickson, a practitioner who had led the spiritual focus of the building project; Emma A. Hawkins, who had initially supported the idea of the temporary structure but apparently had changed her mind; and Anne H. Thomas, one of the longest-serving members. Also among the names were practitioners Lilian Harding, Mary B. LaBee, Nettie E. Morse, Hattie A. Range, plus two former Reading Room librarians, Jessie Estep, a practitioner and leading charter member with Mrs. Baker, and Adela S. Hawley, who had the special distinction of having been a member of First Church of Christ, Scientist, Chicago, Edward Kimball's church and, proving her popularity, having served two years as librarian during the only two years that the job was an elected office. In all, the group leaving included three founders and eight *Journal*-listed practitioners.

As board clerk, Edwin W. Craven accepted the letter of withdrawal. Mr. Craven and Mrs. Baker must have known each other quite well since they were serving together on the board for the second time. Craven, along with Oliver C. McGilvra, was representative of the prominent men who were becoming involved in Christian Science at this time—lawyers, judges, businessmen, consultants, financiers—and who were quickly rising to positions of importance. Since joining the church in 1900, Craven and his law firm, Craven & Craven, had been in charge of purchasing both the lot on Sixth Avenue and the one at Sixteenth and Denny. He had served on the building committee for both of the building projects. Prior to recently going full-time into the practice of Christian Science healing, Craven had been Grand Commander of the Grand Commandery of the Knights Templar of Washington, a popular Masonic fraternal organization that marched military style in local parades. He was accustomed to commanding, and he commanded a certain amount of respect. To Craven, Mrs. Baker's rebellion might have seemed like a challenge to his leadership role in the church, a vote of no confidence—not only regarding the temporary structure he had proposed, but also the new Capitol Hill location he had selected and purchased.[107]

The group withdrawing wanted to return to their previous downtown location. A year before, perhaps with a similar desire, a group of thirteen, including Christian Science Teacher Louisa C. Eaton, had withdrawn to form Third Church. Third Church had services and reading rooms at Third Avenue and University Street, with Miss Eaton as First Reader. First Church began announcing to its attendees that there were three Christian Science churches in Seattle and to see the bulletin board for more information—a gesture of support for the new Third Church. But this church was probably already having problems, and before the end of the year they would disband, which the *Christian Science Sentinel* reported as being "for the best good of the Cause of Christian Science." It was an important warning for the wise. Even during this era of rapid growth in Christian Science church attendance and membership, the mere act of forming a new branch did not ensure success, and neither did having a central location where Christian Science activities had previously flourished. However, Mrs. Baker's group had what it took to build a successful Christian Science church. They had done it before. If the city had not recently annexed Ballard with its tiny Christian Science church, and if not for the briefly operating Third Church, Mrs. Baker's withdrawing group might have been the second in Seattle, but recent events required it to take the name Fourth Church.[108]

The clerk responded promptly with a letter of response to Mrs. Baker and all the other signers.

> Your withdrawal from membership has been received, and accepted, and in compliance therewith your name has been dropped from the roll.
>
> In the matter of your withdrawal from First Church of Christ, Scientist, Seattle, the Board of Directors regret that it seemed to you desirable to do so, but extend to you good wishes and a Godspeed.
>
> By order of the Board of Directors,
>
> E.W. Craven, clerk[109]

Now the board had work to do. There was a vacancy to fill on the board. They needed replacement ushers, Sunday School teachers, and an evening reading room attendant.

The board was also planning for an upcoming Christian Science lecture. They had just learned that Mary Brookins, a member of the Board of Lectureship, was in town because of the AYP Expo, and that she was available to lecture on July 11. They wanted to secure the Moore Theater if that was possible. They needed to decide who would do the introduction and have 1,500 invitations printed.[110]

The board decided to send a lecture invitation to the new Fourth Church.

Alaska Building at Second Avenue and Cherry Street

Paul Dorpat collection

Looking down Second Avenue at the Alaska Building

Postcard

The view from the top of the Alaska Building, 1904

Paul Dorpat collection

13

Independence Day (1909)

Having withdrawn their membership from First Church, the forty-two newly independent Christian Scientists wasted no time in establishing Fourth Church of Christ, Scientist, Seattle. Having made the conscious decision to establish their church permanently in the center of Seattle urban life, Fourth Church would embrace a role of active civic engagement. Perhaps more than any other Christian Science church in Seattle, the activities and progress of this branch church were consistently reported in the Seattle newspapers. Their first headline appeared in the *Seattle Times* on July 4, 1909: "To Build New Church." "In view of the constant growth of Christian Science in this city," the notice in the *Seattle Times* explained, "it has been deemed expedient to establish Fourth Church of Christ, Scientist. In order that the place of meeting may be readily accessible to residents of outlying districts, a lease has been taken of Arcade Hall."[111]

The timing was auspiciously serendipitous. Independence Day had special significance to Mary Baker Eddy and the early Christian Scientists. Eddy's first ever newspaper advertisement for instruction on her healing system was published in Boston in 1868 on July 4. Eddy formed her first organization, the Christian Science Association on July 4, 1876, the centennial of the American Declaration of Independence. In 1897, 2,500 people traveled to Concord, New Hampshire, for a special Independence Day event at Eddy's home, further giving the holiday the quality of a holy day for this new religious movement that so identified with spiritual revolution. Addressing the crowd, Eddy said:

> To-day we commemorate not only our nation's civil and religious freedom, but a greater even, the liberty of the sons of God, the inalienable rights and radiant reality of Christianity, whereof our Mas-

ter said: "The works that I do shall he do;" and, "The kingdom of God cometh not with observation" (with knowledge obtained from the senses), but "the kingdom of God is within you," — within the present possibilities of mankind.[112]

In Seattle, Oliver C. McGilvra had recently drawn a connection between America's founding documents and Christian Science in a public statement. McGilvra's highly prominent father Judge John J. McGilvra was widely known to have had a friendship with President Abraham Lincoln. Oliver had recently told an audience of over two thousand in Seattle at a Christian Science lecture:

> To my mind the most important documents in American history are the three declarations of independence. They are first, the American Declaration of Independence,—being a declaration against the oppression of a foreign power, second, the Proclamation of Emancipation,—being a declaration against a condition of human slavery, and third, the Christian Science text-book, "Science and Health with Key to the Scriptures,"—being a declaration against the bondage of sin, sickness, and death.
>
> The American Declaration of Independence was written by the bravest and wisest men who ever assembled in convention; the Proclamation of Emancipation was written by Abraham Lincoln, the grandest man who ever sat in the Presidential chair, and "Science and Health with Key to the Scriptures" was written by the Rev. Mary Baker G. Eddy, the foremost woman in all the world today.[113]

McGilvra said this for the hundredth anniversary of Lincoln's birthday, a special national holiday when the entire nation was expressing profound appreciation for President Lincoln and his guiding role in keeping the United States of America together through a devastating civil war. Such statements coming from McGilvra, who reiterated his close personal connection to the great American at an overflowing special service at First Church of Christ, Scientist, Seattle, on the occasion of the Lincoln centenary, made them especially noteworthy — at least to Christian Scientists. But neither the social prominence, the legal expertise, nor the bold statements of First Church president McGilvra were enough to keep his own divided church community together.[114]

Over the next few months, several more members of First Church would withdraw to join Fourth Church, most significantly, William K. Sheldon, as soon as he completed his term as First Reader. During his reader term, Sheldon had become a Christian Science practitioner, and he would soon become a Christian Science teacher. Sheldon's Normal Class teacher was Laura Sargent, who had been a member of Mary Baker Eddy's household at the time of the 1897 Independence Day event and who also was, according to one source, first cousin (once removed) to Samuel Adams of American revolutionary fame. The members of Fourth Church were almost certainly aware of this, and it must have given special significance to the timing of their 1909 organizational efforts.[115]

It was also beneficial that the formation of Fourth Church coincided with special events surrounding the world's fair. During the summer of 1909, Seattle was full of visitors and activity because of the Alaska-Yukon-Pacific (AYP) Exposition being held on the University of Washington campus. On Independence Day, besides the big fireworks show, the focus at the fair and throughout the city was women's rights. About 600 members of the National American Women's Suffrage Association from all over the country had come for the publicity opportunity of the AYP Expo. Washington voters were considering giving women the vote, and the woman suffrage leaders were holding a convention at the AYP to promote their cause. Other supportive events were going on too, like the climbing team from The Mountaineers Club that planted an AYP flag atop Mount Rainier along with a pennant with the motto, "Votes for Women." These activities culminated in an official AYP "Suffrage Day" on July 7. Well-known women suffragists gave talks at several large Christian churches and the Jewish synagogue. Mary Baker Eddy's church made the news along with the ones hosting the suffrage leaders because of the Independence Day announcement by the Christian Scientists forming Fourth Church and also the Christian Science lecture by Miss Mary Brookins for the following Sunday, July 11, sponsored by First Church of Christ, Scientist. First Church was able, for the first time, to rent the Moore Theater, Seattle's "largest and best theater," for the Brookins lecture, even with popular actress Ethel Barrymore on the stage there that week. The lecture was "packed," and the *Christian Science Sentinel* reported that a man came to the lecture on crutches, who "required help in getting comfortably seated," and then afterwards "walked out normally, carrying the crutches in one hand." All these happenings—the activities and visitors for the AYP Expo, the focus on women's voices in Seattle, and this publicized report of healing so like the stories of healings in the Bible—could only have helped the launch of the new Fourth Church. They began holding church services the day of the Brookins lecture.[116]

DEDICATION

The hall rented by Fourth Church was on Second Avenue between Union and University Streets, just a few blocks from the Moore Theater, and around the corner from the floundering Third Church of Christ, Scientist. Their Christian Science Reading Room was in the nearby Empire Building, where William K. Sheldon had his practitioner office. The Empire Building was a twelve-story high-rise on Second Avenue at Marion Street, near the Marion Building, the previous location of the First Church reading rooms, and near the Burke Building where First Church held its building committee meetings. The Marion block of Second Avenue was the cultural center of Seattle where all the big festivals, parades, and public ceremonies happened. The Empire Building, built in 1906, was one of the best-known buildings in the city. Like the "terra cotta-trimmed, elegant" Burke Building, the Empire Building was owned by civic leader Judge Thomas Burke. Burke had had helped Seattle secure the role of the leading city on Puget Sound through his involvement in the development of the local railroads. He was the attorney for the Great Northern railway company, owned by James J. Hill, the "Empire Builder." Judge Burke "personally supervised the selection of the Italian marble" used throughout the interior of the Empire Building. Starting in the summer of 1909, Burke's building became a center for Christian Science activity in Seattle with the opening of the reading room.[117]

To conduct Fourth Church services, the members elected Helen E. Cushing to Second Reader. Helen was the wife of former president of the Port Angeles & Eastern Railroad, Charles A. Cushing, who had been instrumental in the development of rail lines on the Olympic Peninsula and a car ferry connecting Port Angeles to Victoria, British Columbia—and had consequently been given the honor of introducing a Christian Science lecture in Victoria at the Victoria Theatre. The elected First Reader was Charles Warburton Ireland, a recent immigrant to the United States from Ireland. He came with his wife Charlotte and two young adult daughters. In 1901 when Charlotte started reading Mary Baker Eddy's book, Charles was a self-described "scoffer and almost an infidel." As to Christian Science, he later explained, "I at first regarded the subject as nonsense." But he testified that shortly after he started reading the book, he was healed of "severe rheumatic trouble and lame back" and incurable "liver complaint." After one week of reading, this inveterate smoker since his youth lost all desire to use his pipe. Continuing his study of the book, he said his old friends started telling him he looked twenty years younger. "I can conscientiously state that I feel it," he wrote. "My whole thought has been changed." The Ireland family joined First Church of Christ, Scientist, Seattle, in 1903, and they all left together in 1909 with the Fourth Church group. Charles had been working at People's Savings Bank, but soon after his election to First Reader, he began advertising locally as a Christian Science practitioner. His new practitioner office was on the seventh floor of the Empire Building, just down the hall from Sheldon's office.[118]

In returning to their downtown cultural roots, Fourth Church also returned to high-priced downtown hall rentals. They wanted to build a church edifice, but first they needed to build up their congregation. They expected rapid growth—if only because First Church, which seated less than 800, was already nearing its capacity. The downtown hall that Fourth Church rented was initially configured to seat about 500. Between the Brookins lecture, the AYP Expo, and the continuing growth of interest in Christian Science in Seattle, the large crowds anticipated did come. By the end of the year, the board arranged with the Arcade Hall management to increase the hall's seating capacity to 1,000. Fourth Church was successfully established, and may have even already seemed to rival First Church.[119]

14

Temporary Structure (1909)

D uring the month of July 1909, while so many residents of Seattle were enjoying the cultural activities at the Alaska-Yukon-Pacific Exposition, First Church was building their temporary structure. Members of their church community—men, women, and children—pitched in to help complete the project. One historical sketch later recounted, "Women were seen on their knees nailing down strips of carpet in the aisles. Men were doing the rougher work." On August 1, they held services at their new location. The local newspaper reported:

> The wanderings of First Church of Christ, Scientist, will cease today when services will be held at eleven o'clock in the temporary structure erected within the walls of the proposed new church building at Sixteenth avenue and Denny way, where they will be continued until the new building, to cost $100,000, is finished.[120]

Quickly built of wood over just a few weeks, the structure was referred to as "our summer kitchen" by a visiting lecturer. The thin wooden walls did not provide the congregation with "quiet, both as to the elements and passing traffic." Heated by an old-fashioned wood stove, it must have felt a bit like camping. When seasonal changes brought the long nights, frequent rain, and chilly dampness characteristic of late autumn in the Pacific Northwest, they lost a few more members to Fourth Church.[121]

Autumn also brought the annual election meeting with its required rotation in office, resulting in several new members on the executive board. At the new board's first meeting on December 14, with an unarticulated nod to Mrs. Baker, they made a conscious decision to work differently than the previous board. The board unanimously adopted a resolution,

> That it shall be the general policy of the Directors in their delibera-
> tions in all matters pertaining to the . . . welfare of this Church, if
> there is not perfect unity of thought, if there is a dissenting vote,
> that we drop the question until a later meeting, each one working
> metaphysically to bring out the sense of harmony, oneness; thereby
> securing demonstrated work for this church.[122]

The new board wanted to start building the permanent edifice as soon as possible. Their big problem was how to pay for its high cost. They still needed $80,000 to start building, more than twelve times the cost of their chapel on Sixth Avenue. The board got to work on trying to find a way to move forward that would promote unity.

The membership elected Edwin W. Craven to First Reader, giving him the honor—and the challenge—of conducting Sunday services and Wednesday meetings for the next three years in the breezy temporary structure for which he had advocated. Serving with Mr. Craven as Second Reader was Miss Eugenia H. Deamer, a relatively new member from Pennsylvania, and a new practitioner. Oliver McGilvra was unanimously re-elected president, so he would continue his leadership role at membership meetings. The following year Mr. McGilvra became chair of the board, the most powerful position in a Christian Science church.

Not long after this, Second Church, which had once been the recipient of leftover money from First Church's lecture fund, returned the favor. On January 4, 1910, the Ballard congregation began contributing to the building fund for First Church. Those members explained:

> Our membership is not large, yet we realize that the little we may
> do, if given in love and with the right thought, will be a help to our
> sister church in completing the edifice which is so much needed.
> Our Master said, "I am not come to destroy, but to fulfill;" and we
> are striving to reflect the Christ-spirit, the Christ-love, which assists,
> constructs, establishes, and supports every work that is needed in
> the giving out of this truth which is doing so much for humanity
> throughout the world.[123]

Through this small gesture of charity, the little Ballard church expressed a welcome spirit of cooperation. The precedent they set would have a long-lasting result.

First Church was making comparatively slow progress on its edifice that was "so much needed." As far as church building, the other areas where Julia Field-King had planted Christian Science had borne much more fruit than Seattle, despite its earlier start.

While they were building their temporary structure, the Christian Science periodicals featured dedication services for a recently constructed edifice in London, a new more expansive church home for First Church of Christ, Scientist, London. The previous edifice, the first Christian Science church in Europe, dedicated in November 1897 shortly after Mrs. Field-King's arrival in London, was already outgrown. This new one near Sloane Square was described as "a vast white building" with "lofty arched roof" and a "long white sculptured gallery circling the wide auditorium, the beautiful organ towering upwards." It cost $400,000 — twice the price of the original Mother Church edifice in Boston.[124]

Likewise in St. Louis, Field-King's students' congregation had outgrown their 600-seat stone church on Pine Street built for $35,000, and they had already completed and dedicated another much larger church on Kingshighway Boulevard for $150,000. They completed the twelve hundred seat auditorium in time for the 1904 St. Louis World's Fair. Both the St. Louis and London churches were rewarded with dedicatory letters from Reverend Mary Baker Eddy for their significant church building successes.[125]

Obviously, in Seattle there was no grand new Christian Science edifice to impress visitors to the 1909 AYP Expo. There were no dedication announcements for the temporary structure on Capitol Hill. It was briefly mentioned in the Christian Science periodicals, but they received no congratulatory letter from their Leader.[126]

While the temporary structure was being constructed, *The Seattle Times* reported on Eddy's 88th birthday. The article clarified that Eddy did "not think much of birthdays" and that there were no special observances of the event in Boston or anywhere else. The article noted that she was in her usual good health, still following her usual daily routine, and still doing her usual work. For a woman of her age, *The Seattle Times* reported, she was "remarkably vigorous and active" — "notwithstanding the recent reports alleging her to be dead or very near to death." Just before her birthday, a letter from Eddy was printed in the *Christian Science Sentinel*, and in part in the *Seattle Times*, denying that she was sick, incapacitated, or dead.[127]

In the years since the 1906 dedication of The Mother Church Extension, Eddy had received a lot of negative publicity. Humorist Mark Twain published a book ridiculing Christian Science and its leader. *McClure's Magazine* published a series of unflattering biographical articles. The sensational *New York World* launched a series of highly critical articles, including claims that Eddy had died and people in her organization were hiding her death from the world for devious purposes. Eddy was, in fact, alive and well, a fact easy to prove. But this was not the last time a false report was published. Wild claims by newspapers were common in those days because they boosted profits. Eddy constantly had to deal with this type of public relations problem. This sort of thing impelled her to launch her own newspaper in 1908, *The Christian Science Monitor*, to exemplify fair and accurate journalism, its motto, "to injure no man, but to bless all mankind."[128]

Along with the media attacks, a highly publicized legal battle was mounted against Eddy over control of her very substantial estate. Her opponents, which included several family members, sought to have Eddy declared mentally incompetent. From Eddy's perspective, the issue was fabricated for the purpose of discrediting Christian Science and its founder. Eddy decisively won the legal battle. She also received positive publicity from *Cosmopolitan* and *Arena* magazines, among others, and a favorable biography by Sibyl Wilbur. Meanwhile, she faced many other internal battles over control of her rapidly growing organization. Some of her students were leading rebellions or struggling to gain personal power.

In Seattle, although Allen H. Armstrong had no news of church dedication to share with his Leader, he wanted to express his continuing loyalty, to support and cheer her through her trials and tribulations—perhaps hoping to receive a reply letter. In June 1910, his students sent a letter of gratitude to Eddy by telegraph. Again in October, Mr. Armstrong and his whole association of students from Washington telegraphed a message of love and loyalty. They did not receive any response from their extremely busy leader. As with the gift package of Puget Sound salmon, Eddy's staff probably never showed her the telegraphs from Seattle.[129]

Few if any of the Christian Scientists in Seattle had ever had any direct contact with Mary Baker Eddy. They had never received any letters from her or seen any public recognition that she even knew their branches existed. They could only find the personal connection with her that they seemed to desire through reading her published writings. They could read her Communion Sunday address from several years earlier when Eddy briefly spoke from the balcony of her home in Concord, New Hampshire, to ten thousand visitors—a moment captured by a photographer for posterity. The address itself was published along with the remark that despite the open-air venue, (and total lack of any kind of amplification), "Mrs. Eddy's strong, clear voice was distinctly heard even by those a long distance removed." Through the Christian Science periodicals, even those in Seattle clearly received her message.

My Beloved Brethren:—I have a secret to tell you, and a question to ask. Do you know how much I love you and the nature of this love? No: then my sacred secret is incommunicable, and we live apart. But, yes: and this inmost something becomes articulate, and my book is not all you know of me. But your knowledge with its magnitude of meaning uncovers my life, even as your heart has discovered it. The spiritual bespeaks our temporal history. Difficulty, abnegation, constant battle against the world, the flesh, and evil, tell my long-kept secret—evidence a heart wholly in protest and unutterable in love.

The unprecedented progress of Christian Science is proverbial, and we cannot be too grateful, nor too humble for this, inasmuch as our daily lives serve to enhance or to stay its glory. To triumph in truth, to keep the faith individually and collectively, conflicting elements must be mastered. Defeat need not follow victory; joy over good achievements and work well done should not be eclipsed by some lost opportunity, some imperative demand not yet met.

Truth, Life, and Love will never lose their claim on us. And here let me add:—

Truth happifies life in the hamlet or town;
Life lessons all pride—its pomp and its frown—
Love comes to our tears like a soft summer shower,
To beautify, bless, and inspire man's power.

With everlasting love,

Mary Baker G. Eddy[130]

15

Pastor Emeritus (1910)

On Monday, December 5, 1910, it was in all the newspapers: "Mary Baker Eddy is dead." This time Boston paparazzi reporters had not invented this news to sell newspapers or to goad the reclusive religious leader into doing an interview with them to prove otherwise. This time she really had departed. The timing of her passing, late on a Saturday night, made it impossible for the press to scoop the internal communication network of Eddy's organization. The Christian Scientists in Boston were the first people outside of Eddy's household to know. They heard about it at their regular Sunday church service the next morning.

The *Seattle Star* found it remarkable that only a brief announcement was made by the First Reader:

> It becomes my duty to announce that Mrs. Eddy passed from our sight last night at a quarter before 11 o'clock, at her home on Chestnut Hill.[131]

Aside from this desk notice, it was an otherwise normal service. It was just as noteworthy to the *Seattle Star* that in Seattle there were no signs of mourning, no special services, no eulogies—not even a mention of Eddy's passing was ever made at any of the local Christian Science churches, according to the news report. It was only at churches of other denominations that Eddy's death was discussed, and "in each instance the ministers bestowed a generous measure of credit and praise upon the aged leader," according to the *Seattle Star*, which used extra-large print for their headline, "Mrs. Eddy Passes," with a large portrait. The drawing was not flattering, but the accompanying words of the article were. The *Star* called her "a remarkable woman" and suggested that her accomplishments surpassed those of Martin Luther and other significant religious reformers.[132]

Among other tributes from the press, the *Tacoma Times* put the news of Eddy's passing on the front page, top and center, with the same large portrait and a long article. They described her as founder of one of the great world religions, estimating the number of her followers in the United States alone at about one million. They grouped her with Jesus, Mohammed, Buddha, and Joseph Smith. Likewise, the *Spokane Press* considered Eddy's passing front-page news.[133]

The *Seattle Times,* however, apparently did not deem Eddy's passing as especially newsworthy. They relegated the news to page 12. The article was comparatively short and full of information suggesting negative connotations—the type of focus typical of her harshest critics. The *Seattle Times* attributed her death in her ninetieth year to lack of medical attention. Perhaps Editor-in-Chief Alden J. Blethen received some complaints from readers because a few days later an editorial took a much different tone:

> Mary Baker Eddy is dead—and in her death one of the most interesting characters of modern times has passed away. Even an "unbeliever" must pay tribute to the force and influence of this wonderful woman.
>
> There are those who scoff at her death—claiming that she taught the doctrine that there was no such thing as death. But it will be remembered that there have been those in all times who scoffed at those who could not verify in realism the theories of an ideal.
>
> This is not intended as a discussion of Christian Science in any of its phases. We are treating of the woman herself, rather than of anything which she taught or sought to teach.
>
> Christian Science today is known all over the world, and it is safe to say that this fact is due almost entirely to the work of this wonderful woman who has finally succumbed to those human ailments which she denied so long and so strenuously that she was about ninety years of age before she lost the power longer to combat.
>
> There are at least only two or three persons in a century of the history of the world who have developed such a following as this aged woman commanded. Most women, in similar conditions, would have arrogated to themselves a sort of regal authority and royal splendor. But this woman lived simply and quietly—not in poverty—not in luxury—but in comfort.
>
> Her pleasures were few and her wants—not many. Offered almost idolatry by some of her followers, she accepted little in the

way of homage, and what she did accept she accepted rather as a vindication of her teachings than as a tribute to her personality.

And yet it will be as a "personality" that at least the "unbelieving" world will remember her at the present. She was a wonderful woman![134]

Even one of Eddy's harshest critics shared some surprising words of admiration with readers of the *Seattle Times*. Georgine Milmine, who had recently done an "exhaustive study" of Eddy's life and published an extremely unflattering biography, wrote:

Mrs. Eddy, in the space of half a lifetime, succeeded in establishing a new faith and a new church, besides acquiring great riches and worldly honors, and her powers increased to the end of her life. This, surely, is a new record in religious history.[135]

The Christian Science community in Seattle made a public tribute in their own way. While introducing a Christian Science lecturer at the Moore Theater on January 15, 1911, to "an audience which taxed the seating capacity of the theater," William K. Sheldon of Fourth Church paid homage to the founder of Christian Science:

Six weeks ago, there passed forever from mortal view a woman to the record of whose life-work, a record of unexampled, benevolent, beneficent achievement, there was paid such a tribute by the public press as has never been accorded to the work of any private individual at the close of an earthly career; and pulpits which do not accept her system of theology, and individuals who do not accept her system of therapeutics, unite with the press in saying that this is a better world today because Mary Baker Eddy lived and labored and loved . . . and as the result of her discovery and of her labors, throughout the entire world today unnumbered thousands rise up and call her blessed.[136]

Christian Scientists in Seattle and everywhere were entering a new phase for their movement. Over many years Eddy had been preparing them for this. She had been giving her Boston church officials more and more responsibility, and providing them less and less personal guidance, pointing them instead to her writings and encouraging them to follow her simple rules and guidelines—and to *not* consult her. After the dedication of The Mother Church edifice in 1895, when she ordained the Bible and her textbook as impersonal pastor of the church worldwide, Reverend Eddy became Pastor Emeritus.

At the next annual business meeting of The Mother Church, on June 5, 1911, in the report from the Board of Directors, the Clerk, John V.

Dittemore, emphasized the importance of continuing to follow their leader:

> Christian Scientists have more to be grateful for than any other people, but their heritage will only be secure by their untiring vigilance. Let us remember that our Church Manual represents the inspired demonstration of Mrs. Eddy; that its by-laws are adequate to cover every need in the progress of our movement; and let us strive, whether we be church officers, practitioners, or lay-members, to obey its provisions in spirit as well as in the letter, and maintain its integrity inviolate for the benefit of the ages to come.[137]

Bliss Knapp, the secretary of the Board of Lectureship, read telegrams from branch churches in the United States and three other continents. Members representing seven cities gave progress reports. Seattle, Washington, was one of the featured cities, and Allen H. Armstrong gave the report. The mood of the meeting was "characterized by confidence and encouragement." Christian Scientists had every reason to be hopeful.

"The past year has recorded the greatest growth in the history of our church," Mr. Dittemore announced, referring to the increase in church membership. "Our board of lectureship is carrying the gospel of scientific Christianity into all parts of the world." That year alone, according to their report, approximately 700,000 people attended Christian Science lectures. But what was most significant was the number of dedicated Christian Scientists. Dittemore explained:

> The prosperity of the Christian Science movement being dependent upon the healing of the sick and upon what Mrs. Eddy has described in *Rudimental Divine Science* as its more "emphatic purpose,"—the healing of sin,—no better indication of our progress can be given than to note the increase in the number of persons devoting themselves solely to the practice of Christian Science.[138]

By this time, there were more than 4,800 full-time practitioners of Christian Science healing worldwide advertising in the *Christian Science Journal*. In Seattle alone there were more than 50, and the number was continuing to increase rapidly. These full-time healers were often the ones serving as readers, on the executive boards, and on the building committees.

Not long after Armstrong returned from Boston, work began on the new building for First Church of Christ, Scientist, Seattle. On October 17, 1911, they laid their cornerstone. The edifice would be their "temple of Bedford limestone," their tribute to God, to Jesus Christ, and to their

Leader, Mary Baker Eddy. Their use of the word temple conjured Eddy's spiritual interpretation of the biblical word "temple," which included in her definition, "the superstructure of Truth; the shrine of Love," and also "a material superstructure, where mortals congregate for worship." As a forward step, building on their previous work, this project would be their superstructure.[139]

Although they could no longer consult Eddy by letter, telegraph, or personal visit, anytime any church member had a question about how to proceed with church business, they had her writings to study and prayerfully ponder. She would always be their Leader and their Pastor Emeritus.

Mary Baker Eddy portrait by J.A.J. Wilcox in
Science and Health with Key to the Scriptures, **38th edition**

16

Joint Activities (1911)

Irst Church of Christ, Scientist, Seattle, may have laid a cornerstone, but not much else was happening on the construction of their stone temple. They had raised nowhere near enough funds to pay for the building, and for years now the membership had been going through democratic wrestling trying to find a workable way to finance the project they could all agree on. At the end of 1911, the progress of Christian Science in Seattle may not have seemed very impressive. There were four Christian Science congregations—First Church on Capitol Hill, Fourth Church downtown, the tiny Second Church in Ballard, plus a new small Christian Science Society in the recently annexed Rainier Valley in the southeast—four congregations, but no edifices. First Church was still holding services at an inactive construction site in a drafty, uninsulated temporary structure heated by a woodstove. The three other congregations were still renting halls. Furthermore, the future of Christian Science might have seemed very uncertain.

After the articles about her death in December 1910, Reverend Mary Baker Eddy continued to make headlines in Seattle, but the coverage was more negative. The tributes from the press were followed by ongoing coverage of the funeral arrangements, unusual in the amount of detail. The focus on cemetery, grave, and casket might seem to highlight the ironic fatality of this spiritual teacher who had so famously declared that there is no death. When the funeral was over, newspapers chronicled sensational conflict and scandal of the sort that had always seemed to follow Eddy's career.[140]

There was a lawsuit over her will, and a sensational splash from Augusta Stetson, one of Eddy's most problematic students, whose name was known to Seattle newspaper readers. Mrs. Stetson made headlines with bold claims of Eddy's ability to overcome death just like Jesus. Eddy will return in the flesh, Stetson promised. Boston church officials immediately publicly denounced Stetson's statements, but the press continued to publish articles on the topic. *The Seattle Times* printed a full two-page spread including Stetson's statements under the headline, "Do the Dead Come Back?" in a tabloid-style unusual for *The Seattle Times*, mixing images of deathbed resurrection from Eddy's illustrated poem *Christ and Christmas* with haunting images of ghosts, spirit writings, mediumship, and other weird claims of the paranormal. It was presented in a way that would make any Christian Scientist shudder in dismay. Eddy had consistently spoken against spiritualist mediumship. There was a chapter in her textbook called "Christian Science versus Spiritualism" and a recurring church sermon topic denouncing necromancy. But upon even glancing at the pages in the *Times*, skeptics might have felt affirmed in their worst suspicions about Christian Science.[141]

Then the *Seattle Times* reviewed a book by Frederick W. Peabody, the Boston attorney involved in lawsuits against Eddy who had become an anti-Christian Science lecturer. The *Seattle Times* described Peabody's book as a "complete exposure of Christian Science" as a "bogus healing system," essentially witchcraft.[142]

Meanwhile, news commentators were speculating on the future of the Christian Science Church without its powerful leader at the helm. "The vitality of her message will meet the supreme test now," noted one independent voice. Some said Eddy had left behind a faulty organizational design that posed "a great dilemma" for her followers. Experts were predicting the downfall of the church, either from power struggles and schisms, or a slow but certain decline. All the predictions about the certain failure of Eddy's church might have seemed very credible. Christian Science might have seemed certain to fade away into historical oblivion.[143]

It was at this moment of uncertain future that the Christian Scientists in Seattle fulfilled the promise they had made to each other when there was only one church. Back in 1907, they had resolved to work together cooperatively. Following through on that resolution now seemed imperative.

In July 1911, First Church initiated the first joint activity by proposing to Fourth Church that they combine their reading rooms. They both had reading rooms downtown, and they were only a few blocks apart. By combining, they could accommodate more people in nicer and more spacious rooms with longer operating hours, and they would no longer compete with each other. The initial invitation was only the start of a long process of consolidation. It took nearly a year to plan the location, leases, staffing, oversight, develop operational rules, then get approval from the membership bodies of both churches.[144]

In May 1912, the new joint Christian Science Reading Room opened in the Empire Building on Second Avenue. The *Christian Science Journal* reported this development as being "a long step forward in Christian Science work in Seattle." This new Reading Room comprised five connecting rooms on the eighth floor. It had newly carpeted floors and newly purchased furniture. Both churches payed $140 per month into an operating budget covering rent and the salaries of two full-time staff. All other expenses, such as cleaning, printing, and stock, plus wages for two additional part-time staff were paid for by profits from the sale of literature from the Christian Science Publishing Society. The manager in charge of the new joint reading rooms, the Librarian, Alma Durant Bixby, reported to the members, "One cannot visit the [Reading Room] today without realizing the advantage of such beautiful surroundings and with out feeling gratified at having the Cause of Christian Science represented in the heart of a growing city in so refined and quiet a way."[145]

The new reading rooms may have been quiet, but they were also active. Sales totaled at least $1,000 a month, more than $2,200 in December. Mary Baker Eddy's book *Science and Health with Key to the Scriptures* was their biggest seller. They consistently sold more than 100 copies a month. They also sold hundreds of pamphlets and many other items. Visitors borrowed books from their lending library.[146]

Mrs. Bixby was introduced to Christian Science around 1902. She had been struggling with neuralgia, frequently experiencing such great pain that even morphine tablets could not safely dull it. She testified that after being introduced to the Christian Science concept of God as Love, and Love as the only power, she had an overnight healing. She took up the study of Eddy's textbook. In 1909 she moved from Juneau, Alaska, to Seattle and became a member of First Church. Just before getting the job as librarian, she was advertising as a Christian Science practitioner. At the reading rooms she would have frequent opportunity to encourage many others in their spiritual journey.[147]

On Labor Day 1912, they inaugurated open hours on Sundays and holidays, from 2:00 to 7:30 p.m. Sometimes only one or two people came, but the librarian felt that if even only one person visited, the Reading Room had fulfilled its purpose. On other days of the week during the first year, sometimes every seat was occupied in all five rooms.

They used one of the five rooms for a variety of purposes. It was a place for storing extra stock, a private office for the librarian, and an overflow study room for visitors. They also used it as a boardroom, for committee meetings, and interviews with prospective church members. The joint Reading Room became a regional hub, a place where members of First Church and Fourth Church, as well as others in the Christian Science community, came into frequent contact with each other. The staff described increasing use of the Reading Room over time:

> One of the most noticeable features of its growth, is the increased attendance of its readers. By readers, I do not mean those who read from 15 to 20 minutes, watching all who enter, but the readers who read from the standpoint of studentship, who consult the dictionary for the meaning of words and for their different shades of meaning, and who study the Bible concordance and the concordance of Science and Health. There are many, many more who are studying in this manner than there were last year. The questions asked show a general awakening and a broader outlook.[148]

Another cooperative effort initiated in 1912 was a distribution committee for Christian Science literature. Its office was also in the Empire Building. The committee met twice a month on Saturday evenings. Heading up this committee initially was Dr. Walter S. Padget. Dr. Padget was one of the most prominent members of Fourth Church. He was soon to be elected First Reader. A well-connected member of Seattle high-society, he and his wife, Virginia Walsh, were often mentioned in the newspaper for their involvement with clubs and charities. Even their recreational activities were newsworthy — automobile tours to national parks and Southern California, a trip to Hawaii, and a Mediterranean cruise. Professionally, Padget was also prominent as a dentist. He was an advocate for the advancement of the profession of dentistry. His office was in the Medical Arts Building, and he gave talks on dentistry. When he first learned about Christian Science, he was immediately interested in it. He later publicly shared that several of his family members had significant healings. He continued being a prominent Seattle dentist, even after becoming a Christian Scientist. An advocate for the advancement of Christian Science also, as the first chair of the first joint literature distribution committee in Seattle, Dr. Padget oversaw the launch of a remarkable organizational effort with a strong sense of mission.[149]

As early as the 1890s, enthusiastic new Christian Scientists everywhere had made systematic surveys of public and private libraries and reading rooms and made great efforts to place Mary Baker Eddy's book, at times overcoming obstacles of resistance. One "zealous Christian Scientist," on his travels, single-handedly put the book "in hundreds of public places throughout Europe and the East," the *Christian Science Journal* reported, "so that the earth has virtually been encircled with the message of good-will contained therein." The Seattle joint literature distribution effort would do similar placements in their local area of Eddy's books. However, a major thrust of their outreach efforts was one being encouraged by Boston officials, a focus on increasing circulation of *The Christian Science Monitor*.[150]

From its very beginnings, the literature distribution committee was thinking long-term, keeping careful record of locations and frequency of their distribution in each district. Allen H. Armstrong had initiated the first literature distribution, called the "Missionary Committee," in 1901. He gave this new joint outreach committee its start with a $105 gift. Dr. Padget's team gave one-year subscriptions for the *Monitor* to two fire stations, the Women's Department at the Seattle Public Library, and the Army post at Fort Lawton, and 2,000 copies of the special Thanksgiving issue of the *Monitor* to business offices in the city.[151]

Starting in January 1913, the four churches began contributing to the joint distribution committee based on the size of their membership through a monthly per capita tax. The largest contributions by far, because of having the largest membership by far, came from First Church. With these expanded funds, they expanded their reach. They gave *Monitor* subscriptions to the Rainier Club, the Arctic Club, the Press Club, the University Club, the Athletic Club, the Masonic Library, a veterans home in Port Orchard, the Fifth Avenue car barn (a main transit station for Seattle's trolley system), more fire stations, a children's foster care institution, and area prisons and jails.

After placing literature at the county jail, Margaret Mason Walker was asked by the wife of an inmate to talk with her husband about Christian Science. She did, and she left him with a copy of Eddy's book. He started reading it to his cellmates, and soon several men became interested enough to request a church service. A few weeks later, with the help of the jailer, simple services were given at two tanks. Over the next couple of years, they expanded this "Church Extension" work to the county jail, including the women's area, the newly built King County Jail, the city jail, and the municipal home for unemployed men. Fifteen volunteers left immediately after their Sunday service to conduct services at the jails. By 1915, this group became a separate joint committee, chaired by Mrs. Walker, who by this time was a practitioner. They expanded prison outreach to "The Willows," a detention farm in Redmond for men convicted of family desertion, and a similar farm near South Park. They sent literature to the McNeil Island Penitentiary in the south end of Puget Sound and the state penitentiary in Walla Walla in southeast Washington.[152]

They made a special outreach effort to the University of Washington, including the dormitories, the Faculty Club, and the University YMCA, sending personal messages to officials, such as this one:

> You know that the *Monitor* is not a religious or denominational paper, but is an effort to answer the demand for clean journalism, and that it is an up-to-date paper, filled with the latest news of America and of all foreign countries, authentic and free from party or religious bias. Its distinctive feature is that it is free from all reports of vice and crime. The standard newspapers of the east have given the *Monitor* high praise, and we believe that all the students will find it of real value, whether they are interested in diplomacy or sports, or anything in between. We shall be glad to know that the *Monitor* is placed on file in your reading rooms where it will be readily accessible to the students.[153]

They placed the *Monitor* in all the major hotels and boardinghouses, the Salvation Army barracks, the halls of the Industrial Workers of the World labor organization, logging camps, and the Pike Place Market. They put bundles of copies onto boats at dock—ferries, fishing fleets, and government ships—headed for local Puget Sound destinations and Alaska, including Kodiak and the Aleutian islands. Eventually, one way or another, they would learn that the literature had been received and appreciated. For their local efforts, the committee could share more details of interactions with the literature.

> Although several thousand papers are distributed at the ship yards, very few are thrown away. Sometimes, however, the papers are torn up and thrown violently on the ground, and sometimes they are thrown at the feet of the distributors. On one occasion a man who took the paper threw it into the air, saying—"I don't want that paper," another man right behind him caught it before it reached the ground, remarking, "I do." These rebuffs are salutary; they make us work all the harder, and the next visit to the yard is always followed by joy and gratitude.[154]

The distribution workers gave away hundreds of "marked" copies of *Monitor* issues to target groups when the issue contained specific articles that would be of interest to their work. They targeted school teachers and administrators, business owners, theaters, bankers, legislators, lawyers, women's groups, and artists.[155]

As people in Seattle became more familiar with the *Monitor*, more visitors came to the Reading Room to purchase copies. Sometimes they complimented the fair coverage of the controversial topics of the day. One customer "stated that he had for years read the *London Times*, that he had always considered it the best paper published — 'But,' said he, 'She will have to take a back seat for the *Monitor*.'"[156]

Some of the recipients of the *Monitor* eventually became interested in learning more about the thinking behind the newspaper. But regardless of whether *Monitor* readers ever came into a Reading Room, or ever had any active interest in the religion or the healing practice, there was a bigger benefit, as touched on in one report:

> As a result of the activity thus inaugurated, there is apparent an awakened interest in the great work the *Monitor* is engaged in, that of destroying the unreasoning prejudice against Christian Science, or rather the antagonism existing against a mistaken idea of what Christian Science really is. This awakening thought is rendering it possible for the *Monitor* to accomplish its missionary work in our midst.[157]

The committee continued trying to help church members understand their work, its impact, and the value of the *Monitor*. In the next annual report, they explained more emphatically:

> By far the most important result of our work cannot be estimated in dollars and cents. . . . Commercial bodies, mercantile establishments and business men, whom we could scarcely approach a year ago, are now eager to lend us a helping hand, voluntarily offering information, assistance and advertising not obtainable before. A better knowledge of our work and our great daily paper, "The Pioneer of Clean Journalism," is rapidly breaking down prejudice born of ignorance, and this harbinger of good news is making a place for itself and is doing that which nothing else has done toward creating a demand for clean journalism and a wholesome respect for Christian Science.[158]

Another joint activity begun in 1912 was a lecture committee. Each of the churches held at least one Christian Science lecture every year, sometimes several. Each lecture was a major expense and publicity effort. Fourth Church proposed that they do some coordination. The first year they focused on merely preventing scheduling conflicts. The second year, with a team of 15, they coordinated publicity. For Bliss Knapp at the Hippodrome, the committee distributed fliers, putting 158 event notices citywide. They put fliers in the display windows of grocery stores, barber shops, furniture stores, restaurants, music stores, shoe shops, train stations, jewelers, florists, plumbers offices, art galleries, variety stores, and even the old curiosity shop.[159]

Along with all the other joint activities, a finance committee was formed in 1912, "to devise ways and means to raise sufficient funds" to pay for First Church's temple and to offer advice on financing methods. They reported later that year, "The Committee has held many meetings and worked in perfect harmony—really seven individuals with one mind." The committee encouraged all four of the congregations to devote their first Sunday collection to the building fund of First Church. They also enlisted financial support from Christian Science Societies beyond Seattle and they put a collection box at the Reading Room.[160]

Thanks to the efforts of the joint finance committee and all the other joint activities, and with the financial support of the other Christian Science churches in the area, in 1912, after being in their temporary structure for more than three years, First Church could finally begin construction on their stone temple. In appreciation of the "unity and cooperation" and financial help, the members of First Church resolved to return the favor to the other churches in the future: "[W]e pledge our moral, financial, and spiritual support in all the constructive work for the cause of Christian Science in Seattle."[161]

In the introduction for a joint lecture at Arcade Hall, Oliver C. McGilvra, whose influence seemed to contribute to division only a few years earlier, now expressed what this new spirit of cooperation meant to the Christian Science church members at this critical period. McGilvra explained:

> Biblical history is replete with examples of the wisdom of unanimity of action in the cause of Truth. It was not until the multitude had come together on the day of Pentecost and were of one mind that they received the message of the Spirit with its blessing. It was not until Joshua and his followers had compassed the city of Jericho seven times and had joined in a mighty shout that the walls fell.[162]

Likewise in the history of Christian Science in Seattle, they were not able to build their church edifices, not even First Church, until the branch churches developed a spirit of unity through joint activities.

Empire Building on Second Avenue at Marion Street
Marion Building in lower right corner

Paul Dorpat collection

Second Avenue on a parade day with Empire Building in background

Paul Dorpat collection

17

Temple of Bedford Limestone (1914)

I t took a couple of years for First Church of Christ, Scientist, Seattle, to complete their stone superstructure. In the first phase of construction, they completed the walls for the basement level Sunday School and constructed a temporary roof over it. They used this basement building for their auditorium as well as their Sunday School. Besides holding their regular services there, they also held Christian Science lectures, including one by William R. Rathvon. Mr. Rathvon had lived in Mary Baker Eddy's household in Chestnut Hill, Massachusetts. While Rathvon was in Seattle, he might have shared some of his personal stories with the members of First Church—reminiscences of his close work with their Leader "in the last few years of her earthly activity" of the sort included in *We Knew Mary Baker Eddy, Volume II*— adding another dimension to their understanding of their Leader, and their tribute to her, their "temple of Bedford limestone" and New Hampshire granite.[163]

By spring of 1914, the building was almost done. "Simplicity and dignity" were the "chief attributes of a very harmonious design," according to one description of this "imposing" new edifice. The auditorium was "designed in simple restrained renaissance feeling which gives great dignity and repose to the interior. . . . A sunburst in the centre of the ceiling with ample window openings on three sides amply light the room in day time. . . . The windows are glazed with opalescent glass of [iridescent] tone giving the effect of sunlight even when the day is gloomy. The lighting at night is entirely indirect, no fixtures of any kind being visible. It is one of the most successfully lit rooms in the Northwest."[164]

The *Seattle Times* published an article on the final decorating touches of the edifice in May. First Church hired Edward Joseph Holslag, a mural artist most famous for his work in the Congressional Library in Washington, D.C. Mr. Holslag had also painted a biblical mural for a Christian Science church in Kansas City, Missouri. The *Times* reported:

> During the past ten days Mr. Holslag, directing his working staff, has evolved a decorative scheme ensemble for the interior of this building, so beautiful in effect, so soft in tone and altogether harmonious as to awaken instant admiration. One views the completed sections of the decorators' art with a sudden realization that here is in reality an absence of decoration as ordinarily seen; yet in its stead an expression in wonderfully soft color tones that pays compliment to the classic architecture and accentuates the beauty and dignity of the whole interior.[165]

The *Seattle Times* described the interior as a "remarkable departure" and a "welcome relief as compared with the conventional and ordinary church interior." It was a common acknowledgement of the fresh, innovative approach taken for Christian Science buildings. As one commentator in this period wrote:

> Whatever may be said of Christian Science as a religion or a cure either for or against it . . . there is no question that in the architecture of its church buildings it has set an example that every denomination should follow . . . [Scientist] churches, large and small, all over the country, are not only a wide departure from the traditional church architecture, but they are most satisfying to the eye and to the sense of fitness. If Christian Science does no more than reform church architecture it will assuredly not have lived in vain.[166]

The first services in the completed edifice were set for June 7, 1914. Oliver C. McGilvra conducted the services as First Reader. In the auditorium, the acoustics were described in one account as "excellent for the voice and no suggestion of echo or reverberation comes when the splendid organ peals its peons of praise in loudest exultation."[167]

A press release for the opening of the new church was sent by Charles A. Griffith, the current chair of the board, who had played an important role in the construction of the building.[168]

The article in the *Seattle Times* about the opening services said that "as little ostentation is desired as possible." It explained, "These services will not be dedicatory . . . as it is not fully paid for." To pay for construction, the board, under the leadership of Mr. Griffith, had issued $80,000 in 10-year bonds—a mortgage against the property. Half of the bonds still needed buyers, the article mentioned, and they were offering an attractive 7 percent return, backed by the property that was now worth $200,000. The building ended up costing twice their initial budget. Their building was comparable in cost to the original Mother Church in Boston.[169]

The pioneering First Church had successfully completed what Allen H. Armstrong had expressed as a hope fourteen years earlier: a monumental work of architecture "worthy of the city and the cause we love." They had done their best to follow the example set by Reverend Mary Baker Eddy both in the healing practice and in church building. This was the first "prayer in stone" of the Seattle Christian Scientists.[170]

Anna Friendlich wrote in her 1908 article, "Church Building in Christian Science" that the "first appearing of a Christian Science church building in a community often provides a source of surprise and astonishment to the outside world, since no appeal to the public has been made and no pulpit chiding have heralded its coming." She continued:

> Inside the Christian Science fold the excitement is not less. A burst of gladness and wonder arises in every heart when the great work is finished and this tabernacle of Truth is with men. To the modest band of workers a great miracle has been wrought, like the manna shower in the wilderness.[171]

In a letter to a branch church in Cleveland upon completion of their edifice, Mary Baker Eddy concluded her dedicatory message:

> The praiseworthy success of this church, and its united efforts to build an edifice in which to worship the infinite, sprang from the temples erected first in the hearts of its members — the unselfed love that builds without hands, eternal in the heaven of Spirit. God grant that this unity remain, and that you continue to build, rebuild, adorn, and fill these spiritual temples with grace, Truth, Life, and Love.[172]

After the opening services for the Seattle church, Griffith made it clear to the members what the next focus needed to be, using the language of a newly popular recreational activity in the Seattle area, mountaineering:

> In completing this structure we have but reached the summit of one of the foot-hills on our journey onward and upward. The mountain, our real goal, is still in the distance, and other foot-hills are to be scaled before we will have attained the heights where we can say,

with Paul, 'I have fought a good fight, I have finished my course, I have kept the faith.' Having reached the summit of Mount Completion we can now see clearly that the next stage of our journey is to lead us to Mount Dedication. It doesn't look far or difficult of attainment, but we should remember that between here and there lies the valley of Self Denial, and we should also remember that, while we may have faith, both individually and collectively, that we can reach yonder point, 'faith, without works, is dead.' If we would dedicate this Church our faith should be expressed in our deeds. May we not then, each and all, with increased love for God and man, press onward until we can say conscientiously, 'Henceforth there is laid up for me a crown of rejoicing.'[173]

The congregation now had its next goal: to pay off its debt. The work of the building committee was done. The membership unanimously gave their thanks to the committee in a motion, and the board expressed their appreciation in a letter:

Your individual efforts directed by the one Mind, have always been put into expression to produce in the physical structure that which does in the highest way express beauty, harmony, permanence.

This completed structure is a proof to us that the foundation in each individual consciousness must have been the rock, Christ Jesus.

Our Leader tells us, . . . that church is "The structure of Truth and Love; whatever rests upon and proceeds from divine Principle." That individually and collectively your thoughts have rested upon and proceeded from divine Principle, is evidenced in our church building. "The structure of Truth and Love" that you have built in each individual consciousness, is externalized to us in the beautiful way that you have accomplished your work.[174]

To their designing and superintending architect Charles H. Bebb, the board of directors formally expressed "their highest appreciation, confidence and thanks for the masterly design, high art, courtesy, generosity and integrity shown during the period of years covering this construction work." To the board, the structure represented "the highest accomplishment of architectural art and design, standing in its completeness as symbolic of 'a house founded upon a rock' — beautiful, harmonious, permanent."[175]

Their new building made history. In the voluminous classic history of Seattle by Clarence B. Bagley, published shortly after the completion of the First Church edifice, the new stone temple for Christian Science was given the honor of a full-page photograph, along with a brief historical sketch—how they started in 1896 with seventeen charter members, how Edward Kimball, described as a close friend of Mary Baker Eddy, had drawn a large attendance when he lectured in Seattle, and how the membership had grown so rapidly that other churches were established. Bagley described the church as "a beautiful structure," and as having "a very large attendance."[176]

Attending a Christian Science church service was not the only way to see the beautiful new building. Not long after opening services, there was a well-publicized Sunday afternoon organ concert, with Miss Leona Langdon, organist, and Mr. Worth Densmore, tenor soloist, free to the public, "its motive being to promote interest in organ music and to enable music lovers to hear the fine three-manual organ."[177]

In their own internal records, First Church was remarkably silent on any description of the building or the opening services. They did not overtly relish whatever praise they may have received for their edifice. What seemed to matter most to the record keepers was that after nearly twenty-five years of meeting in temporary locations, the members finally had a permanent home.

They had shown Seattle that Christian Science had come to stay.

Temple of Bedford Limestone (1914)

First Church of Christ, Scientist, Seattle

18

Seismic Disturbance (1914)

Anna Friendlich in her article "Church Building in Christian Science" wrote that besides the surprise and wonder, the first appearing of a Christian Science church also creates a "seismic disturbance in the mental and moral realm. It shakes established beliefs,—faiths, doctrines, traditions, institutions." And so it did in Seattle. With the appearance of the edifice for First Church of Christ, Scientist, Christian Science became more visible in the city skyline. It also became more visible in the local newspapers. The other Christian churches noticed, and their clergy were speaking more publicly about Christian Science and its founder, Reverend Mary Baker Eddy.

As the joint activities for Christian Science outreach were ramping up, and as the huge stone temple on Capitol Hill was nearing completion, local Christian leaders launched a major effort to encourage "a greater fellowship" among Christians. Nine Protestant denominations came together to discuss ideas for cooperation. The effort culminated in a "great series of unity revival services" organized by the four largest downtown churches for the weeks leading up to Easter Sunday, 1914. It was a movement significant enough to warrant special mention by Clarence B. Bagley in his history of Seattle. To advertise the revival meetings, the leaders planned a variety of "attention-getting features to attract the general public." They placed advertisements in the newspaper. They used balloons and banners. They put fliers on the windows of automobiles parked downtown. A music band marched through the streets to "summon the people to church."[178]

The Christian Science churches were not invited to the Christian unity meetings. The focus for the interdenominational audience at the first big unity meetings was "fierce denunciation of Christian Science."

A sermon by Reverend Dr. Mark Allison Matthews, D. D., was the most newsworthy part of one of the first events. Bagley described the Rev. Dr. Matthews as "one of the most eminent representatives of the clergy in the United States," who, since coming to Seattle in 1902, had built up First Presbyterian Church into "the largest membership of any Presbyterian congregation in the United States." One *Seattle Times* reporter covering the series described Rev. Matthews as a "vitriolic-tonged Georgian" who held audiences spellbound, "a forceful—well-nigh hypnotic—speaker." For years Matthews had been speaking out against the new religious movement, conveying his disparaging tone in print through parenthetical question marks, "Christian (?) Science (?)"—religion so-called. He referred to it as "Eddyism," and statements of healing by the "Eddyites" as "exaggerated and false." Besides discouraging people from seeking cure of disease from Christian Science practitioners, Matthews emphasized that in Christian homes women should focus on raising large families. He "declared that Christianity is strong and masculine, not weak and effeminate, the most manly principle ever espoused or taught." Christian Science had "done so much to blacken society and damage the home and virtue." It was "branded by the speaker as blasphemous, immoral, licentious and murderous, and was held up in the most scathing terms as one of the infamous influences arresting the development of the orthodox church." According to Matthews, Mrs. Mary Baker G. Eddy's teachings denied "every fundamental principle upon which the hope of salvation rests." He advised,

> Hold to your Bible and leave alone that which pretends to be a key
> to it, but which is immoral and born in licentiousness.[179]

Reverend Matthews' words of denunciation in *The Seattle Times* received a swift response from John M. Henderson in a letter to the editor. Mr. Henderson shared that he grew up in the same denomination as Matthews and had also attended divinity school. He, too, had once ridiculed and criticized Christian Science. But after facing a death sentence from his doctor, and receiving no benefit from the prayers of his friends and family in the orthodox church, "as a last resort, and under protest," a Christian Science practitioner was called. He quickly regained health. Now, not only did he identify as a Christian Scientist, he defended Christian Science in his role as Committee on Publication for the State of Washington. Henderson had some strong words for Matthews:

DEDICATION

The Pharisees were "orthodox" and they cried out against Jesus, even though His teaching was everywhere supplanting sin and suffering and sorrow with joy and peace, health and holiness. . . . The same mental habit obtains in our own day, and it is therefore easily explainable why it is difficult for one whose mind is absorbed in the effort to win the world to certain creedal enunciations, to see good in Christian Science, even though the elevating and purifying influences of this science are as present in every community as the sunshine.[180]

Notwithstanding the message of Henderson's protest letter, the unity revival meetings continued over the next two weeks, with nightly sessions at the First Methodist Episcopal Church edifice— which, ironically, was designed by an architect who was a Christian Scientist. The *Seattle Times* gave the events the leading headlines on the religion page of the newspaper day after day. "Great Unity Revival Series Will Open This Evening," and similar promotional messages in extra-large lettering spanned the full width of the page above news articles detailing every session. News coverage included large photograph portraits of all the participating pastors and artists' sketches of each of the pastors in action at the events, striking dramatic gestures as they addressed attentive audiences. Reverend Ralph Atkinson, "acknowledged to be the foremost leader of revival music in the country," promised "a monster choir composed of the best voices from the four churches participating . . . Presbyterian, Baptist, Congregational, and Methodist Episcopal." The events received an extraordinary level of publicity—in every way far beyond the small notices, usually at the bottom of the page, given by the *Times* to Christian Science lectures. But despite the hype, according to reporter John Evans, the actual events did not quite achieve expectations:

The beginning of the series was far from auspicious. The audience was less in number than the average attendance at the downtown churches on the glorious Sunday nights in summer when the lakes and the islands call more loudly than the hard-backed pews. The pledged choir of one hundred voices dwindled to a dozen . . . What was lost in numbers, however, was made up in enthusiasm. . . . Every individual had sung as though life and future hung in the balance, dependent on volume of sound and intentness of purpose.[181]

At the second meeting of the series, the audience size was "a considerable improvement over the numbers present on the opening night." Even so, at the close of the evening, the audience was "awakened rudely" by Reverend Matthews. Matthews, "his eye searching accusingly," aimed his finger at those attending until they "quivered" and "wriggled uncomfortably." The audience received a harsh scolding. "You are expected to go back to your homes and your churches and your stores and banks and factories and shops and talk to men about Christ and bring them here." As to the next revival event, "If it is not packed," he told them, "it will be . . . evidence that you went home and went to sleep." The revival pastors wanted to light fireworks in hearts with the gospel, to shake the city like an earthquake.[182]

Even with the new recruitment effort, after the first week, turnout was disappointing. Revival leaders added a series of noontime events at the Orpheum Theatre and shared that there was something special happening at these meetings. "The very atmosphere seemed surcharged and electrified with the presence of a divine power," the *Seattle Times* reported. The meetings were sure to be packed by the end of the series. However, if they ever achieved this goal, it did not make the news. The revival meetings were eclipsed by standard notices about upcoming Easter services throughout the city.[183]

Around this time, in an internationally syndicated column published in *The Seattle Star*, Pastor Russell often discussed Christian Science. He considered it to be promoted by "the Adversary, Satan, with a view to confusing the people and leading them away from the Truth." Around this time, Pastor Russell wrote a series of articles denouncing Mary Baker Eddy's teachings. In his article, "Christian Science: Is It Reasonable?" he wrote:

> The growth of Christian Science has astonished the world. Its teachings appeal to a very intelligent, well-to-do class of people, of considerable mental independence. The physical healings of either themselves or their friends seems to have been more or less associated with their conversion to their cult. Their realization of the cure brought them the conviction that there is a supernatural power outside of man, and aroused a religious sentiment such as they had never known before. It seems to them that they have started a new life.
>
> . . . Let us give Mrs. Eddy credit for desiring to be logical; but let us notice that her language was confusing when she said, 'There is no death, no sickness, no pain.' . . . But since Mrs. Eddy and Christian Science fail to recognize and state these facts clearly, it follows that however attractive her teachings may be to some people, they cannot be relied upon because they are off the true founda-

tion—recognizing neither the facts of sin and death, nor the necessity for redemption therefrom by Jesus' sacrifice or for the coming Restitution.[184]

Russell made the case that Christian Science was in conflict with the Bible, and the fact that "Mother Eddy" had succumbed to death proved that her theories had "failed to the highest degree." There were other ways Christian Science was getting negative publicity. *The Seattle Star,* a paper that tended toward sensationalism and seemed especially hostile to Christian Science at this time, printed an extra-large headline on the front-page about a "woman healer," a reader at a Christian Science church and "leader of that cult," associated with disruptive events, including the discharge of a gun, a divorce suit, and rumors of infidelity. The facts printed in the article were based on assumptions about circumstantial evidence, but suggested reason to be suspicious of Christian Scientists. Other headlines in Seattle newspapers told of legislators in other states working to outlaw the professional practice of Christian Science healing.[185]

The Christian Scientists in Seattle might have found comfort in Reverend Mary Baker Eddy's dedication letter to First Church of Christ, Scientist, in Atlanta, Georgia. As reported by the *Boston Globe,* this church that erected the first Christian Science edifice in the southern states had been "attacked by pulpit and press, and openly expressed opposition accompanied every step made by the Scientists in the direction of their new church." This church had been growing rapidly when Rev. Matthews was living in Georgia. To this embattled church for the dedication of their Georgia granite edifice in 1898 on Easter Sunday, Rev. Eddy wrote:

> Be patient towards persecution. Injustice has not a tithe of the power of justice. Your enemies will advertise for you. Christian Science is spreading steadily throughout the world. Persecution is the weakness of tyrants engendered by their fear, and love will cast it out. Continue steadfast in love and good works. Children of light, you are not children of darkness. Let your light shine. Keep in mind the foundations of Christian Science—one God and one Christ. Keep personality out of sight, and Christ's "Blessed are ye" will seal your apostleship.[186]

In Seattle, their enemies did advertise for them. Even with all the negative publicity, new people continued to embrace Christian Science. Orison "O.J.C." Dutton exemplified this. Mr. Dutton was well known in Seattle. Besides his work as a real estate agent and investor involved with many civic organizations, he had run for public office and was a friend of the former mayor of Seattle. He and his wife had recently spent two months in Yellowstone National Park with the former mayor and an entourage of other members of Seattle society. Mr. Dutton had been an active Episcopalian, a vestryman at Saint Mark's parish. He told his story while introducing a Christian Science lecturer at the Hippodrome in April 1914, just after the great unity revival meetings.

> For many years I was a scoffer at what I understood Christian Science to be, and had I been told ten years ago that some day I should make remarks in public in favor of this subject, I should have replied emphatically: "Never! Not I!"
>
> About five years ago I was in attendance at a lecture given in this city by one who claimed to be able to expose the teachings of Mrs. Eddy as false and blasphemous.[187]

Dutton may have been referring to the October 13, 1909, free lecture entitled "Christian Science Exposed," given by "celebrated anti-Christian Science lecturer" Frederick W. Peabody of Boston. Shortly after the foundation was laid for the First Church temple at Sixteenth and Denny, the *Seattle Times* reported that Baptist ministers in Portland were working with medical physicians to "prevent further inroads on denominational and professional work by Christian Scientists." Their plans included bringing Mr. Peabody to the area. Rev. Matthews hosted and introduced him in Seattle. Peabody called Christian Science a "new-old witchcraft" and its founder "a charlatan, a heartless and avaricious despot, pretender and author of the greatest get-rich-quick concern ever conceived." The *Seattle Times* called Peabody's lecture a "scathing denunciation of Mary Baker G. Eddy couched in vitriolic terms." But the denunciations did not have the desired effect on Dutton. As he told the Hippodrome audience in 1914,

> The whole discourse appealed to me as unfair and unjust, tearing down the beliefs of others, giving nothing of comfort or help in their place. I determined then and there to investigate for myself, with the result that every hour of my life is one of gratitude for that decision.
>
> In our family of six many benefits have come to us through the application of the Principle of Christian Science, and it has been applicable not only in a physical and spiritual way, but in a business way, solving my daily problems and lifting me out of the bondage of fear and limitation.[188]

O.J.C. Dutton and his wife, Pearl Blackburn Dutton, joined a Christian Science church and become actively involved in a very public way. The Duttons sent their children to The Principia School, the boarding school for Christian Scientists in Saint Louis. Mention of Principia and the comings and goings of the Duttons between Seattle and Saint Louis was regularly reported in the society page of the *Seattle Times* over the next few years.[189]

Not every local clergyman denounced Christian Science entirely. Reverend E. Tremayne Dunstan at the West Seattle Congregational Church the made news for attempting to be more evenhanded in his remarks about Christian Science in sermons. As reported in the *Seattle Times,* in what he called "a sermon that will please nobody," he noted the rapid building of hundreds of Christian Science churches across the country, "some of them cathedral in proportions." As to the spiritual teachings, the pastor said,

> I have tried to rid my mind of everything in the nature of an unreasoning prejudice against that which is new and have never taken part in the denunciations of Christian Science which orthodox preachers have frequently made. . . . Frequently I have spoken appreciatively of Mrs. Eddy's teaching, and because of this some of my friends have been just a little fearful as to my own position.

Rev. Dunstan firmly denied that he had embraced the doctrines of Christian Science but he "frankly declared that he found much to admire in the new church." Above all, he expressed appreciation of the influence of Christian Science on other Christian churches:

> It is a spiritual idealism which has leavened the thought of millions of people and has completely changed the lives of the great majority of these. Never since the apostolic days has a religious movement spread so quickly. . . . It has forced men from the old mental ruts and has helped them to think. And above all, it has helped to restore our faith in the indwelling Christ who is the source and secret of all power. . . . There has been restored to the church, though partially as yet, that faith in God as a living presence and power which was the source of the church's early triumphs. Christian Scientists believe, and with them now many others, that God has power to heal the body and to answer prayer today as in the days of the Lord's appearing. There can be no question that the primitive church accepted, literally, the word of the Master when, speaking of his own works of healing, he said, 'Greater works than these shall he do.' For centuries the church, because of its lack of faith, narrowed the scope of that promise to the apostolic age, or explained

away its meaning by declaring that the work of God in saving the soul is greater than the work of God in healing the body. But we are beginning to understand that we must put no limit to the power of the Almighty if we really believe in a living God.[190]

The Christian Scientists could hardly have said it better. Dunstan observed that some "neglected truths" of Christianity were now "being voiced from multitudes of pulpits in the older denominations," but that "it has been too late to stop the exodus of thousands of our most intelligent hearers."

One of the most visible ways the new converts to Christian Science were publicly putting their newfound trust in the unlimited power of God to the test was in the erection and dedication of church buildings. Public denunciations and criticisms of Christian Science were not going to put a stop to that work.

DEDICATION

First Methodist Episcopal Church, Seattle

Postcard

First Church of Christ, Scientist, Seattle

Clarence B. Bagley

19

Spreading Branches (1914)

As soon as the Capitol Hill branch completed its edifice, the downtown branch moved forward with its own building project. The next month, July 1914, Fourth Church of Christ, Scientist, purchased a double lot on the southwest corner of Eighth Avenue and Seneca Street. This area just up the hill from the business district was known as First Hill. This centrally located district was being rapidly developed for apartment buildings at the time, a newsworthy building boom. The *Seattle Times* mentioned the purchase for the new Christian Science building project as "illustrative of the activity in that part of the city."[191]

The site was only a few blocks from the original Christian Science chapel on Sixth Avenue that had seated 500. Fourth Church had much bigger plans, out of necessity. The previous year they had outgrown Arcade Hall and moved their services to the newly constructed Hippodrome at Fifth and University. The Hippodrome could accommodate thousands. In its first year of operation, *The Seattle Times* described the Hippodrome as the "Madison Square Garden of Seattle . . . the home of fun—wholesome, dignified, clean," and as having a "high standard." It was a dance hall, a vaudeville theater, and a venue for carnivals, conventions, and civic ceremonies. On Sunday mornings and Wednesday evenings, the Hippodrome was a sanctuary for Fourth Church. Initially, they set it up to seat 1,500. They could significantly expand seating capacity for lectures, and they held many at this new venue. Bliss Knapp, Willis T. Gross, Reverend William P. McKenzie, Jacob S. Shields, William R. Rathvon, and Professor Hermann S. Herring, all spoke there on Christian Science to large audiences.[192]

At this time changes were happening for the other Christian Science congregations too. In Ballard, Second Church had recently moved to a new location. Originally formed in 1902 by "a few students of Christian Science," their small membership initially purchased a building "known as the old Catholic church building" and remodeled it for their use for church services and a reading room. It was on West 58th Street, a residential area. But they had since moved to a more visible location in the commercial district, the Scandinavian American Bank Building on Ballard Avenue at Vernon Place.[193]

In the southeast end of Seattle, the small Christian Science society in the Rainier Valley had recently moved northward. Originally organized in 1911, they initially held services at Socialist Hall in Hillman City. Now they were meeting in Columbia City at Modern Woodmen Hall, a second-floor room in the Weed Building on Rainier Avenue near South Ferdinand Street. Georgianna Elouise Wiestling, a single woman supporting herself as a music teacher, a former member of First Church and a founding member of Fourth Church, was now serving as its First Reader. Like Ballard, Columbia City was a separate small town annexed by Seattle in 1907. An electric railway connected it to Seattle. The area was rapidly growing, and the Christian Science church was now active in the center of its commercial district.[194]

Meanwhile, back on Capitol Hill, First Church was getting settled in their new church home. For the first time in their history, they could keep all their records in one place. They had an office in their new church, and the board had its own private room. Their treasurer and bookkeeper were working together to put their financial records in better order. There were no more construction expenses, only some minor ongoing maintenance and cleaning costs. Future contributions to the building fund would go towards paying off their mortgage.[195]

At the December 8, 1914, annual membership meeting for First Church, board chair Charles A. Griffith gave a report on the activities of that eventful year, which he declared "marks an epoch in our history." Besides completing their church building in early June, that fall two new Christian Science churches were formed at the initiative of the board. Even with the new stone temple, which they initially claimed seated as many as 1,300—the largest auditorium in their history—and even with holding two services every Sunday, at 11 a.m. and 8 p.m., the building could not hold the number of people who wanted to attend. The Seattle church body needed to expand again. In the southwest end of the city, in a district called West Seattle, a small group formed a new Christian Science society that met at the West Seattle Masonic Hall on

California Avenue in the commercial center. In the northeast part of the city, the newly formed University District Christian Science Society had just held its first meeting at University Masonic Hall, overflowing their 300 seats from the very first meeting. Speaking of these new churches, Mr. Griffith assured the members in his report. "While each has drawn members from our own congregation, we have experienced no diminution in either membership or attendance." The attendance in the Sunday School had "practically doubled in the past twelve months," requiring the church to hold two Sunday School sessions instead of one. Addressing any lingering concern about paying off the mortgage on their church property, Griffith continued:

> Our ability to go forward with and complete our work is not lessened, but rather increased, here again proving the accuracy of our Leader's assurance that 'Giving does not impoverish us in the service of our Maker, neither does withholding enrich us.' . . . As the need develops for other organizations in other sections of the city, and each such need is properly met, we shall find that we have more, not less, that we are richer, not poorer.[196]

Church building was only beginning. More edifices were needed. Growth in attendance was accelerating. The earlier words of Rev. Mary Baker Eddy were clearly relevant:

> *Beloved Brethren*: — the spreading branches of The Church of Christ, Scientist, are fast reaching out their broad shelter to the entire world. Your faith has not been without works, — and God's love for His flock is manifest in His care. . . . Abide in His word, and it shall abide in you; and the healing Christ will again be manifest in the flesh—understood and glorified.[197]

There were now six Christian Science churches in Seattle, and more would be formed soon. There may have already been an expectation that branches of Mary Baker Eddy's church would eventually spread to every district in Seattle.

20

Declarations of War (1914)

At their December 11, 1914, election the members of First Church of Christ, Scientist, Seattle, in their collective wisdom, once again put Allen H. Armstrong on the board. The board members then nominated Mr. Armstrong for the position of chair. Prior to the board vote, however, Armstrong asked his fellow board members for time to explain what he felt he must work for. He saw an urgent need for a debt-free church—dedication—at the earliest possible date. He would not accept the position of chair—or even board member—if there was not unanimous agreement on making this the highest priority. The board quickly agreed with Armstrong. But there remained a question of whether all the members in the church were in agreement with the board on this goal.[198]

The effort to reach the summit of "Mount Dedication" as proposed by Charles A. Griffith just after opening services for the new edifice, had apparently lost its momentum because of internal contention. That fall, the board and membership were focused on a round of changes to their organizational bylaws having to do with accounting procedures— staff support for the Treasurer, systems for paying expenses, financial audits, and reports to the members. There were amendments, and amendments to amendments, and vote tallies that showed divided opinion on the changes. Church financial records had not been kept in good order during the building project. There had been unpleasant "surprises" along the way. The biggest surprise might have been the final cost for the building. Their stone edifice on Capitol Hill had ended up costing nearly twice the original budget. The board held special meetings to address criticism of the handling of church finances. The treasurer, clerk, and bookkeeper were now working together on how to track "every liability and asset" according to standard accounting practices.[199]

The debt on the building was a serious concern. Even with their large and growing membership, a mortgage of $80,000 was a huge burden. They risked losing ownership if ever unable to make mortgage payments. But it was not fear of loss that motivated Armstrong and the other board members to pay off the debt quickly. There was a spiritual impetus behind the focus. This was another opportunity to prove that faith that could move mountains.

The members were called to attend a special meeting the evening of Friday, February 26, 1915, in the Sunday School room of the church. "A full attendance is desired," the call letter stated. To prepare for the meeting, members were requested to read a recent article by Dr. Edmund F. Burton in the *Christian Science Sentinel* entitled "Support." The article was about taking a spiritual view of church and financial supply, the importance of looking to God for support through "unswerving obedience and trust."[200]

What Armstrong said that evening in the Sunday School was so significant to the members that his notes were preserved in the church files for posterity. Armstrong addressed the members:

It is customary for one in accepting an important post of duty to make a statement of his purpose and policy. With us as a Christian Church, the case is somewhat different, for our purpose is defined to Christian Science.

I believe it is wise, however, and both fitting and expedient, that I state, briefly, the ideal before me, in accepting the present office. This ideal relates to the purpose for which this meeting is called: — namely, to inaugurate the activity that must eventuate in the dedication of our church building.

If the church and its chosen executives have a common purpose, a common ideal, and are agreed in a general way as to how this purpose is to be attained, harmony can prevail. If, however, such agreement does not obtain, then no harmony is possible.

A sense of right is one of the strongest incentives to human action and endeavor. Hence, if differences of judgement or opinion arise as to what is the right, or the thing to do, or the right method to pursue, the mental collision is sharp and painful. This is one reason why individuals, with the best of motives, pain each other.

Again, should those who are to act for you pursue one ideal while you in thought and purpose pursue another, the results cannot be happy.

DEDICATION

The purpose of this meeting is therefore chiefly that your board may come to a clear agreement with you upon the accomplishment to be endeavored and thus prevent waste of time and emotional energy. ...

This purpose is first: The dedication of this church-building at the earliest possible date. Second: The constant education of ourselves, and of the congregation, to this end. I have used the expression "constant education" because of the tendency of the age to postpone, to neglect, or to forget what is essential to the spiritual welfare of both ourselves and mankind. . . . If it is necessary for us as individuals to watch, it is necessary for us as a whole to watch, lest this work of dedication drag, and we be found unfaithful stewards.

Again, if it is wise for us individually to examine ourselves and to see our mistakes as error, it is wise for us as a body to do so, that we may accomplish the end, namely: the forsaking of the error. I mentioned the education of the congregation, also, because the membership of the church does not exceed one third . . . of the congregation. This remaining two thirds . . . must be educated into, not their duty, but their privilege.

Full publicity though without begging must be given to the conditions of this problem. They, as well as ourselves must learn the truth of the statement contained in *Science and Health*, . . . [Giving does not impoverish us in the service of our Maker, neither does withholding enrich us. We have strength in proportion to our apprehension of the truth, and our strength is not lessened by giving utterance to truth.]

As students of this way, we find it a part of our own emancipation to enlighten others. To this end this structure is erected. . . . The mental elements involved show the task of completion of the first permanent structure for Christian Science in the city to be a difficult one. To a peculiar degree, its citizens are devoted to commercialism.[201]

Armstrong had written on the concepts of mental elements that hindered and the need to open thought to possibility in his article "Present Salvation" in the *Christian Science Journal,* in which he expounded on Saint Paul's statement, "Now is the accepted time: behold now is the day of salvation" (2 Cor. 6:2) by discussing how a limiting false concept among physical scientists had previously hindered the development of a new wireless technology. He wrote:

Wireless telegraphy was just as much a possibility a century ago as it is to-day; but it was not then a mental possibility. No law of mechanic, of mathematics, or of electrical science has changed in the slightest. The human apprehension of these has, however, changed very greatly; hence the different results.[202]

In this same way, Armstrong suggested the Christian Scientists of First Church needed to "escape from the human limitations" by honestly examining their own thinking, confessing their sin, and forsaking it — both individually and as a collective body — including "pride in certain traditions of Christian Science." He continued:

> This First Church is mentally pioneering the way that others may follow. The multitudes must be allowed to hear the truth and to learn how far its power exceeds the power and the accomplishments of blind belief and fear, in every department of consciousness. Three other structures are needed now and if we will complete our task, these structures will go forward, for mortal resistance will be weakened by our victory. We are working for Christian Science first; for this church in particular only because it stands first in the order of undertakings. The completion will be more difficult than that of any succeeding structure because it is the first.
>
> Because of these considerations, we are under the necessity of taking council with each other. We must study the letter on this point and pray for the spirit, that its saving power may be known. . . . We cannot purchase high heaven, but, on the other hand, we cannot receive from heaven while the human self and human desire hinders us from maintaining the divine ideal.

The more open hostility to Christian Science following the completion of their edifice might have given rise to some concern for their future. In his speech Armstrong expressed some wariness of the activities of other religious groups working against them, including special concern about high officials who had recently moved to Seattle.

Armstrong shifted to an analogy of warfare. Fighting had broken out that summer in Europe with a succession of declarations of war, invasions, and battles. The United States was not involved, and most Americans preferred it that way. But the newspapers were filled with news of war. Concern about the spread of the fighting, a possible shift of power in Europe, and the potential impact of war even in Seattle was on everyone's mind in the fall of 1914. In making his case for early dedication, Armstrong had argued that just as England had needed to strengthen itself against a rising German empire or suffer as German

vassals, so the members of First Church needed to muster themselves
to withstand the opposition and rise to the challenge.

> Thus, you see, we must enter the struggle which raises every de-
> partment of human consciousness above its present condition of
> bondage to sensible belief, or suffer the more appalling cost of de-
> feat in the full toll of fear, sickness, and death. . . . The weapons of
> this warfare are not carnal but we nevertheless must be earnest,
> persistent and skillful in their use.

As to paying off their mortgage,

> If we had only ourselves as an organization to think of this might be
> done at our leisure, our convenience. At this point, the human ele-
> ment and the demand clash.

After hearing Armstrong's speech, the membership moved, seconded,
and passed this resolution:

> Resolved that the members of this church do hereby express our
> hearty approval of the purpose and method expressed by our Pres-
> ident's address and that by our vote we give expression of our in-
> tention to cooperate with our Board of Directors to the end that this
> church edifice may be dedicated at an early date and that Truth
> may have its perfect expression in our midst.

Now, with a renewed sense of resolve and a spirit of unity, the
board could move forward toward the goal of dedication.

"The battle is on," Armstrong declared. "Not a battle of hate against
hate, but a battle of Love against hate."[203]

21

A Woman's Religion (1914)

The board for the newly formed University District Christian Science Society got organized. During the month of December 1914, they set up a bank account and accounting books. They purchased 18 dozen folding chairs and four dozen hymnals, and they began making monthly payments to support the jointly maintained downtown Christian Science Reading Room. They put an advertisement for their church services in the *North End News*. They appointed a member to get one sign for the door of their rented room and one to put out by the sidewalk.[204]

Because attendance had unexpectedly overflowed the 300 seats they had set up in the University Masonic Hall at the first church services on Sunday, November 29, the board members saw potential for even more people at their next church services. They wanted to send a "circular letter" to students at the University of Washington. The University kept records on students' religious preference and made this information available to official student groups. Edward Dill, one of the two men on the five-member board, had already had a meeting with the Secretary of the University Young Men's Christian Association, the YMCA. Now the board directed clerk Ruth F. Anderson to ask the secretary of the University YWCA, the women's group, for a list of university women interested in Christian Science. Established in 1895 by Ella Chamberlain for Bible study and missionary outreach to local immigrants, the YWCA was the first women's organization established on campus. Whether or not the YWCA helped the Christian Scientists was not recorded. There may have been an expectation of cooperation because of their shared interest in advancing the social status of women.[205]

DEDICATION

The influence and leadership of women in Christian Science and in particular in the U-District society was significant. Rev. Mary Baker Eddy's church organization had included equality of the sexes as a foundational principle since its beginning in the 1870s. The new U-District society was unmistakably and overwhelmingly female. Started by a woman, it was organized by a team of three women, its first business meetings were chaired by a woman, and its first board had a woman majority. All three officers in charge of the Sunday School were women. The First Reader was a woman, with a man assisting as Second Reader. Having so many women in church leadership roles was unusual for Christianity at the time, but not for Christian Science societies and churches.

The Christian Science church was a pioneer in the extent to which it put woman's voice into the pulpit. Whenever possible, a man and a woman served together in the readership. In 1910, about 60 percent of the First Readers throughout the world were women. There was a general tendency for the First Readers at the largest churches to be men, and the smallest churches sometimes had two women readers. At this time in Seattle, the readership was remarkably gender balanced. In Seattle, the rapidly growing list of Christian Science practitioners, the closest role in the Christian Science church to clergy, showed a gender ratio of about 90 percent women, the same as was true globally.[206]

In these early Christian Science churches in Seattle, women typically comprised a supermajority of the members. This U-District branch had perhaps a larger than usual female supermajority. The female leadership in the organization reflected the makeup of the membership.[207]

Christian Science was widely perceived as a "peculiarly woman's religion." In 1901, the *Christian Science Journal* published an article called "Woman's Religion" that illustrated how this female image was sometimes an obstacle for its acceptance.

> The statement is often made that Christian Science is a 'Woman's Religion,' and it is said in a way that would carry with it a slur and a suggestion that by virtue of its being so dubbed it would fully justify one wasting no thought or time upon it; and would also result in securing its everlasting doom.[208]

A clergyman whose wife was healed of invalidism by Christian Science wrote the article. After the healing, he took up the study of Mary Baker Eddy's book, but he struggled with the idea of its author being a woman.

I found myself unable to accept Mrs. Eddy, and I tried to separate *Science and Health* and Mrs. Eddy. The more I tried the more Mrs. Eddy seemed to pervade every part of it, until at last my opposition to her overshadowed all else, and I abandoned the whole thing in bitterness, anger, and disgust. After several years of struggle it began to dawn upon my consciousness that possibly it was my own conceit and some jealousy, with a few other pungent ingredients mixed in, which were making Mrs. Eddy the mark for my spleen and keeping me out of the Truth. I took *Science and Health* again, locked my old self-conceit in a dungeon where it could not be seen or heard, and a new light dawned upon me. . . . From that moment my life changed and my demonstration came.

Those who were so energetically establishing Christian Science had embraced the idea of a new religion founded by a woman. The radical notion of a democratic church that empowered its women might have been at least part of what made Christian Science so appealing to women. People in Washington were unusually supportive of women's rights, allowing women to vote sporadically since 1883 and permanently since 1910 — ten years before the Constitutional Amendment that gave women voting rights nationally. Seattle and the University District were especially supportive. The first graduate of the University of Washington was a woman. Seattle had the first woman mayor of any major United States city, Bertha Knight Landes, and she lived in the University District. So considering how supportive the University community had been of women's higher education and active involvement in civic life, the immediate appeal of the new Christian Science church was understandable, especially among young women. Several wives of prominent faculty and administrators at the University would soon join the Christian Science church. On an official list from the University during that era, nearly four times as many female students as men selected Christian Science as their church preference.[209]

There was some concern about the imbalance of gender within the Christian Science movement, as shown by Eddy's article "Men in Our Ranks," published in the 1910 *Christian Science Journal* and *Sentinel*:

A letter from a student in the field says there is a grave need for more men in Christian Science practice. I have not infrequently hinted at this. However, if the occasion demands it, I will repeat that men are very important factors in our field of labor for Christian Science. The male element is a strong supporting arm to religion as well as to politics, and we need in our ranks of divine energy, the strong, the faithful, the untiring spiritual armament.[210]

DEDICATION

Perhaps to present a more gender-balanced image to visitors, the ushers in Christian Science churches were consistently predominately men for many decades. As the number of men increased within the membership, it became customary to elect a man to the more prominent First Reader position. The small minority of men within the ranks of full-time Christian Science practitioners were the ones most often selected to be lecturers. Also, men filled most of the leadership positions at The Mother Church in Boston. This gender-balanced image may have helped recruit more men to membership at branch churches.

Even with men holding prominent positions within the Christian Science organization, women made up the overwhelming majority of voters within the democratically run branch churches, and so controlled the most important decisions, such as whether to build a church—a topic that would soon be raised within the new University District Christian Science Society.

Their rental of University Masonic Hall was serving their needs at present, but they would very soon need a larger room. Eventually they would want their own building, something as grand and elegant as First Church of Christ, Scientist, on Capitol Hill—to present this new religious movement, this "woman's religion," in the best possible way to the public. For now, the mostly-female members of the U-District branch of Eddy's church focused on outreach to the University community, through every way available to them. They were preparing for church growth, and it was already happening.

22

Church Growth (1915)

Within six months after being formed, the University District Christian Science Society had outgrown their first meeting place at University Masonic Hall. They needed to find a larger space nearby. They continued to rent the Masonic Banquet Hall for their business meetings, but by May 1915, they were holding Sunday services and Wednesday meetings in the second floor public hall of the newly built University State Bank Building at the corner of Northeast 45th Street and University Way.

This intersection was a new commercial center, a highly visible and convenient corner in the heart of the U-District. It was at the end of an electric trolley line heading northeast from downtown Seattle. Nearby intersecting rail lines ran east and west. Some of the largest buildings in the city outside the downtown core had recently been built there as apartments for students and faculty.

The University District was part of a grand civic vision for promoting and developing Seattle into a prominent American city, the commercial capital of the Pacific Northwest—a world trade center with a focus on Asia and the Pacific Rim. The spirit of Seattle's ambitions was symbolized downtown by the Smith Tower, which opened on July 4, 1914. A symbol of the information technology innovation that the Smith-Corona typewriter represented, the Smith Tower, besides being Seattle's first skyscraper, with an astounding 35 stories, was the tallest building in western America. In the University District, Seattle's ambitions were expressed in the 1909 Alaska-Yukon-Pacific Exposition, the world's fair that had drawn four million visitors. Because of the AYP Expo, the forested acreage owned by the University of Washington was transformed into a parklike campus of Olmstead design, oriented for spectacular views of Mount Rainier. After the Expo ended, many of the large elegant pavilions designed by leading architects were used for college classes. Near the west entrance of the campus, a commercial area was developed with hotels, transportation infrastructure, paved streets, and sidewalks. Beyond the commercial area, forests and farms were being developed into commercial buildings and residential neighborhoods. Seattle was transforming into a bustling city with elegant architecture, and the University District was one of the most actively developing areas. This Christian Science church was intentionally planted in the heart of the University District. It would grow along with the district.

That summer on Friday, July 9, 1915, the society held a Christian Science lecture at the bank building, with financial and logistical support from the other branches. They invited Bicknell Young, an especially talented and popular lecturer. Young had given Christian Science lectures all over the United States since 1903. He had lectured all over Europe, including England, Scotland, Wales, Ireland, Germany, France, Italy, the Netherlands, and Holland, as well as Mexico and Australia. After living in London for nearly four years, Young moved back to Chicago where he was able to respond more easily to requests for lectures throughout the United States. On previous trips to Seattle he had given lectures at the city's largest venues: the Moore Theater, the Grand Opera House, Dreamland, and the Hippodrome. He could certainly fill the comparatively small hall in the University Bank Building, which could seat 950 people.[211]

Young was an especially good lecturer for the university community because of his "scholarly manner" that set him apart from the provocative style of the recent revivalist series. As one reviewer put it,

> Mr. Young indulges neither fervor of language nor flights of oratory, nor does he appeal to the emotional side of human nature. His lecture is scholarly, logical, clear, and convincing. His arguments were within the grasp of even the simple child, yet he sounded the depths of philosophic and scientific research.

Another newspaper reporter concluded:

> If all doctrinarians would present their case in the spirit which characterizes the lecture of Mr. Young, there would be some rational thinking that would do the world a lot of good, whether it establishes permanently the Christian Science thought or not. In these days of rant and fury, it is certainly refreshing to be able to listen to

a scholar who treats his subject rationally, and his hearers as if they were possessed of a fair supply of good sense and understanding.[212]

Whenever Young's lectures were printed in full in local newspapers, those issues would sell out. The Christian Science Publishing Society sold reprints of his lectures as pamphlets in English, French, German, Swedish, and Norwegian.[213]

Besides the appealing content of his lectures, Young had the confident stage presence of an experienced performer. He was described as "a man of striking personal appearance" who had "a rich, musical voice." Prior to going into the full-time practice of Christian Science, Young was a well-known baritone singer. People in Seattle might have been to his performance of Handel's Messiah in Tacoma in 1897.[214]

But even with his scholarship and stage presence, Young presented himself with a sense of holy dignity appropriate for his religious topic. As one report put it, "One might have thought it was an orthodox Presbyterian that was lecturing, as he dealt with the Gospel story, with prayer, and the love of God, albeit he was in frock-coat instead of clerical garb." His ministerial quality was perhaps a family characteristic. Bicknell Young's full name was *Brigham* Bicknell Young. Raised a Mormon, he was named after his famous uncle Brigham Young, who had served for 30 years as president of The Church of Jesus Christ of Latter-Day Saints, in Salt Lake City, Utah. Bicknell's father, Joseph, was also a high-ranking church official, and as was typical for early Mormon officials, he practiced polygamy. Bicknell's mother, Jane Bicknell Young, was his father's first wife of seven. She had been part of the Mormon community from its beginnings in upstate New York. She was along for all the westward moves by wagon train to Ohio, then Missouri, then Illinois, until the Mormons finally established themselves in the western desert of Utah where they were safe from religious persecution. Bicknell, the youngest of his mother's eleven children, was born in Salt Lake City in 1856 during the first decade of Utah settlement. As he was growing up, Salt Lake City was growing into a major city. As a young adult, having exhausted the musical training options in Utah, Bicknell studied in London at the Royal College of Music. After graduating, he married one of his teachers, Eliza Muzzacato, an Italian who was ten years his senior. Young had been baptized into the Mormon Church and was active in the religion as a youth, but during his time in London he stopped identifying as a Mormon. Muzzacato's Catholic background may have been a factor. But according to one source, he had already become agnostic. Bicknell maintained friendly ties with his Mormon friends and family in Utah, and for several years he and his wife lived in Salt Lake City, but by 1890, they left Mormon country for Chicago.[215]

The Youngs moved to Chicago to advance their musical careers, but this was when Bicknell's new career in Christian Science began. Chicago became a stronghold of Christian Science after Mary Baker Eddy's visit there in 1884. Bicknell became seriously ill, and he was healed by a Christian Science practitioner. Both he and Eliza became Christian Scientists.[216]

Bicknell's conversion to Christian Science had a big impact on his family. His brother Seymour, a medical doctor by profession, stayed with the Mormon church, and, following his father's path, became a high-ranking polygamous Mormon church officer. But his mother and six sisters all left the Mormon Church for Christian Science.

At the 1897 dedication service for First Church of Christ, Scientist, Chicago, when Edward Kimball was First Reader, Bicknell sang a solo composed by Eliza for the occasion. At that dedication, at which the overflowing audience filled even the standing room and entrances at all four dedication services, he was among the first to hear Reverend Eddy's longest and perhaps most significant branch church dedicatory address. The address included a statement about the potential to halt or even reverse the aging process—a message that proved to be provocative and even controversial. Eddy wrote:

> [I]f wisdom lengthens my sum of years to fourscore (already imputed to me), I shall then be even younger and nearer the eternal meridian than now, for the true knowledge and proof of life is in putting off the limitations and putting on the possibilities and permanence of Life.[217]

Eddy revisited her challenging statement about aging in an address for the Christian Science church in her home town, Concord, New Hampshire—at which, when they later dedicated their new church edifice, Bicknell Young was given the privilege of reading Eddy's address at the dedication services. Following the Chicago statement, the Concord audience heard:

> The statement in my letter to the church in Chicago, in substance as follows, has been quoted and criticized: 'If wisdom lengthens my sum of years to fourscore, I may then be even younger than now.' Few believe this saying. Few believe that Christian Science contains infinitely more than has been demonstrated, or that the altitude of its highest propositions has not yet been reached."[218]

Eddy taught that an understanding of Christian Science "even in small degree" would increase longevity. It was a message that Mr. Young took to heart. As a Christian Science teacher, he challenged his students to rethink aging. He would tell them:

> There is no more age than there is death. Age is one of the most persistent *diseases* in human belief. . . . Are you going to take part in it, or are you going to take part in the demonstration over it? It is not a question of years. Years haven't a thing to do with it. It is not in years, or of years. Eternity is all there is. Just the everlasting now; there is no time at all.[219]

Young's mother took Christian Science class instruction from him, and it seems she put the teaching into practice effectively, as she was noted for her extraordinarily long life. Jane and four of Bicknell's sisters—two of whom became Christian Science practitioners—moved to Tacoma, Washington. When Jane Bicknell Young died in 1913, she was believed to be the oldest woman in Washington State. She was known to be both a widow of a leading figure in Mormon history and a pillar of the Christian Science church for 30 years—one of the first "women of prominence to enroll as an adherent of Mary Baker G. Eddy"—and the mother of Bicknell Young. A *Seattle Times* article on her life accomplishments focused on her "remarkable vitality":

> Aside from a slight deafness she suffered none of the ailments of old age. Until a few weeks ago she was as active physically and mentally as a woman of 60 years and went about the city unattended, visiting relatives and returning social calls. On these occasions she resorted to the use of the street car no oftener than those only half her age. Highly educated and cultured, she retained a keen interest in the affairs of the world to the last, and at 98 her conversation sparkled with brilliancy . . . Her memory was unusually retentive to the last and her fund of personal anecdotes covered a period of more than eighty years.[220]

So when Bicknell Young lectured in the University District, on top of his other credentials, some may have known him as Jane Young's son.

But even beyond all his aforementioned strengths as a lecturer, one more is worth special mention, and that is the inspiration that audiences felt. When he read Eddy's dedicatory address at Concord, it was so "finely read," his "musical voice so perfectly modulated and his faultless enunciation," and he had such an ability to speak Eddy's words as though they were his own, it was reported that many in the overflow

123

congregation were moved to tears and "received a strong spiritual uplift." This spiritual uplift was an effect that audience members felt during his lectures, too, even resulting in physical healing. As one person testified in the *Christian Science Sentinel*:

> [W]hile listening to Mr. Bicknell Young's lecture on Christian Science, my foot hurt me so that I could hardly keep still, but from that evening it was healed. The corn disappeared, and my foot became normal in size.[221]

At the Friday evening lecture on July 9 in the University District, the hall was packed. It gave another boost to the vitality of the newest of the Seattle branches of Mary Baker Eddy's church—this University District church that would celebrate its centennial.[222]

The rented space at the University Bank Building in the heart of the growing district continued to meet their need for a church home after the lecture. But as member Eileen Gormley later explained, "The members knew there were still more progressive steps to take." They already had a building fund. In January 1915, only a few months after they held their first church services, they started setting aside the collection from the first Sunday each month with the goal of someday having a church building of their own. Soon they would be ready to start, thanks in part to the church growth they experienced from the lecture.[223]

**Looking north on University Way NE at NE 45th Street
University State Bank Building on right**

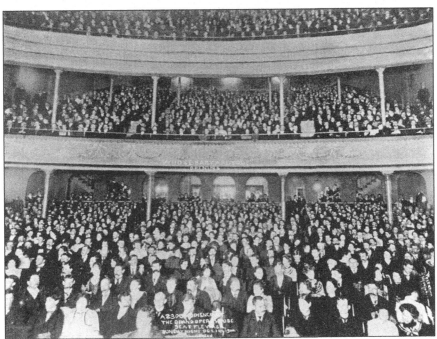

Seattle's Grand Opera House in 1900

Paul Dorpat collection

23

First Unit (1915)

On Sunday, August 29, 1915, First Reader Thomas Franklyn Hoyt, invited the entire congregation of Fourth Church of Christ, Scientist, to stay after the service to hear a message from the chair of the building committee. A few months earlier, the membership decided to move forward with the building project. The decision was unanimous. The Hippodrome was meeting an immediate need for the growing congregation, but it was hardly an ideal place of worship. It was meant to be temporary. Now, after six years of renting public halls, the members were ready to build a permanent church home.

Although not specifically named in the available records, the chair of the building committee and the leader of the spiritual aspect of the building project was almost certainly William K. Sheldon.[224] Mr. Sheldon had recently become a Christian Science teacher. He also had professional experience with building projects. He grew up in Rutland, Vermont, which had a booming stone industry. Like his father before him, Sheldon had worked as a marble dealer. He may have become involved with Christian Science while working at a stone quarry in Massachusetts. After that, he moved to Seattle, became a Christian Science practitioner, and was almost immediately elected to First Reader at First Church. For such a large congregation with so many Christian Science practitioners and teachers already within the membership to have elected a new member to the most prominent office, Sheldon must have been perceived as having an outstanding understanding of Christian Science, even before he became a Christian Science teacher. At First Church, although he was not on the building committee, Sheldon had been involved with the project. He helped select the stone used in the Capitol Hill edifice. At Fourth Church, Sheldon served as chair of the building committee in the early phase of the project.[225]

Fourth Church was fortunate to also have on the building committee Frederick S. Sylvester, who was known for his business skill. The president of Sylvester Brothers, a wholesale grocery company, he had been active in business ventures "with characteristic enterprise" since arriving in Seattle in 1889, the year of the great fire. He, along with his business partner, his brother George, and both of their wives, had been involved in the Christian Science church from its start in Seattle in 1896. His successful grocery venture had grown in parallel with the church, and now he owned substantial wealth and a good understanding of accounting. He too would play an important role in the early phase of the building project.[226]

The members of Fourth Church already knew all about the financial side of the church. They heard financial reports at membership business meetings every quarter. But so many among the large congregation at the Hippodrome had never applied to join the church formally as members. Fourth Church may have had a higher percentage of non-members than any other branch in Seattle. These regular attendees may not have understood what it cost to keep the church going. The building committee chair gave them a primer, because the church had an urgent need.

The pressing issue was the final payment on their mortgage for the lot at Eighth Avenue and Seneca Street. It was due on October 15. The church did not have funds on hand to make that payment. They had borrowed money to make the previous mortgage payment, and the church was running a deficit on their regular expenses. Since some in the congregation may not have known about all the activities the church was supporting, the chair openly shared their financial obligations with the Sunday assembly.

Each year Fourth Church was contributing $300 to the Committee on Publication for public relations and lobbying, $1,400 to the joint literature distribution committee, and $1,900 to the joint Reading Room in the Empire Building. Their Christian Science lectures were costing $750, and the regular church services ran about $12,000 for rental and salaries. Because they were still making payments on their building lot, they also had the extra expense of mortgage interest and property taxes, which added more than $1,500 to their expenses that year.

The new branch churches in the outlying districts in Seattle had drawn many away from Fourth Church, yet the congregation continued to grow. But even so, collections on Sundays were not sufficient. The church was two months behind on its bills. To make the final mortgage payment, pay off the recent credit draw, cover their back expenses, and eliminate their budget deficit, they needed $7,500 immediately. Once this was done, they could get a building loan to start work on their edifice. Eventually, they would be relieved of the extra expense of rent. Most importantly, having their own edifice would provide "a place of worship that will reflect love."[227]

Considering all this, the building committee chair asked the congregation to give special thought to the Sunday collections for the next six weeks. Even after meeting this goal, they must not become passive in their desire for a church home. "In [Christian Science] we cannot stand still. We must progress," he emphasized. This was only the beginning of their financial needs. The chair concluded:

> This statement is made without any sense of complaint or criticism, and is commended to your consideration, measured entirely by your sense of gratitude for benefits received and your interest in broadening our activities for the benefit of suffering and sinning humanity.
>
> It is the desire of every [Christian Science] church to present in the best way possible to the community in which it is located the Christ Truth which makes men free, and releases them from bondage including debt. The building and paying for so many beautiful [Christian Science] Churches in the short space of time since this movement was inaugurated has been the marvel of the whole world.
>
> [Christian Science] is a philanthropic and Christian movement, the activities of which are far reaching in their influence and power for good, beyond the possibilities of estimate. It is a work neither hard [nor] burdensome, for it is based on the Divine principle, Love, which Mrs. Eddy tells us . . . [is] "universal and impartial in its adaptation and bestowals." Therefore, we have no sense of hesitation in calling the attention of all who have felt the transforming healing influence of [Christian Science] (both Church members and regular attendants) to the righteous demands of this work, and ask the substantial hearty support of one and all, which will insure the carrying forward of these activities in a manner worthy of so great a cause.[228]

Contributions did increase. Fourth Church met the financial goal, and the church claimed title to the corner lots at Eighth and Seneca. By December, the architect was working on preliminary designs in preparation for the January membership meeting. The committee selected George Foote Dunham for the design work. Mr. Dunham had been professionally trained in Chicago by Solon Spencer Beman. Like Mr. Beman, Dunham was a Christian Scientist. He was based in Portland, Oregon, which was not ideal for this Seattle project, but Dunham was proving an ability to work remotely and travel to the building site as necessary.[229]

Dunham quickly designed a plan for building in phases. The first unit was a temporary auditorium in the daylight basement where the Sunday School would eventually be. In its unfinished state, it could seat about 1,000. The basement ceiling would be designed with this in mind and covered with a simple wood roof to keep the space dry. The first unit would cost about $25,000. They could use the basement auditorium while the second unit, the final auditorium and foyer, was being constructed above them. Unlike the temporary structure built by First Church, this temporary auditorium would have concrete walls and a concrete ceiling. It would be the final building, just without its final finishes.

For the complete edifice, they were considering a design similar to First Church, but bigger and more expensive. Their initial permit to the City of Seattle was for a 2,500-seat auditorium in a $250,000 building — an edifice nearly twice as large as what had just been built on Capitol Hill, at more than twice the initial budget. This proposed megachurch was reported in the news, putting everyone on notice about the expectation of continued expansion of Christian Science in Seattle.[230]

The members of Fourth Church voted to move forward with the first unit. They approved Dunham's design unanimously. Members and friends of the church worked "valiantly" to see the basement project through to completion while keeping their services going without interruption. They paid their expenses promptly while construction was underway.[231]

At the same time, Fourth Church had another immediate focus and expense. Hermann S. Herring was coming from Concord, New Hampshire, to give a Christian Science lecture for them—the first of two during the year 1916. This one completely filled the Hippodrome. For their next lecture by George Shaw Cook later that year, they held the event at the even larger Arena. More than 5,000 attended.[232]

Meanwhile, war was breaking out in Europe, disrupting lives, especially the lives of European Jews. Civic leaders in Seattle were trying to raise awareness about the crisis. A relief fund was started to help those made homeless and destitute—the Jewish refugees fleeing Europe.

129

DEDICATION

Many prominent Seattle citizens, businesses, and churches contributed. True to the congregation's new embrace of a spirit of financial generosity, even philanthropy, the largest contribution by far came from Fourth Church.[233]

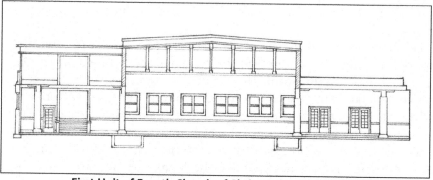

First Unit of Fourth Church of Christ, Scientist, Seattle
Daylight basement auditorium, future Sunday School
Drawing: Christina Safronoff

24

Incorporation (1916)

The members of the University District Christian Science Society looked forward to building a church with hopeful expectations, but before they could purchase any real estate, they needed to formally organize. They needed to become a legally recognized entity—a corporation. At the September 1915 quarterly business meeting, the members decided to take steps toward incorporation. As part of that process, they would upgrade their organization from a society to a church—a Church of Christ, Scientist.

This raised the issue of establishing a Christian Science Reading Room because all Christian Science churches were required to have one. They were already supporting the jointly maintained Reading Room downtown in the Empire Building, but at the end of 1915 the new Third Church began discussing the idea of establishing their own Reading Room in the University District. The membership decided that "at such time as the Society has provided sufficient funds and feels that the time has come . . . for the Reading Room to be established that this be done."[234]

The next issue to resolve was their name. "Third Church of Christ, Scientist, Seattle," had already been used by the group whose short-lived organization was dissolved in December 1909. Consequently, for several years Seattle had a First, Second, and Fourth church, but no Third. Since two other Christian Science societies had already been formed in Seattle, in West Seattle and Columbia City, the University District society was the seventh Christian Science congregation formed in Seattle, and the *Seattle Times* referred to it as seventh in an article about the rapid growth of the newest Christian Science churches. It might have been expected that the University District Society should be called Seventh Church. But that would leave a number gap in the list of Seattle churches in the *Christian Science Journal* directory ever after, a continuing reminder that a Christian Science church had failed. The U-District Society contacted church officials at The Mother Church in Boston and all the other Seattle churches about the issue of numbering. All gave their approval for the re-use of the name "Third." So the group moved forward with that name and sent in the forms for incorporation to the Washington Secretary of State. The corporation was officially created December 22, 1916.[235]

When Third Church incorporated, they rented two connecting rooms in the University State Bank Building for their reading room. The initial advertised hours were noon to 9:00 p.m. every day, except on Wednesdays they closed early at 7:00 p.m. before the Wednesday testimony meeting. It was also open Sundays from 2:00 to 7:00 p.m. Their listing in the *Christian Science Journal* as Third Church first appeared in early 1917.

Not much was added to the building fund for the newly incorporated church, because there was a need to devote the first Sunday collection to a special relief fund run by The Mother Church. The fighting that had begun in Europe in 1914 had escalated. As a Christian Science publication later put it, "Hell's stores were opened, and an anguished world convulsed."[236]

The war had spread to more countries, becoming a world-wide war. The Mother Church had started a war relief fund in October 1914, to which all branch churches and societies were invited to contribute. Initially, the focus was financial support in affected countries for Christian Scientists who were under great distress. The war disrupted the economy, businesses closed, jobs were lost, entire industries were effected, and buildings were destroyed. Men were called away for military duty. Families had to find new homes and income sources. William D. McCracken, a member of the Christian Science Board of Lectureship, traveled to Europe to organize relief efforts. Fund managers reported that the charitable love expressed through the gifts of money and supplies helped recipients overcome the grip of fear, enabling them to take their own independent steps toward improving their situation. By December, the relief effort was expanded to anyone impacted by the war.

It was an issue of debate in America to what degree the United States should strengthen its military defenses or take part in the war — if at all. On this question the Christian Science church was not silent. In 1916, the *Seattle Times* reprinted a statement from a *Christian Science Monitor* editorial. Mary Baker Eddy was in local headlines again, with her own words, and those framed in a positive light — possibly a first for the *Seattle Times*.

> Mrs. Mary Baker Eddy, founder of the Christian Science Church, is quoted by the Christian Science Monitor as an advocate for national preparedness of the navy and army against invasion. In one of the most remarkable editorials which has appeared in the greatest of the Christian Science newspapers, the words of Mrs. Eddy, written by her in 1908, are quoted thus:
>
> "It is unquestionable, however, that at this hour the armament of navies is necessary, for the purpose of preventing war and preserving peace among nations."
>
> The editor of the Monitor argues that since evil in the world has not disappeared, but threatens to overwhelm good, the doctrine of non-resistance cannot yet be accepted in the world.
>
> The "Monitor" squares the proposed military preparedness with the doctrine enunciated by Mrs. Eddy. In conclusion it declares:
>
> "The absolutely vital question, therefore, for a nation on the eve of preparedness appears to be that there should be in its thought no dream of conquest, no idea of preparedness for aggression. When a great nation prepares for war it should prepare with the conviction that it will never need to put out its strength, but it should prepare so as to be able to defend that which is good."
>
> This stand is declared to be the only scientific one to accept.[237]

Not long after the first official listing for Third Church of Christ, Scientist, and its new Reading Room appeared in *The Christian Science Journal* directory, the United States officially entered the world war. Just after midnight, on April 6, 1917, the residents of Seattle learned that Congress had passed a war resolution. *The Seattle Times* had said it would blow its whistle when it passed. So when the five whistle blasts were heard distinctly throughout the city that night, people knew exactly what it meant. Another blast at 10:15 the next morning announced that President Woodrow Wilson had signed the bill into law. That day, headlines on American military mobilization took the place of the newspaper masthead on the front page of *The Seattle Times*. It was all "a very suitable way of telling the people that a history-making epoch has arrived."[238]

A political cartoon on the editorial page of the *Times* showed an oversleeping Uncle Sam abruptly waking by the alarm of war from his slumber on the pillow of pacifism. The *Times* called for unity:

> The United States today is at war. Whatever division in sentiment there may have been in the country yesterday, there can be none

today. In the face of a common enemy, this people can no longer be pro-this or pro-that. They must be Americans—simply and solely. . . . The time for action has arrived. Yet, though the hours be few and precious, there still is a little space for sober consideration of the future. First, let us remember this: Having entered upon war, the United States must emerge from it a victor. We have enunciated certain principles in the defense of which we are taking the field, constructively at least. When the struggle ends, those principles must be the principles upon which peace is concluded. We have announced our determination to overthrow a system of autocratic militarism, which menaces popular government throughout the world. The United States alone—not England, France, Italy, or Russia—must assure the triumph of that noble idea.[239]

At the Annual Meeting of the members of The Mother Church in Boston in early June, William D. McCracken, who was then President of the church, likewise called for unity and action to support the war effort:

The need of the hour is powerful and loving cooperation. The enemy stands at the gates, and those within the protecting shelter of The Mother Church are more than ever under obligations to support each other. . . . Cooperation means working together for the same end. It certainly involves the rejection of all apathy, indifference, or sluggishness. There should no question in our minds that our duty to God involves loyalty to a righteous government and to its constituted authorities. . . . Those who enjoy the protection of a government in times of peace should be willing, by their alertness to duty, to protect that same government in times of war. . . . This is the time when we can encourage each other and sink our differences of human opinion out of sight. We are members of a church which has become world wide and is calling under its beneficent shelter the sick and the sinning everywhere. In order to do justice to them we must learn to do justice to each other. We can assume in every instance that the motive which actuates our brother is a good one; time will test it. . . . We are an army of Christian Scientists. The United States has called Americans to war for the protection of certain ideals. Let us ask ourselves the question, . . . Are we laggards, or are we filling our places individually, praying daily as well as giving freely of our activities as God outlines for the protection of the free institutions which must spread to all nations of the world? . . . Are we real soldiers, keeping step together, shoulder to shoulder, eyes straight ahead, saluting the commandants in strict attention to the commands of our Leader to love one another, to be fruitful in season and out of season, holding our standard so high that it fills the sky and resounds around the world with its helping and saving power.[240]

Within sixty days, the entire Christian Science movement in the United States was organized and at work, able to respond quickly to any needs. In every state an appointed War Relief Committee organized sub-committees in every town and city where a Christian Science church or society existed. They recruited 2,000 volunteer war relief workers, hired 200 full-time employees, plus ten chaplains. They organized thousands of helpers to produce comfort kits of hand-knit sweater vests, socks, blankets, hats, scarfs, and toiletries for civilians affected by war and soldiers heading off to battle. They purchased and operated sixty-nine automobiles and two small ships. They set up organizational headquarters, supply centers, and volunteer cooperatives. A church report later explained:

> Even to a group so accustomed as are Christian Scientists to seeing the so-called impossible accomplished, the progress of the work of this Committee during the later months of 1917 and the earlier ones of 1918 was astonishing.[241]

One way the committees supported the troops was in the establishment of Christian Science Welfare Rooms at every military training camp. The welfare rooms were similar to Christian Science Reading Rooms, and sometimes they used that name on signs. Their primary focus was support and spiritual training of soldiers from Christian Science families, but they offered any visitor a quiet place to read and write, "a cordial welcome and an atmosphere of refinement and culture." They had desks and tables for reading and writing and were decorated with the homey touches of couches, easy chairs, curtains, elegant lamps, bouquets of flowers in vases, potted plants, and often had fireplaces and pianos. On the walls were hung framed pictures of Mary Baker Eddy and The Mother Church edifice in Boston.[242]

The welfare rooms offered Christian Science literature and books for studying the Bible lesson. They could double as an auditorium for church services on Sundays and Wednesdays. They often had private rooms for counseling and Christian Science treatment. They provided a meeting place for visiting family members, and were used for hymn sings, social activities, and holiday parties.

These welfare rooms were established throughout the United States, in Canada, England, and France. They were in rented rooms, tents, or buildings erected for this purpose. The war relief workers at the training camps did anything they could to support the soldiers. Helpfulness was the keynote of their efforts. They offered rides to soldiers, delivered copies of *The Christian Science Monitor* to anyone interested in the news, engaged with everyone on base, they talked with soldiers about their personal challenges, and gave free Christian Science treatment to anyone who asked. They visited hospitals, stockades, and prisoner of war camps. The staff for the welfare rooms often lived on-site. As later described in the Christian Science Publishing Society book *Christian Science War Time Activities*, the workers were up with the birds in early dawn, and often active with their work until midnight. Many of these war workers were *Journal*-listed Christian Science practitioners or First Readers at local branch churches.

Mr. C. Macklem was in charge of the Washington State committee, which planned for a Christian Science Welfare Room at Camp Lewis, the Army base south of Tacoma. This Welfare Room started out as two tents in a grove of trees. Forty Christian Scientist soldiers built a small cottage in ten days. Then a larger building was built at the cost of $6,120, and the cottage became a residence for the workers. Built in the bungalow style, it had a large main room with a fireplace at the end for reading room and auditorium, a separate writing room, and two private rooms for Christian Science treatment.

In Washington State, there were four official welfare rooms. Besides the building at Camp Lewis, there were rooms at the naval bases in Bremerton and Port Townsend, and one in southern Washington in Vancouver. There was also an unofficial welfare room supported and operated by individual Christian Scientists in downtown Seattle called the "Christian Science Soldiers' and Sailors' Hospitality Club." This independent welfare room in Seattle was organized by Orison "O.J.C." Dutton.[243]

Mr. Dutton was a new member of Third Church. Not long after Congress declared war and just after Mr. McCracken gave his recruitment message to Mother Church members, while thousands of young men were enlisting for military duty, Dutton enlisted in the army of Christian Scientists. By signing the membership book at Third Church on June 19, 1917, this civic-minded former Episcopal vestryman fully dedicated himself to his new religion. Dutton was elected to the board that fall, then board chair and church President. During the year 1918, Dutton would be extremely active in supporting his new church, including taking charge of the Camp Welfare work for Third Church. On top of all his new church duties, Dutton would establish the Seattle welfare room for soldiers.[244]

Even after becoming so actively involved in the Christian Science church and its welfare work, Dutton continued to also be active in many other civic organizations, including the most patriotic of roles. On July 4, 1917, an Independence Day that *The Seattle Times* declared held "new meaning" that year, Dutton arranged and served as master of ceremonies for "Seattle's celebration of 'Americanization Day'" at Woodland Park, where new United States citizens "pledged their allegiance to the Stars and Stripes."[245]

Other prominent Christian Scientists in Seattle, even with all their regular church activities, and now the welfare work, somehow made time to be involved in other organizational work supporting the war effort. Christian Science teacher Allen H. Armstrong and church officers at First Church of Christ, Scientist, Oliver C. McGilvra and Charles A. Griffith all served as precinct captains in the Minute Men organization for enrolling men in the military reserves.[246]

But as Christian Scientists, ultimately, they would have considered prayer to be the most important way they could support the war effort. Mary Baker Eddy's "Prayer for Country and Church" captured the sentiment, which Dutton as church President read aloud to the membership of Third Church at a business meeting:

> Pray for the prosperity of our country, and for her victory under arms; . . . In your peaceful homes remember our brave soldiers, whether in camp or in battle. Oh, may their love of country, and their faithful service thereof, be unto them life-preservers! May the divine Love succor and protect them. . . . Great occasion have we to rejoice that our nation . . . will be as formidable in war as she has been compassionate in peace. May our Father-Mother God, who in times past hath spread for us a table in the wilderness and "in the midst of our enemies," establish us in the most holy faith, plant our feet firmly on Truth, the rock of Christ, the "substance of things hoped for" — and fill us with the life and understanding of God, and good will towards men.[247]

No doubt the war was on everyone's mind, especially as America entered the fight. Yet even as Third Church provided ongoing substantial support to the Camp Welfare and War Relief Fund, the congregation continued working toward its goal of building a church edifice that it had set from its initial formation, a goal reinforced by its subsequent incorporation. At the start of 1918, Dutton helped the church purchase property for a building. Dutton was a real estate agent and had served on the City of Seattle Planning Commission. He was involved in finding property for other organizations, including a clubhouse for the Broadway Improvement Club and land for a Boy Scout camp, Camp Parsons. With him on the lot selection committee were board members John J. Cavender, an engineering inspector who had previously been a real estate agent, and Clifford H. Anderson, a fire insurance agent. The committee worked quickly, and on January 22, 1918, they presented seven options to the membership. Through a democratic process led by Dutton, after discussion on the advantages and disadvantages of all seven options, the members made their selection. The majority chose a lot just north of the University of Washington campus. It was on the southeast corner of Northeast 50th Street and 17th Avenue Northeast, which at that time was called "University Boulevard." A wide, flat street with a landscaping strip down the center, it led directly to the main campus entrance. The street would later be dubbed "Greek Row" because of the fraternity and sorority houses that were already starting to be built along it. The property selection was ratified at a special business meeting in March. The decision was almost unanimous. They purchased the lot for $4,800. The members offered a vote of thanks to the lot committee for "impersonal, unselfish, and untiring devotion to the cause of Christian Science." The members began holding monthly meetings to discuss church building.[248]

**Christian Science War Relief Building and Workers' Cottage
Camp Lewis, Washington**

Auditorium and Reading Room

Writing Room

Christian Science War Time Activities

25

University of Washington Society (1917)

A s soon as Congress declared war, life at the University of Washington dramatically changed. To prepare students for enlistment, faculty held military-style training exercises on campus and planned for a very different focus for the next academic year. Everything was geared for war service. In the summer of 1917, the United States began sending troops to war. That summer the Christian Scientists who were students at the University of Washington organized. They wanted to start a registered student organization for campus ministry, a Christian Science Organization.

Christian Science Organizations had already been formed at colleges in the Boston area at Harvard, Simmons, Radcliffe, Wellesley, and Smith College; in New York at Columbia and Cornell; in California at Berkeley and Stanford; at the University of Chicago and Illinois; at the University of Michigan at Ann Arbor, and a few others. The students in Seattle saw a need for one at the University of Washington. Perhaps it was the war that motivated them to come together. On Sunday, October 21, 1917, the same day the first American soldiers started fighting in France, they held their first meeting near campus at the home of Mr. and Mrs. Priest. [249]

Arthur Ragan Priest was Dean of Men and one of the most prominent people at the university. Mr. Priest had led a major reorganization of the university to prepare it for a new era of growth. He was Professor of Rhetoric and Oratory. He ran the debate team, which had recently won the Pacific Coast championship. He was Phi Beta Kappa and Phi Delta Theta. He was also First Reader at First Church of Christ, Scientist.[250]

Arthur's wife, Willa Trent Priest, was also a prominent member of the university community in her role as wife of the dean. She often attended social events as a "patroness" along with the wives of other university faculty and administrators. Her associates' husbands included President Henry Suzzallo, President Thomas F. Kane, Professor Edmund S. Meany, and Law School Dean John T. Condon, whose names became commemorated in the names of campus buildings, and Comptroller Herbert T. Condon who was later Dean of Men for many years. Willa was an active Christian Scientist, a member of First Church, a musician at Third Church, and a Christian Science practitioner. She had recently moved her office from their University District home on 16th Avenue Northeast to the tenth floor of the Empire Building downtown. Arthur was advisor for the new Christian Science College Organization. Willa was almost certainly also involved.[251]

Seven students gathered that day at the Priest residence: Ruth Bragdon, Merle Childs, Eleanor Hoppock, Ernest Oertel, Rosamond Parsons, Florence Pettit, and Adele Reeves. Initially, they called their group the Christian Science Society of the University of Washington. Eleanor Hoppock was elected reader and president. Eleanor was mature both in life and in Christian Science. A graduate student in the College of Education and a teaching fellow in the French Department, she already had a teaching certificate from the University of Paris and had traveled extensively in Europe. Eleanor had been introduced to Christian Science ten years earlier, around 1906, when her family was living in Minneapolis. "It appealed to me instantly," Eleanor later wrote, "and since then has always been the church of my choice." Her seven-years-younger sister, Adele, who was a senior at the University of Washington, later shared,

> When Christian Science was introduced into our home . . . I did not foresee the tremendous influence for good which it was to bring me and to several members of my family. Since our whole-hearted acceptance of Christian Science it has indeed been a 'pearl of great price.'[252]

Eleanor and her sisters had attended Sunday School, and they also received instruction in the practice of Christian Science at home from their mother, who was First Reader in Wenatchee just before the family moved to Seattle. That Eleanor accepted the role of Reader at the college organization was significant because she had overcome the fear of speaking in public. She had found it difficult to give testimonies at church, as she would later explain:

Error tried to tell her that she had never spoken in public and that, to speak convincingly, one must have the natural ability to express one's self, an ability which she believed she lacked. For many weeks she allowed this argument to govern her. Finally, after a week of struggle, she went to the Wednesday evening meeting resolved to rise to her feet though fear told her it would be impossible for her to say a word. Love did not desert her, however, and once on her feet, the words came to her. Thereafter she never again let fear prevent her from acknowledging help received in Christian Science.[253]

While this event probably happened before the Hoppock family moved to Seattle, the act of standing up to share a personal story of healing at a large church like First Church in Seattle with its 1,200-seat auditorium packed to capacity, without the benefit of electrical amplification, must have been intimidating to many people. Eleanor successfully applied what she learned from Christian Science to this and other much more serious situations she would soon face.[254]

The members of the new college organization elected an executive board, which appointed several committees. One of their first actions as an organization was a financial contribution to the Camp Welfare Fund set up by The Mother Church to support the troops. They also circulated copies of *The Christian Science Monitor* around campus and gave subscriptions to the campus libraries. They wanted to put on a Christian Science lecture, but that would have to wait until after the war.[255]

A big question for this new organization was where to hold their meetings. For the rest of fall quarter, they held their meetings in the homes of their members about twice a month on Sundays at 3:00 p.m. Meanwhile, they worked on finding a public meeting location that they could advertise. They asked Comptroller Herbert T. Condon about having their meetings on campus. Condon was friendly towards these Christian Scientists. His wife, Maud, would soon become a member of Third Church. Mr. Condon advised the students to ask permission from the university president, Henry Suzzallo. Apparently, Mr. Suzzallo was not as friendly to Christian Science, because when Suzzallo granted them permission they saw it as a significant victory—the result of fervent prayer. Starting January 1918, they held their meetings on alternate Thursday evenings in Meany Hall in room 110. The Christian Science Society at the University of Washington was finally established with regular advertised meetings in a public place. But not long after this achievement, they lost both their advisor and their reader-president to war service.[256]

America was ramping up its military, and more than 60,000 men in Washington State would join the military. At the University of Washington more than 1,500 students and 53 staff and faculty took leave of absence for war service. Even those who continued their educational activities took on extra projects to support the war effort. Many campus buildings were used for training, supporting, and housing troops. Curriculum changed to war-related themes. Everyone was encouraged to conserve food and be thrifty with money. Organizations of all kinds held fundraisers to support the troops. Freshman and sophomore women were required to spend at least two hours a week manufacturing bandages. They converted sphagnum moss, which was abundant in western Washington, into surgical dressings for the Red Cross. Everyone was involved in some way with the war effort, including the Christian Scientists.[257]

After a huge goodbye banquet with representatives from every student organization and activity, Arthur and Willa Priest left for Paris in February 1918. Washington State Governor Ernest Lister appointed Arthur to officially represent Washington in France, and Willa was his secretary. The Priests were put in charge of a headquarters for financial, communication, and logistical help for the troops. Their son Harold, who was already in France as a lieutenant in the US Infantry, was one of the first servicemen they greeted upon their arrival in Paris.[258]

Both Eleanor and Adele Hoppock also headed for Paris. While the overwhelming majority of Americans in the military were men, there were also what the *Seattle Times* called the "petticoated soldiers." Eleanor and Adele Hoppock were among them. They were both traveling in Italy when the war first began, and considering their practical experience with European culture and fluency in French, German, and Italian, they had valuable skills and experience they could contribute to the war effort. The Hoppock sisters were two of the five University of Washington women in the United States Signal Corps. The *Seattle Times* reported that Adele Hoppock had "such high standing in her studies that she was given a special diploma," so her enlistment ended her college experience. After a month of training in San Francisco, the two Hoppocks were sent to serve in France as telephone operators, handling calls for troop movements and medical supplies. They worked long hours, and there were no substitutes available. During nineteen months of service, they never missed a single day of work. Adele testified of an overnight healing of a severe throat cold during an especially demanding time in her work, and also overcoming the need for glasses. Stationed within 13 miles of the front, she was publicly commended for

143

bravery. She stayed at her post while under attack from air raids, working inside a burning building until ordered to leave. "I was protected in every way," Adele later explained. "I am sincerely grateful for all the . . . teaching I received in the Sunday School; and for attendance at a Christian Science Society in a university during my last year of school." Eleanor also testified of healing and protection during the war, saying, "divine Love went with me every step of the way." At the end of the war, Adele served as a telephone operator in Versailles at the Peace Conference.[259]

The college yearbook for 1918 was called the "War Edition." It was "sincerely and appreciatively" dedicated "To Washington Militant; to that spirit of loyalty and patriotism which has inspired so many of our men to give themselves to their country." The entire yearbook focused on wartime themes. A large center section covered military activities in detail—Army, Navy, Aviation, and Ambulance—with page after page of male students and faculty in uniform with articles about their preparation efforts and wartime assignments. A few of the war-theme pages showed the female side of the student body. One article, entitled "On To France," told about "campus belles" who traded knitting needles at home for oaths of allegiance and service abroad. The article included a photograph of Adele in her long-skirt uniform. Near the front of the yearbook was a full-page pencil drawing, a head and shoulder close-up of a beautiful young woman wearing a military uniform, her long hair loosely pulled back and partially tucked into a ranger-style hat. She had a subtle smile of gentle confidence on her face. Beneath the portrait was the title, "'Washington Militant' (Drawn from life)." The Hoppock sisters expressed that spirit, and this artistic representation bore a striking resemblance to Adele.[260]

"Washington Militant" (Drawn from life)
University of Washington *Tyee* "War Edition" 1918

26

Influence and Inspiration (1918)

T he world war did not stop progress on church building in Seattle. Having purchased a building lot near the main entrance to the University of Washington in March 1918, the members of Third Church of Christ, Scientist, seemed determined to continue moving forward with their construction project. But under the guidance of Orison "O.J.C." Dutton, Board Chair and President, in April as American troop involvement in European battles intensified the board suspended the monthly discussion meetings on church building. Perhaps members were stretched too thin. Mr. Dutton was the Third Church committee for Camp Welfare ministry activities on military bases, which kept him very busy. Many members of their church community may have been away supporting war efforts, and the remaining members may have had more duties than usual with the usual church work. Church services and their Christian Science Reading Room seemed to be operating as normal. But in the fall of 1918, the Mayor of Seattle required all church activities be suspended because of influenza.[261]

In 1918 and 1919, the word influenza had a meaning that conveyed a special terror throughout the world. Merely saying the word struck fear in people's hearts, because this was not the common seasonal illness. This influenza was a novel virus, a new variant on the usual contagion. Sometimes referred to as "the grip," it was associated with a grip of fear. It had unusual symptoms and was known to be deadly, not only to the most vulnerable people in society—small children, the elderly, and the malnourished—but to healthy young adults. As the world war entered its fifth year, a pandemic began, triggering another world-wide war being fought within hospitals and homes, an assault on humanity by a mysterious new disease often described as an attack.

A short article later published in the *Christian Science Sentinel* pointed out that influenza is an Italian word meaning influence. In her *Church Manual*, Reverend Mary Baker Eddy had warned members against "influencing or being influenced erroneously." The article by Horace C. Jenkins called "Influence" stated that Eddy's warning could be creatively interpreted to "mean not to catch or pass on this very erroneous influenza" — this very erroneous *influence*. Taking this interpretation of influence seriously could bring inspiration and healing, something the whole world desperately needed in 1918 for influenza — and the fear of it. [262]

In Seattle, the first report on the novel virus was published in the back pages of the *Seattle Times* on May 28, 1918. It was a brief dispatch from London about a "mysterious epidemic" in Spain that had spread to "at least 40 per cent of the population" and even the king of Spain was feared to have "fallen a victim to it." "The symptoms resemble influenza," the brief article explained, "but many persons afflicted with it have fallen in the streets in a fit." Because newspapers in neutral Spain were the first to openly report on the outbreak, it became known as the Spanish flu. The disruption and death toll of the world-wide military conflict had been massive, among the most deadly in human history, but the influenza pandemic may have been worse.[263]

This influenza spread rapidly through the military camps and transports. Soldiers who had long endured terrifying hazards of brutal battlefronts quickly succumbed to influenza. As troops returned home, the contagion broke out in their own communities and rapidly spread through every city and town. Ultimately, hundreds of millions of people in nearly every country in the world were affected. What made the Spanish flu especially alarming was the inability of modern medicine to offer effective help to victims. This failure was publicly admitted by the eminent Dr. Victor C. Vaughan, who had been touted by the *Seattle Times* as "one of the most distinguished members of his profession in the country" during one of his recent visits to Seattle.[264]

Dr. Vaughan was early on the scene when this strain of influenza made its deadly debut in America among troops at Camp Devens near Boston. Dr. Vaughan was in charge of the communicable disease section of the Surgeon General office of the US Army during the world war. He had faced many types of epidemics in many military camps, both during the current war and previously as a military doctor during the Spanish-American war. His medical expertise was *Epidemiology and Public Health*, the title of the two-volume book he later authored. During peacetime at the University of Michigan Medical School where he was Dean of medical faculty, the nationally known physician established several medical journals, published prolifically on his medical research, and served as President of the American Association of Physicians and the American Medical Association. Statements by such a pillar of the medical field carried weight. Vaughan had been an early advocate of the theory of disease that microscopic organisms known as germs cause communicable disease through physical transmission. Germ theory represented the most advanced application of science to medicine. From his study of Spanish flu mortality rates, he came to a very alarming conclusion: "If the epidemic continues its mathematical rate of acceleration, civilization could easily disappear from the face of the earth." Medical science provided dire predictions but little practical help in the life and death battles going on in the hospitals. He famously said, "The saddest part of my life was when I witnessed the hundreds of deaths of the soldiers in the army camps and did not know what to do. At that moment I decided never again to prate about the great achievements of medical science, and to humbly admit our dense ignorance in this case." Vaughan's experience with the Spanish flu, according to one account, "compelled him to question his very faith in medical science."[265]

As the influenza epidemic spread across the United States in the fall of 1918, government authorities faced unprecedented challenges with few guidelines and little time to prepare. New health rules were published regarding air circulation, personal hygiene, and prohibiting crowding. Emergency hospitals were set up to handle the surge in patients, quarantines were imposed on entire military bases and cities, in some places regulation surgical masks were required when going outside the home. Public venues were shut down in a desperate attempt to prevent contagion. In some cities special police squads were tasked with enforcing the health rules. These were serious matters concerning public health, because doctors were making little progress in curing patients.

While medical practitioners were at a loss as to how to treat Spanish flu, Christian Science practitioners were confident in their solution, not only for prevention and cure of the disease for individuals, but to bring about the end of the epidemic. Although Eddy had been gone for eight years, they had her writings to consult. In 1906 she had written an article called "Personal Contagion," which began:

At a time of contagious disease, Christian Scientists endeavor to rise in consciousness to the true sense of the omnipotence of Life, Truth, and Love, and this great fact in Christian Science realized will stop a contagion.[266]

To the Christian Science practitioner, the treatment of Spanish flu was no different than treatment of any other problem, except for the intensity of the fear surrounding it. Eliminating fear is an important aspect of Christian Science treatment. Normally healing work is done privately, between practitioner and patient, but in the case of the pandemic, perhaps because the newspapers were such a significant factor in conveying fear, Christian Scientists mounted a public relations campaign. They took their spiritual teachings on contagion to the public more assertively than ever before to address the fear that was gripping the world. To their world view, elevating collective consciousness would help not only the work of Christian Science practitioners but even those under medical care. Eddy had earlier written in an article called "Contagion," "If only the people would believe that good is more contagious than evil, since God is omnipresence, how much more certain would be the doctor's success. . . ." Through this outreach, Christian Scientists publicly challenged the medical system, which claimed to have all the answers but obviously did not. They specifically challenged germ theory. After so many years of having to defend against lobbyists working to outlaw the healing practice of Christian Science on the claim of its inferiority to medical treatment, the pandemic gave Christian Scientists a kind of public relations opportunity that supported their view of what would bring about an end to the pandemic. Dr. Vaughan's statement on the "dense ignorance" of medical science in facing the influenza pandemic was a potent statement to quote in letters to newspaper editors. To scoffers at the healing claims of Christian Science, this campaign might have seemed ridiculous, futile, even infuriating. Even some Christian Scientists may have privately disagreed with the media tactic taken by the Christian Science Publishing Society. But the message had its supporters, including people with medical credentials willing to speak out publicly. One such person ready to challenge germ theory was Dr. H. Walton Hubbard, of Spokane, Washington.[267]

Dr. Hubbard had a successful medical practice for nine years before he changed his approach to the treatment of disease. Even while he was in medical school, he concluded that there was a "mental factor in disease which was almost if not entirely ignored by the medical profession." When he began his medical practice, he further explored this idea. He hypothesized that at least some diseases have at least some mental influence. With time and experience, he classified more and more diseases as mental. Eventually he concluded that *all* diseases had "a mental origin." His exploration had nothing to do with Christian Science, and in fact, he had not even considered it. But as he saw more evidence of mental influence on disease, he began studying all the books he could find on mental healing, including *Science and Health with Key to the Scriptures* by Mary Baker Eddy, the textbook of Christian Science. He concluded that Eddy's healing system completely differed from all the others because "Christian Science does not depend on any power inherent in the human mind, but draws all of its power from a divine source above the human mind." For five years he continued his medical practice while he continued studying Christian Science. He witnessed healings as a result of prayer "where the evidence couldn't be questioned." He saw "cases which were hopelessly incurable from a medical standpoint perfectly and permanently healed through the application of [Christian] Science." Even with this, however, he did not immediately accept it. "On the contrary," he later explained, "it quite alarmed me! . . . I had devoted many years of time and effort in becoming a physician and in acquiring a busy and successful practice, and I saw that to accept Christian Science it would be necessary for me to give up the practice of medicine, and nothing was farther from my mind at that time." But when his own son's life was in mortal danger from disease, he relied on prayer. By simply applying what he had learned from reading Eddy's book he successfully healed his infant son of a severe case of diphtheria for which medical means had nothing more to offer and there was little hope of recovery. As he gained more experience in healing, he concluded that the results of Christian Science treatment were "incomparably better" than medical care. Gradually he lost all confidence in material medicine. Eventually, he gave up his medical practice to become a Christian Science practitioner—following the footsteps of Drs. Francis J. Fluno, Abraham A. Sulcer, and John M. Tutt, who all gave up successful medical practices to become Christian Science practitioners, teachers, and lecturers. Hubbard continued to have kind feelings for medical doctors and recognized their unselfish efforts to alleviate sickness and suffering. He remained sympathetic to doctors who opposed the practice of Christian Science, but nonetheless Hubbard became an outspoken critic of germ theory.[268]

Dr. Hubbard shared his new views through lectures starting in 1916 when he was appointed to the Christian Science Board of Lectureship, which brought him from Spokane to Seattle and all over North America before and during the pandemic. Christian Scientists quoted him in letters to newspaper editors, such as this one by Robert G. Steel in the *Grand Rapids News*, reprinted in the *Christian Science Sentinel*:

> [The] statement that "the germ theory of disease is as firmly established as the principle of mathematics" would be at once startling and disconcerting if it were true. It is a man made theory, purely and simply, and is refuted by very many eminent medical men and investigators. Dr. John B. Fraser of Toronto conducted one hundred and thirty-three experiments with various kinds of disease germs (nineteen with germs of pneumonia), in attempts to [produce] the disease in human beings from the germs. In no case was he successful, and his conclusion was that while germs may be the product of disease they are decidedly not its cause. Dr. Walton Hubbard states the case very nicely when he says that because polliwogs are in a mud puddle, it does not prove that the polliwogs made the puddle, since they are there because it is a good place for polliwogs. The biochemists have repeatedly shown the fallacy of the germ idea, and have proved that while it may be a very pretty speculative theory, it is very far removed from a scientific fact. A medical theory of to-day becomes a medical fact tomorrow and a medical discard the next day, and so the change goes on as it has constantly done throughout almost forty centuries of medical history. . . . There are very many noble, self-sacrificing men in the medical profession who have performed herculean services during the prevalence of the epidemic. Unfortunately their efforts have been circumscribed by the limitations of matter, and matter has always proved a broken reed in times of stress.[269]

Peter V. Ross, in a letter to *The Enquirer* in San Francisco, after using Dr. Vaughan's "dense ignorance" quote went on to say:

> [I]t is interesting to note that Dr. F. L. Kelly, of the state bacteriological laboratory at the University of California declares that "we do not know anything more about the disease to-day than we did one hundred years ago; there is no known cure or preventative." Of course no one blames physicians for not understanding the influenza, but the average person is wondering why he should be delivered into the hands of health officers and be forced to submit to masks and other indignities when it is admitted that such officers do not know how to cure or prevent the disease, and in fact stand helpless in its presence.[270]

The *Christian Science Sentinel* reprinted a news article from the *Oakland Enquirer* about experiments at Goat Island by Naval doctors studying the influenza germ. The story told was that fifty sailors volunteered for an experiment where they were exposed to flu germs in every way believed to cause the disease so the medical staff could study the transmission and development of the disease in their laboratory. The article concluded:

> But no cases developed among these fifty sailors! . . . The medical men confessed themselves baffled. All their ideas of the disease were turned topsy-turvy. . . . The doctors are still wondering. The explanation, however, is simplicity itself, for it was proved by each one of these fifty young men. The fifty young men volunteered to act as subjects upon which to be experimented. This showed clearly that they did not fear the disease . . . . [T]hey could not acquire what they did not fear. Since their fear of the disease was gone, the disease was absolutely nonexistent, even though every effort was made to force it on them. . . . Medical men are now acknowledging this condition. They are the first to tell patients to eliminate fear. When this is done, their work is done. There would be no cases of influenza if every person in the state would do as these fifty Goat Island sailors did; namely, eliminate fear of the disease.[271]

The *Sentinel* reprinted a similar article on the Goat Island experiments from the Cleveland *Plain Dealer* and commentary from the *New York Herald* on a similar experiment in Boston that produced neither disease among the volunteers nor an effective vaccine from the blood of people who had recovered.[272]

Christian Scientists put their theory of immunity to the test during the pandemic according to several stories briefly mentioned in the Christian Science periodicals. In Spokane, the largest city in eastern Washington, many in the city became sick, despite Spokane's chief public health officer Dr. John Anderson ruling the city with "an iron, health-minded fist." Dr. Anderson strictly banned all gatherings, public or private, indoor or outdoor, small or large, and required use of surgical masks in public, yet there were so many influenza cases they opened an emergency hospital at the 50-room Lion Hotel downtown at First Avenue and Lincoln Street near the Deaconess Hospital. Spokane had an active Christian Science community centered a few blocks away in the Hutton Building at First Avenue and Washington Street, where First and Second Churches of Christ, Scientist, had a joint Christian Science Reading Room and Dr. Hubbard and several other practitioners had offices. In years past, they had hosted Christian Science lectures by both Dr. Fluno and Dr. Sulcer. The local influence of these former medical doctors may have given Christian Scientists in Spokane a special confidence in their disbelief of germ theory. They petitioned the city to be able to continue holding services at their two local churches because there they were "engaged in the healing of the sick." Their request made the local news when it was denied on the grounds that the city "could not consider the character or purpose of a meeting but prohibited all meetings, no matter what their object." Meanwhile, the hospital at the local military base, Fort George Wright, was overwhelmed with suffering soldiers. There was a shortage of nurses, the nurses were exhausted, sometimes having to work around the clock with no rest, and many became sick themselves. Urgent appeals were made for any available nurse to come help. According to Dr. Hubbard, "an appeal was made to the Christian Scientists in the community, because they were the only ones who were unafraid." They did come to help, "scrubbing floors and doing any work that needed to be done. They kept the hospital in operation, and they did not get influenza." The former medical doctor concluded, "Their consciousness of divine Love destroyed the belief of contagion and proved that Love triumphs over fear." A Red Cross director formally thanked the Christian Scientists "for the splendid aid rendered during the Emergency Epidemic" at the Fort George Wright hospital.[273]

A similar story was told by Mr. Steel about a Naval Training Station in Great Lakes, Illinois, where he said the company commander asked any Christian Scientists to step forward to volunteer to work as nurses in the hospital and they did so without contracting influenza. Zona Marie Carruthers shared her personal experience as a nurse at the Camp Mills Army base in Mineola, New York, where there were more than 4,200 cases of influenza, overwhelming the medical staff and overflowing the hospitals into 50 additional tent wards erected to handle the emergency. Ms. Carruthers wrote:

> When the Government called for nurses in 1918 I was ordered to join the Army Nursing Corps at Camp Mills, Long Island, where I stayed one year. Every day, Christian Science proved to be a constant help to me; and during the epidemic I was so grateful to be helping, not only with my hands, but with right thoughts; for through knowing the truth I was able to help my coworkers and those who were struggling with sickness and sore grief. Later I became a Christian Science nurse.[274]

Myra Atkinson of Ranger, Texas, claimed to have been the only nurse unaffected in the hospital where she worked. Mrs. Atkinson attributed her protection from contagion to the help of a Christian Science practitioner. Mary E. Moser was one of many Christian Scientists who nursed patients in private homes. Miss Moser shared:

> ...I helped to nurse five who were afflicted in my sister's home. Protection was given me through this trying time, and I learned something of the unreality of disease and how to bar my thought against its entrance. I am very grateful for the loving help and guidance of the practitioner during these experiences . . . .[275]

The Christian Science Publishing Society claimed a "great mass of evidence accumulated to show the physical healings" of disease, including influenza, by Christian Science Camp Worker and soldiers in its publication *Christian Science War Time Activities*. One of many letters from Camp Workers stated:

> One of the things for which we are most grateful is the fact that our boys were able to help the others during the recent epidemic. One of them had charge of thirty-six others. The first night he went to each patient and tried to allay his fear and to reassure him. The doctors soon began to turn to him and he was put into a position of considerable responsibility and usefulness.[276]

At the Portsmouth Naval Yard in Virginia, a camp welfare worker arrived when the influenza was at its peak.

> Upon reporting to the Commandant, it was learned that that hospital was congested, and there was a shortage of nurses, due to sickness and recent detachments, creating a serious situation. The services of the Worker were volunteered and accepted, and in the hospital spiritual work was combined with the material care of sick nurses and men in the influenza wards. Wards of terror-stricken men, witnessing the deaths of comrades, were calmed and encouraged, and many patients thought to be very ill were found up and dressed the next day. Sick nurses stopped taking medicine and in some cases requested the [Christian Science] textbook. The death rate at once diminished and in twenty-four hours reached the zero mark.[277]

To the Christian Scientists working to stop the epidemic by elevating human consciousness above fear to the omnipotence of God, church services supported protection of life. When Boston health officials recommended bans on gatherings, the Board of Directors of The First Church of Christ, Scientist, in Boston, The Mother Church, issued official statements of disagreement. In the same spirit, Bicknell Young, then First Reader at The Mother Church, wrote to the *Boston Herald*:

The utterly helpless attitude of the health authorities and physicians generally seems to indicate that they are hopeless to overcome the disease, and are convinced that it must run its course and wear itself out. Those who look beyond matter for the cause and cure of disease see that the great need of the hour is pure Christianity, and yet at the very time when the gospel of Christ in all its practical strength and helpfulness is most needed it is proposed to close the churches.[278]

On October 8, just as health officials across the country were implementing police-enforced bans on public gatherings, *The Christian Science Monitor* published an editorial intended "to help stem the tide of fear which is the most serious factor in perpetuating the present epidemic":

Fear is the most prolific source of all evil. Of course if fear were understood in its full metaphysical significance, it would be understood to be the provoking cause of all evil of every sort. But even from the ordinary point of view of the world, fear, when it communicates itself to numbers, is capable of causing greater disaster than any other phase of the human consciousness. . . . Some day the world will come to see that what it calls contagion is a mental contagion, and that what it calls infection is the infection of one mind from another. Orthodox medical practice today largely recognizes this, but it draws back from the logical consequences of its own admission, and endeavors to shelter itself in a halfway-house, which is built partially out of mind and partially out of matter. . . . Let any person who has been brought in contact with the conditions of today ask himself frankly whether it is not fear which is playing such fearful havoc in the world. Everywhere men and women are afraid. Afraid in the areas of war of a storm blast that may at any moment strike over them; afraid within the orbit of the air squadrons of the sound of the terrible engines whirring in the darkness overhead, and of hearing the bombs explode all around; boys sleeping fearfully in the trenches, waiting for the summons in the gray morning to go over the top, and men and women sleeping in towns and villages, miles and thousands of miles away, fearful of what in that very moment may be happening to those they love; men and women at sea, waiting as it were for the explosion of torpedoes; or even men and women in immediate physical safety, wondering what effect the war is going to have on their incomes and their lives. A great fear has stricken the world, and it is little wonder if out of this fear there have emerged pestilences and diseases which have mounted on the winds of fear, and scattered their seeds in every direction. In such circumstances what would it be expected that a Christian community should do? . . . [S]hould it not naturally fling wider open the doors of the churches, confident that in doing right, by worshiping God, no ill could touch it? . . . The church which closes its doors practically proclaims its impotency, and the admission is a terrible one when it is made in the hour of a nation's need.[279]

The *Monitor* concluded its editorial with the classic theatrical line, "Surely it was a wise man who once said, 'A mad world, my masters!'" and emphasized the message with the provocative headline, "A Mad World." This editorial was reprinted in major newspapers. An explanatory note added, "It is hoped that by recalling to the community the power of Christian prayer to stop the ravages of disease the necessity of opening the churches will be seen and that their opening will be demanded, thus proving that the facts do not belie the statement upon the coinage of the Nation: 'In God We Trust.'"[280]

The *Monitor* editorial received some negative reactions from Christian clergy who supported the health bans on church services. This provided opportunity for a round of response letters, like this one by Steel in the *Grand Rapids News,* later reprinted in the *Christian Science Sentinel:*

Rarely is one allowed the doubtful privilege of reading a letter from the pen of a minister of the gospel so replete with statements which dishonor God, discredit Christ Jesus, and repudiate the whole Bible, as the one which appeared in a recent issue attacking the editorial, "A Mad World," reprinted from *The Christian Science Monitor.*

It is the height of absurdity that after nineteen centuries of Christian teaching and in the most thoroughly Christianized nation in the world, the churches should be closed because of the fear of a so-called epidemic and the foolish belief that the power of God has suddenly become less than that of a microbe.[281]

In the same spirit, a letter by John M. Dean first published in *The News Scimitar* in Memphis, Tennessee, included this challenge to the churches:

. . . If the Bible is true, the house of God should be preeminently a place of safety, and now is the time of times to test it. Is an all-powerful God powerless against disease microbes, and can they take possession of the churches to His exclusion? Is Christianity good for fair weather but not for foul, and must prayer be understood as mere lip service? If this is true — if prayer is unavailing and

God is not "a very present help in trouble" — the world would suffer no loss if the churches were to remain closed permanently.[282]

Another opportunity for challenging germ theory presented itself in the virtual endorsement of the Christian Science approach by the influenza public health committee in Des Moines, Iowa, near the hard-hit military base Camp Dodge. Emphasizing a message similar to what U.S. President Franklin D. Roosevelt would one day tell the nation, that "the only thing we have to fear is fear itself," an article from the *Monitor* sent to newspaper rooms throughout the country blamed fear for the spread of influenza and suggested that the fearless Christian Scientists at Camp Dodge had proven their immunity. The Des Moines public health committee was comprised of the former Mayor, the superintendent of schools, the secretary of the Chamber of Commerce, the president of the trades and labor assembly, a pharmacist, and three medical doctors, and it was chaired by the acting health officer for Des Moines, city sanitarian, Dr. William C. Witte. Dr. Witte was quoted as saying:

> Many people have thought themselves into their graves. When one continually thinks that he has Spanish influenza or any other disease . . . then, it is quite probable he will, because he has not the right attitude of mind. . . There is no question, that by a right attitude of mind these people have kept themselves from illness. . . . Fear is the first thing to be overcome, the first step in conquering this epidemic. I am not a Christian Scientist, but I believe an application of their principles will materially aid in preserving the health of the community. They did not originate with the [Christian] Scientists, but are to be found by anyone who will take the trouble to read his Bible.[283]

Attorney Howard W. Byers, Corporation Counsel for Des Moines, recommended "that newspapers prepare editorials citing the immunity which Christian Scientists enjoy from influenza, and urging the use of common sense and a calm attitude of mind in conquering fear of infection." That recommendation "was indorsed by the committee as a whole, and newspapers were asked to quote the committee to that effect." Mr. Byers added, "I would recommend that if anything be printed in regard to the disease it be confined to simple preventive measures — something constructive, rather than destructive."[284]

Byers' recommendation was in line with the teachings of Eddy, who founded *The Christian Science Monitor* in 1908 to raise the standard of journalism, and who long before the 1918 pandemic had offered commentary on the harmful power of mental suggestion that newspapers wielded over the public:

> Many a hopeless case of disease is induced . . . not from infection nor from contact with material virus, but from the fear of the disease and from the image brought before the mind; it is a mental state, which is afterwards outlined on the body. The press unwittingly sends forth many sorrows and diseases among the human family. It does this by giving names to diseases and by printing long descriptions which mirror images of disease distinctly in thought. . . . A minutely described disease costs many a man his earthly days of comfort. What a price for human knowledge!

> Looking over the newspapers of the day, one naturally reflects that it is dangerous to live, so loaded with disease seems the very air. These descriptions carry fears to many minds, to be depicted in some future time upon the body. . .

> We should master fear, instead of cultivating it.[285]

Newspapers throughout the country reprinted the *Monitor*'s Camp Dodge article under their own headlines, such as "Fear Responsible for Spread of Influenza," "Anti Fear Campaign Urged by [Christian] Scientists," and "Quit Thinking about Influenza." The Camp Dodge story and the Des Moines health committee were further quoted in letters to newspaper editors reprinted in the *Sentinel*, assuring that Christian Scientists everywhere got the message. Meanwhile, a wave of appeals, pleas, and protests arose throughout the country as bans on church services were imposed by cities and states on their citizens. Special indignation was expressed when churches were forced to close but taverns were allowed to continue operating—consumption of alcohol apparently having been deemed a more essential business than the spiritual uplift of religious worship. An advertisement paid for by Christian Science Churches of Oregon, quoted the *Monitor* editorial and Dr. Witte to make their plea to the general public:

> [A]t the very moment when the churches should be filling the minds of the people with peace and reassuring them of the impotence of evil, it is proposed that these churches shall be shut, and that the admission be made that it is dangerous for men and women to congregate to worship God for fear the Lord's arm is so shortened that He cannot contend with microbes. . . . Let the church doors be opened and unobstructed worship proceed in a Christian land.[286]

Appealing to a higher sense of law, at least one Christian Science branch church challenged the local laws banning church services as being unconstitutional. In Los Angeles, when the Mayor banned all public gatherings, all Churches of Christ, Scientist, in the city united in protest of "disease . . . being so industriously promoted through . . . mesmeric fear" and in a petition to the city council to be allowed to resume holding services in support of the need "for the dissemination of a universal understanding of omnipotent Divine power, reliance upon which effectually aids in destroying the dread of contagion." Similar petitions were made in other cities. As the Christian Scientists in Portland, Oregon, explained:

> The efficacy of Christian Science to prevent and heal disease is universally accepted. Christian Scientists know that they can be of greater service in overcoming the wave of fear now sweeping over this country, by maintaining their regular services.[287]

Like Spokane, Los Angeles had a special connection with medical doctors turned Christian Scientists, since both Dr. Fluno and Dr. Sulcer practiced and taught in California.[288] After the City of Los Angeles rejected the petition, Ninth Church of Christ, Scientist, on South New Hampshire Street announced its intention to challenge the ban by holding church services on Sunday, November 3. In response, Mayor Frederick T. Woodman warned that he would enforce the strictest interpretation of the closure law. Mayor Woodman publicly declared:

> I want it distinctly understood that, while I have every respect for religious organizations, I also have every respect for the laws I am charged to see enforced. . . . [T]he chief of police will have a force of policemen at every Christian Science church door tomorrow with orders to see that those doors are not opened to any gathering for services or for any other purpose.[289]

That Sunday, the board members entered the Ninth Church building three hours before the service time. They held a private conference while a crowd of people gathered outside and a parade of hundreds of cars, "travelling in a slow stream, drove past the building and vicinity." Right at 11 o'clock the church doors were unlocked and a few people quietly entered the building. The police responded as directed. The five board members, all prominent members of Los Angeles society, were "technically arrested" on charges of violating a health ordinance. All were immediately released except board chair Harry P. Hitchcock, who declined to pay $5 for bail and so the jailer held him in custody until the hearing the next morning. Mr. Hitchcock was following the legal strategy devised by Judge Robert M. Clark, legal counsel for the Christian Scientists. They intended to expedite a constitutional ruling on the Ninth Church case by taking this test case to the California State Supreme Court and then immediately on to the U.S. Supreme Court. However, they never had their day in court in Washington, D.C., because their hearing was delayed until after the closing order was rescinded.[290] Ninth Church nonetheless made an impact. The dramatic story made the front page of the *Los Angeles Times* and it made the news in places like Seattle. Christian Scientists throughout the world would read about it over the next few months in the *Christian Science Sentinel*.[291]

In Evanston, Illinois, near Chicago, where according to a report from Ernest C. Moses in the *Sentinel*, churches were ordered to close but other public places were allowed to remain in operation, another Christian Science church challenged the ban by holding services. As to their desire "to test the legality of the restriction," Mr. Moses explained:

> Christian Scientists . . . are not without sympathy for the health authorities in their endeavors to meet epidemics of fear and disease; for they recognize the difficulties which the officials encounter, and would aid rather than obstruct every right measure. I am sure that your citizens who are Christian Scientists will, with good will and regard for their neighbors, gladly work for better health in Evanston and cheerfully cooperate with civil requirements based on the law rightly constituted and administered.[292]

It was not only the Christian Scientists protesting and challenging the bans. Churches of other denominations responded in a variety of ways. Episcopal churches in Pennsylvania united in a public statement of disagreement. A Catholic minister made national news for a $50 court fine for conducting church services in defiance of the ban.[293]

Instead of engaging with police, attorneys, and courts, many Christian Scientists protested through prayer and spiritual study. Maude M. Greene shared her personal story of how the bans caused her to elevate her thinking about church:

> When the order came that, on account of an epidemic situation, all churches must be closed, I experienced a considerable sense of resentment and rebellion. . . . As is invariably the case with students of Christian Science, refuge was sought in the textbook, "Science and Health with Key to the Scriptures," and on page 583 was found the definition of church. I supposed that I already knew a good deal about this definition, but soon discovered that I had only made a

beginning. As I read the familiar words, "The structure of Truth and Love; whatever rests upon and proceeds from divine Principle," there came like a flash the realization that no one ever had been or ever could be deprived of "the structure of Truth and Love;" that this structure is a divine idea always present in the spiritual consciousness of man; that church is something vital in one's own consciousness, and something of which he can never be deprived. The doors of this structure have never been and can never be closed; they are forever and eternally open; no "ban" ever has been or ever can be put upon that which "rests upon and proceeds from divine Principle," for it is the expression of eternal, unchanging, ever present, ever operative law, that law which forever denies and casts out utterly the belief of disease of any name or nature. . . . Then I appreciated, as never before, the fact that the Christian Science church, as it stands to-day, represents that divine manifestation which the spiritual concept of church has brought to mankind; that it is the expression of that concept improved and bettered in human consciousness because of the activity and law of the right idea of church.

In "great gladness of heart," Ms. Greene, alone at home, read through the list of citations from the Bible and Eddy's writings that comprise the Sunday sermons in all Christian Science churches, which are published in advance for individual study. Her view of church changed. She explained:

[R]ight there the church service was held in its entirety, and its doors were open wide. . . . it was an indescribable joy to know that I was taking the healing activity of this church with me, and there came into my experience a higher and holier sense of church membership than I had ever known, and it was impressed upon me that I could only really "belong" to the Church of Christ, Scientist, as it first belonged to me, —was really a part of me. The experience meant much, for I repeatedly saw this consciousness of church cast out the devils of fear and of an epidemic disease.[294]

The prayerful protest illustrated by Greene may have been the predominate one taken by Christian Scientists in Seattle. City officials in Seattle had the benefit of learning from the experience of early hotspots like Boston. On September 28, 1918, the Washington State Board of Health met in Spokane to discuss the situation and how to prevent a local epidemic. Washington State Health Commissioner, Dr. Thomas D. Tuttle, shared what he had learned from a meeting of health authorities in Chicago:

The outstanding feature of discussion . . . was the evidence that whatever efforts were made the spread of the disease was only retarded and not prevented. As one health officer very aptly expressed the situation: "One can avoid contracting the disease if he will go into a hole and stay there, but the question is how long would he have to stay there? The indications are that it would be at least for a year or longer."[295]

As a practical matter, even in Washington, even with six weeks of warning, it seemed the best they could expect was to try to flatten the mathematical curve predicted by epidemiologists. But before local health board officials could take preventative action there were local cases. Only days after the Spokane conference the first Spanish flu death in the state was reported in Seattle at the University of Washington Naval Training Station on Portage Bay and there were 650 new cases. The following week, Camp Lewis near Tacoma reported 100 cases and the Naval Shipyard in Bremerton reported several hundred more. When the *Seattle Times* announced on Saturday evening, October 5, that Mayor Ole Hanson, Board of Health official Dr. J. S. McBride, and Chief of Police J. F. Warren ordered all public gatherings banned until further notice, it was stated as being necessary to protect not only the public but also "the army of men working in the shipyards and on other war work." The closure order was drastic, but it was a "patriotic duty" to ensure that the epidemic did not affect the local military production needed to win the war. Dr. Tuttle's emphasis was on prevention, a simple thing if the order were supported by "the intelligent and conscientious cooperation of every citizen."[296]

The Seattle closure order was not without controversy, however. The Superintendent of Schools objected to closing schools, and Corporation Counsel W. F. Meier questioned the legal basis of such an order. Regardless of objections, Mayor Hanson was prepared to enforce the order. An "Influenza Squad" of police was charged with breaking up crowds and enforcing the ban on spitting. Initially churches were allowed to hold services outdoors, a concession that seemed to satisfy local religious leaders. A spokesman for the city's Protestant clergy, declared that "Seattle churches unhesitatingly will obey the mandate barring the usual indoor church services. . . . I don't believe there will be any insurgents." Rev. Edward J. O'Dea, Catholic bishop of Seattle, announced that all the city's Catholic churches would hold open-air mass. The Christian Science churches "expressed their intention to comply cheerfully with the closing edict," a sentiment voiced by Florence Lewis, clerk of Fourth Church of Christ, Scientist. The *Seattle Times* quoted Miss Lewis as stating, "Christian Scientists are, first of all, obedient to the laws of the land, and it will be our loving duty to comply in all the particulars with the requests of the city officers."[297]

Seattle Police Department "Influenza Squad"

Paul Dorpat collection

The two largest open-air services in the city were held at First Presbyterian Church and Saint James Cathedral. Rev. Dr. Mark A. Matthews, the Presbyterian pastor, planned a "great patriotic-religious gathering" with special music from an army singing squad and a naval band on the south side of their church on Seventh Avenue between Spring and Madison Streets. But the gathering turned out to be "rather small," probably because of the short notice, Rev. Matthews said. It rained that Sunday morning. It was impossible to play any instruments in such cold, wet weather and the song leader for the program was unable to sing. The Catholics turned out en mass for open-air mass at Seattle parishes. The "common thought" among Catholic adherents "was that more severe scourges and prohibitions . . . had failed for centuries to stop the divine services of the Catholic Church." At Saint James Cathedral, which held seven hourly masses that day, as reported in the *Catholic Northwest Progress*:

[A]ttendance ran from a couple of hundred to a thousand souls. . . .
Seats had been arranged to accommodate all, lights were strung

163

from tree to tree, and the superb Catholic choir filled the air with sacred music to the accompaniment of an organ. While bared heads bowed in the falling rain at the tinkling sanctus bell, the non-Catholic spectators looked on and wondered. It was beyond their comprehension.[298]

They kept masses short that cold morning because, as reported by The *Seattle Times*, "the clergy did not want to keep the members standing in the wet for any length of time." Protestant Church leaders were hopeful that with more advance notice more churches could organize outdoor services and attendance would be higher. But they did not have the opportunity because that week the Mayor banned even outdoor church services. This apparently triggered a negative response by local religious leaders. As reported by the *Seattle Star*:

> Scores of clergymen from different city districts have laid siege to the offices of the city health physicians with requests to be allowed to address their congregations under the dome of heaven, and been refused. Dr. McBride saying, "Religion that won't keep for two weeks to save people's lives isn't worth having."[299]

If Board Chair and President O.J.C. Dutton at Third Church of Christ, Scientist, in Seattle even entertained any discussions about holding open-air services, it was never mentioned in the board or membership minutes. It is hard to imagine Christian Scientists in Seattle wanting to stand in the cold autumn rain to hear their Bible Lesson read aloud when they could read it for themselves at home as Greene had done. Nor did Mr. Dutton seem to entertain any discussion about strategies for challenging the ban. The *Seattle Times* did not publish the article about Camp Dodge, the *Christian Science Monitor*'s editorial, nor any letters challenging germ theory. Besides assurance of cheerful compliance with health rules, local newspapers focused on Dutton's latest organizational initiative, the "Christian Science Soldiers' and Sailors' Hospitality Club."

Dutton was in charge of a Chamber of Commerce volunteer effort to find affordable housing in Seattle for war industry workers. His appointment to "take charge of the Camp Welfare Work" for Third Church resulted in a similar effort. His Hospitality Club project was to provide beds for Christian Scientists in the military. On Sunday, September 29, Dutton held an afternoon meeting at the Metropolitan Theatre to "present to Christian Scientists and their friends plans for a soldiers' and sailors' hospitality club soon to be opened in Seattle." The project was officially independent of the Christian Science churches, a point that was repeatedly emphasized. With financial support from individuals, Dutton secured the second and third floors of a downtown building on Fourth Avenue at Pine Street. The space, which had been "unoccupied for some time," was remodeled to provide a large hospitality room for entertainment and job placement services for discharged military men, a room for quiet reading and writing, and a dormitory with 200 beds, for "night-and-day operation." Furnished with donated items, it was "a simple, plain, comfortable place, as homelike as possible." Administrative headquarters for the operation were in the Empire Building along with the joint Christian Science Reading Room, at least sixteen Christian Science practitioners, and so many other Christian Science church activities.[300]

When Dutton organized the hospitality club, he may not have realized what life and death risks he would face. Even before the club opened he had a brush with death while he inspected the unfinished space with the city sanitary engineer and fire marshal. The *Seattle Times* reported that an unidentified man in a nearby hotel fired two gun shots in quick succession. The shots "fired pointblank" went through a window on the street side, the bullets "passed about a foot above the heads of the three men," left the building through a window on the alley side, hit the brick wall of the adjacent building, then fell to the ground. But this startling incident paled in comparison to the epidemic that broke out in Seattle just as the Christian Science hospitality club was preparing to open. However Dutton handled club management, he must have faced many challenges and perhaps many brushes with death. It is probably safe to assume that like so many others he was praying daily with Psalm 91, finding comfort and confidence in the Bible's promise of deliverance from both "the arrow that flieth by day" and "the noisome pestilence" through trust in omnipotent God. As the Psalmist wrote: "Because thou hast made the Lord, which is my refuge, even the most High, thy habitation; There shall no evil befall thee, neither shall any plague come nigh thy dwelling." (Ps 91:3, 5, 9-10) The club was in operation for eighteen weeks—essentially the same period as the pandemic. During those four and a half months, according to the *Seattle Times,* the club accommodated 6,850 overnight stays and 21,000 day visits. Dutton's appointment in December to a Chamber of Commerce committee tasked with offering help to the Mayor for the influenza situation in Seattle likely reflects positively on his management of his many civic projects during this challenging time, including the Christian Science Soldiers' and Sailors' Hospitality Club.[301]

Immediately after the ban on public gatherings was lifted at the end of November, Third Church along with all the other Seattle branches put on two well-publicized Christian Science lectures, as their way of "offering at this time the healing and constructive message of Christian Science."[302]

In the Christian Science periodicals, among the thousands of testimonies of healings published, there are many hundreds that mention healings of influenza. About two hundred specify or indicate Spanish flu, several from the Seattle area. These personal stories were published during or immediately following the pandemic, over the next few years, and over many decades afterward. What is most remarkable about their stories is the quickness of their cure. Testifiers often stated that they had neither long recovery and nor any lingering "after-effects." They were well in a few days, two days, one day, overnight, a few hours, one hour, even a few minutes, or less. Sometimes they described the healing as instantaneous.[303]

One of the first published, in the January 4, 1919, issue of the *Sentinel*, was a dramatic story from a soldier at Camp Dodge, the Army base in Iowa featured in the *Monitor* dispatch. Marven L. Scranton recounted defending himself from an influenza attack through prayer. His experience was perhaps part of the basis for the famous claims of immunity of the Christian Scientists:

> I had seen several of my comrades walk out of rank, fall over, and be carried to the hospital overcome by the disease; so when I began to feel ill, fear overwhelmed me with the suggestion that I was getting it. We were all out on reveille formation one morning when everything seemed to get black before my eyes and I could scarcely stand alone, so stood there leaning on my rifle. I was gradually becoming unconscious when I heard some one, as though far away, telling me to move over and stand at attention, so I moved over and straightened up the best I could, all the time declaring the truth. Within fifteen minutes everything cleared up, the cloud lifted, and I was completely healed. . . . my quick delivery from the attack of influenza and the fear of death has caused me to be most grateful. At that time over half our company was in the hospital and very few escaped the disease entirely. That I was one of those who escaped I owe entirely to Christian Science.[304]

For several of the published healings it seems their condition was so severe that the testifiers described experiencing something like death prior to being healed. One testifier described becoming detached from her body, observing it from outside of it. Another wrote of waking in the night to the "sense of having been close to the shadow of death." This testifier then stated plainly, "My wife tells me that to mortal sense I had every appearance of one passing on." Another testifier wrote:

> Upon the arrival of the practitioner I seemed to be passing through the belief of death — the last enemy to be overcome. To one who does not understand Christian Science it would seem a miracle, but when we know that all things are possible to God, it no longer becomes one. I was brought back to life. . . . I fully realized that death is what Mrs. Eddy says it is . . . — "an illusion."[305]

While most of the people who relied on Christian Science treatment were already familiar with it, for some it was their first experience with it. Some had Christian Science healings while under a medical doctor's care. Others called a Christian Scientist because no medical doctors were available to help them. Martin Verheul had lost confidence in his medical treatment:

> We knew little of Christian Science in 1918 when the influenza epidemic struck our entire family. We called our family physician. The medicine he prescribed for me seemed to make me worse instead of better, and so I destroyed it all. We called a Christian Science practitioner for help for all of us, and we were healed. That was the end of material remedies in our home.[306]

Christian Science practitioners were available for help over the phone, but they often made home visits during the epidemic. One person told of a practitioner staying at her bedside for twelve hours one night. In a published testimony of healing of a "severe attack of influenza" by E. R. Cose, from East Aurora, New York, in expressing his appreciation for his quick, complete healing, wrote:

> I am absolutely convinced that the Christian Science practitioners, in their consecration and vigil against the enemy, disease, are as truly soldiers as were our American boys on the firing line.[307]

Louis J. Scherz testified of being healed during a church service. Mr. Scherz had been struggling with influenza for two weeks. Since the services were suspended where he lived in Plainfield, New Jersey, despite not feeling well he traveled twenty-five miles to New York City to attend a Wednesday evening testimony meeting and a Christian Science lecture the next evening. "From that time I felt no further effects of the illness," he wrote.[308]

The published testimonies are only a sampling of the healings that may have been shared at Wednesday church meetings. In a response to criticism from *The Christian Century* that Christian Science churches remaining open "was a discourtesy to the health authorities," Ernest C. Moses of Chicago, Illinois, shared:

> During the recent epidemic in this city alone, at the Wednesday evening testimony meetings of the Christian Science churches, fully attended throughout the epidemic period, hundreds of testimonies were given of the healing of cases of influenza. . . . These proofs of the healing power of God in Christian Science explain why Christian Scientists advocate that the "life interests of the people" require that civil authorities refrain from interference with the practice of religion, since the authorities rely upon medical advisers who prefer to work from the standpoint of fear of evil, rather than from the standpoint of faith in God.[309]

Presumably, a similar profusion of testimonies were being shared in every city where there were Christian Science churches. It would be difficult to even estimate how many people might have claimed healing of Spanish flu through Christian Science. Perhaps it could be said that, like the Apostle John's statement about the healing acts of Jesus, that "if they should be written every one, I suppose that even the world itself could not contain the books that should be written." (John 21:25) But some attempt was made to count them in some areas when the practice of Christian Science healing was once again under attack.

With so many testimonies of healing of influenza shared in the Christian Science periodicals and at church services, it might seem as though everyone who relied on Christian Science was healed, but unfortunately, not everyone recovered. One case of a boy who died under Christian Science treatment led to criminal charges for the Christian Scientists involved. Although this case was dismissed by the judge, the surrounding public controversy spurred Christian Scientists to publish statistics showing that the "morbidity . . . and mortality among Christian Scientists was not nearly so great as among others." These figures published in local newspapers were republished in the *Sentinel*. The *Oregonian* published following letter by A. O. Freel in defense of Christian Science in the case of the boy who died:

> Because the methods employed by Christian Science in healing the sick do not happen to agree with the preconceived opinion of a judge in a police court about how the sick should be treated, is small reason for his accusing the Christian Science practitioner and the parents of a deceased boy of criminal neglect in the care and treatment of the boy, who is said to have died of influenza. The

judge in dismissing the case is reported to have said that, in his opinion, the boy would not have died if he had received reasonable medical treatment.

In making this statement the judge is assuming an unenviable responsibility. Especially is this true as no evidence was introduced to show neglect in the care of the boy. Such a conclusion in this event could be arrived at only on the assumption that under "reasonable medical treatment" all similar cases of influenza recover. But such is not the case. Within a period of little more than a year, more than two thousand cases have proved fatal under medical treatment in Oregon.

In fact Christian Science treatment has proved itself to be many times more successful than has medical treatment in the healing of influenza wherever statistics have been gathered. As a fair example of the relative value of Christian Science treatment in healing influenza, the statistics from California are as follows:

In that state during the months from October, 1918, to March, 1919, inclusive, Christian Science practitioners treated 23,418 cases of influenza and pneumonia. Of this number 66 cases proved fatal, or about two and four-fifths fatal cases for each thousand cases reported. During the same period the figures compiled by the state board of health covering 305,856 cases show that of this number 20,904 were fatal. This shows a mortality of sixty-eight per thousand of all cases reported. In other words, Christian Science treatment in California proved itself to be about twenty-four times as successful as medical treatment in healing influenza and pneumonia during the epidemic last year.[310]

In response to another "gratuitous fling at Christian Scientists" in a health officer's report on the epidemic, Albert F. Gilmore shared his New York statistics in the *Rochester Times-Union*:

Careful investigation in the city of Rochester reveals the fact that of the two hundred and eight cases of influenza in which Christian Science treatment was resorted to, but one resulted fatally. In the light of the utter failure of the medical profession to check in any degree this epidemic until it had spread through every section of our country, and that it did finally literally "burn itself out,"—to quote a leading medical journal,—it is not exactly easy to understand where a medical practitioner can find warrant for attacking another system of healing which had, in the case of the epidemic, a notably successful record.[311]

Hugh S. Hughes, Jr., shared these Wisconsin figures in the *Milwaukee Sentinel*:

> [S]tatistics in Wisconsin show that over six per cent of the cases under medical treatment were fatal, while statistics gathered from forty-five cities in Wisconsin, including Milwaukee, show that under Christian Science only two-tenths of one per cent were fatal.[312]

John Randall Dunn cited an article in an unnamed Midwestern newspaper as his source for these figures:

> [N]ational statistics covering the influenza epidemic of 1918 show that while one in every sixteen cases under medical treatment passed on, under Christian Science care only one case out of every five hundred and thirteen proved fatal.[313]

While some medical doctors might find these undocumented statistics questionable and continue to equate reliance on Christian Science treatment to negligence, it is unquestionable that the influenza pandemic did not hinder the popularity of Christian Science as a treatment of disease, because the number of professional practitioners continued increasing. At least some in the medical field recognized the influence of fear as harmful. The *Sentinel* quoted a report from the State Board of Health in Nevada on the epidemic as concluding:

> The quarantine and mask questions [for Spanish influenza] have both been tried; neither one has proved successful . . . there can be no question of doubt but that fear so reduced the powers of resistance that many became easy victims, and "fear" should have been entered in the death certificate as the remote cause of death.[314]

The growth of the Christian Science movement only accelerated after this global health emergency. The Committee on Publication of Colorado as quoted in the *Sentinel* noted an overall benefit from the pandemic experience in the level of dedication among Christian Science adherents:

> The epidemic of fear, spoken of as the "flu," which was spread by and in mortal mind on the wings of suggestion, forced Christian Scientists to more consecrated effort, with generally favorable results, and afforded opportunities to the committee on publication for voicing the truth through the press, thereby calling the attention of the public to the only antidote for fear; namely, divine Love and its ever operative law.[315]

Eddy's words written in 1899, must have seemed even more mean-ingful to Christian Scientists who served in the emergency hospitals in 1918:

> Beloved Christian Scientists, keep your minds so filled with Truth and Love, that sin, disease, and death cannot enter them. It is plain that nothing can be added to the mind already full. There is no door through which evil can enter, and no space for evil to fill in a mind filled with goodness. Good thoughts are an impervious armor; clad therewith you are completely shielded from the attacks of error of every sort. And not only yourselves are safe, but all whom your thoughts rest upon are thereby benefited.[316]

Applying this sentiment to the pandemic, in his 1919 *Sentinel* article "Influence," Horace C. Jenkins wrote:

> We may always rejoice that the seeming affliction is simply an op-portunity to prove to a watching world, weary with the long night of cruel dreams, that the image and likeness of God, the real man, is free from all malign influences. Gratitude and joy clothe man with invincible armor. Jesus expressed gratitude for the assurance of the uninterrupted operation of Principle even before he commanded Lazarus to awaken from that deep sleep called death; and equally striking was his insistence on the necessity for joy even on the part of those above whose material perception he was about to ascend. Such gratitude and joy must be included in the equipment of each one who has enlisted to help "reinstate primitive Christianity and its lost element of healing" (Manual, p. 17). A Christian Scientist may, therefore, rightfully claim exemption from being influenzaed, for he is daily seeking and finding refuge from all erroneous influ-ences "in the secret place of the most High," in whom "we live, and move, and have our being."[317]

In Detroit, Michigan, where for at least one Sunday the Christian Scientists apparently successfully held church services despite a local ban, even a critical commentator expressed the spirit of Eddy's teach-ings when he wrote in the *Detroit Times*:

> The evening following the issuance of the health commissioner's edict against the Spanish influenza, the avenues in the vicinity of every Christian Science church in Detroit were fairly choked with the motor cars of the communicants of this faith. Being exempted by religious scruples from service in the fight with material weap-ons against epidemic, this flourishing church filled its sanctuaries, quite oblivious of trepidation about overcrowded meeting places.

The Christian Scientists not only deny bodily ills, but they deny microbes admittance to their prayer meetings by filling them so full there isn't room left for a germ to edge in.[318]

Medical experts at the time were concerned that until a vaccine was found Spanish flu would continue to afflict people, but in fact the epidemic came to an end. Whether the influenza simply burned itself out, as some suggested, or the Christian Scientists succeeded in rising in "consciousness to the true sense of the omnipotence of Life, Truth, and Love," as Eddy had instructed, in 1919 this most deadly form of influenza disappeared from among the human race as suddenly and as mysteriously as it had appeared.[319]

The pandemic was fading when two Christian Science churches dedicated their new buildings. The special services on Easter Sunday in Rockford, Illinois, "attended by an assemblage that filled the auditorium," and Edmonton, Alberta, Canada, were "occasion for rejoicing among the local Christian Scientists." Likewise were they cause for joy by those all around the world when the *Christian Science Sentinel* printed their dedication announcements.[320]

In Seattle at Third Church of Christ, Scientist, which was still holding its services in a rented hall in the University State Bank Building, the members were inspired to begin their construction project on their lot on "Greek Row." Just before Easter Sunday 1919, there would be a membership motion to move forward with church building, thus launching a city-wide building boom of Christian Science churches that did not stop until there was one built in nearly every district in the city.

In regards to the influenza, in official church records at Third Church, there was never any mention of anything about it in any of their meeting minutes. It is unclear whether any meetings were ever held on how to handle the closure order. Their internal records, which detailed so many operations of the church, left no record of any discussion. No special tributes were ever made, nor any memorial events officially organized. It was almost as though to them the pandemic never happened.

27

Membership Motion (1918)

In the middle of the night on November 11, 1918, residents throughout Seattle heard a whistle blow, and knew what it meant. The war was over. That morning, Seattle celebrated. "By a sort of spontaneous combustion of Seattle's heart and soul," the *Seattle Times* reported, "Parades of Joyous, Shouting, Happy Workers . . . Let the World Know that Peace Has Come."

> There never was anything like it in Seattle before—today's celebration of the end of the world war. . . . By 10 o'clock this morning the city was delirious with joy and Second Avenue a howling, shrieking bedlam of men and women, boys and girls, walking and riding, or just standing still and cheering. . . . The greatest demonstration in the city's history began at 8 o'clock and in two hours a monster impromptu parade developed on Second Avenue. It had no head nor tail and for once there was no grand marshal to announce 'the details.' It was democracy in full tilt. From one end of Second Avenue to the other, auto trucks, private cars, delivery wagons, laundry wagons, even garbage wagons, sounding sirens and girls ringing bells, blowing horns and trailing anything that would add to the noise. . . . Perfect sunshiny weather made possible a celebration of maximum enthusiasm and display. . . .

The Governor of Washington proclaimed the day a legal holiday, but, as this news article put it, "Seattle beat him to it." As a "spectacular climax for Seattle's unforgettable day of rejoicing" over the peace declaration, the *Seattle Times* hosted a big fireworks display to "mark the end of the biggest of all wars." The prevalent sentiment was that the end of this war meant the end of all wars.[321]

It would be many months before all the troops would come home. The peace treaties still needed to be negotiated, and a new League of Nations would be established to promote permanent peace. Over the next several months, life in America slowly returned to normal.

For the Christian Science community, church operations also returned to normal. But as a result of their war-time activities outreach efforts, Christian Science had advanced and spread. By the end of the war, the Christian Science War Relief and Camp Welfare network of workers and volunteers had distributed 40,000 copies of a pocket-sized edition of *Science and Health with Key to the Scriptures* to people in the military, and so Mary Baker Eddy's book was "read in bunks and hospital beds and freight cars, as well as in forests and trenches at the front." War relief workers placed the Christian Science text-book in portable libraries shipped overseas by the American Library Association. They gave away Bibles, hymn books, pamphlets, Christian Science magazines, and six million copies of *The Christian Science Monitor*.

Christian Scientists had collaborated with the Red Cross, engaged with chaplains from other religions, developed relationships with military officers, and gained access to hospitals, naval ships, and lighthouses. They supported other welfare organizations that provided war relief. As the committee report later published in *Christian Science War Times Activities* concluded:

> Christian Scientists have sometimes been charged with being self-centered and lacking in interest in that which concerns the general welfare. While they themselves knew the falsity of such statements it is, nevertheless, cause for gratitude that such misconceptions have been largely corrected in public thought by the war time activities of our movement.[322]

The committee reported other benefits for the Christian Science movement. The churches most involved had increased attendance at church services and lectures. There were more testimonies at Wednesday evening meetings, more activity at reading rooms, and church collections received more generous financial contributions. The war relief work engendered more active communication between branch churches, which resulted in a greater spirit of unity and cooperation.

The Christian Science building at Camp Lewis would continue to operate for many years. Other Christian Science war relief organizations were closing down, or being transformed. The organization managing the Christian Science Soldiers' and Sailors' Hospitality Club was dissolved. Orison "O.J.C." Dutton sold its furniture and fixtures and turned all remaining funds over to the Christian Science War Relief Fund. The club facility at Fourth Avenue and Pine Street would continue to operate in a similar capacity of providing homelike temporary quarters and job placement services, but run by the Salvation Army and so now it would be open to "all discharged soldiers, sailors and marines." In Port Townsend, the Christian Science War Relief Rooms were converted to a Christian Science Reading Room. A new church was formed to support the new reading room, which was in a former saloon. The war relief worker stayed an extra few months to help organize the new church and serve at the reading room. The worker wrote, "It has occurred to me that the War Relief work was the bud and the new church the flower."323

In Seattle, the flower of the new church in the University District was blossoming. Changes had been happening for Third Church since the end of the war. They had to move their Christian Science Reading Room, which had been on University Way near Northeast 42nd Street. With Mr. Dutton in charge of the relocation project, he moved the Reading Room into two connecting rooms in the University Bank Building at 45th and University where they held their church services and where their Reading Room had been originally. Now both church and Reading Room had the same address. The building owners would not allow them to put a sign on the exterior of the building to advertise the Reading Room, so they put gold lettering on their windows. The new location for the Reading Room was easy for church goers to find.

There had been a few problems with the auditorium related to sharing the hall with clubs, dances, and other community functions. Now there was some contention within the membership over space used for the Sunday School. They were subleasing two rooms for $1 per Sunday from R. Ella Hensley. Mrs. Hensley was a full-time practitioner and a founding member of Third Church. Besides being the church's original First Reader, she was reading for services in jails and prisons through the Church Extension program. She had been renting office space in the University State Bank Building since shortly after Third Church moved its services there in 1915. The Board received letters of complaint about the room share from two members, who referred to bylaws in the *Church Manual* by Mary Baker Eddy. The Board members prayerfully considered the issues individually, then they discussed the issues together at their next meeting. The Board disagreed with the complaints on all points. The Clerk sent response letters explaining the Board's interpretation of the bylaws. They referred to Mary Baker Eddy's book *Miscellany* from a chapter called "Peace and War," which included articles called "Other Ways Than By War" and "How Strife May Be Stilled." Both members also received follow-up personal visits from a Board member. This apparently settled things down. The Board considered moving the Sunday School to the Reading Room, but then decided against it. They continued renting Hensley's office. But problems with their rental space may have fueled the desire to erect a custom-built church of their own with a room for every function, where they would have complete control, and where such issues were less likely to arise.[324]

Nothing had happened with their building lot during the war. Now that contributions to the War Relief Fund were no longer necessary, they could dedicate their first Sunday collection once again to their own building fund. It was time to consider the next steps. On Wednesday, April 15, 1919, just before Easter Sunday, a special meeting of the membership was held in the University Bank Building after the regular Wednesday evening testimony meeting. Board Chair and President Dutton called the meeting to order. It began in the normal way with silent prayer followed by the slow and thoughtful audible repetition of the Lord's Prayer. Then, launching into the business at hand, President Dutton announced that the meeting had been called for the purpose of taking action on building a church edifice.

After some discussion of various ideas and approaches, individual members began to propose actions to be voted on by the membership. First, a proposal was made to appoint five members to a building committee to oversee construction of the church. But, that motion was withdrawn. Putting first things first, a bigger question was put to the members: Were they were ready to start a building project?

It would be a huge financial commitment for this new church, which already had so many regular expenses: their room rentals, salaries for readers, musicians, and librarian, plus the per capita dues for the joint activities all the Seattle churches supported together. Building a church would not be easy.

After more discussion, they decided to vote by secret ballot. This ensured that everyone was truly and thoughtfully voting their individual conscience—a prudent approach, considering the importance of this decision, the level of commitment it would require, and the tremendous long-term effort it would set in motion. When the ballots were collected up and counted, President Dutton announced the results of the vote. Overwhelmingly, the members voted "yes." They were ready to build a church.

The next item for discussion was how to proceed. A motion was made and seconded that a building committee of five members be elected by the membership. The mover referred to the Church Building section of the *Church Manual*, the rules for Christian Science churches established by Reverend Mary Baker Eddy, which states:

> There shall be a Building Committee consisting of not less than three members, and this committee shall not be dissolved until the new church edifice is completed.[325]

Whoever was elected to the building committee would have a difficult responsibility throughout an unknown duration. It was a serious commitment. But this motion was withdrawn. Instead, the membership decided to hold elections two weeks later. The special meeting was adjourned.

With all the discussion and parliamentary process that had taken place, it must have already been quite late at night, probably well after ten o'clock. No doubt many members were ready to go home. But there was urgent business on a different topic. Consequently, Dutton convened another special meeting to hear an important letter from the Christian Science Board of Directors at The Mother Church in Boston.

There were conflicting views among Boston officials over the relationship between the Christian Science Board of Directors of The Mother Church and the Trustees of the Christian Science Publishing Society. It would soon make headlines in the *Seattle Times:*

> Christian Science Leaders in Fight: Litigation Started in Boston Court to Determine Control of Publishing Company

Two days later, another internal conflict would make local headlines. A branch church filed litigation against officials of both the Boston church and the publishing company. This case involved questions over the relationship between The Mother Church and the branch churches and who held the highest authority now that Rev. Eddy was gone.[326]

Third Church members instructed their clerk to reply to the Directors of The Mother Church with a letter expressing loyalty to the *Church Manual* and faith and confidence in the Board of Directors. Beyond that, the members were not sure how to respond. The meeting was adjourned. For now, the members were focused on building a church.

The monumental task of building would have to be accomplished without the extraordinary organizational skills of Dutton, who had done so much for Third Church and the regional Christian Science community throughout the wartime period. Shortly after the members of Third Church decided to build, Dutton wrote a letter to the Board "requesting permission to withdraw from active service" as Board member, Sunday School teacher, and usher, "because of leaving the city." He and his wife, Pearl, were planning to drive their motor car nearly 4,000 miles from Seattle through Yellowstone National Park then continuing over "awful . . . muddy" country roads to St. Louis. They expected to live in St. Louis for two years while their children Virginia and Harry John completed high school at The Principia School for Christian Scientists. Their youngest son, Orison Marshall, would also enroll at Principia. Mary Kimball Morgan, the school founder, a Christian Science practitioner who had since become also an authorized Christian Science teacher, was actively overseeing the expansion of the programs and facilities at the campus on Page Avenue. The Principia Alumni Association had recently started outreach to support fund raising and admissions. They took a promotional film on the unique school around the country "to tell its story in a new and vivid way to the thousands of persons who were interested in knowing more about its activities." Enrollment had grown to several hundred students, many of whom boarded in the school dormitories. The Dutton family was leaving Seattle to join this growing community involved with inspired educational activity for Christian Science youth. The Board Clerk sent a letter of appreciation to Dutton in accepting his resignation. The Duttons would return to Seattle after their St. Louis sojourn and after touring more regions of the country. But for now, it was time for other members of Third Church to step up.[327]

The most important roles were those about to be filled for the special group referred to as the building committee. At some branch churches the Board appointed members to the Building Committee, but at democratically robust Third Church the membership elected them. There would need to be another membership motion.

28

Building Committee (1919)

The members of Third Church of Christ, Scientist, Seattle, elected a youthful team to the building committee—representative of the University District and the church membership. On the committee were two women, Ruth A. Densmore and Helen R. Lantz, and three men, Horace P. Chapman, Robert A. DeCou, and Byron B. Haviland. The committee held its first official meeting on Tuesday evening, May 6, 1919, at the Lantz residence. All five members were present. They elected officers by secret ballot. Mr. DeCou was elected chair and Mrs. Densmore secretary. The committee would spend a lot of time together, and this first meeting in the comfortable environment of the Lantz residence offered an opportunity to get to know each other.[328]

Although Ruth Densmore was young, she was mature in her work for Christian Science. She had been involved in Third Church since its beginnings in October 1914. She had helped organize the first meetings, was elected to the first board, had served as church clerk, on the music committee, and as a Sunday School teacher. Even before joining Third Church, Mrs. Densmore had ten years of experience with church work. She was about 16 when she joined First Church. She was there as they outgrew the chapel on Sixth Avenue, through the moves and the temporary structure, and she had seen the Capital Hill construction project go from concept drawings to completion. While a student at the University of Washington, she was a member of the Phi Beta Phi sorority, involved in the women's tennis club, the Women's Chorus, the Women's League, the Montana Club, among other activities. She often held leadership roles. After graduating in 1911, Ruth went to graduate school in Berlin. When she returned, she worked as a teacher for a few years before marrying Harvey B. Densmore, a professor of Greek at the University of Washington, a Rhodes Scholar, and a friend of Herbert T. Condon. This well-educated housewife was entrusted with correspondence for the Third Church building project. The meeting minutes she kept were orderly and clear, consistently detailed and descriptive — an exceptionally thorough record of building committee activities.[329]

Like Mrs. Densmore, Helen Lantz had been a member of Third Church from its beginnings, and she was also originally from Montana. In fact, Montana was her middle name. Mrs. Lantz had been a student at the university with Mrs. Densmore, class of 1911. Her focus was writing. She was a founding member of the journalism sorority Theta Sigma Phi, an editor for the campus newspaper, *The Daily,* and a writer for the university literary magazine, *The Washingtonian.* Helen was also on a debate team and ran for student government. She continued her studies in the graduate program, then worked as a reporter for a few years, living at home with her parents. Helen had recently married a University of Washington law professor, "Judge" Harvey Lantz, a man 25 years her senior who had been admitted to the United States Supreme Court bar. Mrs. Lantz continued to be active at the university as president of the Alumnae Association. Helen had some familiarity with building projects. Her father, Hiram Benjamin Ross, was a local carpenter and building contractor, and like Mrs. Densmore, she had been a member of First Church during its building project. Mrs. Lantz also brought familiarity with the professional practice of Christian Science to the building committee, since her mother was a practitioner.[330]

Horace P. Chapman was relatively new to Christian Science and Third Church, but he had previous experience in church work, having served on the board of trustees at the University Congregational Church. His professional background was in the business of shipping and international trade. He had come to Seattle from Farmington, Illinois, in 1887, at about the age of 15. He got involved in shipping during the Klondike gold rush. Now he was sales manager for the Charles H. Lilly Company, the largest grain dealer in the area. Mr. Chapman was well connected socially with prominent businessmen and community leaders through his active involvement in several Masonic organizations, including the University Lodge, professional organizations relating to shipping, and more recently, now that his son Horace was a teen, the Boy Scouts. These connections might prove useful in the upcoming construction project. Chapman was also serving Third Church in the demanding role of treasurer.[331]

Byron Haviland had only recently joined Third Church. He and his wife, Bessie, had previously been members at First Church. Mr. Haviland grew up in the Midwest in a farming family. Both his parents were Canadian, and in his early adulthood, when he and Bessie were first married, they lived in Victoria, British Columbia. At that time, Byron had had no interest in any church organization. But in 1906, after being diagnosed with Bright's disease and told it was incurable, he looked into Christian Science. He later wrote that by pondering the first line of the Christian Science textbook, "To those leaning on the sustaining infinite, to-day is big with blessings," he concluded that the reward of heaven did not follow death, as the "orthodox religions" taught, but was available in the ever-present now, and he was healed. He and Bessie joined with other Christian Scientists in Victoria, and in November 1910 helped reorganize the society as First Church of Christ, Scientist, Victoria. Byron served as Second Reader. Around 1914, the Havilands moved to Seattle. Byron had been working as a foreman at a shipyard. But when he joined Third Church in 1918, just before his election to the building committee, he became a full-time practitioner of Christian Science.[332]

Robert Austin DeCou had joined Third Church in 1917, right before the building lot was purchased. At that time, he had just completed his three-year term as First Reader at Second Church in Ballard. He and his wife, Stella, and their three young children had already been living in the University District for about two years. Mr. DeCou worked as an accountant at Lindquist-Lilly, the men's clothing store on the second floor of the Joshua Green Building, where Allen H. Armstrong had his practitioner office. He had also been secretary of the joint lecture committee, which put him in regular contact with key people at all the other branch churches. DeCou was financially secure and had a seemingly ideal family, but he had faced great difficulties earlier in his life. Originally from Iowa, his father, a farmer, died when Robert was very young. He and his brother were raised by their mother. As a young adult Robert got a job at a printer in Lincoln, Nebraska, married, and started a family. But his wife Genevieve died, leaving him alone with a newborn baby girl. He and his five-month-old daughter, Genevieve, moved with his older brother and his mother from Nebraska to Seattle, where they lived together in Ballard until Robert remarried. Perhaps what made this young accountant worthy of the responsibility of chair of the building committee was a quiet strength of character refined through hardship. In the role of chair, DeCou would outline the agenda, set the meeting tone, and guide the discussions and decision-making for the committee.[333]

This building committee was described as "well-balanced." As was typical for Christian Science building committees it was gender balanced. Each member brought different skills and perspectives. They were all fully committed to fulfilling their assignment. Although the board held higher authority in the church, they took a "'hands off' policy" toward the building committee, offering aid when needed, but never obstructing. The building committee began by discussing "certain fundamental principles of church building." They had assured the membership that they would work "just as rapidly but no more so than the church membership were willing to go." As a committee member later explained, they would make "no plans and strove not to outline beyond the unfoldment of Wisdom to meet present demands." The initial expectation was that they would pay for the construction with funds on hand. Intending to follow the examples set by The Mother Church building projects, no debt would be incurred.[334]

They agreed to make some recommendations to the board about how the building committee should conduct its business, such as banking and payment of bills. They also requested the board put "an immediate end to the undesirable and as it feels unwise" publicity for their "proposed building operations." Just a few days earlier, two Seattle newspapers carried "rather detailed reports . . . regarding the church [they] were to build." Under the headline "Build New Church," the *Seattle Star* informed readers, "Plans for the construction of a new building for Christian Scientist church of the university district have been completed and work will begin soon." Within 24 hours, building committee members were being contacted by architects about the project. First Church and Fourth Churches had publicized their building projects along the way, and apparently someone at Third Church sent out a press release. But the Third Church building committee believed it would be better not to do this kind of publicity. Perhaps out of concern for the negative reaction over the Capitol Hill edifice still in recent memory, they preferred to keep this building project out of the news.[335]

They initially planned to hold their meetings once a week at the Reading Room at the University Bank Building. But as they began working on design, they needed more flexibility in meeting time and location. For the first few weeks, they met several times a week and often downtown at offices of architects and suppliers, and the offices and homes of different building committee members. They made a special visit to the Seattle Public Library, where they were given a private room to look over and discuss "a number of books dealing with plans and descriptions of various church buildings."[336]

They interviewed several architects: Charles H. Bebb and Carl F. Gould, who had worked with First Church of Christ, Scientist, over many years on their Capitol Hill building and were the architects for the University of Washington; H. Percy Sharpe, a local architect who advertised primarily as a home builder; Frank H. Fowler, an engineer and architect; and George Foote Dunham, who had recently designed Fourth Church.

The decision for the architect was quick and apparently easy. They selected Mr. Dunham. Dunham "impressed the committee with his businesslike and thorough handling of the questions that arose" in interviews. They also liked that he was "a Christian Scientist" with "much valuable experience in designing and building Christian Science churches." He was based in Portland, Oregon, which made it inconvenient to work with him, except he was already making frequent visits to Seattle to work with Fourth Church and passing through on the way to Victoria, where his church design would soon be under construction at Chambers Street and Pandora Avenue across from Harris Green, and Spokane, Second Church on the north side of the city on West Indiana Avenue at West Post Street.[337]

Concerns had been expressed by members to the committee about whether they could build a large enough building on the lot to accommodate current church attendance. The committee "carefully considered all sides of this question," and concluded with a recommendation to the members "that the church continue its plans to build on this site without further doubts as to its adequacy." During the summer of 1919, design work quickly moved from concept to preliminary plans for a church design that would provide "maximum seating capacity from the space" they had "to work with." Dunham shared with the committee that he felt "an unusual sense of freedom in working" on the plans for Third Church, which he attributed to "splendid" prayer support by the building committee. He prepared a watercolor architectural rendering of the design for membership review at a September 30 meeting. The members approved the plan by a vote of confidence in the building committee. The original watercolor was framed and hung in their Reading Room, and as was common for church building projects, postcards were printed for use by members.[338]

With the big decision on the architect made, the committee settled into a regular pattern of meeting weekly at noon on Mondays at Byron Haviland's practitioner office in the Empire Building. Besides being a

convenient location for connecting with building industry profession-
als, and besides being in the primary hub of Christian Science activity
in Seattle, Haviland's office was on the tenth floor, just down the hall
from William K. Sheldon, who was involved with the Fourth Church
building committee, allowing convenient sharing of information about
their building projects. From this elevated location in one of the tallest
buildings in the city, they enjoyed an unusually expansive view.[339]

Working together with Dunham, the committee requested bids for
excavation and foundation work. Progress was happening quickly,
right on schedule for optimum seasonal timing for the construction cy-
cle. On the financial side of the project, however, there was a problem.
The first Sunday collection was earmarked for the building project.
Their funds were growing. But the amount in the building fund was
nowhere near enough to cover even the excavation contract.

The committee reconsidered its approach. Perhaps waiting until all
funds were on hand was not the right approach. An important goal of
this project was to overcome any sense of limitation. Having funds on
hand would be proof of having overcome limitation. But over the next
several meetings, there was much discussion about whether insisting
on having *all* the funds on hand before beginning "did not carry with it
a sense of limitation which would probably prove a hindrance in the
building work." The need for a building was "being more and more
felt." The committee members all believed it was time to start construction, knowing that since, as Mary Baker Eddy wrote, "Divine Love always has met and always will meet every human need," they could
count on having the funds available when they were needed.[340]

After more discussion, they decided to ask the membership to allow
the work to proceed regardless of the amount in the building fund,
with the expectation of the funds becoming available while construction was underway. A membership meeting was called, and the members agreed to go ahead with the first contract, but nothing more until
that contract had been fully paid for. With this official approval, the
building committee could now begin building.

184

**Architectural rendering of Third Church of Christ, Scientist, Seattle,
by George Foote Dunham**

Third Church of Christ, Scientist, Seattle

29

Foundation (1919)

I n early December 1919, the building committee of Third Church of Christ, Scientist, Seattle, accepted the lowest bid for the excavation and foundation work. That lowest bid was from Neil McDonald, the same construction contractor used by Fourth Church. The cost was about $13,000, plus there were architectural fees to pay. They only had $3,500 in the building fund, but despite their shortfall, they moved forward with the work.

First Reader Frank H. Plumb read a notice at church services that month: "The work on the first part of the construction on the new church edifice is well under way. Funds are necessary to complete this first contract." A similar message was mailed out to all the members. The building committee was confident that every need would be supplied. They asked members to pray for the building project daily.[341]

Unfortunately, not enough funds came in soon enough to continue the construction work. Now they faced a dilemma. They could not do any more contracts because of the constraints put on them by the membership, but it was impossible to complete the work for the first contract because of the need to hire other specialized contractors to install plumbing, oil tanks, and heating ducts before finishing the foundation work.

Meanwhile, the lawsuits involving The Mother Church were escalating. Referred to locally as "the Boston situation," they would later be known as "The Great Litigation." During March 1920, a series of headlines related to the conflict were seen in the Seattle newspapers, including one about 100 employees of the Christian Science Publishing Society walking away from their jobs in protest.[342]

A conference was called of all the Christian Science churches in Washington State. Representatives were meeting in Spokane. Third Church in Seattle was not inclined to take sides or get involved in the controversy in any way. The membership directed their elected representative for the conference to not take any action and to strictly follow the *Church Manual*. This foundational issue was consuming the attention of the board and the membership. The building project needed to be put on hold.

The building committee halted the construction work. They spent the first quarter of 1920 figuring out how to wrap up this phase of construction. There were many unexpected and now urgent construction and contract issues. The board had to take out loans to make final payment on the foundation work. The contract with Mr. McDonald needed to be renegotiated. It took a few months of intensive work to resolve all the problems caused by the sudden stop. Once everything was settled, there was nothing more they could do until the church paid off all debt.

The building committee continued to meet every Monday noon at Byron Haviland's office in the Empire Building. For several weeks their meetings were short. There were only a few small details of business to discuss. Each week the question was raised as to what the focus of the committee should be. The next steps were not clear. A general sense of confusion was noted in the minutes. Then in April, about a year into the project, they changed their approach.

Up to this point, their meetings had always begun with silent prayer and saying aloud the Lord's Prayer before launching into the business of the meeting. Ever since 1914, this was how it went at all their church meetings—board, membership, and committees. Occasionally, the meeting chair would read an extra something from the Bible, Mary Baker Eddy's writings, or Joseph Armstrong's book about building the original Mother Church edifice. But now that it seemed impossible to do anything further, the building committee decided, at Helen Lantz's suggestion, to devote the entire next meeting to what they called "purely metaphysical work"—Bible study and prayer.[343]

At the meeting on April 29, each of the five members brought readings from the Bible or Mary Baker Eddy's writings to share, ponder, and possibly discuss. They decided to continue this approach, with the addition of a unifying topic for each meeting. Throughout the summer they met each week, sharing the fruits of their individual spiritual study. The purpose of this work was to gain a clearer understanding of *building* as spiritual idea. Ruth Densmore carefully recorded each

187

weekly topic and every citation shared by each of the members in their meeting minutes. She occasionally recorded how inspiring the meetings were to the committee members. They were satisfied that progress on church building was indeed continuing through their individual and collective metaphysical work. They were getting a clearer view of the spiritual nature of the foundation of their church.

30

Queen Anne Hall (1920)

Seventh Church of Christ, Scientist, Seattle, wrote to The Mother Church in Boston on April 4, 1920. The "final step in our demonstration of readiness" has been accomplished, the clerk explained. They were applying for recognition as a new branch of The Mother Church. Normally, this meant setting up a listing in the directory of churches in the *Christian Science Journal,* exchanging friendly official greetings with the other local branches, and then focusing on the routine business of running a church. But these were not normal times. Their letter to the Board of Directors in Boston also included special assurance of their continuing loyalty.[344]

It had taken five months to organize Seventh Church. The letter suggested that this was remarkably slow—"according to calendar time." But they were now rejoicing over obstacles overcome, the biggest challenge being the establishment of a reading room—something that would always be difficult for the Queen Anne branch and the other Seattle churches in residential areas. "The united thought has been one of obedience to the Manual of The Mother Church," the clerk of Seventh Church wrote. That they were starting out as a church, not a society, was an unmentioned remarkable accomplishment in itself that showed significant organizational strength. They had thirty-seven charter members, all members of The Mother Church except one, and among them were seven *Journal*-listed Christian Science practitioners.[345]

They had the blessings of the branch churches from which they had come. On October 24, 1919, a group from the Queen Anne district had petitioned the boards of both First and Fourth Churches. First Church had such a large amount of debt from construction of their edifice that some members felt the Queen Anne residents should wait until the church was dedicated before forming yet another branch church in Seattle, and so when fifteen people met to discuss the idea of starting a new church, "some opposition developed." But the proponents argued that a new church would "relieve the condition of overflow" at the services of First Church. Furthermore, it was difficult to travel from Queen Anne Hill to Capitol Hill. Because of Seattle's hilly terrain and water ways, the route was circuitous. Going to church on the public trolley system included a transit connection downtown. Parents were hesitant to take their children on such a long journey, and so they were "being deprived of the opportunity to attend Sunday School." For the family-oriented Christian Scientists living in Queen Anne, a local church was "quite essential." The boards of First and Fourth Churches both agreed with the petitioners and offered their "hearty approval" and "loving co-operation."[346]

The approving board letters were shared at a meeting on November 7, 1919, at Queen Anne Hall, in lower Queen Anne at First Avenue West and Roy Street. They sent a reply to First and Fourth Churches:

Thanking you for the hearty good wishes which you have extended to the new organization and with every assurance of a desire to work for the united progress of the Christian Science movement in the city of Seattle, and in the world at large, we are very sincerely yours.[347]

They held the next meeting on November 18. And so began a succession of frequent business meetings over the next several weeks, often starting at 8 p.m. and continuing until 11 p.m. The members of the new group each pledged a regular monthly contribution to give the board an initial budget to work with. They were already committed to long-term financial support of the church, even a building project. The collection from the first Sunday of each month would go to a building fund, beginning with the first church service on January 4. They put "just a simple little notice" in the newspapers about the new Seventh Church, "the latest addition to the number of Christian Science churches in Seattle."[348]

At the first service, the audience filled every one of their 300 chairs, and a few had to stand. Charles A. Griffith, board chair at First Church during building construction, now served as First Reader for Seventh Church. Edna Lyman Scott was Second Reader. The subject of the sermon that week was "God," and members found the citations "appropriate and inspiring to this new expression of church." Ernest Worth sang a solo called "It Is Enough To Know," accompanied by his wife on piano. They collected about $310 for their building fund. The board reported:

> The unselfish contributions of many volunteers, the sense of divine leading actuating the Board, and the harmonious co-operation and democracy felt in all the deliberations of Seventh Church, helped immeasurably to make the occasion a success in a large way.[349]

This very harmonious beginning for Seventh Church, however, was occurring during an increasingly divisive period for the larger Christian Science Church community. The "Boston situation" may have previously seemed as distant rumblings—not something that should involve people in Seattle. This was no longer the case. The Seventh Church letter to Boston asking for recognition coincided with an eruption of controversy worldwide.

Earlier that week, the members of Seventh Church met with their board to help them decide if they should send a delegate to a State conference of Christian Science Churches, to be held in Seattle the next day, March 30th, "for the purpose of considering what steps best to take in the matter of the problems existing between the Board of Directors of The Mother Church and the Publishing Society." Of special concern was the fact that Seventh Church was not yet a recognized branch church. After "considerable discussion," the members resolved to ask their First Reader, Mr. Griffith, to attend the Tuesday conference and report back to them.[350]

After the Wednesday testimony meeting following the conference, the members gathered to hear about the event. As the membership business meeting began, they were all reminded by the president of Mary Baker Eddy's "Rule for Motives and Acts," that "neither animosity nor mere personal attachment should impel the motives or acts of the members of The Mother Church." Principle, not personal feelings, should be their guide. There were many reports to consider. They had received a letter from a branch church in New York. There were verbal reports of actions taken in other parts of the country. Griffith gave his report on the Washington conference. Several other members also gave brief talks. Over the next few weeks, they received the official conference minutes, a letter from the chair of the Washington conference, a circular from the Board of Directors of The Mother Church, a telegram from the Trustees of the Publishing Society, and a *Boston Post* article. Then they received a letter from other delegates from the Washington conference, with a letter enclosed from a similar conference of delegates in New York State, along with a petition.[351]

The issue was heating up. The Seventh Church board members were united in their disapproval of some of "these ambiguous, cryptic and insinuating letters" they were receiving from Washington delegates. They welcomed "honest criticism and information if set forth in comprehensive terms," but they were "unalterably opposed to any propaganda that would interfere with individual demonstration according to the Manual of The Mother Church." It seemed to them that by trying to give advice to practitioners and branch churches, the conference "had enlarged its activities far beyond the powers conferred" to them. They were not sure they wanted to support any more state-wide church conferences.[352]

In the spirit of the unity that had characterized all their organizational work, Seventh Church unanimously decided to take action regarding their Reading Room purchases. Until the Publishing Society was again following the *Manual of The Mother Church,* Seventh Church would only stock for sale the writings of Mary Baker Eddy and a few other specific items. But it did not seem consistent to the members of Seventh Church to take individual action. They received more letters, including one from the joint literature distribution committee announcing possible closure of their offices in the Empire Building.

Seventh Church decided to write a letter to all the Christian Science churches in Seattle, recommending "unified consideration" on the issue of literature. They called for a meeting of the Seattle boards.[353]

31

The Plan (1920)

In early May 1920, Third Church of Christ, Scientist, Seattle, become aware that First Church was trying to pay off their construction debt as soon as possible so they could dedicate. The members of the building committee at Third Church now had a much deeper appreciation of the challenges of church building. Here was an opportunity to help support the Seattle pioneers of Christian Science, the congregation from which Third Church came.

They saw two options. They could request to have the financial need of First Church announced by the First Reader at church services, hoping that people would contribute to First Church individually. Or they could send funds collectively, as Third Church.

The building committee had come to see church building as an expression of unity. They interpreted the recent slowdown in contributions to their building fund as a symptom of disunity. A collective contribution to First Church seemed the best way to unite in oneness. As they continued their discussions, the idea of collective effort expanded into an even grander vision for cooperative church dedication. They wrote a letter to the board asking them to call a meeting of representatives from the boards of all the Seattle churches to discuss this idea.

The board did not immediately respond. After a few weeks, the committee sent another letter to the board. They wrote, "[T]he Building Committee is convinced that action is imperative." The board clerk replied that there were no extra funds on hand to give to First Church, and they already had a lot of meetings on their calendar. In other words, the answer was no. But the response letter suggested that the building committee was, of course, always free to take questions directly to the membership body.[354]

Feeling strongly about the importance and urgency of this idea, the building committee members discussed how to present to the membership what they now referred to simply as "The Plan." They decided to make a motion at the upcoming business meeting. In preparation, they sent a letter to all the members:

Dear Friends,

Since that meeting of the church membership when it was voted that no further contracts be let until the indebtedness incurred in the first contract should be paid, the building committee has been impelled to consider church building from a metaphysical standpoint exclusively. . . .

As an unfoldment of our metaphysical work we here present to you the outline of a plan for the continued steps of our church building and we ask you to consider this and if possible vote upon it at the semi-annual meeting June 15.

Quoting from page 264 of *Miscellaneous Writings* [by Mary Baker Eddy], "Unity is the essential nature of Christian Science. Its Principle is One, and to demonstrate the divine One, demands oneness of thought and action."[355]

Their plan was to direct the board to write letters to all the Christian Science churches in Seattle inviting them to join in "unified support for constructing Christian Science church edifices." First Church was built, but not yet paid for. Third and Fourth were only partly completed. Fifth and Sixth had plans drawn and wanted to start construction. Under the proposal, the Seattle churches would focus on one building project at a time until it was complete and dedicated, and then move on to the next mutually agreed-upon project. All churches would contribute their first Sunday collection of each month—their own building funds. A committee of representatives from each of the churches would coordinate the effort so that the "Seattle field" could "devote its entire effort and resources for church building to this unified action." The proposal reflected the same spirit as the cooperative support that had been given to First Church when it was under construction. "The Plan" simply added a system for coordination.[356]

In June, the membership approved The Plan. Third Church began sending monthly contributions to First Church. The board sent letters to the other Seattle churches and societies inviting them to join with them in the cooperative effort to help First Church dedicate.

The building committee continued its weekly metaphysical meetings. For their spiritual study they focused on the topics of "unity," then "foundation," and then "walls." As they waited for responses from the other churches, they saw a need for "protective work for the seed which had been sown — the idea of unity — to know that it could not be reversed or destroyed."[357]

By early August, responses from the other Seattle churches had come in. Seventh Church wanted more information. Fourth Church appreciated the spirit of the invitation, but felt they could not agree to the proposed form. First Church was grateful for the effort to bring about unity and they would take it under consideration, but they would have to respond later. Second and Sixth Churches were not interested in The Plan at all. Fifth Church never responded.

Still feeling a sense of urgency, the building committee asked their board to confer with the other Seattle churches to find a way to do co-operative dedication that everyone could agree to. But the board had other urgent issues needing their attention.

On August 4, 1920, Third Church had another special meeting on the Boston situation. The conflict within the Christian Science Church had been making the news, both for the events surrounding the lawsuit and the resulting division, as Boston church employees, individual members, and branch churches worldwide took sides.

Previously, the members of Third Church had decided to take no action on the issue until the Supreme Court of Massachusetts made its ruling. But on this night they took a stand. In a rising vote, with members standing up to be counted, they decided to boycott the Christian Science Publishing Society. They canceled their advertisements in the *Christian Science Journal* and discontinued their subscriptions to all the periodicals. They would use those funds instead to support the Board of Directors of The Mother Church.

All the Seattle churches were united in this boycott. The boards had met and agreed. There would be no listings for Seattle churches or practitioners in the *Christian Science Journal* directory until the conflict was resolved.

Nothing more would be contributed to any building fund until the Boston conflict was resolved. The building committee dedicated themselves once again to their metaphysical work.

32

First Church Dedication (1920)

A formal invitation was sent out to the Christian Science community. It was a simple white folded card printed with special calligraphy style writing:

First Church of Christ, Scientist
of Seattle, Washington
Cordially invites you to attend the
Dedication
of its
Church Edifice
Sunday, November twenty-first
Nineteen hundred twenty

The big event, held the weekend before Thanksgiving, was announced in the *Seattle Times* and other local newspapers:

Will Dedicate Church
Christian Science Edifice Free From Debt
Services Tomorrow in Building on 16th
Avenue that was Started in 1909

Dedication of the First Church of Christ, Scientist, at 16th Avenue and East Denny Way, will be held tomorrow at 11 a.m., 3 p.m. and 8 p.m., with suitable services, according to the announcement today. The public is invited to attend the ceremonies . . .

"Earth was first turned for the building of this church in 1909," reads a statement from the church authorities. "The building was completed in October, 1914, at a cost of $170,000. The structure is of

Indiana limestone and the interior is beautifully harmonious, the ideal of the building committee being that no single feature of the decoration would be conspicuous and thus attract attention from the supreme purpose for which the building was created, namely, of presenting the message of Christian Science from the platform."[358]

Seattle Christian Scientists had reached a significant landmark in the development of their movement. They had achieved the high goal put forth by Allen H. Armstrong twenty years earlier to build "a structure worthy of the city and the cause we love." The self-described "little band of beginners, who struggled along" prior to Armstrong's arrival was now a large, thriving congregation overflowing the 1,200-seat auditorium and 700-student capacity Sunday School they had completed only six years earlier. The *Seattle Star* hailed their edifice as "one of the finest church buildings in the city." The growth of the congregation had already resulted in six more Christian Science churches in Seattle. Joining Armstrong were now about one hundred full-time professional Christian Science practitioners in Seattle alone, more than twice the number of chiropractors listed in the city directory. There were now three other Christian Science teachers—Mrs. Edith S. Alexander, John E. Playter, and William K. Sheldon—ensuring that the number of dedicated Christian Scientists in Seattle would continue to grow for many years to come.[359]

That they were able to pay for this building was remarkable. When they started planning their construction project, based on the rate of contribution to the building fund at that time—about $500 a month—they estimated it would take 20 to 40 years to pay for the project. Their initial design was a $200,000 project—comparable in cost, quality, and seating capacity to the original Mother Church edifice. But whereas people all over the world had contributed to the Boston building project, only local Christian Scientists had contributed to this building project. Even if they had used the cheapest materials available, reducing the cost to $100,000, the estimate was ten years. But they opted to build the church as they really wanted it to be.[360]

By building in phases over several years, they were able to pay for much of the construction as it was being built. The temporary structure was part of that financial strategy. But there still remained $80,000 in debt. Despite the turmoil, conflict, and even attack they might have felt through this period, they paid off this 10-year mortgage in only six years—with some help from the other branch churches in the area.[361]

DEDICATION

At the dedication service on Sunday, November 21, according to one source attributed to the *Seattle Post-Intelligencer*, First Church was "packed to capacity," and "hundreds of people were turned away"—"[n]early 4,000 people in all attended the three services." The report continued:

"In humble gratitude this church is lovingly dedicated to God and His Christ," were the words of dedication, spoken by the first reader. The pronouncement was received by the great congregation in awed silence. No other reference was made to this dedication, the regular Sunday service being conducted immediately afterward.[362]

It was also noted that all funds for the building were from free-will offerings. First Church of Christ, Scientist, Seattle, had established a local movement and persevered in achieving the stability and visibility of a permanent location. They had set a high standard for Christian Science church building in Seattle. They had proved what was possible. As Allen H. Armstrong had said in introducing a Christian Science lecture at the start of their building project,

The people of this church and denomination occupy at present a unique place in the Christian world, because they have entered into a conviction that the statements of the Scriptures are true, and that the salvation therein promised is a present possibility. . . . Science confirms these declarations with the irresistible logic of demonstration.[363]

To Armstrong the completion and dedication of their church building was a scientific demonstration. They were pioneering a way for others to follow. Already more building projects in Seattle had been started. They also needed to prove their understanding of Christian Science by completing their buildings and dedicating. They would need to challenge and overcome every sense of limitation. It must have been generally expected that the University District branch, Third Church, having already built a foundation, would be next.

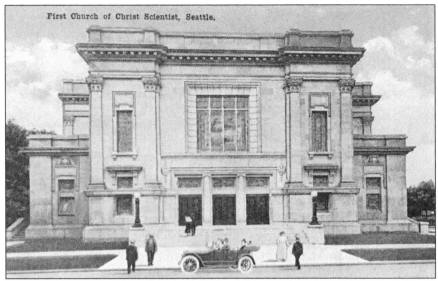

First Church of Christ Scientist, Seattle.

First Church of Christ, Scientist, Seattle

Postcard

The Mother Church Extension, Boston

Christian Science Publishing Society (1923)

33

Building Fund (1920)

t the regular Monday noon building committee meeting on November 22, 1920, at Byron Haviland's practitioner office on the tenth floor of the Empire Building, only four of the five members were present. Robert DeCou, committee chair, began the meeting with readings from the Book of John about how branches cannot bear fruit unless they abide in the vine of Jesus Christ (John 15: 1-8), followed by a published letter by Mary Baker Eddy to a branch church including similar imagery of branches needing to bear fruit.

Although there was no mention in the meeting minutes about the Third Church building committee members attending the dedication of First Church the previous day, it is hard to imagine any of them would have missed the big event. But rather than invigorate them in their own work, somehow a deep sense of discouragement had set in. The status of the building committee became the focus.

Mr. DeCou presented two propositions for discussion. The question was whether the committee should resign, or simply discontinue the regular meetings. The minutes record that "the work of the committee seemed for the present to be finished" because "it looked as if there would be no resumption of building activity for the present." It seems that at least one member of the building committee was read to quit.[364]

So far that year, the only thing that had happened at the building lot was some cleanup after complaints from neighbors of the "unsightly condition" of the premises. It had taken almost an entire year to pay for the first contract for the excavation and foundation. Having recently made the final payment, they could now move forward with construction under the constraints the membership had given them, except there was nothing in the building fund, and church collections were no longer being contributed to it.[365]

When the building committee had recommended sending the first Sunday collection to First Church, they expected that immediately after the dedication those funds would be redirected to their own building fund. Instead, just before the dedication service, the membership voted to start sending the first Sunday collection to Boston to the Board of Directors at The Mother Church to help pay their legal fees. Nothing would be added to the building fund for the foreseeable future.

Maybe one or more member of the building committee had interpreted this decision by the members of Third Church as lack of interest in the building project. Maybe they took it as a vote of no confidence. Maybe they felt they were falling short compared to the obvious recent success of First Church, or they were feeling burdened by other responsibilities at church or in other areas of their lives. Maybe the committee had been criticized. Maybe they were feeling that their metaphysical work that year—week after week of spiritual study and prayerful effort—had been ineffective.

The details of the discussion that day were not recorded. Perhaps they revisited the bylaw in the *Church Manual* on church building that states that the committee "shall not be dissolved until the new church edifice is completed." However their discussion went, the result was an informal resolution that it was "the feeling of the members present" that "the meetings should be continued and the committee remain intact unless the church membership saw fit to remove us for any reason."[366]

They immediately returned to their metaphysical work. The subject for their next meeting was "Substance." The following week the topic was "Activity," then "Guidance," and after that the focus was "Rejoicing." They read the rest of Joseph Armstrong's book on the building of the original Mother Church together, one chapter at a time.

They had probably all read a recent article in the *Christian Science Sentinel* by their architect's wife, Violet Webster Dunham, about how she overcame "a stubborn physical ailment" that had been very discouraging to her. She had been earnestly working to find physical relief through prayer for several days, without apparent result. Then as she was watching laborers working to break up concrete blocks, she gained a fresh spiritual insight. As she explained it:

> Faithfully they hammered away without any immediate results, but after many measured blows, the blocks would suddenly break apart. Then came the analogous thought: Those men are working at

a problem, and they know the answer; hence they are not discouraged by the seeming slowness of their task. They do not need to know which blow is going to break the concrete; but they do know that each blow counts, and so they continue until the result is attained. It is not the first blow nor the last which does the work, but it is the steady, persistent effort, and each and every blow has been needed to bring about the breaking of the solid stone. Like a flash came the spiritual awakening which enabled to her to declare, almost aloud, that every word of truth has power.

Many days had been devoted to solving this problem, seemingly without any change in the condition, yet every declaration of the reality of good and of man's right relation to God had done its work, and every declaration was needed. Then a deep sense of gratitude for the positive Principle . . . took the place of the discouraged thought, and with righteous desire for further unfoldment, study of the textbook was joyfully taken up. There was no sense of the passage of time, but within a very few moments absolute freedom was manifested.[367]

Like the laborers working steadily and persistently to accomplish their task, as seen through the perspective of Mrs. Dunham's inspiration, the building committee continued its weekly metaphysical meetings with no break for any holidays.

34

Election Meeting (1920)

The members of Third Church of Christ, Scientist, Seattle, met Tuesday evening, December 21, 1920, in the University Masonic Hall for their annual business meeting. President O.J.C. Dutton opened the meeting promptly at 8:00 p.m. in the usual way, with silent prayer followed by the Lord's Prayer. The church clerk, Jean K. Cole, read the minutes from all five of the membership meetings of the past three months, including the two special meetings on the Boston situation. The members approved the minutes as recorded.

The first item of business on the agenda this evening was the election of the most important of all the church officers: First and Second Readers. The president read the qualifications for readers from the *Church Manual* by Mary Baker Eddy. In the Christian Science church, readers are not clergy. There is no specific training or certification required. They are not leaders. Aside from being members of The Mother Church, readers simply need to "read understandingly and be well educated," and to "devote a suitable portion of their time" to preparing for the Sunday lesson. The First Reader is also responsible for conducting the Wednesday testimony meetings. An important part of reader preparation is spiritual. As Eddy wrote, "They must keep themselves unspotted from the world,—uncontaminated with evil,—that the mental atmosphere they exhale shall promote health and holiness, even that spiritual animus so universally needed."[368]

According to their bylaws, a two-thirds majority of ballots cast was needed to elect a reader. As was customary, there were no campaigns, no nominations, nor any speeches. Those present were simply given a list of eligible members and a blank card on which to write one name during a period of silence. A team of three members appointed by the president collected up the ballots for counting. The process repeated until someone received enough votes.

On this night, the vote for First Reader resulted in the election of Ralph E. Forbes, who was just finishing up his two-year term on the board. The vote for Second Reader resulted in the election of Ruth A. Densmore, the secretary of the building committee.

The issue was raised whether a member could, or should, serve in two church offices at the same time. Building committee member Horace P. Chapman had also been serving as church treasurer for the past three years. It was decided by a vote of the membership that building committee members were not eligible to serve in any other capacity, elected or appointed, except usher and Sunday School teacher. They extended a thank you to Mr. Chapman for his years of work as treasurer and released him from that duty, allowing him to more fully focus on the building committee. There was no mention at this point of Mrs. Densmore.

This annual business meeting also included voting to admit new members, hearing committee reports, and conducting other church business. Probably going late into the night without finishing the church business, they adjourned, then continued the meeting the next night after the Wednesday testimony meeting, and again the following Wednesday, December 29.

Meanwhile, Mrs. Densmore continued attending the weekly meetings with the building committee, as usual. Her new duties as Second Reader would begin just a few days later, on January 2, and no doubt she and Mr. Forbes were already actively working together, planning and practicing. This holiday season was an unusually active period for church work for Densmore, and as she began shifting her attention to preparing for services, there may have been some uncertainty about whether or how long she would also be expected to continue her work with the building committee.

Finally, probably very late on Wednesday the 29th—after reports from the treasurer, the secretary, the superintendent of the Sunday School, the Reading Room librarian, the church extension representative on work in the prisons, and the Washington Committee on Publication—a motion was made to elect a replacement for Mrs. Densmore on the building committee. The members elected the church clerk, Mrs. Cole, who was busy taking the meeting minutes and was just finishing her two-year term on the board. There being no further business, a motion to adjourn was duly carried. The building committee team, which had worked so closely together for so long, had a new member.

35

Call Letter (1921)

When the new year 1921 came around the building committee held its first Monday noon meeting on January 3. Ruth Densmore did not attend. The previous day they heard her read the Scriptures to the Third Church of Christ, Scientist, congregation at the University Bank Building as their new Second Reader, a change that no doubt would have stirred some cheerful conversation as they settled in to their meeting. Since Mrs. Densmore had been their secretary, they now needed a replacement. By voice vote, they elected their journalist member, former editor for the *The Daily*, Helen Lantz.

Their new committee member, Jean K. Cole, was originally from Milwaukee. She had lived in Seattle for about ten years. Her husband, George Seaverns Cole, had come from Chicago to teach law at the University of Washington. He was on the faculty while Mrs. Densmore and Mrs. Lantz were students. Mrs. Cole had been a music teacher then, offering instruction from her home in the University District, but now she was in the full-time practice of Christian Science. Her office was in the Leary Building. After completing her two-year term on the board, she might have hoped for less active duties at church. However, the building committee had the potential to be even more active and demanding than board work once they started construction again. For now, they were only doing metaphysical work, and this new committee member came prepared to share.[369]

There was recent activity around the building site—evidence of progress. The neighbors near the building lot wanted to pave the alley and were asking Third Church to sign a petition to the City of Seattle. The committee unanimously agreed to support the improvement. Horace

Chapman was appointed to take it to the board with a letter from the building committee recommending favorable action.

The group started talking about their building project, and after some discussion, they came to another unanimous decision. They agreed that "the time had arrived in which to go ahead with the actual construction." The question was how to go about bringing this development to the attention of the membership. At this point Robert DeCou shared his prepared reading selections, which included Mary Baker Eddy's statement in a letter that seemed relevant to the ongoing Boston situation:

> All is well at headquarters, and when the mist shall melt away you will see clearly the signs of Truth and the heaven of Love within your hearts. Let the reign of peace and harmony be supreme and forever yours.

And this from *Science and Health*:

> There is to-day danger of repeating the offence of the Jews by limiting the Holy One of Israel and asking: "Can God furnish a table in the wilderness?" What cannot God do?[370]

Next, Mrs. Cole read Mary Baker Eddy's article "A Word to the Wise," written when the foundation of The Mother Church was complete but there were not enough funds on hand to build. Eddy's directive to complete and fully pay for the church edifice during the calendar year 1894 was done. Eddy admonished those (and future) Christian Scientist church builders:

> No doubt must intervene between the promise and event; faith and resolve are friends to Truth; seize them, trust the divine Providence, push upward our prayer in stone, — and God will give the benediction.[371]

The committee approved this selection as "a fitting reference" to include in a call letter to the membership. The building committee encouraged their members to "push upward" their "prayer in stone" in the University District. The membership needed to decide between building a temporary auditorium in the future Sunday School in the basement—as First and Fourth Churches had done—or moving forward with the final walls and roof. The committee provided cost estimates from the architect for both approaches. Either way, they wanted to proceed with construction immediately, despite, once again, having nowhere near the funds needed to pay for the work.

At a special meeting in February, the membership authorized the building committee to move forward with the walls and roof of the permanent church edifice. They also established a separate fund for The Mother Church. Members who wanted to contribute to the Boston legal fees could put their contribution in a special envelope. The first Sunday collection would once again go to their own building fund.

Over the next few weeks, the building committee continued their metaphysical study with a focus on the topics of gratitude, tithing, and church. But now at their meetings, they also had business to discuss as they analyzed costs, reviewed bids, and looked at brick and tile samples.

Cole shared a letter she had received. It was a personal account of a church built by a relatively small membership of modest means. The writer described how in February 1916, when they outgrew their location and found it impossible to find anything else that was suitable, they focused on unity of thought. Then, after seven meetings, the decision was unanimous to move forward with building. The members of this building committee had no experience with construction, yet they built successfully. Purchasing the lot in June, and starting with only $2 in their building fund, they broke ground in August and completed the church edifice in time for the Thanksgiving service in November. Within one year of starting the project, they had fully paid for it. The letter concluded, "We have had numerous inquiries as to how we did it and it is difficult to say except that we demonstrated every step of the way." The writer pointed out four steps in the process of "demonstration": 1) need, 2) unity, 3) supply, and 4) "realization of no hindrance to Mind's activity." The Third Church building committee saw so much value in this testimony that they put the entire letter into the minutes.[372]

The committee took their metaphysical approach to the entire membership at two special meetings, the first focused on unity of purpose, the second on supply. At each meeting, the hour was spent sharing "helpful and inspiring" ideas and "individual proofs of spiritual supply."[373]

In early April 1921, they signed a contract for construction of walls and roof. That month the First Reader announced at church services, "Actual building of Third Church of Christ, Scientist at the corner of 17th Avenue and East 50th Street has been resumed." The need for extra contributions was made known to the congregation. Contributions were growing. By May, there was $2,900 in the building fund. But they needed $46,500.[374]

They wrote letters to the members explaining the urgent need for more funds. They held more special meetings and gave the members citations from the Bible and Eddy's writings on "supply" to study every day. Contributions to the building fund increased, but on June 1 there was still not enough money to pay the full construction bill.

Meanwhile, the other Seattle churches were considering Third Church's proposed "Plan" for a cooperative system for building church edifices. First Church had called a meeting to consider establishing a joint building fund, but apparently no decisions were made. Third Church was still on its own.[375]

Initially, the building committee had promised not to spend money faster than funds were available, but after construction began, "because of a better understanding of the problems . . . in building operations and of clearer metaphysical unfoldment," they later explained, they asked the members to reconsider. These Bible citations were shared at a membership meeting that spring:[376]

"the God of heaven, he will prosper us; therefore we his servants will arise and build." (Nehemiah 2: 18-20)

"Behold the Lord's hand is not shortened, that it cannot save; neither his ear heavy, that it cannot hear." (Isaiah 59:1)

After some discussion, the members voted to allow more flexibility for contracting for the walls and roof. They even gave permission to borrow money if necessary.

Borrowing money was not easy. Apparently, some banks were not interested in doing business with them. They had to search to find "institutions friendly to Christian Science." Also the membership wanted to build in phases, but banks would only loan for a complete building. They needed the money immediately, but bank mortgages took time to process. The board was able to get a small loan to cover some expenses, but the overall financial problem remained unsolved.[377]

By early July, the building committee had made no progress on financing. They were faced with "seemingly impossible conditions." Horace Chapman "expressed his earnest conviction that under the circumstances it would be only honest to stop the work." The others on the committee, however, disagreed. They "declared that the time had not yet come to acknowledge defeat." They must be "faithful over a few things," as explained in the Bible (Matt. 25: 21). The majority voted to "investigate every possible source of light on this problem." They devoted themselves to prayerfully listening for a way to move forward.[378]

36

Cornerstone (1921)

I t was 6:00 a.m. on Wednesday, July 13, 1921. The five members of the building committee, the seven members of the board, the contractor, foreman, and head mason quietly assembled at the corner of Northeast 50th Street and 17th Avenue Northeast, the building site for the church edifice for Third Church of Christ, Scientist, where the foundation had been quietly awaiting its structure the past eighteen months. That summer morning this small group gathered for a ceremony. They were laying the cornerstone for their church.

It was the "earnest wish" of the building committee that the ceremony be "held as quietly and with as little publicity as possible." They held the private service in the early morning "to avoid curiosity seekers," as Byron Haviland later explained.[379]

Traditionally, many churches and organizations have celebrated the laying of cornerstones with large gatherings and special ceremonial shovels, but Reverend Mary Baker Eddy required a different approach for Christian Science churches. In the *Church Manual* was a bylaw:

> No large gathering of people nor display shall be allowed when laying the Corner Stone of a Church of Christ, Scientist. Let the ceremony be devout.[380]

At the cornerstone ceremony for Third Church, it was later recounted,

> Even Nature's voices were silent during that early morning hour and the absolute stillness of the mist-wrapped earth gave fitting tribute to the sacred occasion.[381]

The two official readers came prepared with special reading selections. When she was on the building committee, Ruth Densmore had taken part in the decision-making for the cornerstone and church inscription, so it was beautifully fitting that she was there as Second Reader. The First Reader, Ralph Earl Forbes, started the ceremony by leading the group in repeating together the "Daily Prayer" from the *Church Manual*:

"Thy kingdom come;" let the reign of divine Truth, Life, and Love be established in me, and rule out of me all sin; and may Thy Word enrich the affections of all mankind, and govern them![382]

Mrs. Densmore then read these brief selections from the Bible:

Psalms: (Psalms 118: 21-24)

I will praise thee: for thou hast heard me, and art become my salvation. The stone which the builders refused is become the head stone of the corner. This is the Lord's doing; it is marvelous in our eyes. This is the day which the Lord hath made; we will rejoice and be glad in it.

1 Corinthians: (1 Cor. 3: 6, 7, 10, 11)

I have planted, Apollos watered; but God gave the increase. So then neither is he that planteth any thing, neither he that watereth; but God that giveth the increase.

According to the grace of God which is given unto me, as a wise masterbuilder, I have laid the foundation, and another buildeth thereon. But let every man take heed how he buildeth thereupon. For other foundation can no man lay than that is laid, which is Jesus Christ.

Mr. Forbes, read these selections from *Science and Health with Key to the Scriptures* by Mary Baker Eddy:

The Bible teaches transformation of the body by the renewal of Spirt. Take away the spiritual signification of Scripture, and that compilation can do no more for mortals than can moonbeams to melt a river of ice. The error of the ages is preaching without practice. . . . Our Master said, "If ye love me, keep my commandments." One's aim, a point beyond faith, should be to find the footsteps of Truth, the way to health and holiness. (241:13, 21-24)

The chief stones in the temple of Christian Science are to be found in the following postulates: that Life is God, good, and not evil; that Soul is sinless, not to be found in the body; that Spirit is not, and cannot be materialized; that Life is not subject to death; that the spiritual real man has no birth, no material life, and no death. (288:20)

Jesus established his church and maintained his mission on a spiritual foundation of Christ-healing. He taught his followers that his religion had a divine Principle, which would cast out error and heal both the sick and the sinning. (136:1-5)

Our Master said to every follower: "Go ye into all the world, and preach the gospel to every creature! . . . Heal the sick! . . . Love thy neighbor as thyself!" It was this theology of Jesus which healed the sick and the sinning. It is his theology in this book and the spiritual meaning of this theology, which heals the sick and causes the wicked to "forsake his way, and the unrighteous man his thoughts." (138:27-2)

CHURCH. The structure of Truth and Love; whatever rests upon and proceeds from divine Principle. The Church is that institution, which affords proof of its utility and is found elevating the race, rousing the dormant understanding from material beliefs to the apprehension of spiritual ideas and the demonstration of divine Science, thereby casting out devils, or error, and healing the sick. (583:12-19)

Then the group stood in silence while the workmen installed the cornerstone and cemented into place and adjusted the terra-cotta tile facing bearing the inscription:

THIRD CHURCH OF CHRIST SCIENTIST, 1921 A.D.

After silent prayer, everyone present united in repeating aloud the Lord's Prayer with Mary Baker Eddy's spiritual interpretation.

> Our Father which art in heaven,
> *Our Father-Mother God, all-harmonious,*
>
> Hallowed be Thy name.
> *Adorable One.*
>
> Thy kingdom come.
> *Thy kingdom is come; Thou art ever-present.*
>
> Thy will be done in earth, as it is in heaven.
> *Enable us to know, — as in heaven, so on earth, — God is omnipotent, supreme.*
>
> Give us this day our daily bread;
> *Give us grace for to-day; feed the famished affections;*

And forgive us our debts, as we forgive our debtors.
And Love is reflected in love;

And lead us not into temptation, but deliver us from evil;
And God leadeth us not into temptation, but delivereth us from sin, disease, and death.

For Thine is the kingdom, and the power, and the glory, forever.
For God is infinite, all-power, all Life, Truth, Love, over all, and All.[383]

And as later recounted,

When the benediction had been pronounced, each went his way in silence, feeling that God was still speaking.[384]

37

Walls and Roof (1921)

After laying the cornerstone for the new church edifice for Third Church of Christ, Scientist, the building committee asked the membership "how the financial obligations were to be taken care of." The contract for the walls and roof was signed, and construction was beginning. Now they needed $18,000 to pay for it.[385]

"The ideal church will be objectified in this edifice just to the degree that we, as Christian Scientists, apprehend and live this ideal," wrote the chair of the building committee. "Our present conception of this ideal will meet our present need." The members were expected to make their own individual demonstration of supply in order to increase their contributions to the building fund.[386]

In response, individual members voluntarily pledged amounts they would commit to paying. One building committee member later recounted that "The women sold jewelry and did housework to earn money to contribute to the church." They raised $6,000 during July and August 1921. But they still needed significantly more.[387]

They needed more than was coming in through the first Sunday collection. Nothing could come from the general fund, because the church consistently spent every penny received for normal operating expenses. It was uncertain when they would begin the next phase of construction. The building was now just a shell without doors or windows. It was not secure. Their general contractor, Neil McDonald, recommended the church hire a night watchman to protect the building materials while construction was in progress. At Jean Cole's suggestion, they asked members to volunteer. And so, as Byron Haviland later explained, "the women came each night and sat in the church to watch against vandalism." It was an ongoing duty that lasted for about a year, according to Mr. Haviland, as he told the story years later. Mrs. Cole, who lived only four blocks away, volunteered to regularly inspect the building site.[388]

In November 1921, the building committee and membership once again considered several options for moving church services into the unfinished building, as First and Fourth Churches had done. Their current meeting place at the University Bank Building was "unsatisfactory, and too small." It was becoming "inadequate to handle the steadily increasing membership." But ultimately Third Church decided the savings in rent was not worth the extra effort and cost of finishing the building while occupied. So they continued to hold services in the bank building. In the meantime, they were "looking earnestly for Principle, the guide of all right activity, to point the way."[389]

As the members looked for direction on how to move forward with the building project, it would have been natural for them to listen especially carefully on Sundays and Wednesdays to their First Reader Ralph E. Forbes—not for leadership on what actions to take, but for comfort, spiritual insight, and inspiration. In his role as First Reader, Mr. Forbes chose scriptural selections to begin each Sunday service, the hymns, and on Wednesday evening he created a sermon of his own using passages from the Bible and Mary Baker Eddy's writings. He was digging deep in his own spiritual study, working to "read understandingly," as instructed by Rev. Eddy through the *Church Manual*.[390]

Forbes was familiar with building projects. His professional background was in the lumber industry. But since he began studying Christian Science, he had begun thinking differently about building. As he explained:

> I soon came to the conclusion that whatever I had gained in the way of material success and position was founded on an unsubstantial base,—that I had built my wall on a foundation of sand,—and the desire to change to a more solid foundation at once was very strong. However, thanks to the advice of helpful friends, I did not throw down the entire wall before starting on the more substantial basis, as in my untempered zeal I might have done to my sorrow; but I have been trying ever since to change my wall from the sandy foundation of human will to the rock of Christ, very slowly, one brick at a time. . . [391]

Forbes, testified about overcoming chronic headaches and a tobacco habit of fifteen years through Christian Science. He had embraced this new way of thinking. Now, as First Reader, he guided the entire membership through a collective change of thought, one church service at a time.

The ongoing legal battle between the Trustees of the Christian Science Publishing Society and the Board of Directors of The Mother Church continued to work its way through the Massachusetts court system. No doubt this was very much on the thought of all the Christian Scientists in Seattle.

For the members of Third Church, that fall of 1921, with their foundation and cornerstone laid, walls and roof built, but the building otherwise just an empty shell, they focused on spiritual study and prayer. They had the opportunity to shift to a new way of thinking about church building, as Forbes, put it, "one brick at a time."

Third Church of Christ, Scientist, Seattle, under construction
Third Church of Christ, Scientist, Seattle

38

Final Plans (1921)

On November 24, 1921, a series of minor headlines in Seattle newspapers was major news for church members. "The Christian Science Controversy" was over. The Massachusetts Supreme Court handed down a ruling in favor of the Board of Directors of The Mother Church. In early 1922, the First Reader at Third Church of Christ, Scientist, announced that the Christian Science Publishing Society was now under the control of the Board of Directors. The *Christian Science Monitor* and the other periodicals could once again be purchased through their Reading Room. The Christian Science churches in Seattle had been running a large weekly advertisement in the local newspapers for locations and service times. They discontinued this and renewed their listings in the *Christian Science Journal* directory. Having united in their support of the Mother Church, within the Seattle congregations there might have been some expression of happiness over the ruling, that right was done. But, there was at least one local Christian Scientist who had sided with the Publishing Society Trustees, and that publicly. Regardless of how individuals might have felt about the issues, there must have been a collective sigh of relief that the court battles were finally over. Reverend Mary Baker Eddy's church and her governing *Church Manual* had survived a supreme test.[392]

In the spring of 1922, Third Church was ready to move forward again on their building project. To finance the remaining construction, they decided to mortgage the land. The membership imposed requirement to pay for each phase separately made it impossible to get a conventional mortgage loan from any bank. As an alternative method of borrowing money, they sold $50,000 worth of bonds at a time. It helped that their new church treasurer, Miss Bertha Vera Sandall, had experience handling mortgage bonds and worked at the company selected to act as trustee for the bonds. But as a board member later explained, it was "not possible to market these bonds in the usual way." Instead, "with the aid of the other churches in the city," the loan money they needed came quickly from "friends, mostly students of Christian Science." At Third Church, the First Reader announced at services that bonds were available for sale from the treasurer at church and at the Reading Room.[393]

The building committee expressed enthusiasm over the speed at which the bonds sold. But now they had to face sobering problems of managing the construction project. It seemed their biggest problem was the architect. With his busy travel schedule, George Foote Dunham had not been available to supervise the construction as originally expected. Furthermore, the committee had never received the complete plans with design detail. They described the preliminary drawings as "extremely indefinite." The committee and construction crew had to work from the preliminary plans—they had to improvise. As they did, they were shocked to realize that some things had not been considered at all in the design, such as access to the organ loft—"a serious error," according to the representative from the Kimball Organ Company—and there were other problems. They were not happy with Mr. Dunham's plan for heating or lighting. The lobby floor vibrated when walked on. After heavy rains the roof leaked. The building contractor was not happy with the drainage design. It seemed that "numerous unforeseen expenses" were arising, adding several thousand dollars to the construction cost. When the committee talked with Dunham about these issues, secretary Helen Lantz recorded that he gave "only vague, evasive replies."[394]

In the meeting minutes, Mrs. Lantz wrote:

> Those of the Committee present felt convinced of two things: first that individually and as a Committee the members must rise higher in the demonstration of service through a clearer realization of "Church" as taught in our textbook in meeting the problem confronting them. Second that some definite action must be taken soon regarding the architect.[395]

For the "definite action" to be taken, Robert DeCou conducted an investigation. He concluded that Dunham's work on design and artistic effect was excellent, but in the more practical details he was sorely lacking. Unfortunately, this architect "was inclined to take advice of people who were not experts." The building committee had a frank talk with Dunham about their desire to put the work "in other hands, deducting accordingly from his commission." The architect countered with a promise to consult more with experts. He had just returned from travels back East where he had the opportunity to study the design details of several churches. After consulting with an "expert engineer," he assured the committee he would produce the detailed plans the contractor needed to estimate the building costs for the next phase. He did send updated plans, but the building committee still needed to improvise details as construction was underway.[396]

Meanwhile, committee members worked intensively on all the other finishing details that still needed to come together at the right time. They were having meetings several times each week to make decisions, in addition to carrying out their own individual assignments between meetings—communications with vendors, taking field trips to suppliers, and visits to the building site. Then there was the problem of supervision of the construction. Once construction was underway, Mr. DeCou was spending most of his days managing the details of the work. The chair raised this issue for discussion at a meeting one evening at the reading room. The other members saw this imbalance of workload as unfair. This could not continue. They had no budget to hire anyone to supervise, nor could they pay a committee member to do the work, so they concluded together that "the time had come for each member of the Committee to wake up to his responsibilities and be willing to sacrifice his personal and private interests." They agreed to a new procedure where the contractor would call Mrs. Lantz whenever there was a need for a decision, and she would call the other members by telephone to get a decision within a few hours. All members would stand in readiness to visit the church and take turns doing daily inspections.[397]

At this point, they recorded a "sense of burden and confusion" and concluded that these "were errors which had arisen to becloud the vision of Church as understood in Christian Science." They reminded themselves yet again how important it was in their work to devote at least a few moments at each meeting to reading from the Bible and Eddy's writings. During the final phase of construction, the whole membership met once each month after the Wednesday evening testimony meeting for "spiritual giving" to support the building going on. The long-desired church edifice for Third Church was finally nearing completion.[398]

39

Opening Services (1922)

The completion of the new edifice for Third Church of Christ, Scientist, Seattle, was announced in the local newspapers the day before the opening services on Sunday, November 12, 1922. The morning, afternoon, and evening services would be presided over by Ralph E. Forbes, First Reader, and Ruth A. Densmore, Second Reader. The headlines in the newspapers foremost noted the cost of the building—$100,000 including the furnishings. The *Seattle Times* and *Seattle Star* similarly described the three-story building as:

> cement construction, finished in brick veneer and terra cotta trimmings. The wide entrance is adorned by five Ionic columns. . . . Interior finishes are of wood work, ivory enameled. Pews are of light oak. Windows are made of art glass, while an indirect lighting system has been installed. A three-manual Austin pipe organ will be installed soon, but it has not been received yet.[399]

It had been almost exactly eight years since their first church service at the University Masonic Hall. While newspaper readers were learning about the upcoming opening services and the new edifice, the building committee had its own focus. Their minutes recorded:

> The day before the opening of the church found the members of the Committee busy getting the building swept and garnished for the initial services. During the entire week members of the Committee had been in almost constant attendance at the church supervising painting, cleaning, carpet-laying, furniture placing, landscape gardening, etc. Much still remained to be done, but at noon time the Committee found a quiet corner of the auditorium where they

paused for a few moments of silent thanksgiving followed by Mrs. Cole's readings.[400]

The committee learned that the board appointed them all to serve as ushers in the foyer. Jean Cole's readings included the phrase "the spiritual modesty of Christian Science" as the jewel of church building. Christian Scientists valued modesty. But even so, the church members and visitors would certainly want to voice their appreciation to this team of five who had so faithfully accomplished so much. They could do so individually in the foyer before and after the services.[401]

The building committee had proved their dedication. They held at least 253 meetings over a period of almost four years. Their ongoing work had required "the study in detail and often at great length such matters as wall construction, arches, curves, ornamental detail, floor construction, lighting equipment, heating and ventilation, color effects in walls, trims and glass and in all manner of furnishings," and research into church pipe organs, which "required especially careful consideration." They had had "many problems and trying experiences." They later reported that diligent spiritual preparation and study of the Bible and Mary Baker Eddy's writings "removed many mountainous difficulties" along the way. And now, their work was essentially done, giving "eloquent testimony to His direction."[402]

"One is greeted with a warm sunshiny effect in the church auditorium," later wrote Eileen Gormley, the first historian at Third Church. The "sunshiny interior" was exactly what the building committee and architect had been trying for. The color scheme of the walls and curved ceiling was designed to "shade up gradually just as we see the color of the sky, darker at the horizon and looking up it seems to grow lighter." The "beautifully shaded and mottled effect in amber and opal" of the art glass windows suggested "sunshine and soft, fleecy clouds." The "Greek motif" of the building expressed "simplicity and purity, symbol of Truth." Miss Gormley described the Corinthian style as "majestic and yet pure and simple, as is Christian Science itself." The opening event was "a time for gratitude and joy in the demonstration of the Truth, which stood clearly before the eyes of all and which was understood more clearly in the thoughts of those who had worked and watched."[403]

The members of Third Church expected their attendance and membership to continue to grow. When this small band of members decided to design the auditorium to seat 840 congregants and the Sunday School to serve 700 children, they were confident that it would "not be possible to build a Christian Science church that will not soon be filled for the same reason that the law of God maintains a balance between supply and demand." Starting from the opening Sunday, Third Church held two services, 11 a.m. and 8 p.m., as First and Fourth Churches had been doing for several years.[404]

There were still many more details to attend to that kept the building committee as active as ever. There were bills to pay from the construction workers and suppliers and decisions to make about insurance. There was a contract dispute to resolve with the subcontractor for the plastering and a disagreement to settle with their architect over his final bill for construction supervision and travel expenses. There was linoleum to install, concrete landings to build for the front entrance, and a sidewalk to repair. There were more furnishings to buy: umbrella racks for the vestibule, special wrought iron lamps to custom design, and a grand piano rental needed until the organ could be installed. Then there were the customer service issues surrounding the organ, with months of ongoing communications to prevent further delivery delays. The committee needed to persistently monitor the organ progress until it was installed.

The report of the building committee at the semiannual membership meeting June 1923 gave a reflective summary of their process:

> From the beginning of our work as a committee we have sought to make every step taken an unfoldment of God's plan. We have endeavored to be humble enough so to lay aside our own wishes that we all should be of one mind and that the mind of Christ before reaching any least decision. In this endeavor we many times found it necessary to bring our five differing opinions to harmonious agreement before proceeding.
>
> May we all profit by the lessons learned in this work and add charity to charity, to patience more patience, and to spiritual purpose greater wisdom and zeal, and in so doing prove with ever greater certainty that the true church is a spiritual structure which heals and saves.
>
> We are confident that the work done is God's work from the selection of the design to the carrying out of the detail thereof. This fact is further proven in the united, consecrated support given by the members to every problem referred to them and the spiritual unity manifested throughout the entire period of building.

Respectfully submitted,
Building Committee[405]

DEDICATION

Early in July, the building committee met at the church for a final inspection of the organ installation. They carefully checked over the instrument with the specifications. Then a prominent local organist, Mr. W. H. Donley, the organist at First Presbyterian Church, put on a private organ concert for them, so they could hear the instrument's "possibilities." Mr. Donley gave them "more than an hour's recital demonstrating the flexibility of the instrument, its tonal beauty and richness of combinations." The committee members were pleased that the organ was "truly beautiful and satisfying." They expressed this sentiment in a final letter to the board.[406]

With this, their work was done. The meeting minutes were wrapped up and the building committee disbanded.

Third Church of Christ, Scientist, Seattle, auditorium

Photo: Dale Lang

Auditorium art glass windows (lower)

Photo: Dale Lang

40

Second Unit (1922)

"Dear Little Wildflower," the letter began. It was one of the first of many letters Paul J. Jensen would write in his role as secretary of the building committee for Fourth Church of Christ, Scientist, Seattle. This friendly letter was an invitation to a meeting on May 10, 1922, at the Empire Building to launch the work on the second unit. The letter was to architect George Foote Dunham, but it seems there was already an expectation that his wife, Violet, would be the one to receive the letter and take action. Although Mr. Jensen's later letters would address her more formally as Mrs. Dunham, there would always be a cheerful tone of familiarity and camaraderie in their frequent correspondence, even during this period of the most intense pressure when so many critical elements needed to come together quickly. During the summer of 1922, as the Fourth Church second unit construction was ramping up, the architect was of necessity on extended travels in the East. Dunham was awarded the design for Sixth Church of Christ, Scientist, Saint Louis, and he had already committed to being there for the start of the project. It was not certain when he would return. He left Violet in charge of the Fourth Church project.[407]

Back in the fall of 1921, around the time the Boston litigation was finally resolved, the membership of Fourth Church had told the building committee to "get busy." As far the membership was concerned, the committee already existed, despite having been inactive for several years, and it was time to start working again. The church had paid off the debt on the first unit, and the members were ready to move forward with the second unit. The membership wanted to see a final design, a cost estimate, and a plan for financing the project. But most of all, they wanted to see a completed church edifice.

William K. Sheldon relayed the directive to "get busy" to Dunham in a letter. But it was not so easy to instantly start up this major construction project. First of all, the architect was on extended travels again. But the building committee was not quite ready to start work either. They needed a new chair. Mr. Sheldon had taken the lead on the building work after the former chair Frederick S. Sylvester was elected First Reader. Even though the first unit construction was done, Mr. Sheldon had had to deal with quite a lot of building issues. Even after the congregation moved services into the daylight basement in March 1917, there were ongoing problems with the building—leaks, seepage, and dampness. The problems were due primarily to the fact that the building, being unfinished, was not fully waterproofed. The exterior walls had only a temporary covering of "a swabbing of hot asphalt" instead of its intended terra-cotta tiles. The concrete walls absorbed rain, as did the concrete floor. Sheldon had overseen resolution of these issues, but his work as a Christian Science practitioner and teacher also demanded his attention, and now he needed to leave the city for an extended period. As much as he had valued his involvement on the building committee since his appointment in 1915, after getting the project going again he tendered his resignation. He asked for the pardon of the members for insisting that they accept it. There were, after all, many other highly qualified people among the membership.[408]

By early May 1922, the building committee had a new chair, Charles T. Hutson. Mr. Hutson had proved himself highly capable in everything he did throughout his career in law. Originally from Wisconsin, after graduating from the University of Wisconsin Law School, he had begun his legal practice in the Wild West—in Pasco, Washington, when it was "all dust and had no paint" and the only place in town to bathe was a zinc tub by the railroad pump house. His first law office was in a tiny shack. The "rough-and-ready citizens" often brought guns to meetings, and he at times had to travel 40 miles by horseback at night to conduct his business. The remote location of his start in law did not hinder the advancement of his career, however. From his modest private practice in wheat country, he became county prosecutor, then entered the Washington State legislature as a senator. At the time, he was the youngest person ever elected to the State Senate. When President Theodore Roosevelt visited Pasco, Hutson was at the top of the list of the welcoming committee. When a new Assistant United States Attorney position was created for the western district, Hutson was the first one appointed. Hutson moved to Seattle in 1907 after taking this federal prosecutor position. It may have been shortly after his resignation from that position five years later that he came into Christian Science. His wife died after a lingering illness, and he, now solely responsible for their two young daughters, also had a serious health problem. His bronchial asthma was so severe that "after exhausting all known remedies" his physicians advised him to "leave Seattle and try other climates." Instead, he tried Christian Science and was completely healed within a few weeks.[409]

Hutson's public debut as a Christian Scientist coincided with the first unit building project for Fourth Church. The *Seattle Times* took notice when the former Assistant United States Attorney began introducing Christian Science lectures in Seattle. "Happiness, however interpreted, is the goal sought by all," Hutson had told the audience of more than 5,000 people at the George Shaw Cook lecture at the Arena on Sunday, September 10, 1916. As reported in the *Christian Science Sentinel*, Hutson's introduction continued:

> For hundreds of years theory upon theory for the amelioration of the sufferings of the human race have been advanced, and in practical operation they have failed to accomplish the result sought. . . . Then Christian Science was discovered, — an agency found so potent for good that in the short space of fifty years it has extended to all the world, and its followers are numbered in the millions. When its teachings are accepted, understood, and demonstrated, inharmony and discord disappear and happiness is attained.[410]

Hutson had found the happiness he had been seeking, and although he continued his career in law in private practice, he began also working for the cause of Christian Science, actively and openly, as did his brother, Roy J. Hutson, head of a fuel company and partner in a new paper pulp mill in Edmonds. When Charles Hutson was appointed to the building committee, Roy had just completed a term as First Reader at First Church. A decade hence, Charles would be First Reader at Fourth Church. Starting in the spring of 1922, when the Fourth Church building committee began to "get busy," Hutson was in charge of this critically important work. He was especially well qualified to organize and run the meetings because of having served in the state legislature and as chair for at least one political convention. His building committee meetings were run formally, efficiently, and effectively.[411]

There were other changes for the re-activated building committee. Miss Jessie Estep continued on the committee, but resigned from her role as secretary. Her replacement, Paul J. Jensen, was a secretary by profession. An immigrant from Norway, he was the clerk at one of the finest hotels in Seattle, the Frye Hotel on Yesler Way, and managing secretary for a statewide organization for the restaurant industry. Also on the building committee team, they had Christian Science practitioner Emma Augusta Hawkins, who had two years of experience on the building committee at First Church. Others involved for at least part of the building process included Dr. Walter Padget, the dentist, who had completed his term as First Reader; Fred Brubaker, the manager at the barbershop in the New Washington Hotel at Second and Stewart; Hiram K. Ball, an Alaska gold rush miner turned real estate agent; Ben S. Booth, an embalmer with a successful undertaking business; Mr. Russell, and Mrs. Pratt.[412]

At the meeting on May 10 at the Empire Building, George Dunham attended before heading east. Mr. Dunham's presence must have been reassuring to the newly activated committee. They officially authorized him for the project. There had been enough concern about working with an out-of-state architect that they had consulted with Robert De-Cou, former chair of the Third Church building committee, about his experience working remotely with Dunham. On this Fourth Church project, Dunham would be more consistent in his visits to the building site. He would visit Seattle about once a month, unless traveling. Dunham would also be in much closer communication with Neil McDonald, the construction contractor, with whom he had previously worked on the Fourth Church first unit and the Third Church edifice. McDonald's construction crew was just then finishing up the work on Third Church. Fourth Church would get the best crew and price if they started work on July 5. McDonald needed several working blueprints of the final design as soon as possible to provide a cost estimate for the upcoming membership meeting on June 12.

In discussing the project with Dunham that day, the committee made some design changes. Most significantly, they chose steel roof trusses instead of wood. The cost was significantly more, but it would make a stronger building. This meant a major revision of the plans that Mr. Dunham could not be directly involved in because of his travels. It would be up to Mrs. Dunham to oversee the work—Violet, the "dear little wildflower."

Violet expressed a spirit of sweetness and modesty, but both her architect husband and the building committee seemed to have complete confidence that she could do the needed work for this largest and most expensive of all the Christian Science churches in Seattle. That Violet was a Christian Scientist was apparent from phrases used in her letters to the building committee. She cheered the "unity expressed" by the

members, expected the work to "progress harmoniously," and re-
marked that the "beautiful edifice is to be brought into expression."
Violet grew up in Stockton, California, and attended Mills College, a
women's college in Oakland. Always a busy career woman, Violet
started out as a secretary for her lawyer father, and within a few years
she was working for a judge of the United States Circuit Court of Appeals in Portland, Oregon. She met George around 1914, just a few
years after he moved to Portland from Chicago and started his own
architecture business. The two married in 1915 on Valentine's Day.
Around the time she met George, Violet testified of being healed of
"chronic stomach and bowel trouble" and a "lifelong throat trouble"
through the work of a Christian Science practitioner. Then, after doing
her own year-long study of Mary Baker Eddy's textbook, Violet testified about overcoming the need to wear glasses, as well as the instantaneous healing she had experienced of a "stubborn physical ailment,"
proving the effectiveness of "steady, persistent effort." By the time Violet was put in charge of the Fourth Church building project, she was a
dedicated Christian Scientist, and was serving as Second Reader at
Sixth Church in Portland, where she and George were members. Her
communications suggest that part of her work for the Fourth Church
design project was spiritual, prayerful. Violet was known for her
"boundless energy." One associate later described Violet as "the original go-girl," sharing how her "infectious enthusiasm makes all her activities successful." She would need that energy for the launch of the
Fourth Church project, guiding the building committee in these critical
early months of the project.[413]

When faced with choices, the building committee often went with
the better—and more costly—option. Besides choosing steel trusses
over wood, they chose full terra-cotta exterior tiling instead of brick
with terra-cotta trim, and they chose tile for all four sides of the building instead of finishing with painted stucco on the two less visible
sides, as Third Church had done. They chose granite front steps over
concrete. They chose copper roofing for the dome over tin. They even
splurged on hot water for the sinks in the readers bathrooms and two
drinking fountains in the halls. So many extras added tens of thousands of dollars to the cost of the project. The one cost-cutting decision
they made was to eliminate the two electric fireplaces the architect had
originally planned for the foyer.

The building was going to be very expensive, and they had nowhere
near the amount needed in their building fund. They needed to raise
$30,000 to qualify for a mortgage for $75,000 from Seattle Title and

Trust Company. But this would only get the project started. They would need more funds later. At the June 12 membership meeting, through a proxy vote, the members approved the project with Dunham as architect and McDonald as contractor. The committee was "joyfully on its way in the good work of completing its building." They prepared a statement to be read by their First Reader at church services requesting more generous contributions from the congregation. Jensen notified Mrs. Dunham that the project was approved and the committee wanted "to proceed with full speed ahead."[414]

Violet had already done a preliminary design of the steel trusses, but had been holding off on final design work for the membership approval. Now that they had approval, Violet was under pressure to produce the revised design. "Please hurry plans. McDonald at a stand still" were the only words in Jensen's June 28 letter to the architect's office. McDonald's crew finished the Third Church project earlier than expected, and they had already moved to the Eighth and Seneca job site. McDonald needed the plans for final cost estimation. Violet sent two sets of preliminary plans for McDonald to work with while she was completing the design revisions. There were twenty-seven steel trusses to design. Violet supervised two engineers and two draftsmen who were working and checking calculations as fast as they could. She even had them working (against their objections) on Monday, July 3—what might have otherwise been a four-day holiday weekend. She tried to help them as best she could. Meanwhile, she was taking phone calls from steel contractors competing to be the suppliers. There was a little tussle over the steel contractors because McDonald had his own ideas about the best steel supplier. Hutson ended up having a long-distance telephone conversation with George. This brief quarrel over cost, quality, reliability of delivery, and authority over subcontractors seemed to shake Violet's self-confidence a bit. "Am doing all I can to get Mr. Dunham back—he is doing all he can too," Violet wrote to the building committee. But despite the intense pressure, Violet completed the work and sent the final plans to Seattle on July 3—right on schedule for the originally planned July 5 start date.[415]

As soon as the construction work began, Fourth Church moved its services to the Wilkes Theatre at Fifth Avenue and Pine Street. The Wilkes Theatre, built in 1909, was a live theater playhouse that also showed movies. The managers had announced plans for a major remodel of the 1,600-seat theater to turn it into "a modern motion picture palace" with new seats and curtains and "a blaze of electric lights" outside on Fifth Avenue. But these plans were not fulfilled; instead, the theater became a place for civic meetings, political rallies, and on Sundays and Wednesdays, a Christian Science church. Church representatives had searched the city for an alternative meeting place, and this was the best they could find. Fourth Church announced its temporary move with a large display advertisement in the *Seattle Times*. Then they held a Christian Science lecture by former medical professional Dr. John M. Tutt at their new Wilkes Theatre location.[416]

At a regular weekly building committee meeting that summer, Hutson shared that he had been approached by two labor union managers who wanted to discuss the union affiliation of the workers on the Fourth Church building project. They were concerned that some of the workers were not members of any union. This issue was a contentious politically polarizing one. Seattle had strong labor unions and a history of unions showing their strength through strikes and other forms of activism. Just a few years earlier in 1919, there had been a massive general strike involving more than 65,000 workers that had brought Seattle to a standstill for five days. The event had threatened to turn violent, even revolutionary, establishing a reputation for Seattle as a stronghold of socialist ideology similar to what triggered the Communist revolution in Russia in 1917. In subsequent years in Seattle, tensions continued between the working class and large business owners. Having been so involved in politics—and not necessarily on the side of the unions—Hutson would surely have seen this as a highly sensitive issue for this large, diverse congregation and also for his new career in private law practice. At the committee meeting, Hutson pointed out that according to their construction contract, decisions on hiring and wages were entirely the responsibility of Neil McDonald. Anyone concerned about union rules needed to talk to Mr. McDonald. To prove this point beyond any doubt, the chairman was about to read the contract out loud to the committee when McDonald came into the room.

McDonald came to the weekly building committee meetings to give progress reports and discuss issues with the committee. He was "asked for his version of the labor situation" as it concerned the church. At this, McDonald "merely smiled." He assured the committee that all the workers were union except for the common day laborers, and they were receiving union scale wages. With the exception of those two union managers, "every one is satisfied." McDonald said, "Leave it to me." That was the end of the issue.[417]

By mid-July, McDonald was discussing the concrete pour for the auditorium floor with the committee. It was still many weeks ahead, but some important decisions were best made first. He needed to know the heating system design and the type of organ so the air ducts could be framed into the concrete floor. There were still questions about plumbing and wiring to be resolved.

To assist the project, Violet was in communication with the building committee, the architect, the contractor, the engineers, and the city building department. She made sure everyone involved had the plans, the specifications, and the recommendations they needed. Violet sent a Portland heating engineer up to the Seattle building site to consult with McDonald. She assured the committee that this building would have good ventilation. They were checking over the shop drawings from the steel contractor and planning out the placement details of the terra-cotta exterior tiles. "We feel that the work is progressing nicely, and without any delays," Violet reported.[418]

The most critical parts of the design were done on schedule, as expected. The architect's office had much smoother communications and working relationship with Fourth Church than they had had with Third Church. Violet had successfully overseen the launch of the second unit project. But the building committee wanted to hear from the architect himself. He had been gone longer than expected—two full months. "Where is my little friend George Foot, I miss his smiling countenance?" came a friendly letter "unofficially" to Violet mid-July. Ten days later, the question was repeated more officially and with a less friendly tone. It was relayed that Mr. Hutson needed to reach Mr. Dunham directly, urgently. Unfortunately, it was difficult to know exactly where he was. Violet had received a wire from him that he was headed back by train via the Canadian route. He was expected to arrive in Seattle at the Frye Hotel the next Sunday, July 30. That meant he could meet with the building committee that Monday.[419]

Violet wrote back apologetically to Jensen, "He has been detained much against his desire, but all things work out, and we will surely be glad to have him home again."[420]

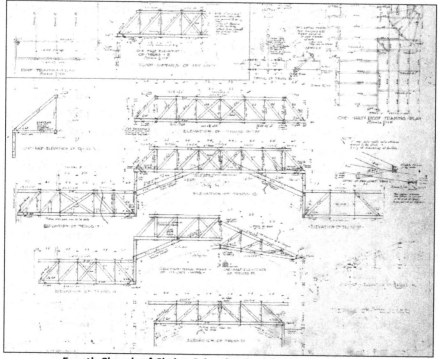

Fourth Church of Christ, Scientist, Seattle, roof truss plans

41

Elevation (1922)

The urgent issue at the noontime building committee meeting on Monday, July 31, 1922, was the question of the alley grade at the back of the Fourth Church of Christ, Scientist, Seattle, building. Neil McDonald, their construction contractor, was in attendance at the meeting at Charles T. Hutson's law office in the Hoge Building, as was George F. Dunham, their architect, just returned from more than two months travel in the East. There was a concern that the design of the church might need to be altered because of possible changes to the elevation of the alley, and this raised further issues about the supervisory responsibility for the construction project. Mr. Hutson, the chair, wanted Mr. Dunham to explain the alley grade he used for the design for the first unit of the building five years earlier, because the city engineer's office had no specific grade on record and apparently the city was now considering making street elevation changes. That could affect part of the new church building. Besides interior changes possibly needed, production of the terra-cotta tiles was being delayed until the question of the alley grade was resolved. Mr. McDonald had stopped all work on the project. Hutson wanted to know who made the alley grade and by what authority?

Through the discussion that followed, the committee learned that the city had not yet formally decided the alley grade when the first unit was constructed. Dunham had based his whole building design on a grade level determined by Mr. Duffy, the engineer hired for the first unit. Someone needed to speak with Duffy to find out how he determined the grade level. Hutson was of the opinion that if Duffy got the grade from the city, the city was legally responsible. Fourth Church had already had to deal with an issue of financial liability relating to the alley after construction of the first unit. The sidewalk had settled near the alley. The City of Seattle Department of Streets and Sewers believed it was caused by water flow from the basement excavation tunneling under the sidewalk. Since the city considered this to be the fault of Fourth Church, they were responsible for repairs. Now the church was dealing with additional issues over the alley because of a paving project for Spring and Seneca Streets. Considering how much regrading work had been going on in downtown Seattle in previous decades, sometimes resulting in architecturally significant first-floor entrances of major buildings ending up far below or above the eventual sidewalk level, it was a serious concern with potentially long-term unfortunate and somewhat embarrassing ramifications. This brought construction work to a halt.[421]

There were further questions about who was ultimately responsible for decisions on the project. In the discussion, Dunham explained that he charged 6% of the total project cost when he did both the design and superintendency. When he supplied only the plans, he took 4%, plus extra charges as needed to cover his expenses for consultation. This was the arrangement he had with Fourth Church. Dunham simply said he preferred the 4% plan. By implication, this put responsibility for the alley grade on the building committee. Hutson then asked McDonald if he could continue on the construction work. McDonald said he could as soon as he received the alley grade and some other design details.

That week Hutson spoke with Duffy about the original grade level. The City of Seattle had a half dozen different grade levels on file for this alley, and none of them could be said with any certainty to be final. But as far as Duffy could tell, the grade from five years ago was still the one being used by the city. At their next meeting, the whole committee met at the construction site and walked along the alley, devoting the entire meeting to this important issue. They inspected the part of the building that might be impacted by future changes to the grade. They decided that the only practical solution was to continue using the alley grade tentatively given by the city engineer's office five years earlier. They were of the opinion that "this will eventually be THE permanent level."[422]

Having finally settled the question, the project could move forward again. The building committee could now focus on making the next urgent decision.

Elevation (1922)

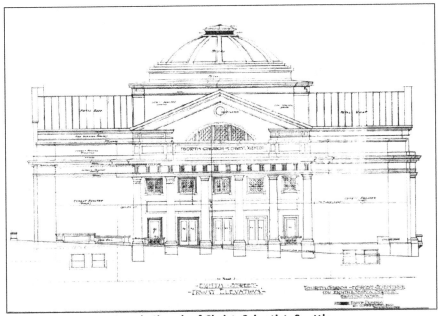

Fourth Church of Christ, Scientist, Seattle
Eighth Street - Front Elevation

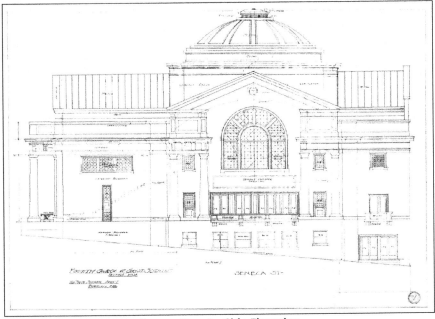

Seneca Street – Side Elevation

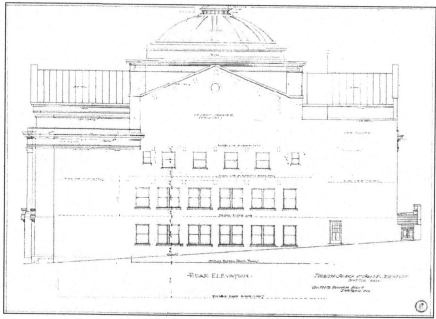

Alley Side - Rear Elevation

42

Terra-Cotta (1922)

The day after the building committee for Fourth Church of Christ, Scientist, made their noontime inspection of the alley, they made another field trip. At nine o'clock on the morning of Tuesday, August 8, 1922, the building committee plus several board members assembled at the corner of Second Avenue and Madison Street where two trolley lines crossed. The members may have traveled to their meeting place using public transportation, and perhaps they could have taken the train line called the "interurban" south toward their destination, but instead, for their morning journey together, Neil McDonald and Ben S. Booth provided for their use two automobiles—referred to as "machines." The party of ten traveled about thirty miles south to the town of Auburn, where they visited the manufacturing plant of the Northern Clay Company.[423]

Out of all the bids for supplying the terra-cotta tile for siding the new church edifice, the two lowest bids were essentially the same price. The committee left it to Mr. McDonald to decide, and he selected the Northern Clay Company over the Denny Renton Company, which had provided the tile for Third Church. The terra-cotta was a large portion of the construction budget. Using terra-cotta instead of brick added $12,000 to the cost. Putting terra-cotta on all four sides of the building added another $6,000. Northern Clay's winning low bid was about $34,000—a sizable portion of the entire project cost, which started out at $100,000, but with all the extras added had risen to $150,000—and would continue to rise.[424]

Terra-cotta was a very popular siding for commercial and public buildings at that time. The ceramic tile facing was less expensive than stone, lighter than brick. It was an effective fireproofing, and it was resistant to water stains and air pollution. Prior to 1905 when the Auburn factory became the first local manufacturer, terra-cotta was very expensive because it had to be shipped from the East Coast. But now that there was an affordable local supply, all the best new buildings in Seattle were using it. The Frederick & Nelson's Department Store, the Coliseum Theatre, the Joshua Green Building, the Dexter Horton Building, the Olympic Hotel, the Northern Life Tower, the Federal Office Building, and the Washington Mutual Savings Bank building, all were sided with terra-cotta, all from the Northern Clay Company.

The Northern Clay Company used clay dug along the Green River near the plant. The tiles were custom designed to fit each building. The clay was laid out in the drafting room, cut to a precise size allowing for shrinkage, artistically crafted in the modeling room, then coaxed to a uniform thickness in the plaster of paris room. In the pressing room, a cast for a mold was made with which the tile could be mass-produced. The tiles were glazed in a satin finish, primarily in ivory white, but colors were also available for ornamental highlights. The factory had three high-temperature terra-cotta kilns, heated with coal from the local mines of Black Diamond. The firing process for each batch took several days.[425]

The reason for the Fourth Church visit to the plant was simply to select the color for the tile. The group looked at many color samples. There was a special room for this purpose, but the members took the samples outside so they could see how the tile looked in natural daylight. In the sunshine "the delicate coloring effect" was "more pronounced." They spent about an hour looking at the samples before deciding. They picked a satin finish in an ivory color, "a shade most pleasing to the eye, and which would not reflect glossily in the glare of the sun." The committee's choice was unanimous.[426]

With the terra-cotta tile selection work done, the church group headed back to Seattle. Meanwhile, the manufacturers got to work on their order.

Fourth Church of Christ, Scientist, Seattle, terra-cotta tile

43

Primitive Christianity (1922)

When they laid the cornerstone for Fourth Church of Christ, Scientist, in 1922, the walls on the opposite side of the building, those facing the alley and the adjoining parcel, were already three feet above the second story floor. They started construction for the second unit, the foyer level and auditorium, in July, but did not lay the cornerstone until the end of October. The dramatically uneven wall construction—so out of sequence with the normal order for construction projects—may have been related to the delivery delay for the terra-cotta tiles. A fire in one of the kilns at the Auburn plant had slowed down the manufacturing and some of the work on Fourth Church was being held up as a result. But the cornerstone ceremony and the notice in the newspaper the following day may have been intentionally timed—influenced by a desire to lay the cornerstone and announce it on dates of special significance.[427]

The cornerstone was laid during an "unostentatious service" at 8:00 a.m. on the last Sunday in October. Church officers gathered for a quiet ceremony on the sidewalk at Eighth Avenue near Seneca Street. The focus of popular culture that week was on costume parties, pumpkins, black cats, ghosts, witches, and the general mischief-making associated with Halloween. But Halloween was not the only holiday associated with the end of October. The last Sunday in October has special significance in Christian history. It was Reformation Sunday, a day commemorating Martin Luther's most important written work, his controversial commentary on ways Christianity had gotten off track under the leadership of the Catholic Pope. Luther nailed his *Ninety-five Theses* to the door of the All Saints' Church in Wittenburg, Germany, in protest on October 31, 1517. For this Luther was branded a blasphemer and worse by church leaders. But to those who joined his protest movement, he was a Christian reformer.[428]

The end of October also has special significance in Christian Science history. The very first Christian Science church edifice, built in 1886 in Oconto, Wisconsin, was dedicated on Reformation Sunday. But the significance of the day goes back even farther, to 1875, when the first edition of Mary Baker Eddy's most important written work, *Science and Health with Key to the Scriptures* was published on October 30. Eddy began her chapter "Science of Being" with Martin Luther's famous words: "Here I stand. I can do no otherwise; so help me God! Amen!" Like Luther, Eddy was branded a blasphemer and worse by many Christian leaders. But to those who joined the Christian Science movement, she was a Christian reformer. She protested the prevailing theology that caused Christians to think of Jesus' command to "heal the sick" (Matt. 10:8) as no longer necessary or even possible. Her protest brought her some notoriety among orthodox clergy, some of whom considered her teachings not truly Christian. The laying of the Fourth Church cornerstone was announced in the Seattle newspaper on the anniversary of the first printing of Eddy's book.[429]

An essay by Robert G. Reichert on the architectural style for Fourth Church found in their historical files explained that he believed George Foote Dunham's design was intended to represent church architecture of the second century Roman style. The building expressed the spirit of Reverend Eddy's efforts to "reinstate primitive Christianity and its lost element of healing." Reichert explained, "The 2nd Century was the great Christian healing era," and Eddy's book embodied "her discovery of original Christian healing." Reichert was an architect who had earned his Master's degree in architecture at Harvard, had toured the great cathedrals in Europe, and taught occasionally in the architecture program at the University of Washington. He wrote his essay half a century after the Fourth Church edifice was completed. On the day of the cornerstone ceremony in 1922, Reichert was an infant in North Dakota, but since he moved to Seattle in 1948, he may have personally known some of the members involved in the Fourth Church building project. According to Reichert, Dunham's design was modeled after the Pantheon in Rome. The intention was to emulate this building style used during New Testament era biblical times when the followers of Peter and Paul began establishing meeting places for the Jews who were the primitive Christians, and whose customs and practices at church meetings were "typical of Jewish practice": focused on the reading of the scriptures — as it was at Christian Science church services. "It must be remembered," Reichert wrote, "that the wonderful Gothic pointed arch style buildings which today are regarded as 'churchy' church buildings did not appear architecturally until the 12th Century," and so the Pantheon style was "architecturally considered as the genuine or real Church type." Fourth Church would provide visitors "a very true picture of the original Christian Temple. Here one can walk through the porticoed entrances just the same as did Paul of the Bible."[430]

Around the time he wrote his "Architectural Historiology," Robert Reichert was walking through that second-century-style church portico regularly—after parking his Harley-Davidson motorcycle. Reichert was widely known in Seattle for his motorcycle and biker outfit. He wore black-leather boots and jacket, ripped denim jeans, and a "cap pulled so low you could barely see his eyes." He had such an unusual "tough and cool" look that it was easy to assume, as *Seattle Times* columnist Eric Lacitis did before interviewing him in 1979, that Reichert was a high school dropout thug who had never given up the wild life. "He looked like he could have been Marlon Brando's sidekick in 'The Wild One,' the classic movie about bikers," Lacitis wrote. But whenever Reichert arrived at his destination, he changed into a business suit. Reichert was, though, in fact, a wild one. He did his rule-breaking and hell-raising as an outspoken avant-garde architect. As architecture historian Jeffrey Murdock explained, "Reichert believed that the creation of architecture was a spiritual, artistic process, and he rebelled against the rationalist architectural trends of the mid-20th century." Reichert created provocative residential designs using triangular and trapezoidal shapes that would still look far ahead of their time, even decades later. Eventually, he would be recognized by modern architecture enthusiasts as an "independent visionary," but his unusual designs, especially his own residence in Queen Anne, were not always appreciated by neighbors. Reichert knew something about what it meant to go against norms and traditions. "I paid for it," he later shared. "People would dump garbage on my driveway. Nice people would curse." Perhaps this made him all the more appreciative of the controversy and hostility Mary Baker Eddy faced in her career.[431]

Besides his appreciation of the architectural style of Fourth Church, Reichert also loved to play its organ. Reichert was a longtime church member, a dedicated Christian Scientist. "I religiously don't believe in age," Reichert explained in the interview for the *Seattle Times*. He would ride his Harley and wear his biker outfit for many decades. This "iconoclast artist" had fully embraced the practice of timeless thinking that Mary Baker Eddy taught. Radical thinking would be encouraged in the children who would soon attend Christian Science Sunday School within the Fourth Church walls actively under construction on Reformation Sunday in 1922. The church officers present for the October 29 cornerstone service could only walk through the second-century-style portico that day in their imagination, since construction of the planned columns was still months away. Perhaps those officers also at least momentarily considered the many generations of people of every type and background that would walk through the doors of this church long into the future. Perhaps they also wondered how long it would be before Mary Baker Eddy's reformation would be recognized universally. "I love the orthodox church," Eddy had written, "and, in time, that church will love Christian Science" —words well known by all the members of the Fourth Church building committee.[432]

The cornerstone was placed to the right of the portico, near the farthest right door, where members would enter the building for private meetings. The location for the cornerstone was a last-minute design change by Mr. Dunham. The granite block with its simple engraving, "Fourth Church of Christ, Scientist, A.D. 1922," would quietly offer a reminder of their grand cause each time they entered the building. Construction on the walls on the Eighth Avenue and Seneca Street sides of the building began the day after the ceremony.

To get to this point in the construction, the building committee had passed through the fiery trial of a furnace fiasco. The original heater installed in the basement for the first unit had proved to be inadequate, even for heating only the Sunday School level. For the second unit, the heating system was completely redesigned by another specialist. However, the committee realized that even the new improved furnace would be woefully inadequate for heating the entire building. A "fog of doubt and misunderstanding" enveloped the "astounded" building team. When confronted with the issue at a committee meeting, Dunham was at a loss to explain how his recommended specialist, who was supposedly the best heating engineer west of the Mississippi, could have made such significant errors in calculations. The extra eight to twelve thousand dollars needed to make the changes to provide adequate heating was yet another unexpected expense. The total estimated cost for the construction project had risen to $200,000 by the time the cornerstone was laid. Now they needed to raise $38,000 quickly so they could get another loan for $75,000, in addition to the extra $8,000 that Miss Jessie Estep had recently loaned the church. This meant writing another letter about financial needs for the First Reader to announce to the congregation at services.[433]

In early November Neil McDonald's crew, weather permitting, would begin pouring the concrete for the auditorium floor, a ten-day effort. Ideally, the building committee would have already made the decision on the pipe organ so the right type of blower duct could be framed into the right place before the concrete was poured. The selection of the organ was clearly an important one to the committee, but they had not yet had time to research the options. They immediately started the process. They had sales representatives from several organ companies make site visits to the church so that the committee would at least be aware of possible installation issues before the concrete pour was done. They also asked advice from trusted sources, including local organists.

Then an unexpected issue arose mid-November that put new pressure on everyone involved with the construction project. Urgent action was needed. The managers of the Wilkes Theatre, where Fourth Church had been holding its services, had ordered the Christian Scientists to vacate the building. Negotiations were underway to convert the Fifth and Pine building to a retail department store, and they wanted Fourth Church out by November 20. McDonald promised to rush the work of getting the basement level ready for use again as a temporary auditorium. It was completed just in time for services there on November 26. Fourth Church advertised their return to Eighth and Seneca with a "Removal Notice" in the *Seattle Times*. For the first couple of weeks, including the special Thanksgiving Day service on November 30, church attendees had to walk through the recently delivered stacks of terra-cotta tiles to get to the door.[434]

On December 18, the building committee had a meeting with the board and McDonald. They had already heard sales presentations from three organ vendors. They had already received letters of recommendations from trusted organ owners. As a final step, they heard reports from two expert consultants. Then they voted by ballot. Eight out of the twelve agreed with organist John Hamilton Howe that the Austin Organs company, located in Hartford, Connecticut, and represented in Seattle by Charles J. Whittaker, "offered the most in the way of a church organ." They were very impressed with the Austin presentation. "Obviously, Mr. Whittaker knows organs," clerk Paul J. Jensen commented.[435]

There were still so many decisions to make and so much to do. They hoped to have the second unit ready by the end of the next summer.

Considering that goal, nearly everything was both important and urgent. There was never a dull weekly meeting for the Fourth Church building committee. But even with so much still to do, the building committee took two weeks off in recognition of Christmas.

**Granite cornerstone at Fourth Church of Christ, Scientist, Seattle
laid on Reformation Sunday, Oct. 29, 1922**

44

Art Glass (1922)

T here was one important benefit for Fourth Church of Christ, Scientist, Seattle, from George F. Dunham's extended travels in the East during the summer of 1922. That benefit related to their art glass windows. Mr. Dunham had the opportunity to visit the Dannenhoffer Glass Works factory in Brooklyn, New York, and he came away with some new ideas for the design of the windows for the edifice under construction in downtown Seattle. During one of his visits with the building committee, he shared his new inspiration. The windows would be a very important architectural feature of the church—indeed, the very identity of the building. It was well worth putting top quality into the stained glass. He proposed huge arch-shaped windows. The design was similar to those at Second Church of Christ, Scientist, in the upper west side of Manhattan on Central Park West.[436]

Dunham had specified Dannenhoffer art glass even before his visit to the factory. They were, after all, known to be the largest manufacturers of opalescent, hand-rolled, and drapery glass in the East—and the very best. Church building projects for every denomination throughout the country used Dannenhoffer. As far as Dunham was concerned, no other art glass supplier was even worth considering.

The founder of the Brooklyn company, John Dannenhoffer, was "a pioneer of pioneers in glassmaking." For Dunham to have visited the factory at all was a special privilege, because the details of their processes and formulas was a carefully protected secret. Dannenhoffer was known as "the best color producer in the world," according to the *Brooklyn Eagle,* which explained, "His blending of the different chemicals through which the various colors are made, was something short of marvelous." They started with Massachusetts white sand and then added soda ash, alkali, and metallic oxide. They added other substances to create colors. To make ruby red, they added flakes of twenty-four-carat gold to the mix. The ingredients for each batch were "twirled and whirled round and round," then shoveled into pots and heated to 3,500 degrees. Once everything had melted to a red-hot lump, it was pulled like homemade taffy, flattened out onto a sheet and then gradually cooled in ovens. When extra effects were desired, graceful ripple patterns could be created by pulling and twisting an iron prong through the sheets while the glass was still pliable. Both the company founder and his son John had studied chemistry, but the glass manufacturing process was still viewed as something of an art—with less than completely reliable results. "As one might say in a whisper," John Dannenhoffer revealed in a 1905 interview with the *New York Times*, "there are only two things more uncertain—the mood of a woman and the heels of a mule. We, for instance, never know exactly how the shades will be in the finished product." The high cost for their glass—hundreds of dollars for each window—was due in part to the fact that twenty times as much glass was rejected, broken, and discarded, as what ended up being shipped out for an order.[437]

When Dunham visited the factory, neither the founding Dannenhoffer nor his more ambitious sons John and Nicholas were still running this famous company begun in 1888. A third-generation family member, George Bernard Dannenhoffer, had been sufficiently trained in supervising the secret process that the company was still going. Dannenhoffer Glass Works only manufactured the glass. The glass sheets they produced needed to be cut and the pieces assembled by craftsmen who specialized in the art of stained glass windows. In Dunham's view, the only craftsman in the Pacific Northwest qualified to do a sufficiently "acceptable, artistic job" was David L. Povey, owner of Povey Brothers Glass Company in Portland, Oregon. Mr. Povey had done the work for the Dannenhoffer windows for both First and Third Churches of Christ, Scientist in Seattle. He had proven mastery of a general style and specification for art glass windows that had been used "so often" in Christian Science churches that it was "sometimes referred to as 'Christian Science glass.'" Dunham brought Povey to a Fourth Church building committee meeting in November, and together they presented several sketched ideas for consideration. Then in January, Povey sent a full-size sample window for one of the smaller openings, demonstrating their skillful use of Dannenhoffer glass.[438]

A representative from the Belknap Glass Company came to show some samples and offered a bid to do all the same glass work for about half the price. The building committee was expected, as a general rule, to use the lowest bidder, but they stuck with Dunham's recommendation, at least for the auditorium windows. However, they saved some money by using the lower cost Belknap Glass Company for all the other windows in the church. They placed their order with Dannenhoffer in February 1923 expecting the windows to be ready to install in six months, during the final phase of construction. They ordered "Amber Flesh and Opal glass in light and medium densities." Dunham specified that the windows would be shaded darker at the top of the window, and the source of light would be considered so that the overall appearance would be balanced. They would use only the best grade of the glass, perfectly blended.[439]

The interior decoration color scheme for the entire church was coordinated with the art glass windows. Dunham's wife Violet was involved in the color recommendations. George and Violet brought armfuls of color swatches and flooring material samples to a building committee meeting to show and discuss. They recommended mulberry tone carpet in the auditorium and gray linoleum and grey tile in the foyer. For wall tint they suggested "proper proportions of raw umber, burnt sienna and vermillion," for the woodwork an ivory finish, and for the birch wood pews a brown mahogany wood stain with a rubbed varnish finish.[440]

On April 23, 1923, fourteen cases of art glass were loaded by Dannenhoffer onto the steamer ship *Corbus*, scheduled to leave New York on May 2. The *Corbus* was headed first for the Port of San Francisco—a 5,000-mile ocean journey through the Panama Canal that took about four weeks—and then north, reaching Portland a few days later. Dannenhoffer had to convince this steamer company to prioritize the glass cases to get it on this ship. Even so, the shipment arrived in Portland on June 11, two weeks later than expected, but anticipating its arrival, Mr. Povey was already set up with drawings laid out and marked for cutting the glass so he could start working as soon as the glass was unpacked. The Dunhams made daily visits to the Povey Brothers Glass Company workroom at Fifth and Flanders to make sure the work was staying on schedule. The art glass windows were ready in time for July 5 installation—right on schedule. Povey shipped them to Seattle on Independence Day.[441]

The window installation may not have begun on Thursday, July 5, however, because it was practically a second holiday that year—at least it was in the Seattle area. The same day the art glass windows were traveling from Portland to Seattle, also en route from Portland to Seattle was the president of the United States of America. President Warren G. Harding was on a public speaking tour of the western United States, starting from Saint Louis, the gateway to the West. In anticipation of Harding's arrival to the Puget Sound area, the United States Naval fleet was amassing in Elliott Bay, making for an especially exciting Independence Day for Seattle. The president was scheduled to pass through Tacoma on his way to the Alaska Territory. Seattle residents traveled by car, train, and boat to the Tacoma Stadium where Harding spoke to an enthusiastic crowd of more than 25,000 people standing out in the "cold, drizzling rain" to hear the words of their country's chief executive. Thousands more waited on the streets during "driving, heavy rain," cheering and waving their American flags, hoping to catch a glimpse of the president as he passed by in his flag-draped Cadillac. As the president's ship left the Port of Tacoma headed north, the roar of the crowds on the beaches, it was reported, could be heard two miles offshore. The presidential ship with its battleship escorts detoured briefly through Elliott Bay, then headed north for a three-week tour of Alaska.[442]

When President Harding returned on July 27, it was a very big day of patriotic celebration in Seattle—a presidential holiday. Planned events with the president included a downtown parade with marching band music and special events at Volunteer Park, Woodland Park, and the University of Washington Stadium. Elliott Bay was full of anchored navy ships, arranged in a four-mile line. At the head of all the battleships, the first to greet the incoming presidential ship with a 21-gun salute and the national anthem was an armored cruiser named the *USS Seattle*.[443]

Seattle was feeling its strength. The president's visit showed the extent to which this frontier town had become a world-class city. Some were calling it "Queen City" because of its beautiful parks and boulevards. Other boosters dubbed it "The Wonder City," claiming it to be the youngest city of its size in the world. That summer the residents of Seattle were singing and dancing to a melody called "Seattle Town" by Seattle's own popstar composer Harold Weeks. Mr. Weeks, who was a Christian Scientist and would one day serve on the board of Fourth Church, had been a nationally known ragtime composer since his junior year at Queen Anne High School. Weeks is best known today for his 1918 smash hit "Hindustan," which was widely played by dance orchestras and subsequently became a jazz standard. The *Seattle Times* featured the catchy "Seattle Town" as a local hit that was sure to sweep the nation, as so many of Weeks' other songs had.

DEDICATION

Seattle Town, Seattle Town,
I've a love in my heart for you,
You're my own town, home town true,
And there's no other place like you,
Your harbor fair, Beyond compare,
Is the port where the dream ships all come true,
When away I am always yearning,
For the happy day I'll be returning,
Seattle Town, Seattle Town

Harold Weeks' quixotic ditty expressed a persistent local belief that there was something truly special about Seattle. Besides unusual scenic beauty and abundant natural resources, the city possessed an unrelenting optimism referred to as "the Seattle Spirit." The Seattle Spirit included an imaginative vision for a better future, the enthusiastic promotion of good ideas, a desire to overcome all obstacles, a willingness to work together. Since the early pioneer days of the 1870s, civic cheerleaders noted the Seattle Spirit expressing itself in the efforts to bring the railroad to Seattle, rebuild the city after the fire in 1889, promote the city as the provisioning stop for the Alaska gold rush, create the highly successful Alaska-Yukon-Pacific Exposition in 1909, develop the University of Washington campus, and establish the shipyards. The city boasted continuing rapid growth, one of the tallest buildings in the world outside of New York City, and now its battleship namesake was leading the United States Navy as its flagship. Yet Seattle still had so much greater potential to be realized. The editor of the *Seattle Times*, C. B. Blethen, declared Seattle to be "the loveliest city in which to live in the whole world." A front page headline affirmed the "city's growing supremacy."[444]

Midway through Seattle's celebratory summer of patriotic fervor, this high of civic spirit was sadly sobered by an unexpected and most unfortunate turn. Just after the president left Seattle, tragedy struck. Harding was feeling ill as he boarded the train, and just after arriving in San Francisco, he suddenly died. A shocked nation went into mourning over the loss of a very popular leader. Seattle immediately put its organizational abilities toward planning memorial services for twenty-ninth President of the United States.

On Tuesday, August 7, at First Church of Christ, Scientist, in Seattle, there was a joint meeting of the boards of the seven branch churches. They discussed the idea of holding memorial services for President Harding that Friday, the day of the presidential funeral. Churches of all denominations were planning memorial services, some of them uniting in impressive public ceremonies. Even the Russian Greek Orthodox Church, a community of recent immigrants, "shared in the nation's sorrow." The Christian Scientists unanimously agreed to hold memorial services, but each branch separately. A telegram from the Board of Directors at the Mother Church in Boston pointed them to the order of services used for President William McKinley's memorial service in 1901. The Christian Science Reading Rooms were closed and memorial services were held in their church auditoriums at 11 a.m. Most businesses in Seattle were closed that day, and even the trains stopped for five minutes of silence at noon. As the *Seattle Times* put it,

> from sea to sea, as the nation stilled its busy life a moment in reverence, there seemed to breathe a message from his countrymen, saying: "Well done, thou good and faithful servant."

The seven Churches of Christ, Scientist, Seattle, also united in sending a letter of sympathy to the First Lady, at the initiative of Fourth Church.[445]

Throughout all the unusual events of that summer, the Fourth Church building committee continued its work uninterrupted. For the last phase of construction—the installation of the auditorium flooring, the pews, and the pipe organ—each member of the committee was responsible for monitoring progress at the church one day of the week. Ideally they would have liked to install the pipe organ first, then the auditorium carpet, and the pews last. But the pews arrived first—all 2,025 ½ linear feet of them. They had come by train from the American Seating Company factory in Manitowoc, Wisconsin (about 80 miles north of Oconto, where the first Christian Science church edifice was built in 1886). There was concern that the curved pews might unbend if left stored in the foyer too long, so they asked the Frederick & Nelson flooring department to expedite the mulberry carpet shipment from Philadelphia so they could start installing the pews as soon as possible. There were some delays because the pews did not fit perfectly into the auditorium. According to Dunham, the manufacturer's designer had misread the blueprints. Some on-site modifications were needed. General contractor Neil McDonald wanted to attach the pews to the reinforced concrete floor with smaller bolts than those provided by the manufacturer, which added another delay. But when the church auditorium opened for services, even the pipe organ had been successfully installed.[446]

DEDICATION

The grand opening of the completed building was on Sunday, September 23, 1923. It was a very busy week for the members of Fourth Church. Besides their usual two Sunday services, and their usual Wednesday evening testimony meeting, they held public lectures on Thursday and Friday.[447]

Like the art glass in their church windows, their lecturer, Charles I. Ohrenstein, was from New York. And like Jacob S. Shields, their lecturer at the Hippodrome at the start of their building project in 1915, Mr. Ohrenstein was known to have been Jewish prior to becoming a Christian Scientist. Ohrenstein had previously lectured for Fourth Church in 1917. That Fourth Church so heavily favored the two Christian Science lecturers of Jewish heritage, inviting them for major event series before, during, and after their building project was likely not a coincidence. Their choice of lecturers may have been a nod to the Jewish primitive Christians who, according Robert G. Reichert, inspired the design of their building, and also to the Jewish Christian Scientists who, according to one study, may have comprised as much as ten percent of the members of Christian Science churches in cities like New York and Chicago. At that time, Jews fleeing persecution in Europe were coming to the United States in large numbers. Many of these new Americans found Christian Science appealing. Mr. Shields believed that no one had to give up anything good about the Jewish religion or any other religion to come into Christian Science, it only added to the essence of all other religions. "Christian Science is no more for one or the other faction or creed than mathematics or music," he explained. At a time when Jews often faced some degree of antisemitism even in America, Christian Scientists as a whole were tolerant, sympathetic, and even supportive to Jews—especially at Fourth Church, as shown by its generous and public contribution to the Jewish relief fund prior to the war.[448]

Everyone coming to the church during opening week was among the first to see the new auditorium with its art glass windows. With no religious symbolism, as had become standard for Christian Science branch churches, the windows expressed the beauty of holiness in a way that visitors from almost any religious heritage could appreciate. As for the grand opening, according to the building committee secretary, it was "a humdinger of a success," and the art glass windows "the source of endless praise." Special notes of thanks were sent by the building committee to many of the vendors, especially the art glass craftsmen.[449]

To Neil McDonald, their ever trustworthy and reliable general contractor:

> Using a Biblical term, we are glad to say, 'Well done good and faithful servant.' You have erected a beautiful church building, and all who see it are lavish in their praises. It is our joy to thank you for the personal interest you have at all times reflected in the construction of this lovely 'structure of truth and love.' And even though your work is done, remember that the doors always swing inward for you. Come when you can, we shall always be glad to see you.[450]

To their architect, George F. Dunham:

> It is our pleasure to say for the members of this church that they are happy beyond words with their new edifice. The Sunday School room, the foyer, the auditorium, the exterior—all serve to elicit exclamations of admiration and reverence from members and non-members alike. And with each passing Wednesday, and with each fleeting Sunday, our thankfulness in the privilege of meeting in this beautiful 'structure of truth and love' grows more profound. The large foyer is delightful. It is a most congenial place in which to linger and talk and renew acquaintances. Be sure you have much of which to be proud in the construction of this exquisite church, which exhales in its noble auditorium a sweet sense of peace and love and unity.[451]

To which Dunham responded:

> I am most grateful for your words of appreciation for the finished structure. The architect who sees the finished structure mentally before the drawings are made can surely rejoice in having this structure finally brought into manifestation which is visible to the eye. All who have a part in Christian Science church building will grow through the experience, and for my part I want to express my gratitude for the wonderful work which has been done by all those connected with the building, the helpful cooperation which made it possible for us to bring out the complete expression.[452]

There was no question that the Fourth Church edifice was a magnificent work of architecture. It may have been a question how they would pay for it. At nearly $300,000, it ended up costing nearly three times the original budget. The building committee under the command of Charles T. Hutson gave the members a place to worship that was the best that money could buy. But along with the building that was such a humdinger of a success, the members also had a humdinger of a mort-gage to pay off.[453]

**Second Church of Christ, Scientist, New York City,
on Central Park West and 68th Street**

Postcard

Fourth Church of Christ, Scientist, Seattle, art glass windows

45

Seventh Church Service (1923)

At the November 21, 1923, first meeting of the finance committee at Seventh Church of Christ, Scientist, Seattle, the committee chair, Justice M. Matthews, read a brief article called "Service," consisting of a quote from Warren G. Harding:

> Service is the greatest thing in the human calendar, and the better we equip ourselves, the better we serve, because in the expansion of the mind comes the better understanding of how best to serve. No matter what your fortune in life, the greatest compensation that will come to you tomorrow or next year, or the closing year of your life will be the consciousness that you have somehow been of service, either to your friends, your state or your common country. This is the greatest thing that can happen.

This same patriotic quote from the late US President was included in a section called "Service" in the committee's lengthy report to the church board along with a quote from Mary Baker Eddy, "Giving does not impoverish us in the service of our Maker, neither does withholding enrich us." They apparently intended this pair of statements about service to sweeten the committee's unanimous recommendation to adjust church salaries downward. Before Seventh Church could move forward with building, they needed to overcome a financial deficit.[454]

An alternative approach was being taken on their building project. Perhaps the grand opening of Fourth Church just a few weeks earlier prompted them to take action. For four years, Seventh Church had been meeting at Queen Anne Hall at First Avenue West and West Roy Street. This rented room was also used for dances and club meetings. Seventh Church members wanted a church home of their own, but at

256

the pace their building project was going, it might be a very long time before they even started building. Their immediate problem was financial. They were running a deficit on basic operating expenses. The finance committee was of the opinion that it would not be "proper" to use their modest Building Fund to pay operating expenses, and in fact, they emphasized the need to accumulate more in the Building Fund so they could move forward with building an edifice, "to manifest the progress befitting an active and devoted Christian Science organization." Church salaries were by far their greatest expense. Lowering them significantly would go a long way toward balancing their budget.

Their highest paid church employee was their First Reader. At $75 per month, or $900 per year, Seventh Church was paying in the range of what other Christian Science churches in Seattle were paying their First Readers. Considerably less than many professional jobs, the salary was comparable to what a live-in housemaid earned, or a little less than the starting salary for a grade school teacher. A First Reader might spend many hours each week in prayer and spiritual study to select just the right readings and hymns for church services on Sundays and Wednesday and practicing for a smooth delivery, but it did not need to be a full-time job and much of the work could be done evenings and weekends. Second Reader, a role which had significantly fewer duties, was paid $50 per month, or $600 per year. For someone already in the public practice of Christian Science healing, a reader salary would offer compensation for possibly having to reduce their office hours because of their reader duties. For someone considering going into the public practice, a reader salary provided a steady, although modest, income for three years while he or she established a professional reputation and met the requirements for advertising in the *Christian Science Journal*. An election to the readership was an opportunity to dedicate full-time to Christian Science. But not every reader made this leap, and neither of the readers at Seventh Church were advertising a public healing practice. Seventh Church had such a small congregation—only about 200 adults on a typical Sunday—that the Finance Committee felt this level of pay for readers was not justified. They recommended reducing First Reader salary to $50 per month and Second Reader to $30. Reader salaries would be a little lower than what the Reading Room Librarian and Assistant Librarian were earning, positions which really were full-time jobs. The finance committee felt it would be "unjust" to reduce the salaries for the reading room staff, but that "the expense involved is out of proportion for a church of our size." They recommended instead that as soon as possible Seventh Church negotiate with another branch churches to establish a joint reading room, like First and Fourth had done at the Empire Building. But even with lowering the salaries for their readers, musicians, and the treasurer, something much more significant was needed, because their building fund balance was rising so slowly.[455]

The building committee, under the leadership of John S. Gibson, advocated for "earnest and intensive work" to raise funds. Mr. Gibson did not mean fundraiser events or solicitations. In fact, he recommended that the First Reader stop making "repeated appeals for money" at Sunday services. Gibson favored "a plan that encourages free-will offering." The intensive work he recommended for the membership was, like the expectation for his job as chair of the building committee, primarily prayer.[456]

Several articles on church building were published in the Christian Science periodicals that they had probably all read. The same article by Anna Friendlich that was published in 1908 just before First Church began their building project was republished, reminding readers that before "the walls of salvation" could appear "within the pure heart, . . . [h]eaps of rubbish must be excavated from the consciousness,—love of money, improvidence, sloth, self-indulgence, extravagance, fear of poverty, business superstitions, rainy-day prudence, unintelligent management, all that makes for lack." A new article by Ella W. Hoag emphasized the need to "rise above the temporal, mortal viewpoint of dollars and cents." Most recently, Mildred Spring Case emphasized the importance of individual service as critical to church building:

> The question, Are we ready to build? can be answered only as each individual member asks himself, Am I ready to build? If he looks within himself and finds an honest answer to that question, the aggregate result of the ballot as a whole will show better than any other way whether the membership is ready to undertake building.
>
> Am I ready to build? What does it mean for one to put "Yes" on his ballot? It means that he is ready to do his part; to do constructive thinking, and not destructive; to serve the church better than ever before, for the service rendered in the past is not enough for today; to put God first; to give up material things that the spiritual idea may unfold; to invest whole-heartedly, like the poor widow, in the best and surest of investments,—church building; . . .
>
> The result of the ballot can be safely left in Love's hands; for who would want to build if the membership is not ready? Or who would want it delayed if the time is ripe?[457]

Gibson and his family came from French Canada and now they were naturalized citizens. Gibson was a natural for the building committee because of his professional background in carpentry. He had also begun advertising locally as a Christian Science practitioner. Just a few years earlier he and his daughter Anna published an article in the *Christian Science Journal*, recounting an incident relating to financial security and personal safety that happened when Anna was a teen. In the middle of the night a burglar broke into their home on the lower west side of Queen Anne Hill and entered Anna's bedroom. The man had been searching the house for valuables to steal to support his whiskey habit. Anna opened her eyes to the dark image of a man aiming a gun in her direction. She immediately put to use what she had learned in Christian Science. "I knew that God's child could not be harmed," she shared. After a brief exchange with the man, Anna put her face into her pillow "to realize the truth for a moment." Then she lifted her head and asked, "Do you know whose presence you are in?" After the man replied "no," she proceeded to declare the presence of God. She surprised the man by telling him, "your true selfhood is God's child." She told him that she was a Christian Scientist and gave him a Sunday School lesson. Finally, she took his hand and asked him to "promise to rise above the curse of whiskey." He promised to try and left without taking any of the family's valuables. Anna concluded her story by sharing, "In our family circle the morning was spent in a happy consciousness of the wonderful manifestation of the dominion of spiritual understanding over mortal error." Mr. Gibson, who had seen the intruder leave the house through the pantry window, recounted that his younger daughter Viola had witnessed the whole scene in the bedroom feeling no fear. Corroborating Anna's testimony, he wrote, "We were all very thankful for our experience, and for what we have learned through the teachings of Christian Science."[458]

In his role as chair of the building committee, Gibson had been facing a lack of building funds—to the Christian Science way of thinking, a more subtle but equally aggressive problem. Now Gibson was making an open appeal to the members for more active demonstration of what they were all learning about Christian Science and teaching all the children in their very full Sunday School. To prepare for the January 1924 business meeting, Gibson repeated Ella W. Hoag's words:

Are you as individuals ready to undertake church building? Do you as individuals see a new church?[459]

This represented a fresh approach for Seventh Church after several years of working toward building and not getting anywhere.

Back in January 1920 at their very first Sunday service, by dedicating the first collection to the building fund, they set a clear goal of having their own church building as soon as possible. They considered purchasing an existing building, Bethany Presbyterian Church, which was across the street from their Queen Anne Hall location. They appreciated being able to meet at the Bethany church for their annual membership meeting in December 1921, but when they met there again the following March to discuss purchase of the building, the members decided against it. The Bethany church seemed too small to meet their long-term need. They considered leasing the church as a temporary solution, but instead they continued at Queen Anne Hall. They wanted to stay at the foot of the hill near downtown. The next month they purchased a building lot one block north for about $6,500 and created a five-member building committee appointed by the board. The building committee's assignment was to hire an architect to draw up plans for a church to seat 600 for a cost of $40,000. The work began immediately.[460]

Their architect, by unanimous choice, was Daniel Riggs Huntington. Mr. Huntington estimated that what they really wanted would cost $75,000 for the building, plus thousands more for furnishings and the organ. They could build it in two phases, starting with the basement, as Fourth Church did. The first unit would fit their current budget. But the cost for the complete building seemed unthinkable to this small membership. They asked the architect to create a design for a complete building for $40,000.

Huntington then presented a design concept for a smaller building. The membership was willing to go ahead with this plan, but after several joint meetings of the building committee, the board, and the finance committee, the "overwhelming sentiment" was that they needed to slow down and give "time for thoughtful deliberation." As the financial planning process continued, there was "a growing conservatism" among their members. Concerns about the experiences of other branch churches were influencing them, especially regarding borrowing money. It was no longer difficult to find banks willing to finance Christian Science church projects. Seattle Title Trust Company, the bank that made the jumbo loans to Fourth Church, was willing to work with Seventh Church on a mortgage plan, but the members of Seventh Church were hesitant to borrow. As Gibson had explained, "it has come to our attention that some churches that have disposed of bonds are now facing a situation somewhat embarrassing." It was one thing to borrow funds, and it was another thing to pay the debt off.[461]

It seemed that a building project for less than $10,000 would be more prudent for Seventh Church. In response, Huntington proposed a bungalow-style building to seat 430 people for $11,500. Huntington was a local Christian Scientist and a member of First Church. Although he had only recently become a member of First Church, he had lived in Seattle since 1905 when they were holding services in the bungalow-style chapel downtown on Sixth Avenue. Huntington was almost certainly familiar with the architectural history of the Christian Science community in Seattle, and his bungalow structure was probably similar to that building. The members of Seventh Church approved the plan at a meeting on July 25, 1922, and gave the directive to proceed, knowing there was still a balance of debt on the building lot. Within a few weeks, Huntington provided sketches and a model of the design. At the next meeting on August 16, with a rising vote, the membership authorized the building committee to move forward with the bungalow project.[462]

But after the vote, a hesitancy was expressed among the membership. The board asked the committee to hold off on the final design work. That fall they held more special meetings. There was discussion, but no decisions or directives. Financial concerns were probably expressed, because the building committee scaled down the project even further. For less than the cost of the interest alone on a $40,000 building, they could build a small temporary structure that would serve the church's basic needs until they could afford something better. The concept was similar to the temporary structure that First Church had built at Sixteenth and Denny and had used for three years prior to erecting their stone edifice. Many of the members of Seventh Church had been members of First Church, so had either experienced that temporary structure or had heard about it. This temporary approach, costing between $2,700 and $3,000, would "afford simple and suitable accommodation for a growing Sunday School" and "also serve the needs of the congregation."[463]

In December, they held their annual membership meeting on the top of the hill at Queen Anne Congregational Church on the corner of Queen Anne Avenue and Galer Street. At this meeting all the building options were put on a ballot. There were five propositions. There was the original concept for $75,000, the first unit basement of that building for $30,000, the smaller building for $40,000, the bungalow for $11,500, or the temporary structure for less than $3,500. There was also a sixth option on the ballot to defer the building project. When the ballots were counted, the winning option was to defer. They put the whole project on hold.[464]

Almost nothing happened on the building project during the year 1923, and almost nothing was added to the building fund. The church was generous toward other things. They contributed to the Fifth Church building fund, a significant gift was sent to the Christian Science church in Astoria, Oregon, and a collection was taken for the Japanese Relief Fund organized by The Mother Church for "earthquake, tidal wave, and fire" aid. But there was no progress toward building. There was still debt on the building lot, and the church was still running a deficit for normal operating expenses although the members and attendants were "contributing very generously." At the end of the year at the request of the members, the finance committee was created to study the deficit problem, resulting in lowering church salaries, using better accounting practices, and putting the building fund into its own separate bank account.[465]

In January 1924, Seventh Church began the new year by taking a different approach in their work on the building project. In the spirit of the recently published articles on church building by Anna Friendlich, Ella W. Hoag, and Mildred Spring Case, the new focus was on spiritual practice—looking within. Along with more detailed information on finances and financing, the building committee's call letter asked members to search their own hearts about their own willingness to serve selflessly. Gibson asked the members:

> Are you as individuals ready to undertake church building? Do you as individuals see a new church?[466]

46

The Lot (1924)

I n the spring of 1924, there was a big change for the building committee for Seventh Church of Christ, Scientist, Seattle. John S. Gibson could no longer serve as chair. The board took the opportunity
to change the entire committee. The first order of business for the new
committee was an evaluation of the building location. Too many concerns had been expressed about the lower Queen Anne building site at
First Avenue West and Olympic Place.

The lot was a "prominent and slightly corner," and the dimensions
were right for a Christian Science church. But it had a steep slope,
which meant higher construction cost. The extra foundation work required would cost 20% more than a flat lot. Also, in the years since the
purchase, the character of the lower Queen Anne area had begun to
change. There were plans for apartment buildings that would dwarf
the church and "deprive it of its pre-eminence." There were new parking restrictions that would cause inconvenience. But most concerning,
the number of cars in the city had increased, and the intersection had
become a traffic bottleneck, a dangerous corner. The Sunday School
superintendent was hearing from parents about their anxieties. The
committee explained to the board.

> It is a very undesirable corner on which to dismiss a congregation
> of 600 to 800 people and it will be a dangerous place to turn loose
> over 500 Sunday School children. In the latter case we will assume a
> very serious responsibility and we should pause and think about it.

Furthermore, because of the steep grade of the road, the hardwork-
ing engines of uphill traffic would be heard through the walls, disrupting the atmosphere of services. The new building committee felt that
"church surroundings should be quiet and peaceful."[467]

On the financial side of the building project, they proposed that the church accumulate $10,000, then borrow $20,000 to build the first unit of the most desirable building option, pay off the debt over five years, and then complete the building. The mortgage payments would barely exceed what they were already paying in rent.

> Your Building Committee . . . desires that there be awakened a renewed interest in this phase of our activity and believe that after five years of occupancy of a hall, we should be ready and willing to demonstrate this important step. There should be no reason why we cannot be in our own church home before the coming year ends.[468]

But there was no construction work that year. The members did, however, reaffirm their intention to build, and they added extra Sunday collections to the building fund. Then they started discussing selling the building lot and looking for a new location. At a September 22 meeting, the new direction was clear. More than two-thirds of the members wanted to sell the lot and build somewhere else. This was enough to approve the sale of property, according to state law and their bylaws.[469]

That year for the December annual business meeting, Queen Anne Hall was, once again, not available for their use. Fourth Church offered them use of its building. In appreciation, the Seventh Church members took a collection at the business meeting, resulting in a $25 contribution to the Fourth Church building fund. At the meeting the members looked at pictures and plans of other Christian Science church buildings to get an idea of different architectural styles and costs. Then they called for a meeting on January 19, 1925, to officially approve the sale of the lot. They also passed a motion:

> that our church members give prayerful consideration to spiritual church building, that at our next meeting we unfold to our membership the blessings that have been revealed to us through the study of the same.[470]

But the sale of the property did not move forward. At the meeting, the motion to sell lost. A motion to reconsider the motion lost. Someone asked to reconsider the decision to build somewhere else. The chair ruled that motion out of order. Nothing was accomplished at the meeting. Whatever clarity they had recently gained now seemed lost. The meeting concluded with some "helpful remarks" on spiritual church building, "lovingly presented," and a resolution to hear more in this spirit at the next meeting.[471]

But things did not go much better at the next meeting. At a March 12 meeting on the same topic, the chair began with reading relevant passages from the Bible and Mary Baker Eddy's writings and then opened the meeting up for member remarks on spiritual church building. But instead of inspired sharing, a democratic battle broke out suggestive of internal contention. A member rose with a point of order that the call letter was illegal because not in accordance with Robert's Rules of Order. Another point of order claimed that the call letter was illegal because not in accordance with church bylaws. This unusual focus on parliamentary procedure suggests that in someone's strongly held opinion the letter sent out to the members in advance of the meeting did not technically meet the requirements related to the sale of real estate—or possibly that someone strongly disagreed with selling the lot and was using this tactic to veto the majority decision. Regardless of the motive, there would be no decision on the lot that night. The only further business conducted was a motion to officially adjourn to meeting, which carried.

However, the adjournment did not end the meeting. Enough of a discussion continued that the clerk took formal minutes for the informal discussion. No motions were made, only inspiration about spiritual church building was shared. After saying together the Lord's Prayer, the informal meeting ended.[472]

On April 30, they tried again. Three of the seven board members called for the meeting—suggestive of a deeply divided board. On that Thursday evening, the members gathered once again to discuss the question of selling the lot. The call letter included blank proxy ballots, so even those who could not attend the meeting could vote—a provision of state law, the letter explained. The meeting chair set the tone by reading "A Rule for Motives and Acts" from the *Church Manual*—a reminder to be principled, loving, charitable, and kind during the meeting. The ballots were cast and counted, both the votes of those present and a considerable number of proxy votes. It was far from unanimous, but more than two-thirds wanted to sell. The motion carried, and the meeting adjourned.

Once again, afterward, members continued discussion in an informal meeting on spiritual building that merited recording. Then the discussion closed with silent prayer and the Lord's Prayer. [473]

Finally, it was official—and irrefutably legal. Seventh Church was selling. The building project was making progress again, but it would be at a new location, somewhere else in the Queen Anne area.

47

Architect (1925)

T he new building site for Seventh Church of Christ, Scientist, Seattle, was everything that the former location was not. The lot was flat. It was large enough that the Sunday School could be on the same level as the church auditorium and also have a park-like yard outside the Sunday School doors. It was on a residential street surrounded by single-family houses. It was a safe area for children and quiet—*very* quiet.

The search committee found the property just as the sale of their previous lot at First Avenue West and Olympic Place was closing. In November 1925, information about the site at the top of Queen Anne Hill was presented to the membership. On December 28, the decision was quick and harmonious. The members overwhelmingly favored the new location. The vote was almost unanimous. The lot was purchased for $5,700—considerably less than their previous lot.[474]

At church services in the weeks leading up to a special collection for the building fund, the First Reader gave this desk notice:

> It is with deep gratitude that the announcement may now be made to this congregation that a church site, situated at the corner of Eighth Avenue West and West Halladay Street, served by three car lines, has been purchased by Seventh Church of Christ, Scientist, and that steps towards the erection of a church edifice are now in progress. This "temple" must "first be erected in the hearts of its members—the unselfed love that builds without hands, eternal in the heaven of Spirit." (*The First Church of Christ, Scientist and Miscellany*) and to this end [consecrated] prayer and effort are required.[475]

With the new year came new leadership for the project. A new member, Oscar Marcus Kulien, was appointed chair of the building committee. Mr. Kulien was well-known in Seattle for his work in construction. Often referred to as O.M. Kulien, his business, the Kulien Construction Company, had been building brick homes in Queen Anne and would soon complete a major development project by Denny Way between Western and Elliott Avenues, the Kulien Industrial Center.[476]

Besides his work as a real estate developer, Kulien was an active member of Seventh Church, a ministry worker on the church extension committee that held services at area prisons and at the Camp Lewis army base, and assistant Sunday School superintendent. He was the board chair when the membership was deciding whether to sell their previous building site, and he handled the sale of the property. He had been involved with the building committee since the evaluation of the building site in 1924 that led to its sale. Now Kulien was involved as building committee chair.[477]

Starting in January 1926, there was a new level of activity on the project. Things were moving quickly. First they needed to finally decide what they wanted in a building. At a meeting of the board, finance committee, and building committee, they decided on a recommendation to the membership: a church edifice with an auditorium for 500 and a Sunday School for 325 for the cost of $60,000. If such a church could not be built for that cost, they would reduce the seating capacity, but not the grandeur of the architecture. They recommended a mortgage of no more than $45,000. If there were cost overruns, they would raise more money or defer a portion of the work, but they would not increase the amount of debt. The members approved this recommendation. In the spirit of this fresh start, the members wanted the building committee to also revisit the selection of architect.[478]

If there was any criticism of Daniel Riggs Huntington's work, it was not recorded in the meeting minutes or surviving building committee letters. Former building committee chair John Gibson expressed special appreciation for how generous Mr. Huntington had been with his time, working closely with them as though he were a member of the committee. As for architectural qualifications, Huntington did not lack in any way. He had worked in partnership with Carl F. Gould, a prominent Seattle architect who became the first director of the Architecture Department at the University of Washington. Huntington had served as president of the Washington State Chapter of the American Institute of Architects, and he had worked nearly a decade as Seattle's first City Architect. Given the responsibility of improving Seattle's architectural beauty, he designed several fire stations, the Lake Union Steam Plant, the Sanitary Market by the Pike Place Market, and the University, Fremont, and Ballard Bridges. He had designed the Fremont Public Library, the Washington Street Public Boat Landing on the Seattle waterfront, and the prominent First Methodist Episcopal Church edifice downtown at Fifth Avenue and Marion Street. Huntington's devotion of so much time and care to the Seventh Church building project must have been due more to his dedication to the cause of Christian Science than to any need for architectural work. Even knowing Seventh Church was starting fresh on selection of architects and soliciting new proposals, Huntington gave more time to the project. He sketched a plan concept for the new lot at Eighth and Halladay, and discussed the project at length with the building committee and then again with the board. But Huntington was not selected.[479]

They heard from four other leading architects: Allen, Bader, Fowler, and Horrocks. Both Mr. Allen and Mr. Horrocks had strong support. The committee was divided, however, on the choice and asked the board to weigh in. The board wanted the building committee to come to unanimous decision. Finally, "after lengthy discussions and prayerful consideration," in March 1926 they came to unanimous agreement. Surprisingly, they chose an architect who was not even among those formally considered. They chose Harlan Thomas.[480]

A rising star among local architects, Mr. Thomas was the new head of the Architecture Department at the University of Washington, following Mr. Gould. He was also the new president of the Washington chapter of the AIA. Like Huntington, who Thomas knew from decades earlier when they were both architectural apprentices in Denver, Thomas had designed part of the Pike Place Market, a building called the Corner Market, and other significant buildings in Seattle. He designed the public libraries in Columbia City and Queen Anne. When Thomas came to Seattle in 1906, for his own family home on Queen Anne Hill he designed a Mediterranean-style villa with arched windows and doorways and stucco siding. He and his wife had traveled around the world, taking trips for 15 months and more at a time. He kept a watercolor travelog, which he later exhibited at the Henry Art Gallery. The time he spent in Italy influenced the architectural style of his later work, especially the Chelsea Hotel on West Olympic Place in Queen Anne and the Sorrento Hotel on Madison Street on First Hill. This Italian influence would also be apparent in the design for Seventh Church.[481]

Aside from an emphasis on unanimity, the committee recorded no explanation for their selection of architect. It probably helped that since his early career when he designed Methodist churches in Fort Collins and Boulder, Colorado, Thomas had become quite an expert on "the origins of ecclesiastic design." He gave lectures on the topic. For his most recent project he gave the Seattle Chamber of Commerce building at Third Avenue and Columbia Street the look of an early Christian church. It probably also helped that his wife, Edith, and daughter, Dorothy, had both been studying Christian Science since 1916 and had both joined Seventh Church in 1920. Edith, besides being his companion for world traveling, was also involved in his architecture business. Dorothy, as a child, had come on one of the round-the-world trips and, sharing her father's interest in history, gave a commencement speech as class historian when she graduated from the University of Washington in 1919. Although not a member, Harlan may have been at least a regular visitor at Seventh Church services during its early years. The Thomas family had since moved to the University District, where Dorothy joined Third Church. Although the Thomases were no longer members of Seventh Church at the time of the selection, personal relationships with members of the building committee were probably influential.[482]

According to architect Robert G. Reichert, the architectural inspiration for Seventh Church, like Fourth Church, was primitive Christianity. The building was designed to remind visitors of an earlier era when Christians were healers. Thomas had done a neoclassical design with a white-column portico for Enumclaw City Hall, similar to Fourth Church. But for Seventh Church, he proposed something different, an "Early Christian Revival" edifice. Thomas' concept was a somewhat eclectic combination of elements from some of the earliest Christian churches. He envisioned a Romanesque-style building with three arched entry doors, stucco siding, a two-toned red clay tile roof, and floral-motif stone trim around leaded amber glass windows.[483]

Five construction contractors submitted bids, including Neil McDonald. But despite Mr. McDonald's good relationship with the Seattle Christian Science community and his experience with the Third and Fourth Church building projects, he did not win the Seventh Church project. As usual, McDonald gave a low bid, but they received a slightly lower bid from Charles W. Carkeek, nephew of Seattle pioneer Morgan Carkeek, who would soon have a city park named after him. Abiding strictly by the practice of accepting the lowest bidder, the building committee gave the contract to Mr. Carkeek.[484]

DEDICATION

On May 17, 1926, Thomas came to a membership meeting at Queen Ann Hall. He explained his design with a slide show. Thomas was a masterful speaker, and his use of the latest technology for presentations must have been impressive. On July 28, the members gave authorization to proceed. They announced the project in the *Seattle Times* on August 22 with an architect's drawing of the future structure. The cornerstone was laid on September 22. Construction was quick and apparently uneventful. Members were kept informed of progress through reports at monthly meetings. There was no democratic discussion on the project, except informal acceptance of the decisions of the building committee. Within only a few months, the church was complete. Opening services for the 470-seat auditorium were held on Sunday, February 27, 1927. At Queen Anne Hall, their average attendance had been around 200. At the three opening services—11 a.m., 3 p.m., and 8 p.m.—the "seating capacity was taxed to the utmost, many at each service having to stand." Even regular attendance increased to fill the auditorium. They began holding two Sunday School sessions, both well attended. For a lecture in their new auditorium, "great numbers were turned away." The congregation and musicians appreciated the excellent natural acoustics in the auditorium. The neighbors appreciated the distinctive style of the building. Harlan Thomas had created an architectural gem.[485]

The building project was completed almost exactly on time and on budget. It only cost $2,000 over the original estimate, due to some extras added after the original bid. But because the members could not raise as much money as they expected, they ended up with $10,000 more debt than planned—their total indebtedness being $55,000. Consequently, they would have to do without some of the planned furnishings for a while. They would have pews, not chairs—a considerable savings—and no cushions for the wood pews. Despite the great need in rainy Seattle for umbrella racks in the foyer, the board could not justify the extra expense of purchasing them.[486]

The total cost of the building, with furnishings and landscaping, would be $82,000—"an amount that would have staggered the little group of thirty-seven Charter members a few years before," their initial First Reader and eventual church historian Charles Griffith later explained, "but, in the light of a clearer understanding of principle and the unfoldment of good, it seemed only the natural thing." But the church did not yet have a pipe organ. That major expense was still to be accomplished.[487]

270

Notwithstanding the cost-conscious approach of Seventh Church, they expressed a spirit of generosity even while building. They contributed to Fifth Church in Columbia City and Eighth Church in Lake Forest Park, because they, too, were building.

After the Seventh Church building was complete, there were some leaks to fix. They modified the roof drains and added some extra waterproofing. This showed the need for a maintenance sinking fund, on top of all their other expenses. But overall, the project was successful and the members were pleased. The next year when it was time to elect new readers, their efficient, effective, and dedicated building committee chair, O.M. Kulien, was given the honor of election to First Reader.[488]

DEDICATION

Seventh Church of Christ, Scientist, Seattle

Third Church of Christ, Scientist, Seattle

272

48

Christian Science Teacher (1929)

I t was second only in potential impact for the early Christian Science movement in Seattle to the passing of Mary Baker Eddy. On January 30, 1929, Allen H. Armstrong died. Mr. Armstrong passed on in his home in the Mount Baker neighborhood in southeast Seattle. His student association held a memorial service at the Scottish Rite Temple at Harvard Avenue and Broadway. This dedicated Christian Science teacher, sent to Seattle under Reverend Eddy's leadership, would no longer be there to support the steady growth of Christian Science in Seattle. Teacher William K. Sheldon had also recently passed on. Edith S. Alexander and John E. Playter, who were still teaching, showed special admiration for Armstrong's healing ability and the significant contribution he made in the history of Christian Science in Seattle.[489] Armstrong was not widely known to Christian Scientists beyond Seattle, because he never served on the Board of Lectureship and he wrote only a few articles for the Christian Science periodicals. His entire focus had been the professional healing practice, teaching, and encouraging church building.[490]

Once lagging in the growth of Christian Science, Seattle had far exceeded Tacoma, Everett, Bellingham, and Spokane in the number of both practitioners and churches in the 30 years since Armstrong arrived. Starting from only two full-time practitioners in 1899, by 1929 there were 145 practitioners listed in the *Christian Science Journal* – an average of twelve at each of the twelve branch churches – plus about 20 more listed in the Seattle city directory and a few more in the outlying areas of Bellevue, Auburn, and Edmonds. Seattle population had increased more than four times during the same three decades, growing from about 80,000 residents in 1900 to about 365,000 in 1929. The rapid growth of Christian Science had far outpaced even Seattle's tremendous population growth.

Of the twelve Christian Science congregations in Seattle there was First Church on Capitol Hill, Second Church in Ballard, Third Church in the University District, Fourth Church on First Hill above downtown, Fifth Church in Columbia City, Sixth Church in West Seattle, Seventh Church in Queen Anne, Eighth Church in North Seattle at 104th Street on Dayton Avenue near Carkeek Park, Ninth Church in Lake Forest Park toward the north end of Lake Washington, and Tenth Church in Seahurst Park at the far southwest end. One society was meeting at Greenlake Masonic Hall, and another at Ronald Station, a depot for the Seattle-Everett interurban electric train at North 176th Street. The three churches with the largest buildings—First, Third, and Fourth—held two Sunday services: 11 a.m. and 8 p.m.[491]

Christian Science churches were few in number within the overall religious landscape in Seattle. More than 270 churches and religious organizations were listed in the city directory. For comparison, there were 20 Catholic churches, 21 Baptist churches, 22 Congregational churches, 25 Presbyterian churches, and 26 Lutheran churches. But the twelve Christian Science churches had large attendance. At least several thousand Seattle residents were attending Christian Science services regularly, many more came to the frequent lectures, and even more read lectures published in local newspapers and distributed in pamphlet form. The rise and influence of Christian Science was felt in Seattle. It was evident from so many successful church building projects that Christian Science really had come to stay. Notably, Reverend J.D.O. Powers, a prominent Seattle pastor, was calling for a change of attitude by Christian clergy toward Christian Science. Rev. Powers was quoted in the *Seattle Post-Intelligencer* as saying,

> Instead of damning it and its adherents and calling it bad names, if the church is to save itself, we must study it and incorporate in the practice of the church all the truth it has in its possession.

Powers resigned his post in the Unitarian Church, not to join the Christian Science church, but to start a non-sectarian Christian church. Christian Science was having an influence in Seattle beyond the twelve branches of Mary Baker Eddy's church.[492]

There were eight Christian Science Reading Rooms in Seattle. First and Fourth churches had their joint reading room in the Empire Building in the central business district downtown, open 75 hours a week, most days from 9 a.m. to 9 p.m. Third Church had similar hours at its reading room on University Way at Northeast 45th Street. The Second Church reading room in the center of the Ballard commercial area was open weekday afternoons and evenings. The Fifth Church reading room was in their church edifice on 36th Avenue South at South Alaska Street, next to Columbia Park. It was open on Friday afternoons. The Sixth Church reading room in West Seattle on California Avenue at Southwest Alaska Street was open midday from 11:30 a.m. to 4 p.m. The Ninth Church reading room in their Lake Forest Park church edifice was open briefly on Thursday afternoons. All the Seattle branch churches jointly supported two downtown reading rooms: one in the north end shopping district, and another on the south end near Pioneer Square and the ship yards.

The shopping district joint reading room was in the Shafer Building at Sixth Avenue and Pine Street. The 10-story Shafer Building was among the tallest buildings downtown, and when completed in 1924, it was hailed as the most innovative and modern in the city. Handsomely clad in white terra-cotta tiles, this "imposing skyscraper" had expansive windows and the latest technology for electric lights, wiring, and plumbing. The offices were designed with doctors and dentists in mind. The Christian Science Reading Room opened on the ninth floor and immediately Christian Science practitioners started moving into the building. By 1929, there were thirty: fourteen on the eighth floor just below the reading room, and sixteen more on the fifth, sixth, and seventh floors.[493]

The Shafer Building reading room was initiated by Seventh Church. Maintaining an active reading room had been an especially difficult problem for the Queen Anne church. Initially, their reading room was in the Wells Building at Third Avenue and Pine Street. The next year, they moved it one block to the Seaboard Building at Forth and Pike. Seventh Church struggled with both the cost and the location. They moved it a few years later to the top of Queen Anne Hill on West Boston Street at Queen Anne Avenue. But there was not much activity there, so they closed it. All the while Seventh Church had been trying to recruit a partner, as First and Fourth were doing in the Empire Building. They first approached Third Church, but the University District branch was too focused on construction to consider taking on another project and expense. It took many letters and meetings over several years to work out a viable agreement. Finally, in December 1925, the Shafer Building reading room opened with the support of all the Seattle branch churches. By 1929, it had become almost as much of a hub of Christian Science activity as the Empire Building.[494]

Armstrong never had his office in the Empire Building or the Shafer Building. When the joint reading room was established in the Empire Building, Armstrong moved into the Joshua Green Building at Fourth Avenue and Pike Street. At that time, 1914, the Joshua Green Building was the newest, most innovative and imposing skyscraper in the north end of downtown, second only to the Smith Tower. Joint literature distribution and the *Christian Science Monitor* advertising office moved there from the Empire Building, as did more than 20 practitioners. It became a third Christian Science center in Seattle.[495]

Between Pioneer Square and Occidental Square, an area of downtown with the oldest buildings, was the Maynard Building reading room at First Avenue South and Washington Street. Named after David S. "Doc" Maynard, a city founder whose friendship with Duwamish Indian Tribe leader Chief Seattle resulted in the city's name, the Maynard Building, although only a few blocks south of the Empire Building, served a very different demographic group. It was near the industrial zone and Chinatown. This was perhaps the most racially and ethnically diverse area of the city. Church records called this "a section of the city frequented principally by men out of employment." Also known for its taverns, public bathhouses, brothels, and other such activities, it was essentially Seattle's red-light district. This Christian Science reading room, which opened in October 1928, was staffed primarily by men. Located just above the sidewalk on the second floor of the building, easily accessible to passers-by, it was much more like a storefront than the other reading rooms. It did not anchor a Christian Science professional center like the other downtown reading rooms. There were no practitioner offices in the Maynard Building. The venture was perhaps more of a charity project than a profitable sales outlet for the Christian Science Publishing Society. It provided friendly outreach and a wholesome, uplifting space for visitors. With these three reading rooms downtown, it seems the Christian Scientists were trying to reach every demographic group in Seattle. The joint reading rooms were the only ones advertised to the general public in the *Seattle Times*.[496]

Seattle was not the only city to have joint reading rooms. A dozen others had all-city ones downtown, mostly in the Midwest and far west, and there were at least 10 other cities where two or three branches shared a reading room. But Seattle seems to have been very unusual in the extent of its cooperative approach, with its *three* joint downtown reading rooms.[497]

The other joint activities of the Seattle Christian Science churches had continued to grow since their start in 1912. They supported ongoing activities at Camp Lewis, literature booths at the Western Washington State Fair in Puyallup, and occasional commercial expositions. Besides the regular joint literature distribution committee, there was a committee that put literature onto ships, called the "Harbor, Lakes, and Water Ways Committee," and a committee for placing Christian Science books in public libraries. There was a cooperative committee for managing subscriptions to *The Christian Science Monitor*, a *Monitor* advertising committee, and together the churches purchased bulk orders of special issues. A joint lecture committee coordinated scheduling and organized joint events. They had recently started jointly funding radio broadcasts of lectures. The church extension committee conducted ministry efforts for the local jails, prisons, forced labor farms, and other institutions, and the Seattle churches supported the work of the Walla Walla church at the state penitentiary. An Emergency Welfare Fund provided charitable support for local Christian Scientists. Each of these activities was funded by a separate monthly fee paid by each branch based on membership size.

Nearly all of this organization supporting Christian Science in Seattle—the twelve branch churches, the eight reading rooms, and all the joint committees—were established during Armstrong's three decades in Seattle.

For such a significant local religious leader, Armstrong kept a remarkably low public profile. His name only occasionally appeared in the Seattle newspapers. During the period between the death of his wife Maud in 1908 and his remarriage to Harriett Francis Morton in 1915, he made the society page of the newspaper for attending the theater in the company of McGilvras and Burkes a few times. Judge Thomas Burke was one of the most significant civic leaders in the early decades of Seattle's development. He had encouraged the local business culture of cooperation known as the "Seattle Spirit." Besides being the owner of the Burke Building where First Church of Christ, Scientist, had its building committee meetings, Burke was also owner of the Empire Building, the primary Christian Science center. Armstrong may have become acquainted with Judge Burke through Oliver C. McGilvra, Burke's law partner and brother-in-law. Judge Burke had a reputation for protecting the civil rights of minority groups. He had taken a courageous public stand in defense of Chinese immigrants when they were threatened by riots. The misunderstood Christian Scientists may have benefited from their proximity to Burke. One of the last of the pioneer generation of city builders, this much-loved judge—dubbed "Seattle's First Citizen" by his first biographer—had died in 1925, but he was still in the news in Seattle. In 1929, his many friends commissioned a 20-ton granite memorial for Burke for Volunteer Park. Armstrong, like Burke, was a community builder, one of the last of the pioneer generation of Christian Scientists. But there would be no statues of Armstrong anywhere. His passing was quietly honored in less visible ways.[498]

In the brief article in the *Seattle Times* about Armstrong's memorial service, he was remembered first and foremost as a Christian Science teacher. He was described as one of the leaders of the denomination in Washington since arriving in 1899. The article emphasized his organization of the first Christian Science church in San Jose, California. The typical *Seattle Times* reader probably did not know much about the significance of the San Jose church. Most Christian Scientists, however, would have recognized it as being among the few branch churches that ever received a letter from Mary Baker Eddy for its dedication.[499]

With Armstrong gone, the Christian Science movement was entering a new phase of development. It remained to be seen whether these far-western students would continue to live according to the name, title, and profession "Christian Scientist," as Armstrong had. It remained to be seen whether they would continue in the spirit of cooperation and unity that was so heavily emphasized by the Seattle branch churches during and after The Mother Church's Great Litigation.

Their resolve would soon be tested by the extraordinary challenges they would soon face—the greatest economic depression in the country's history followed by the greatest world war. Their elegant church edifices, even with their large and growing congregations, carried huge amounts of debt—much more than they had ever wanted or planned and perhaps much more than was fiscally prudent. It remained to be seen how they would achieve dedication.

Allen H. Armstrong, C.S.B.

Drawing: Christina Safronoff

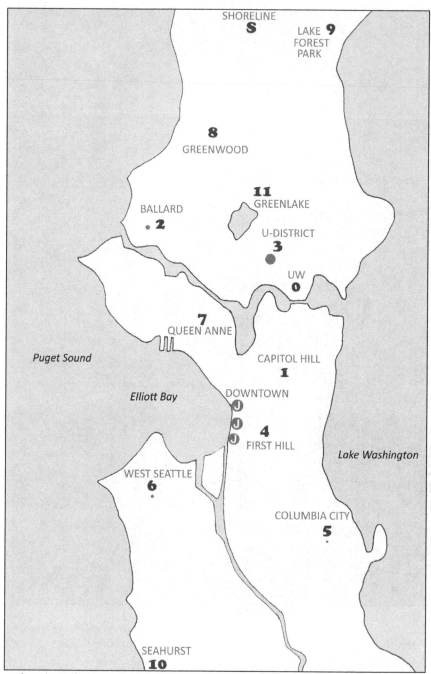

Churches of Christ, Scientist, Seattle, and Christian Science Reading Rooms, 1929. S = Society O = college organization ◉ = Reading Room (dot proportional to operating hours) J = Joint, two or more churches

Looking down Sixth Avenue to Shafer Building on Pine Street
Museum of History and Industry (#1983.10.345.2)

Joshua Green Building at Fourth Avenue and Pike Street
Museum of History and Industry (#1983.10.2876.1)

49

Afterword (2019)

Part 1 of *Dedication: Building the Seattle Branches of Mary Baker Eddy's Church, A Centennial Story* covered forty years, from just after the Great Seattle Fire through the Great War and the Great Litigation to just before the Great Depression. Diverse people played different roles in the development of the Christian Science movement in Seattle, and the branch churches united through a wide variety of joint activities, a tradition which continues to the present day. The four churches that are the focus of the story constructed their buildings: First Church of Christ, Scientist, on Capitol Hill, Third Church in the University district, Fourth downtown, and Seventh atop Queen Anne Hill.

Along the way there were many challenges for each of those building projects and much debt was taken on. But the challenges facing these church congregations are only beginning. At the end of 1929, when the stock market crashes and the Great Depression begins, there is an extra dimension to this story. This is when the joint dedication committee becomes active—the committee that inspired my storytelling and the research project that became this book. That committee report provided me the basic story arc for the next two decades of *Dedication*. There is so much more forgotten history to share, so many more stories to tell, so many more colorful people to introduce to the world—and so many more buildings to build.

Initially, I intended this project to be short—a year at most. I developed the first draft of the manuscript quickly—amazingly quickly. I had never written so much so quickly. But in retrospect, that was only the bare bones of the story. I began to see value in fleshing it out— providing more context and detail and featuring personal stories and backgrounds for the individuals involved. My own surprise at the events and church culture a century ago impelled more careful study. As more branch churches gave me access to their historical files, a fuller story emerged. Individuals shared their stories, information, and documents. I spent a month in the summer of 2018 in Boston visiting the research rooms at The Mary Baker Eddy Library and Longyear Museum. I found answers to research questions, adding depth and detail to my understanding of early church dynamics. New elements of the story developed. By the end of the first year of research, what began as a short sprint had turned into an ultra-marathon.

As the Part 1 story was developing, I found audiences for specific chapters and story aspects, in Seattle and beyond. I discovered that this seemingly obscure local topic had potential for a broad global audience. I had the opportunity to give presentations about my research at international academic conferences for scholars of religious movements, the Center for Studies on New Religions, in 2018 in Taiwan and in 2019 in Italy. There I found an appreciative audience and new insights into the dynamics of religious movements. To prepare for those presentations, I sought out local opportunities to share chapters of the story. The enthusiastic response was profoundly encouraging to me.

I created a podcast in March 2019. Following the advice of the community of podcasters from "The Podcasting Fellowship," a workshop run by Seth Godin and Alex De Palma where I learned podcasting skills, I truncated the name to "Dedication: A Centennial Story." Recording and posting audio editions of manuscript chapters has served several purposes. I used the recording process to refine my writing. Reading aloud each chapter with a listening audience in mind has helped me to improve the flow of ideas and smooth out sentences. I consider the podcast to serve many other purposes. It is a review draft open for corrections and suggestions. It is a call for additional source material and an invitation for participation through oral history. It is a promotional tool, a way to build an audience prior to publishing the book. It is a way to engage with a regional, national, and international audience—an alternative to traveling the country at great effort and expense. It is also a response to the reality of current culture. Many people interested in this content may not be in the habit of reading books but enjoy listening to audio. Because the podcast format packages each episode as a stand-alone audio program, individual chapters, as separate episodes, can potentially find niche interest groups through podcast catalogs and internet keyword searches. The podcast medium opens up new possibilities for bonus material including author and listener commentary, audience questions, interviews, oral histories, and self-guided architectural tours.

The next part of the 130-year story arc of *Dedication*, Part 2, covers the next forty years, from the Stock market crash in 1929 to the Apollo 14 lunar landing in 1971. I already have a working draft. I need to fill in gaps, learn more about the people involved, frame the events with historical context, and refine the writing. If you know of relevant books, documents, letters, photographs, relics, stories, or events that might contribute to this story, please contact me. Especially needed is information about the 1960s era, specifically, anything relating to the Christian Science Pavilion at the Seattle World's Fair, the Christian Science Reading Room in the Central District, the charter plane from Seattle to the youth meeting in Boston, and Christian Science connections with the early space program.

To those wanting to support this project, anything you can do to spread the word about this research and encourage people to listen to the podcast would be helpful. Please rate and review "Dedication: A Centennial Story" podcast in popular podcast outlets. To learn more about the project, visit my website, www.CindySafronoff.com. Current information on events is posted to Facebook page "Dedication Centennial Story." To make a financial contribution, please contact me via my website.

I hope you've gotten as much out of the first part of the *Dedication* story as I have in researching and writing it.

CINDY PEYSER SAFRONOFF

Cindy Safronoff in 2006 by the cornerstone of
Third Church of Christ, Scientist, Seattle

50

Acknowledgements (2020)

Unlike my previous book, *Crossing Swords: Mary Baker Eddy vs. Victoria Claflin Woodhull and the Battle for the Soul of Marriage*, which I researched almost entirely using books available through my local public library, requiring no help from anyone except a few librarians, to research *Dedication: Building the Seattle Branches of Mary Baker Eddy's Church, A Centennial Story – Part 1: 1889 to 1929* I needed help from many people and many organizations. Since I relied almost exclusively on primary sources, most of which had scarcely if at all been seen by anyone for many decades, it was not such a simple matter to get access to documents. For one private collection, it required climbing a ladder into a less than full-height church attic and spending most of the day there. In several cases my hosts spent many hours of their personal time patiently waiting while I looked through boxes and drawers and photographed records. I could not have written this book without everyone's full support. Furthermore, many of the people who advocated for this research project did so somewhat courageously considering the ground-breaking aspect of this research project.

To illustrate this point, I will share that I did not get access to everything I requested from every collection, and there are very justifiable reasons for this. It is not customary for Christian Science branch churches to make their internal records available for publishing. There are privacy issues, various legal worries, bylaws written locally and those in Mary Baker Eddy's *Church Manual*, public relations concerns, and internal democratic dynamics at work. Any of these factors could lead to an unfavorable decision on a request or restrictions. In all cases, I understand. Honestly, if our positions were reversed, I would hesitate to give unrestricted access to branch church records. I can even follow the reasoning for destroying records. From my perspective as a scholar, however, trying to write branch church history with documents and pages missing is like trying to write a summary of a novel using a copy that has every third chapter removed, random pages torn out, half the names blacked out, and the ending chapters unavailable. You can still get the general idea of the story but could easily misinterpret entire elements of the plot and miss important details. Gillian Gill included her backstory of gaining access to primary source documents in "Research Note" section of the Appendix of her biography *Mary Baker Eddy*, an effort that ultimately led to the opening of the archives to the public via The Mary Baker Eddy Library. Just as I wonder what more insights Gillian Gill could have included in her book had she had immediate full access to records kept by The Mother Church, I wonder what more might have been included in *Dedication*, Part 1.

What is most important is that I gained access to enough records collections, and enough of those with no restrictions, to piece together a very comprehensive picture of how things happened in Seattle. In fact, I had plenty of material to work with. During three years I accumulated more than 15,000 pages of primary source documents. I share my disappointments in records access mainly to explain why the people and organizations I mention have my special appreciation. I hope this discussion might convince branch churches to err on the side of retaining historic records, even if it is not clear how those documents taking up space in the file cabinets could ever be useful to anyone, and to give full unrestricted access to historians. Every page potentially includes at least a clue or two useful for solving one of countless research puzzles.

I feel fortunate to have begun my branch church scholarship project at Third Church of Christ, Scientist, Seattle, which has (I now know) unusually voluminous church records. This church's tradition of verbose meeting minutes that began under Mollie Gerry's supervision in 1914 I suspect may have continued to this day because of the scholarly influence of the nearby University of Washington. Important, too, has been ample storage capacity throughout the church's 100-year history. The addition of the Seventh Church records because of the merger made for an unusually rich collection of branch church records. It was the perfect place for me to begin because of the records. It was also the perfect place to begin because of the members.

Here I begin formal acknowledgements. I must give great credit first and foremost to all the members of Third Church of Christ, Scientist, in Seattle. This book would not have been written had they not given me unrestricted access to internal records and unconditional permission to publish from the records as an independent author—and that on my first request, through unanimous (as I recall) vote by the members, and with very little discussion. I cannot emphasize enough my appreciation for their willingness to be a subject of a great experiment in creating a new kind of branch church history, for better or worse, and their willingness to be transparent. I will always cherish Scott Davis' support for honest, independent scholarship. Special thanks to Mary Davis and Josh Draskovich for freeing up my time during critical periods so I could do the research and writing.

Likewise, I would like to express great appreciation to First Church of Christ, Scientist, Seattle; First Church of Christ, Scientist, Burien; Twelfth Church of Christ, Scientist, Seattle; and the Building and Finance Committee for the Christian Science Organization at the University of Washington for getting on board with this project once it was moving. Each of their collections contributed significantly to the story, and their organizational support contributed significantly to my confidence in the project's potential. Special credit is due to many local individuals who helped me access records including Steven Agnew, Renee Alton, Nathan Blaisdel, Robert and Pamee Hohner, Dale Lang, Josette Lewis, Emily Odell, Carol Olano, Greg Palmer, and Merry Ann Peterson. Many others shared personal stories and documents, and helpful suggestions, including Susan Anderson, Pat Armstrong, Rhea Robertson Buck, William Dunnell, David W. Erickson, Alan Galt, Carolyn Geise, Caroline Harlow, Kathy Blackwell Harper, Joanne Holcomb, Gail Howe-Jennings, Charlotte King, and Janet Wright.

Arts and civics organization Town Hall Seattle was consistently supportive of my efforts. Starting from initial introductions at a building architectural tour, staff showed interest in my research and arranged access to their historical files on Fourth Church of Christ, Scientist, even in the midst of a very busy period just prior to their major renovation project. I had the benefit of help from Shirley Bosier, Michael Breeden, Kevin Malgesini, Jonathon Shipley, and I am especially grateful to their dynamic and visionary director Wier Harman, whose acquaintance I had the pleasure of making through this project. The enthusiastic response of the Town Hall Seattle staff after hearing some highlights of the history of the Fourth Church of Christ, Scientist building encouraged me to make the trip to Boston to see what more could be learned from the archives at The Mother Church, The First Church of Christ, Scientist, through The Mary Baker Eddy Library.

Acknowledgements (2020)

The staff at The Mary Baker Eddy Library went to tremendous effort to open the historic records of disbanded Fourth and Eleventh Churches of Christ, Scientist, Seattle, prior to my visit during the summer of 2018 and helped me with research questions. I owe special thanks to Michael Hamilton, Judith Huenneke, Kurt Morris, and Carl Sheasley. To them and other MBEL staff for all their work behind the scenes, thank you! I would also like to share my appreciation for Alan Messmer in the legal department at The First Church of Christ, Scientist, for his pleasant help working through permissions issues, Mary Baker Eddy Library Fellow Alexandra Prince for research comradery, and the security staff around the Christian Science Publishing Society building, especially Charles, whose friendly interactions helped me feel the love of The Mother Church. While in Boston I also had the great pleasure of doing research in the elegant library at the Longyear Museum. Special thanks go to Sandra Houston for accommodating me on short notice, Kelly Byquist for help fact checking, and Webster Lithgow for sharing insights on story craft. My extended stay in Boston was made possible by my old friends Dave and Judy Carlson and my new friends Lane and Pam Partridge, whose gracious hospitality was extraordinary.

The many staff at University of Washington Libraries Special Collections have been consistently helpful, courteous, and cheerful. I only recently discovered collections in the UW archives relevant to local Christian Science history. I look forward to getting to know individual staff members better as I shift to working on Part 2 of *Dedication* and take fuller advantage of the UW's archives.

I would also like to thank scholar friends, especially Shirley Paulson, who expressed overflowing enthusiasm for my project and opened my view to a broader audience at international conferences for the Center for Studies on New Religions, and who I could always count on to cheer my efforts and successes. Linda Bargmann, Ralph Copper Byron, Susan Humble, Keith McNeil, and Amy Black Voorhees engaged with me in big or little ways or little ways that were big—answering random questions, pointing to sources, offering feedback, opinions, or instruction. Jeffrey Murdock and Jeffrey Williams generously shared their knowledge of architects.

Pat Armstrong, widow of Allen H. Armstrong's great-grand son Cliff, showed me a photo of Mr. Armstrong, the only one that she is aware exists, a snapshot that seems to show a light, humorous side to Mr. Armstrong, but not an image everyone would want to represent such an esteemed Christian Science teacher to the world. Christina Safronoff diligently applied her facial recognition and artistic talents to creating a new more dignified portrait of him, and after many rounds produced the one included in this book, for which I am indebted to her.

Besides sharing some fun personal stories (some of which will likely be included in Part 2), Alan Galt challenged me to raise my literary standards. Thanks, too, to my inspired copy editor, Karen Rathmell, whose humbling insistence that I study *The Elements of Style* by Strunk and White has happily resulted in a noticeable improvement in the quality and speed of my writing. Any typos or grammatical errors found in this book are almost certainly my fault, not hers.

While working on images and permissions, which required some detective work to determine proper attribution, I received quick and friendly help from Jean Sherrard. Along the way, thanks to Jean I had a special opportunity to chat with local historian Paul Dorpat, who for his "Now & Then" column in the *Seattle Times* has a special place in the hearts of many Seattle residents, including mine, and for his website PaulDorpat.com deserves special thanks for helping me visualize the early Seattle cityscape. It was an antique dealer and collectibles seller who helped me solve my most difficult permissions puzzle by putting me in touch with postcard collector John Cooper, whose postcard of First Church of Christ, Scientist, Seattle, is on the front cover. If any readers ever find themselves in the Pioneer Square area, be sure to stop by Michael Fairley's Fair Look Antiques at 81 ½ South Washington, near the Maynard Building.

No words are adequate to express the gratitude I feel for my husband Ross Safronoff, who is unquestionably my biggest fan and supporter. I could not and would not have done this work without his unfaltering support.

Sources

Source materials used in developing *Dedication: Building the Seattle Branches of Mary Baker Eddy's Church, A Centennial Story* include:

Historical files at First, Third, and Twelfth Churches of Christ, Scientist, Seattle; First Church of Christ, Scientist, Burien; Christian Science Organization at University of Washington

Historical files of First and Third Churches of Christ, Scientist, Seattle, held by The First Church of Christ, Scientist, in Boston, MA

Fourth and Eleventh Churches of Christ, Scientist, Seattle, collections at The Mary Baker Eddy Library in Boston, MA

Historical files at Town Hall Seattle

Julia-Field King collection at The Longyear Museum in Chestnut Hill, MA

Keith McNeil collection

Longyear Museum Reports to Members newsletters

Christian Science periodicals (*Christian Science Journal*, *Sentinel*, and *Monitor*) in print bound volumes and digital form, including from Found Volumes, The Ark, and Christian Science JSH-Online (jsh.christianscience.com)

"Seattle Now & Then" articles on PaulDorpat.com

Online encyclopedias, including HistoryLink.org, Wikipedia.com, and InfluenzaArchive.org

Ancestry.com (census data, vital statistics, family trees, city directories, yearbooks, miscellaneous newspaper articles, immigration records, draft cards, and other information)

Online historical newspapers (*Seattle Times*, *Seattle Post-Intelligencer*, *Seattle Star*, and others)

DEDICATION

Seattle Public Library, especially the Seattle Room and Special Collections Online

University of Washington Libraries Digital Collections, Music Library Special Collections, and Special Collections

Archives West (Northwest Digital Archives)

Bibliography

Armstrong, Joseph, and Margaret Williamson, *Building of The Mother Church*, Boston: Christian Science Publishing Society, 1908.

Bagley, Clarence B. *History of Seattle: From the Earliest Settlement to the Present Time. Vol. 1-3.* Chicago: The S. J. Clarke Publishing Company, 1916.

Berner, Richard C. *Seattle 1900-1920: From Boomtown, Urban Turbulence, to Restoration.* Seattle: Charles Press, 1991.

Berner, Richard C. *Seattle 1921-1940: From Boom to Bust.* Seattle: Charles Press, 1992.

Christian Science Publishing Society. *Christian Science War Time Activities: A Report to the Board of Directors of The Mother Church by The Christian Science War Relief Committee*, Boston: Christian Science Publishing Society, 1922.

Copper, Ralph Byron. "Declaring 'What the Pioneer Has Accomplished'," 2004.

Dunbar, Herbert L. *Illustrated Historical Sketches Portraying the Advancement in Christian Science From its Inception to the Present Time, Including some of its Church Edifices.* Boston: Herbert L. Dunbar, 1898.

Eddy, Mary Baker. *Christian Science versus Pantheism.* 1898. In *Prose Works Other Than Science and Health With Key to the Scriptures.* Boston: The First Church of Christ, Scientist, 1925.

———. *Church Manual of The Mother Church, The First Church of Christ, Scientist, in Boston, Massachusetts.* 1895. Boston: The First Church of Christ, Scientist, 1910.

———. *The First Church of Christ, Scientist, and Miscellany.* In *Prose Works Other Than Science and Health With Key to the Scriptures.* Boston: The First Church of Christ, Scientist, 1913.

———. *Miscellaneous Writings, 1883-1896.* 1897. In *Prose Works Other Than Science and Health With Key to the Scriptures.* Boston: The First Church of Christ, Scientist, 1925.

———. *The People's Idea of God: Its Effect on Health and Christianity, A Sermon Delivered at Boston.* 1883. In *Prose Works Other Than Science and*

Health With Key to the Scriptures. Boston: The First Church of Christ, Scientist, 1925.

———. *Pulpit and Press*. 1895. In *Prose Works Other Than Science and Health With Key to the Scriptures*. Boston: The First Church of Christ, Scientist, 1925.

———. *Science and Health With Key to the Scriptures*. 1875. Boston: The First Church of Christ, Scientist, 1911.

Faulkner, Charles Draper. *Christian Science Church Edifices*, Chicago: Charles Draper Faulkner, 1946.

Grant, Richard Southall. *Landmarks for Christian Scientists from Bow to Boston*. Boston: Richard Southall Grant, 1937.

Ivey, Paul Eli. *Prayers in Stone: Christian Science Architecture in the United States, 1894-1930*, Urbana and Chicago: University of Illinois Press, 1999.

Kimball, Edward A. *Lectures and Articles on Christian Science*. Chesterton, Indiana: Edna Kimball Wait, 1921.

Leonard, Jr., Edwin S. *As the Sowing: The First Fifty Years of The Principia*, St. Louis, 1980.

Nesbit, Robert C. *"He Built Seattle": A Biography of Judge Thomas Burke*. University of Washington Press, Seattle, 1961.

Ochsner, Jeffrey Karl, ed. *Shaping Seattle Architecture: A Historical Guide to the Architects*. Seattle and London: University of Washington Press, 1998.

Peel, Robert. *Mary Baker Eddy: The Years of Authority*. New York: Holt, Rinehart, and Winston, 1977. Reprint, Boston: Christian Science Publishing Society, 1982.

———. *Mary Baker Eddy: The Years of Discovery*. New York: Holt, Rinehart, and Winston, 1966. Reprint, Boston: Christian Science Publishing Society, 1972.

———. *Mary Baker Eddy: The Years of Trial*. New York: Holt, Rinehart, and Winston, 1971. Reprint, Boston: Christian Science Publishing Society, 1973.

Schuette, Kim M. *Christian Science Military Ministry, 1917-2004*. Indianapolis, Brockton Publishing Company, 2008.

Safronoff, Cindy Peyser. *Crossing Swords: Mary Baker Eddy vs. Victoria Claflin Woodhull and the Battle for the Soul of Marriage*. Seattle: This One Thing, 2016.

We Knew Mary Baker Eddy (Expanded Edition), Vol. 2. Boston: The Christian Science Publishing Society, 2013.

Woodbridge, Sally B. and Roger Montgomery. *A Guide to Architecture in Washington State: An Environmental Perspective*. Seattle and London: University of Washington Press, 1980.

DEDICATION

Young, Bicknell. *Normal Class Notes of 1937 as taught by Bicknell Young.* Santa Clara: The Bookmark, 2003.

End Notes

Abbreviations and short titles used in end note citations:

The writings of Mary Baker Eddy

S&H	*Science and Health with Key to the Scriptures*
Manual	*Manual of The Mother Church, The First Church of Christ, Scientist, in Boston, Massachusetts*
MW	*Miscellaneous Writings, 1883-1896*
Miscellany	*First Church of Christ, Scientist, and Miscellany*
People	*The People's Idea of God: Its Effect on Health and Christianity, A Sermon Delivered at Boston*
Pan.	*Christian Science versus Pantheism*
Pulpit	*Pulpit and Press*

Source Historical Files

01ChSea	First Church of Christ, Scientist, Seattle, Washington
03ChSea	Third Church of Christ, Scientist, Seattle, Washington
04ChSea	Fourth Church of Christ, Scientist, Seattle, Washington, historical files (collection at The Mary Baker Eddy Library)
07ChSea	Seventh Church of Christ, Scientist, Seattle, Washington, historical files (collection at Third Church of Christ, Scientist, Seattle, Washington)
FHL	Family History Library
LYM	Longyear Museum collection, Chestnut Hill, Massachusetts
MBEL	The Mary Baker Eddy Library, Boston, Massachusetts

| THS | Town Hall Seattle |
| UW CSO | Christian Science Organization at University of Washington, Seattle, Washington |

Magazines and Newspapers

CSS	*Christian Science Sentinel*
CSJ	*Christian Science Journal*
CSM	*Christian Science Monitor*
ST	*Seattle Times*
SS	*Seattle Star*
Sea P-I	*Seattle Post-Intelligencer*

Branch Church

BC	Building Committee
Board	Board of Directors (branch church executive board)
CCS	Church of Christ, Scientist

1 *"essentially democratic"*: Eddy, *Miscellany*, 247.

2 Gormley, Eileen. "Historical Sketch of Third Church of Christ, Scientist, Seattle, Washington," July 21, 1934. 03ChSea; "Robert Gerry's Funeral to Be Held on Friday," *ST*, Oct. 7, 1931, 10.

3 Rice, W.H., Secretary. "Minutes," Oct. 23, 1914. 03ChSea.

4 "Obituaries: Mrs. Robert Gerry," *ST*, May 4, 1942, 19; *"At one time"*: Gerry, Mrs. Robt., testimony, *CSS*, Apr. 8, 1911.

5 *Membership Roll (Register #1)*, 76, 98. 01ChSea; 1910 US Census, Seattle Ward 3, King County, Washington, Roll: T624_1659, ED 0157, 2B, FHL microfilm 1375672; *CSJ Directory* 1910, 1911; *"a forward step"*: Holmgren, Hazel G. to Archives of The Mother Church, Sept. 25, 1967. 03ChSea.

Mrs. Mollie Gerry's parents joined First Church of Christ, Scientist, Seattle in 1907, and she joined when she and her family moved to Seattle in 1909.

6 Rice, W.H. "Minutes," University District Christian Science Society, Nov. 17, 1914. 03ChSea; 1910 US Census, Seattle Ward 10, King County, Washington, ED 0181, 2B; 1910 US Census, Seattle Ward 10, King County, Washington, Roll: T624_1661, ED 0182, 9B, FHL microfilm 1375674; 1914 *Polk's Seattle City Directory*, 885.

7 *"We, the undersigned"*: By-Laws of University District Christian Science Society. 03ChSea.

8 Board Minutes, University District Christian Science Society, Nov. 24, 1914. 03ChSea; Gormley, Eileen. "Historical Sketch of Third Church of Christ, Scientist, Seattle, Washington," July 21, 1934, 2. 03ChSea.

9 Gormley, Eileen. "Historical Sketch of Third Church of Christ, Scientist, Seattle, Washington," July 21, 1934, 2. 03ChSea.

10 *"little-known frontier city"*: "Progress of Christian Science," *CSJ*, Dec. 1912, 536.

11 *"would not be like an ordinary boarder" "many callers"*: Julia Field-King reminiscences, 6. LYM; Location: *Polk's Seattle City Directory*, 1890, 418; *Seattle City Directory*, 1891-2, Corbett & Co, 358.

The boarding house was managed by Augustus Herbert (*Polk's Seattle City Directory*, 1890, 803). Today, although all the original buildings on this block were torn down, Julia Field-King's address still exists, used by the "1111 Third Ave" building, a 34-story office building completed in 1980.

12 *Medical licenses*: Illinois State Board of Health, Apr. 16, 1883. Missouri State Board of Health, certificate #3683, Dec. 22, 1888, Jan. 13, 1894. LYM; *Physician*: Physicians, *Polk's Seattle City Directory*, 1890, 827-828; *Homeophathic physician*: F00639. Mary Baker Eddy Library; *Eddy in Chicago*: Lithgow, Webster. "A Westward Wind: Christian Science Teaching Goes West, Part 1: Chicago," *Longyear Museum Report to Members*, Fall/Winter 2017; *"hoping to find something" "for I had a sincere desire" "I thought Christian Science practice was criminal" "comments on the absurdity"*: Julia Field-King reminiscences, 1. LYM.

[13] *"long-standing diseases"*: Julia Field-King reminiscences, 2. LYM; *"cripple" "my doctor told me"*: JFK, "Open Letters," *CSJ*, Mar. 1891.

[14] *1887 class instruction*: Julia Field-King reminiscences, 1-2. LYM; *"In the first two lessons"*: JFK, "Open Letters," *CSJ*, Mar. 1891.

Julia Field-King took Christian Science Class Instruction in Chicago with Joseph Adams in May 1887 ("Principles of Christian Science," certificate of Julia Field King, LYM collection)

[15] *"The new birth"*: Eddy, Mary B.G., *CSJ*, Oct. 1883. Also, Eddy, *MW*, 15, 16.

[16] *Instruction with Eddy*: "The Students of Mary Baker Eddy," The Mary Baker Eddy Library, 21, 25; *250 students in 1889*: Lithgow, Webster, "A Westward Wind: Christian Science Teaching Goes West, Part 1: Chicago," *Longyear Museum Report to Members*, Fall 2017; *"saw the possibilities of the great Northwest"*: Playter C.S.B, John E., Edith S. Alexander, C.S.B, Harriett M. Armstrong, C.S, "The Early History of Christian Science in First Church of Christ, Scientist, Seattle, Washington," hand dated, "appears to be 1932 or later," 1. 01ChSea.

M.D., C.S.D.: The dual credentials are on Julia Field-King's professional letterhead on letters in the Longyear Museum collection, her "card" (ad in directory) in Aug. 1890 *CSJ*, ix, and Jan. 1893 *CSJ*, xiv. Other Christian Scientists combined Christian Science credentials with medical or dental credentials in the 1880s and 1890s, among them H.I. Bradley in New Haven, Connecticut, Mrs. Katherine T. Betts, in Chicago, Illinois, E.J. Foster-Eddy, Boston, Massachusetts, F.J. Fluno, San Diego, California, E.N. Harris, Boston, L.M. Marston, Boston, Mrs. Lawrence Brown, Boston.

Playter, C.S.B, John E., Edith S. Alexander, C.S.B, Harriett M. Armstrong, C.S, "The Early History of Christian Science in First Church of Christ, Scientist, Seattle, Washington": A draft letter from the directors of First Church of Christ Scientist, Seattle, to the Christian Science Board of Directors in Boston, Nov. 9, 1932, in the First Church Seattle files confirm the 1932 date of this historical sketch, and show that it was done by this appointed committee of three, who "were all familiar with the progress of the Christian Science movement in Seattle," and "therefore, were in a position to most effectively record the early happenings of the church." The effort was undertaken in response to a request from the Boston leadership outlined in the CSS, June 4, 1932 and followed up by Byron B. Haviland, Committee on Publication of Washington in a letter dated Sept. 16, 1932. This historical sketch was probably never sent to The Mother Church, because it exceeded the requested length of 500 to 1000 words. However, it was described as "a very valuable acquisition to our church records" by the Seattle board in a letter to Harriett M. Armstrong (Allen H. Armstrong's widow), Oct. 4, 1932. A similar document four pages shorter but with the same title is in a church history folder at The Mary Baker Eddy Library (Box 530771 Folder 242249—currently viewable only with permission from First Church of Christ, Scientist, Seattle), signed apparently by Mrs. Armstrong and hand dated Nov. 9, 1932. The longer version in the First Church files in Seattle, although unofficial, has been used extensively as an acceptably reliable source, hereafter referred to as "Playter."

17 *Teaching background*: Chas Gross, Lasalle County, Illinois, to Anna J. Kinley, Apr. 3, 1862. Public Schools of the State of Illinois, Mill County, Teachers Certificate, First Grade, Aug. 25, 1873. 1872-1873 Prospectus of Independent College, Plainfield, Illinois. Public Schools of Michigan, Van Buren County, Teachers Certificate, First Grade, Mar. 31, 1876. Ninth Annual Catalogue of the Wisconsin State Normal School, at Whitewater, for the Academic Year 1876-1877, Alexandre Seiler, Zermatt, Switzerland, letter Sept. 23, 1881. LYM; *"teaching so unlike all other teaching"*: Julia Field-King reminiscences, 4. LYM; *"My first class was eager"*: Julia Field-King reminiscences, 6. LYM; *Retirement*: Mary Baker Eddy, "Take Notice," *CSJ*, June 1894.

Renegade students: From her initial exposure to Christian Science in Chicago, Julia Field-King knew and may have briefly studied with Emma Curtis Hopkins, who parted ways with Mary Baker Eddy and became a founding influence of New Thought, including Religious Science. See also, Peel, Robert. *Mary Baker Eddy: Years of Authority* (Holt, Rinehart, and Winston: New York. 1977) 416, n. 123.

18 *"They are learning to live the Truth"*: "Notes from the Field," *CSJ*, March 1891; *"I have taught over one hundred"*: Julia Field-King to Mary Baker Eddy, May 28, 1891. LYM.

19 *Field-King called to edit CSJ*: Editor, *CSJ*, Dec. 1891; King, Julia Field, *CSJ*, Sept. 1892; Julia Field-King reminiscences, 8. LYM; *"vigorous protest"*: Julia Field-King reminiscences, 8. LYM; *"I am such a babe"*: Julia Field-King to Mary Baker Eddy, Dec. 17, 1891. LYM; *"[I]f I really trusted God" "I made no more protests"*: Julia Field-King reminiscence, 8. LYM.

20 *"the new-born babes"*: Field-King, Julia. "A Protest," *CSJ*, Dec. 1891.

21 *"we have no need"*: Glover, *S&H*, first ed., 1875, 166-167.

22 *"CHURCH"*: Eddy, *S&H*, 583.

23 *July 4, 1876*: Mary Baker Eddy Library, "The Mary Baker Eddy Library: A Chronology of Events Surrounding the Life of Mary Baker Eddy," 17, citing as its source Christian Scientist Association, record book, Vol. 1, n.d. EOR10, 1; *"designed to commemorate"*: Eddy, *Manual*, 17; *"The question is often asked"*: "Recruit," *CSJ*, Aug. 1885, 101.

24 *"Let no one say"*: SHC, "Our Church-Building," *CSJ*, Nov. 1887.

25 *"O! Christian scientist"*: Eddy, M.B.G. "The People's God: Its Effect on Health and Christianity," *CSJ*, June 1883. See also, *People*, 14.

26 *"designed to be built on the Rock, Christ"*: Eddy, *Manual*, 19.

27 *Oconto church*: "Church Erected," *CSJ*, Oct. 1886. *"The church"*: Mary C. Swift, "Church and Association," *CSJ*, June 1887; "Voices of a Global Movement: The Building of the Oconto Church," blog post, The Mary Baker Eddy Library; "Laura Ellen Sargent, C.S.D.: Biography," blog post, Longyear Museum.

Laura Sargent, who had been a "semi-invalid" previous to her transformation through Christian Science was asked to come be assistant to Eddy starting in 1890.

28 *"Guided by the pillar and the cloud"*: Eddy, *MW*, 149.

DEDICATION

[29] *"era of church building"*: "Newspaper Comment," *CSJ*, Jan. 1898;

[30] *"There is no life, truth"*: Eddy, *S&H*, 468; *"as the north pole" "Has the time come"*: "Christian Science Churches," *CSJ*, Feb. 1892.

[31] *"the erection of a hall"*: "Notes From the Field," *CSJ*, Mar. 1892. See also: Eddy, *MW*, 150.

[32] *Seattle contributions*: "Treasurer's Report," *CSJ*, Dec. 1, 1891 and Mar. 1, 1892.

[33] *"While reading the definition"*: "Notes From the Field," *CSJ*, Feb. 1892.

[34] Seattle collective contributions to The Mother Church were $6 from "Friends" in Dec. 1891 and $10 from "C.S. Students," *CSJ*, Mar. 1892.

[35] *200*: "Christian Science Churches," *CSJ*, Feb. 1892.

[36] *"radical reliance"*: Eddy, *S&H*, 167; *"no doubt must intervene"*: Eddy, Mary Baker, "A Word to the Wise," *CSJ*, Dec. 1893; Eddy, *MW*, 319.

[37] *"November came"*: Armstrong, *TMC*, 92.

[38] *"Notwithstanding the perplexed condition"*: Eddy, *Pulpit*, 8.

[39] *"repeated as often"*: "Notice" for TMC orig. dedication, Jan. 1, 1895. Keith McNeil collection.

[40] *"Christian Scientists, you have planted"*: Eddy, *Pulpit*, 10-11.

[41] *"There are times when human expression fails"*: "The Dedication of The Mother Church," *CSJ*, Feb. 1895.

[42] *"This house of Love now stands"*: Norcross, Lanson P., *CSJ*, Feb. 1895.

[43] "Their Prayer in Stone," *Seattle P-I*, Mar. 24, 1895.

[44] *"Humbly"*: Eddy, Mary Baker, "Church and School," *CSJ*, Apr. 1895, 1; Eddy, *MW*, 313-316.

[45] *"a deep symphony of love" "when the lesson"*: "The Mother's First Appearance in the New Church," *CSJ*, July 1895, 140.

[46] *"era of church building"*: "Newspaper Comment," *CSJ*, Jan. 1898.

[47] *"Another Christian Science church" "the result, in part at least"*: *CSJ*, Dec. 1895.

[48] *"I send my hearty"*: *CSJ*, Dec. 1895, 367.

[49] *"The Christian scientists of this city"*: "A New Church," *Seattle P-I*, Nov. 8, 1896; the initial public notice of incorporation was Oct. 20. "New Incorporation," *Seattle P-I*, Oct. 20, 1896, 2.

[50] *Seattle Theater*: Dorpat, Paul, "Seattle Now & Then: Looking North on 3rd," May 8, 2011, pauldorpat.com (accessed Jan. 2017); *Polk's Seattle City Directory*, 1905, 41; *Readers: Minutes of the Membership Meetings, March 18, 1904 to October 16, 1914*, 11. 01ChSea; *Irregular*: Playter, 3.

Another early First Reader was Marion S. (Stuart Seaton) Callahan, listed in *CSJ Directory* 1899. Early on there were issues over the requirement of membership in The Mother Church for readers, which resulted in replacing readers.

51 *600-seat*: Copper, Ralph Byron, "Declaring 'What the Pioneer Has Accomplished': Talk at First Church of Christ, Scientist, St. Louis, Missouri," Oct. 17, 2004, 2; "*Seattle has been my puzzle*" "*real Christian Scientists*": Julia Field-King to Mary Baker Eddy, Apr. 22, 1897. LYM.

52 "Notes From the Field," *CSJ*, Apr. 1899.

53 "Free Thought Christian Science," *Seattle P-I*, 1896 (Feb-Oct), 14; "*The work there is so mixed*": Julia Field-King to Mary Baker Eddy, Apr 22, 1897. LYM.

In her letter to Mary Baker Eddy, Julia Field-King attributed the scattering influence to students of "Hopkins, Adams, Mason, Choate etc etc." The *Seattle P-I* in the early 1890s showed advertisements for Christian Science healing and teaching by Mr. & Mrs. E.J. Castle, Mrs. J. Anderson Root, Sophie K. Durant, Mrs. Williams, and Mrs. A.W. Anderson. "The Early History of Christian Science" (Playter, 1, 2) mentioned teaching by Mrs. Emily Webber, Miss Lou Aldrich of Portland, and called Field-King's teaching "inaccurate in her statements" proving herself "unfit" for the opportunity bestowed on her and the inconsistent teaching done in Seattle an "unauspicious commencement."

54 *Sometimes to a fault*: Peel, *Authority*, 416 n. 124; *Eddy to Field-King Association*: Copper, Ralph Byron, "Declaring 'What the Pioneer Has Accomplished': Talk at First Church of Christ, Scientist, St. Louis, Missouri," Oct. 17, 2004, 10; "*Christian Science School*": Anna B. White Baker to Mary Kimball Morgan, Oct. 31, 1899, as published in Leonard, *As the Sowing*, 57; "*school which should establish thought on a right basis*": Leonard, *As the Sowing*, 58.

55 "*unprepared and unworthy*": Peel, Robert. *Mary Baker Eddy: Years of Trial*, Boston: Christian Science Publishing Society, 1971. 221; "*in the great metropolis of the great West*" "*special significance*": "Dedication of the Chicago Church," *CSJ*, Dec. 1897. Also, *Miscellany*, 177-183; "*a true and just reply*": Eddy, Mary Baker, *Manual*, 93.

56 "*Killed by Christian Science*": Seattle P-I, Jan. 2, 1891, 2. Jan. 19, 1891, 3. Feb. 22, 1891, 1. Oct. 4, 1891, 1; "Against Christian Science: Rev. E. F. Keever Discusses an Old Error Revived in this Century," *Sea P-I*, Aug. 22, 1892, 5; "Charlatanry vs. Science," *Sea P-I*, Jan. 31, 1892, 4; "*semi-religious craze*": "Special Service for Women: First M. E. Church Crowded Yesterday Afternoon," *ST*, Mar. 14, 1894, 5.

57 *1600-seat*: Polk's *Seattle City Directory* 1889, 873; "*If you had ever*": "Explains Christian Science," *ST*, Oct. 1, 1889, 12; Kimball, Edward A., *Lectures and Articles on Christian Science*. N.S. Wait Publisher, Chesterton, IN. 1921.

58 "*marked increase*": "Notes From the Field," *CSJ*, June 1899, 214; "*Since Mr. Kimball's lecture*": "Notes From the Field," *CSJ*, Apr. 1899, 59.

59 *Armstrong sent*: Playter, 27.

60 "*A real Christian Scientist is a marvel*": Eddy, *MW*, 294.

[61] 1860 US Census, New Albany Ward 5, Floyd, Indiana, Roll: M653_257, 371, FHL film 803257; 1870 US Census, Greenville, Montcalm, Michigan, Roll: M593_692, 89B, FHL film 552191; 1880 US Census, Dexter, Washtenaw, Michigan, Roll: 609, 297D, ED 238; *U of Michigan*: "Memorial Service Held for Scientist Teacher," *ST*, Feb. 5, 1929, 3; "Great Register of San Diego County," 1884 and 1886, California State Library, California History Section, *Great Registers, 1866-1898*, Collection No. 4-2A, CSL Roll 39, FHL 977094.

[62] *Class with Fluno*: Playter, 4; *Fluno's career*: "World's Need for Truth", *Seattle P-I*, May 27, 1899.

Francis J. Fluno took class instruction in Boston from Mary Baker Eddy.

[63] *"While there have been"*: Armstrong, Allen H., "Steady Growth," *CSJ*, Jan. 1897, 500; *Class with Fluno*: Playter, 4.

[64] San Jose, California, City Directory, 1892, 51; *Fluno's advise*: Playter, 4; "Progress of Christian Science: First Church of Christ, Scientist, San Jose, Cal.," *CSJ*, July 1913; *"brimming with enthusiasm"*: Lithgow, Webster. "And of These Stones": Christian Science and the San Francisco Earthquake of 1906," Longyear Museum blog, Apr. 18, 2016; *"proved to be a stepping stone"*: Playter, 4.

[65] "Articles of Incorporation," Sacramento Daily Record-Union, Mar. 15, 1898, 4; *20 charter members*: *"sound basis" "devot[ing] themselves entirely to the practice"*: "Progress of Christian Science: First Church of Christ, Scientist, San Jose, Cal." *CSJ*, July 1913; "Church Dedications: San Jose, California (First Church)," *CSS*, Aug. 25, 1962.

The Oddfellows (IOOF) Building at 82 E. Santa Clara Street still stands, although no longer owned by the fraternal organization.

[66] Allen H. Armstrong's Normal Class teachers were Edward A. Kimball, Laura Lathrop, Septimus J. Hanna, and Alfred E. Baker, M.D, and his diploma was signed by Mary Baker Eddy (Playter, 4. Confirmed from actual diploma in private collection).

[67] *"exceedingly loath" "loyal to his Leader"*: Playter, 4-5; *"expressing regret"*: "Will Leave For Seattle," *San Jose Evening News*, Nov. 11, 1899, 8.

[68] "Laying of Corner-stone in San Jose, Cal.," *CSS*, Feb. 18, 1905, 391; *"We know that all we have"*: "Letters to Our Leader," *CSS*, Dec. 23, 1905; *"Beloved Students: Word are inadequate"*: Eddy, *Miscellany*, 197. Also, "Letters to Our Leader," *CSS*, Dec. 23, 1905.

[69] The number of people in Seattle advertising in the *CSJ* as being full-time in the public healing practice went from two in 1899 to eight in 1900 (including Allen H. and Maud Armstrong) to fourteen by 1902.

[70] *"patiently and persistently"*: Eddy, *Manual*, 83.

Allen H. Armstrong's student association eventually had five or six hundred members. (Playter, 5)

[71] *Church service locations*: CSJ Directory. "Miscellaneous," *Seattle P-I*, Apr. 1, 1894, 12. "Christian Science," *Seattle P-I*, Feb. 3, 1895, 14; "Christian Science," *Seattle P-I*,

Oct. 25, 1896, 14; *"extreme outskirts"*: Allen H. Armstrong, "Among the Churches: Progress at Seattle, Wash.," *CSS*, Feb. 1901.

Initially ads in the local newspapers were for Christian Science Sunday School, not church services. Later they advertised as a Christian Science Bible Class.

72 *"Christian Science Hall"*: Minutes of the Meetings of Board of Directors, Oct. 3, 1899 to May 18, 1903, 37, 67, 96. 01ChSea; *"The church follows"*: Armstrong, Allen H., "Among the Churches: Progress at Seattle, Wash.," *CSS*, Feb. 28, 1901; *Building style*: From historical photos on PaulDorpas.com; *"Christian Science chapel"*: "Progress of Christian Science," *CSJ*, Dec. 1912; *SS at Noon*: 1901 *Seattle City Directory*; "Real Estate & Building: Public Buildings," *Sea P-I*, Dec. 30, 1900, 8.

73 *"first fruits"*: "Progress of Christian Science," *CSJ*, Dec. 1912; Armstrong office: CSJ Directory, 1905; *Cliff as librarian*: 1901 *Polk's Seattle City Directory*; Playter, 3.

74 *Eddy's bylaws on reading rooms*: Eddy, *Manual*, 63, 75.

A few years prior to 1904, Mary Baker Eddy had established a new rule that all Christian Science churches should have a Reading Room. In that era, many different types of organizations had reading rooms—churches of all types, political organizations, and clubs. In Seattle, reading rooms were grouped in the city directory with public libraries. Christian Scientists in Boston and other parts of the country had been operating and advertising reading rooms since the 1890s. They took a variety of forms, sometimes serving a dual purpose as dispensaries for healing treatment. These earliest efforts were motivated by a desire to "raise the vocation" of Christian Scientists "to a livelihood" ("Notice of a New Departure," *CSJ*, May 1889). But as part of the decision to globalize and standardize this outreach, Eddy apparently wanted the reading rooms that served as sales outlets for the Christian Science Publishing Society and the professional offices used by healing practitioners to be separated. During Allen H. Armstrong's era of influence in Seattle, these two functions, although separated, would operate in close proximity. The Seattle church had advertised a reading room since their initial incorporation in 1896, but it had always been in the same location as their church services. The "regular" aspect of the Marion Building reading room was apparently being in an office building.

75 *By dog sled*: "The Baltimore Sun," *CSS*, June 22, 1899; *"in halls and in cabins" "all the time"*: Jackson, Orrin W., testimony, *CSJ*, May 1904.

76 *Ewing's background*: "A Christian Science Lecture," *Seattle Times*, Mar. 10, 1900, 8; *"Whether you accept"*: "The Lectures: At Seattle, Wash.," *CSS*, Apr. 3, 1902.

77 *"We reverently believe"*: Allen H. Armstrong, "Among the Churches: Progress at Seattle, Wash.," *CSS*, Feb. 1901.

78 *"A friend recently"*: Frain, A.K., "Our Church Edifices," *CSS*, Oct. 16, 1902.

79 *"Recognizing the necessity"*: "The Annual Meeting," *CSS*, June 26, 1902.

80 *"In larger and larger throngs"*: Armstrong, Joseph, and Margaret Williamson, *Building of The Mother Church*, Boston: Christian Science Publishing Society, 1908. 104.

DEDICATION

[81] *"This astonishing motion"*: "The Annual Meeting," *CSS*, June 26, 1902.

[82] *"A considerable sum"*: "The Building Fund," *CSS*, Mar. 24, 1906.

[83] "Among the Churches," *CSS*, Jan. 14, 1905, Sept. 30, 1905; "Letters to our Leader," *CSS*, Dec. 2, 1905. Feb. 10, 1906. May 5, 1906; "Giving to The Mother Church," *CSS*, Feb. 17, 1906, June 9, 1906.

[84] *"normal, unexcited, unstrained"*: Armstrong, 149.

[85] *12 from Seattle*: Johnson, William B., William P. McKenzie, and Willis F. Gross, "The Annual Meeting," *CSS*, June 23, 1906; *"Five thousand"*: Eddy, *Miscellany*, 29.

[86] *"Those of us"*: Eddy, *Miscellany*, 73.

[87] *"Please do not send"*: "Christian Scientists Have All the Money Needed," Eddy, *Miscellany*, 72.

[88] *"Beloved"*: Eddy, Mary Baker G., "Dedicatory Message," *CSS*, June 16, 1906; Eddy, *Miscellany*, 3.

[89] *"The great temple"*: Eddy, *Miscellany*, 45; "The Annual Meeting," *CSS*, June 23, 1906.

[90] *"The First Church of Christ, Scientist"*: "Mrs. Eddy Passes," *SS*, Dec. 5, 1910, 3.

[91] *"the new church embodied a might"*: Armstrong, 103.

[92] *"The Christian Science church rises"*: Anna Friendlich, *CSS*, Nov. 21, 1908.

[93] "Progress of Christian Science," *CSJ*, Dec. 1912.

[94] *Attendance*: "Among the Churches: Seattle, Wash," *CSS*, Sept. 25, 1909.

[95] Letters from Examination Board to First Church of Christ, Scientist, Seattle, 1902 to 1913; Membership Roll (Register #1). 01ChSea; *CSJ Directory*.

[96] *Edwin Randall Hoskins*: Cook County, Illinois, Birth Certificates Index, 1871-1922 [database on-line]. Provo, UT, USA: Ancestry.com Operations, Inc., 2011; US WW1 Draft Registration Cards, 1917-1918. State: Washington; King County; Roll: 1991925; Draft Board: 08; US Census 1910, Seattle Ward 3, King County, Washington, Roll: T624_1659, 12A, ED: 0092, FHL microfilm 1375672; *Polk's Seattle City Directory*, 1906, 606; Membership Roll, 34. 01ChSea; *"the entire church body"*: *Minutes of the Membership Meetings, March 18, 1904 to October 16, 1914*, 56. 01ChSea.

[97] *"Grecian style"*: *Minutes of the Membership Meetings, March 18, 1904 to October 16, 1914*, 51. 01ChSea; *"General style"*: Armstrong to Charles H. Bebb, July 17, 1907, BC minutes, 1, 4. 01ChSea; *"Grecian temple"*: Ibid, 12.

[98] BC minutes, 4-26, 01ChSea; *"connection with the Directors" "over a lengthy period of time" "one of the most interesting"*: Charles H. Bebb to Ruth A. Densmore, May 26, 1919. 03ChSea; *"give architectural expression" "eliminating the language expressed" "radical departure" "precedents"*: "An Architectural Expression for a Christian Science Church," Mar. 6, 1915. (author unknown – possibly Charles H. Bebb, as it was paper-clipped to a letter from him to the Third Church of Christ, Scientist, Seattle, building committee) 03ChSea.

⁹⁹ Membership, Board, and BC minutes, *Membership Roll (Register #1)*, and Examining Board letters, 01ChSea; "The Lectures," *CSS*, Jan. 4, 1908; "To Lecture on Christian Science," *ST*, Nov. 7, 1907, 9; "Judge M'Gilvra No More," *ST*, Dec. 19, 1903, 1; "Laud Their Dead Associate," *ST*, Dec. 26, 1903, 4; "Leaves Estate to His Family," *ST*, Jan. 15, 1904, 4; "Early-Day Mansions: No. 21 – John J. M'Gilvra," *ST*, Jan. 21, 1945.

¹⁰⁰ *"moment of interest"*: "Gifts From Puget Sound," MBEL blog, Mar. 4, 2018. MBEL, B00503.

The "moment of interest" quote is from Allen H. Armstrong to Mary Baker Eddy, 30 April 1909, IC 643.66.008. The same photos are included on a page entitled "Scenes Among The Salmon Fishers of Puget Sound" from a promotional booklet advertising highlights of Seattle's history and culture in preparation for the Alaska-Yukon-Pacific Exposition: "The City of Seattle Illustrated," ca. 1909, E.P. Charlton & Co. (Seattle Public Library, Special Collections).

¹⁰¹ *"remarkable cases"*: Playter, 9; "Among the Churches: Seattle, Wash," *CSS*, Sept. 25, 1909.

¹⁰² *"old methods"*: *Minutes of the Membership Meetings, March 18, 1904 to October 16, 1914*, 68. 01ChSea.

Allen H. Armstrong was in charge of posting bulletins on the progress of the building project at the entrance to the church services. He also put envelopes there for contributions to the building fund.

¹⁰³ *"a long informal talk"*: *Board Minute Book March 31, 1904 to June 19, 1911*, 181. 01ChSea; *"not a Leader"*: Eddy, *Manual*, 32-33.

¹⁰⁴ "Alaska Building," Wikipedia.com. Accessed Nov. 28, 2017. Historical photos from "Seattle Now & Then," PaulDorpat.com.

¹⁰⁵ *"To the Directors"*: *Board Minute Book March 31, 1904 to June 19, 1911*, 182-183. 01ChSea. The same letter is in MBEL (04ChSea) Box 40738 Folder 167137 and Box 40737 Folder 165635.

¹⁰⁶ Membership and Board minutes, Membership Roll (Register #1) and Examining Board letters. 01ChSea; *CSJ Directory*; First Church of Christ, Scientist to Mary Baker Eddy, Dec. 23, 1903. 01ChSea; 1901 *Polk's Seattle City Directory*, 1277; Playter, 2.

¹⁰⁷ *Craven & Craven*: *Polk's Seattle Directory*, 1901, 368; "Knights Templar Parade Colorful," *ST*, May 5, 1921, 1, 5; *Craven's purchase of lot*: Purchase agreement, Oct. 12, 1906. 01ChSea. Also mentioned in Board minutes.

Edwin W. Craven had been in the news as an officer in the Knights Templar as early as 1897. Even after retiring as Grand Commander around 1909 when his first listing appeared in the *CSJ*, Craven continued making the local news for his involvement as former Grand Commander in ceremonial roles in major Knights Templar events. Craven sometimes used his Grand Commander letterhead as notepaper for building committee business. BC minutes, 1, 9, 24. 01ChSea; For a few of Craven's news mentions for public events see "Tacoma News: Grand Commandery of Knights Templar," *ST*, June 2, 1897, 2; "Knights Templar in Session," *ST*, June 21, 1904, 4; "Seattle Knights Go To Everett," *ST*, Sept. 10, 1911, 13.

[108] *"for the best good"*: "Among the Churches: Seattle, Wash," *CSS*, Jan 1, 1910.

[109] *"Your withdrawal"*: Board Minute Book March 31, 1904 to June 19, 1911, 184. 01ChSea.

[110] According to Mary Brookins, First Church Seattle had previously not been able to secure the Moore Theater. "Letters to Our Leader," *CSS*, Feb. 12, 1910.

[111] "To Build New Church," *ST*, July 4, 1909, 19; *"In view of the constant"*: "Christian Science," *ST*, July 11, 1909, 11.

[112] *"Any Person"*: Banner of Light, July 4, 1868, 1; Peel, *Trial*, 10-11; Suber, James R. "'For Our Dear Cause': The 1897 Visit to Pleasant View," Longyear Museum Report to Members (Spring/Summer 2013), 4-11; *"To-day"*: Eddy, *MW*, 251.

[113] *"To my mind"*: "The Lectures," *CSS*, Jan. 4, 1908.

Oliver C. McGilvra also gave a brief address on Abraham Lincoln at First Church of Christ, Scientist, Seattle, on February 22, 1909, at a special centenary service in which he shared that his father's law office was in an adjoining office to Lincoln and they had a warm friendship. Consequently Oliver felt as though he personally knew Abraham Lincoln.

[114] "February 12 To Be Legal Holiday," *ST*, Feb. 2, 1909, 8; "Christian Scientists Observe Lincoln Day: President O. C. McGilvra Delivers Eulogy of Great Leader's Faith and Work," newspaper clipping, undated. MBEL Box 530771 Folder 242249; Oliver C. McGilvra to Miss C. F. Miller, Feb. 22, 1909. MBEL Box 530771 Folder 242249; McGilvra's Lincoln eulogy. MBEL Box 530771 Folder 242249.

[115] Board minutes and *Membership Roll (Register #1)*, 01ChSea; *CSJ Directories*; Playter et al, "The Early History," 1932; US Census 1910 shows Sheldon already as "C.S.B.". *Samuel Adams*: "A Biographical Sketch of Laura E. Sargent, C.S.D., and Victoria Sargent, C.S.D.: Ancestral History," The Bookmark, Santa Clarita, CA. Undated.

[116] *"Votes for Women"*: Becker, Paula. "Alaska-Yukon-Pacific Exposition (1909): Woman Suffrage", HistoryLink.org Essay 8587. Accessed Nov. 19, 2017; "Christian Science Lecture," *ST*, July 11, 1909, 7; "Music Principal Program Today," *ST*, July 4, 1909; *"largest and best theater" "required help"*: Mary Brookins, "Letters to Our Leader," *CSS*, Feb. 12, 1910.

[117] "Fourth Church of Christ, Scientist," *ST*, July 10, 1909, 2; *"terra cotta-trimmed" "personally supervised"*: Polly Lane, "Old to be recycled to new buildings," *ST*, Sept. 6, 1981, 102.

[118] *Cushing Second Reader*: "Members of Fourth Church of Christ, Scientist, Seattle, Washington," MBEL (04ChSea) Box 40737 Folder 165635; "Charles E. Cushing," *ST*, Jan. 16, 1941, 28; "For A Ferry," *ST*, May 27, 1899, 1; "Port Angeles Road," *ST*, Mar. 2, 1900, 10; "The Lectures: At Victoria, B. C.," *CSS*, Mar. 21, 1903; 1910 US Census, Seattle Ward 14, King County, Washington, Roll: T624_1661, 13A, ED: 0215, FHL

microfilm 1375674; *Ireland Family: Polk's Seattle City Directories:* 1902, 688; 1903, 644; 1904, 562; 1905, 659; 1907, 623; 1910, 819; 1911, 717; US Census 1910, Seattle Ward 14, King, Washington County, Roll: T624_1661, 9A, ED 0215, FHL microfilm 1375674; "*scoffer and almost an infidel*": C. W. Ireland, testimony, *CSS*, Aug. 10, 1907.

119 *less than 800*: "History of Fourth Church of Christ, Scientist, Seattle, Washington," undated [est. 1932], 1, 2. MBEL (04ChSea) Box 40737 Folder 165635; "Historical Sketch Read at the Dedication Services of Fourth Church of Christ, Scientist, Seattle, Held August 1, 1937," MBEL (04ChSea) Box 40737 Folder 165635.

120 "*Women were seen*": Playter, 10; "*The wanderings*": "Among the Churches: Seattle, Wash," *CSS*, Sept. 25, 1909.

121 "*our summer kitchen*": Playter, 9; "*quiet*": "Plan Recommended by the Church Directorate for Early Completion of Church Building," *Minutes of the Membership Meetings, Mar 18, 1904, to Oct. 16, 1914*, 103. 01ChSea.

122 "*That it shall be*": *Board Minute Book March 31, 1904 to June 19, 1911*, 209. 01ChSea.

123 "*Our membership*": "Among the Churches," *CSS*, June 4, 1910.

124 "Dedication of a Church in London, England," *CSJ*, Jan. 1898; "*a vast white building*": Seymer, Diane Ker, "Expansion," *CSS*, Jan. 4, 1908; "Dedication of Church in London," *CSS*, July 3, 1909.

125 "Among the Churches: Progress in St. Louis," *CSS*, July 25, 1901; "Church Dedication in St. Louis," *CSS*, Apr. 29, 1905; "Declaring 'What the Pioneer Has Accomplished'," Ralph Byron Copper, 2004, p. 4.

126 "Among the Churches: Seattle, Wash," *CSS*, Sept. 25, 1909.

127 "*not think much of birthdays*" "*remarkably vigorous*" "*not withstanding the recent reports*": "Mrs. Mary Baker G. Eddy 88 Years Old Today," July 16, 1909, *ST*, 7; "*My Beloved Brethren*": Eddy, Mary Baker, "Mrs. Eddy's Statements," *CSS*, June 12, 1909; "Denies Mrs. Eddy is Feeble," June 14, 1909, *ST*, 7.

128 "*to injure no man*": Eddy, Mary Baker, "Something in a Name," *CSM*, Nov. 25, 1908, 8. Also, Eddy, *Miscellany*, 353; "The Mary Baker Eddy Library: A Chronology of Events Surrounding the Life of Mary Baker Eddy," MBEL, 64-80.

129 Allen H. Armstrong to Mrs. Mary Baker Eddy, Oct. 17, 1910. MBEL item 643a.66.009. June 5, 1910 telegraph, MBEL item 643a.66.010.

130 "*Mrs. Eddy's strong, clear voice*" "*My Beloved Brethren:--I have a secret*": Eddy, Mary Baker G., "The Letter of the Pastor Emeritus," *CSS*, July 4, 1903. Also, Eddy, *Miscellany*, 133-4.

131 "*It becomes my duty*": "Mrs. Eddy Passes," *SS*, Dec. 5, 1910, 3.

132 "*in each instance the ministers*": "No Mention of Mrs. Eddy's Death at Local Science Church Services," *SS*, Dec. 12, 1910, 5.

133 "Mary Baker Eddy, Founder of Christian Science Church Dead," *Tacoma Times*, Dec. 5, 1910, 1, 5; "Mrs. Mary Baker Eddy is Dead," *The Spokane Press*, Dec. 5, 1910, 1, 2.

DEDICATION

[134] "Founder of Christian Science Passes Away," *ST*, Dec. 5, 1910, 12; "*Mary Baker Eddy is dead*": "The Passing of Mrs. Eddy," *ST*, Dec. 8, 1910, 6. Reprinted in "Excerpts From Editorial Comments," *CSS*, Feb. 4, 1911.

[135] "Mrs. Eddy Expected to Demonstrate Over Death," *ST*, Dec. 30, 1910, 8; "Reproof for Mrs. Stetson," *SS*, Dec. 30, 1910, 1; "*Mrs. Eddy, in the space*": Milmine, Georgine, "Mrs. Eddy Treated to Down Death Thought," *ST*, Dec. 27, 1910, 11.

[136] "*Six weeks ago*": "The Lectures: Seattle, Wash," *CSS*, Feb 11, 1911.

[137] "*Christian Scientists*": "Annual Meeting of The Mother Church," *CSS*, June 10, 1911.

[138] "*The past year*": "Annual Meeting of The Mother Church," *CSS*, June 10, 1911.

[139] "*temple of Bedford Limestone*": "Progress of Christian Science," *CSJ*, Dec. 1912; *Tribute*: Playter, 10; "*the superstructure of Truth*": Eddy, *S&H* 595.

[140] "Mrs. Eddy To Rest in Cemetery Near Boston," *SS*, Dec. 6, 1910; "Son's Will Rules in Burial of Mrs. Eddy," *ST*, Dec. 6, 1910, 13; "Funeral of Mrs. Eddy Marked By Simplicity," *ST*, Dec. 8, 1910, 11; "Mrs. Eddy at Rest," *SS*, Dec. 8, 1910, 7; "The Funeral of Mrs. Mary Baker G. Eddy," *SS*, Dec. 13, 1910, 3; "To Keep Guards Over Her Body," *SS*, Dec. 29, 1910, 3; "Mrs. Eddy's Body Now Lies in Concrete Grave," *ST*, Jan. 27, 1911, 14.

[141] "Mrs. Eddy Leaves Her Fortune to Church," *SS*, Dec. 9, 1910, 1; "Reported Eddy Wealth Goes Mostly to Church," *ST*, Dec. 9, 1910, 5; "Sons May Fight Church to Break Mrs. Eddy's Will," *ST*, Dec. 11, 1910, 22; "Residuary Clause of Mrs. Eddy's Will Void," *ST*, Jan. 13, 1919, 16; "Another Claim Made in Eddy Will Fight," *ST*, Feb. 8, 1911, 3; "Still Another Wants Part of Eddy Fortune," *ST*, Mar. 21, 1911, 5; "Glover Says Mrs. Eddy Systematically Deceived," *ST*, Mar. 25, 1911, 14; "Mrs. Eddy Expected to Demonstrate Over Death," *ST*, Dec. 30, 1910, 8; "Reproof for Mrs. Stetson," *SS*, Dec. 30, 1910, 1; "Do the Dead Come Back?" *ST*, Jan. 29, 1911.

[142] "Peabody of Boston Denounces Mrs. Eddy," *ST*, Oct. 14, 1909, 13; "Peabody to Deliver Lecture," *ST*, Oct. 20, 1909, 23; "*complete exposure*": "On the Reviewing Desk," *ST*, Jan. 15, 1911, 19.

[143] "*The vitality of her message*": "Predict Downfall of Christian Science," *Tacoma Times*, Dec. 5, 1910, 8; a "*a great dilemma*": "Christian Science Church is Now Facing a Great Dilemma," *SS*, 8.

[144] *Joint RR idea*: "History of Fourth Church of Christ, Scientist, Seattle, Washington," 1932, 2. MBEL (04ChSea) Box 40737 Folder 165635.

[145] "*a long step forward*": "Progress of Christian Science," *CSJ*, Dec. 1912; $140 each: C. Macklem, Clerk to Miss Evangeline Fox, July 23, 1912. 01ChSea; "*One cannot visit*": Bixby, Alma Durant, "Report of Joint Reading Room, Read at First Church Semi-annual Meeting June 6, 1913." 01ChSea.

[146] Bixby, Alma Durant, "Report of Joint Reading Room, Read at First Church Semi-annual Meeting June 6, 1913," 2. 01ChSea; Bixby, Alma Durant, "Monthly Report," (various months, 1912-1913), Christian Science Reading Room. 01ChSea.

147 Bixby, Alma D, testimony, *CSS*, Apr. 24, 1920; Bixby, Alma D, testimony, *CSS*, Apr. 24, 1920; *Membership Roll (Register #1)*, 94. 01ChSea.

148 *"One of the most noticeable"*: "Reading Room Report For Semi-Annual Meeting of First Church of Christ, Scientist, Seattle," June 11, 1915. 01ChSea.

149 *First Reader*: "Rites for Chief Clerk," *ST*, Sept. 28, 1920, 11; "Dentists' Wedding Surprises Friends," *ST*, Sept. 7, 1914, 9; *"Some new phases of dentistry"*: "Society: Social Events," *ST*, Mar. 22, 1914, 3; *Medical Arts Building*: 1934 *Seattle Numerical Street Address Directory*, Seattle Public Library, Special Collections Online; *Conference*: "Society," *ST*, July 12, 1918, 6; Raper, Cecil S. and W. S. Padget, "The Lectures: Introductions to Lectures," *CSS*, May 15, 1926.

Dr. Walter Padget gave a talk on "Some new phases of dentistry" at a Seattle alumni meeting for Northwestern University, attending a national dentist convention in Chicago.

150 *"zealous Christian Scientists"*: Editor, *CSJ*, Nov. 1897; "Revised Science and Health in Foreign Countries," *CSJ*, Aug. 1891; Kinter, Geo. H, "Association Work," *CSJ*, Aug. 1896.

151 Charles W. Colby, Report of the Joint Distribution Committee, Nov. 29, 1912. 01ChSea; H.O. Harvey, "Report of the Joint Distribution Committee, Mar. 7, 1913. 01ChSea; "Missionary Committee": *Minutes of the Meetings of the Board of Directors October 3, 1899 to May 18, 1903*, 98, 99. 01ChSea.

152 H.O. Harry, "Report of the Joint Distribution Committee," Mar. 7, 1913. 01ChSea; Margaret M. Walker, "Church Extension Work" Semi-Annual Meeting, June 11, 1915. 01ChSea.

Volunteers conducting jail services had the special privilege, convenience, and speed of traveling by automobile to the jails to begin holding services at 12:15 p.m.

153 *"You know that the Monitor"*: Unsigned draft letter to Steven M. Piles, Secretary, University YMCA, May 1, 1912. 01ChSea.

154 Roberta Lee Terry, "Semi-Annual Report: Christian Science Literature Distribution Committee, June 1, 1914. 01ChSea; *"Although several thousand"*: Roberta Lee Terry, "Semi-Annual Report of the Christian Science Literature Distribution Committee, May 1 to October 31, 1918." 01ChSea.

155 Eleanor L Morgan, "Report of the Christian Science Literature Distribution Committee, June 1 to Nov. 30, 1914." 01ChSea.

156 *"stated that he had for years read"*: Roberta Lee Terry, "Semi-Annual Report of the Christian Science Literature Distribution Committee, May 1 to October 31, 1918. 01ChSea.

157 *"As a result"*: "Report of the Joint Committee of the Christian Science Monitor." June 1, 1912. 01ChSea.

158 *"By far the most"*: Frank S. Smith, "Report of the Joint Committee of the Christian Science Monitor," Mar. 1, 1913. 01ChSea.

Besides their work with the *Monitor*, the literature distribution committee placed dozens of copies of *Science and Health* and many other related books at the public library. They regularly placed literature in the sitting areas (referred to as "reading rooms" in the source document) of hotels, club rooms, businesses, and major department stores. Martha S. Watkins, "Literature Distribution Committee of the Christian Science Churches and Society of Seattle: Annual Report, Dec. 1, 1913." 01ChSea; It was reported in the *Christian Science Journal* about Seattle, "Here, as elsewhere in the field, the reading-rooms and the distribution of literature have been important factors in the growth of the cause." "Progress of Christian Science," *CSJ*, Dec 1912, 537.

[159] Charles A. Griffith to Members of First Church of Christ, Scientist, Seattle, Wash, Dec. 9, 1913. 01ChSea; Letter to Joint Lecture Committee, June 17, 1913 (and associated notes and letters). 01ChSea; Advertisement for First Church of Christ, Scientist, of Seattle, *ST*, May 7, 1913, 9.

[160] *"to devise ways"*: "Report of the Work of Joint Finance Building Committee of the Joint Boards of the Christian Science Churches and Society of Seattle," Nov. 2, 1912. 01ChSea; The regular financial support of the First Church building project by all the Seattle branch churches starting in 1912 is also mentioned in "History of Fourth Church of Christ, Scientist, Seattle, Washington," 1932, (probably written by Adela S. Hawley, approved by the Board), MBEL (04ChSea) Box 40738 Folder 167137.

[161] "Progress of Christian Science," CSS, Dec. 1912; *"we pledge our moral"*: Minutes of the Membership Meetings, Mar 18, 1904, to Oct. 16, 1914, 128. 01ChSea; *"Resolved"*: Minutes of the Membership Meetings, Mar 18, 1904, to Oct. 16, 1914, 116. 01ChSea.

[162] *"Biblical history"*: "The Lectures," CSS, Aug. 2, 1913.

[163] Jones, John Paul, Bebb and Jones to Isabel B. Grant, Clerk, First Church of Christ, Scientist, Aug. 8, 1949. 01ChSea; *Rathvon"*: "Gives Lectures on Christian Science," *SS*, Jan. 26, 1914, 5; "The Lectures: Seattle, Wash," CSS, Aug. 1, 1912; *"In the last few years"*: *We Knew Mary Baker Eddy: Expanded Edition, Vol II.* Christian Science Publishing Society, Boston, 2013, 513; *"temple of Bedford Limestone"*: "Progress of Christian Science," *CSJ*, Dec. 1912.

[164] *"Simplicity and dignity" "chief attributes" "imposing" "designed in simple restrained"*: "An Architectural Expression for a Christian Science Church," Mar. 6, 1915. 03ChSea.

[165] *Edward J. Holslag mural in Kansas City, MO - 2CCS*: Mimi Stiritz, "Christian Science Churches in Missouri," The Society of Architectural Historians, Missouri Valley Chapter newsletter, Summer 2012, 5; *"During the past ten days"*: "Artists Beautify Scientist Church," *ST*, May 4, 1914.

[166] *"Whatever may be said"*: "Christian Science Churches in Missouri," Mimi Stiritz. The Society of Architectural Historians, Missouri Valley Chapter newsletter, Summer 2012, 1. (quoting Reedy's *Mirror*, June 13, 1907).

[167] *"excellent for the voice"*: "An Architectural Expression for a Christian Science Church," Mar. 6, 1915. 03ChSea.

¹⁶⁸ *Membership Roll (Register #1)*, 82, 83, 124. 01ChSea; Examining Committee report to members, Nov. 29, 1907. 01ChSea; "Report of Joint Committee of The Christian Science Monitor, Covering Period from Apr. 1, 1912 to Dec. 31, 1912." 01ChSea.

Charles A. Griffith first applied for membership in 1907, but the examining committee recommended against admitting him because they felt he had not studied Christian Science long enough. He was admitted to membership a year later, and by 1911 he was in the *Christian Science Journal* as a practitioner and a regular contributor of articles and poems. Griffith first became a *Journal*-listed practitioner in North Yakima, in eastern Washington, where he moved to and lived for about two years before returning to Seattle to live on Capitol Hill and rejoining First Church of Christ, Scientist, Seattle. The Griffiths's practitioner office in 1914 was on the eighth floor near the office of Allen H. Armstrong, who shared his office with two other practitioners. In all, there were at least six Christian Science practitioners working in the building at the time. Both he and his wife, Rubena, became Christian Science practitioners, often sharing an office. In 1914, their office was on Fourth Avenue at Pike Street downtown in the newly constructed 10-story Joshua Green Building where Allen H. Armstrong moved his office. Charles had also been involved in the promotion of the *Christian Science Monitor* through the joint literature distribution committee, reaching out to a variety of local businesses to solicit advertising. A separate office was established for the *Monitor* in the Joshua Green Building.

¹⁶⁹ *"as little ostentation"*: "Scientist Church will Open June 7," *ST*, May 25, 1914.

¹⁷⁰ *"worthy of the city"*: Allen H. Armstrong, "Among the Churches: Progress at Seattle, Wash.," *CSS*, Feb. 1901.

¹⁷¹ *"Inside the Christian Science fold"*: Friendlich, Anna, "Church Building in Christian Science," *CSS*, Nov. 21, 1908.

¹⁷² *"The praiseworthy success"*: Eddy, *Miscellany*, 195.

¹⁷³ *"In completing this structure"*: Charles A. Griffith, letter from board to members, June 12, 1914. 01ChSea.

¹⁷⁴ *"Your individual efforts"*: Board of Directors, First Church of Christ, Scientist, to Building Committee, Dec. 16, 1914. 01ChSea.

¹⁷⁵ *"their highest appreciation" "the highest accomplishment"*: "Resolution in Pursuance of Motion Made and Unanimously Carried at the Regular Meeting of the Board of Directors of First Church of Christ, Scientist, Seattle," Dec. 8, 1914. 03ChSea.

¹⁷⁶ *"a beautiful structure" "a very large attendance"*: Bagley, Clarence B., History of Seattle: From the Earliest Settlement to the Present Time, Vol. 1. 1914, 186.

¹⁷⁷ *"its motive being to promote"*: "Plans Recital at Scientist Church," *ST*, Nov. 21, 1914, 4.

¹⁷⁸ *"a greater fellowship"*: "Special Church Meetings Close," *ST*, Mar. 2, 1914, 10; *"great series of unity revival services" "attention-getting features"*: "Big Revival Will Open on March 29," *ST*, Mar. 21, 1913, 8; Bagley, Clarence B., *History of Seattle: From*

the Earliest Settlement to the Present Time, Vol. 1 (Chicago, 1916), 187; *"summon the people to church"*: "Church Forward Campaign Grows," *ST*, Feb. 10, 1914, 5.

[179] *"fierce denunciation of Christian Science"*: "8,000 Hear Revival Crusade Concluded," *ST*, Nov. 10, 1913, 18; *"one of the most eminent representatives"*: Bagley, Clarence B., *History of Seattle, Vol. 3*, 958-959; *"vitriolic-tonged Georgian" "a forceful — well-nigh hypnotic — speaker"*: John Evans, "Calls Apathetic Saintly Walkers in Their Slumber," *ST*, Apr. 3, 1914, 14; *"Christian (?) Science (?)"*: Rev. M.A. Matthews, "Dr. M.A. Matthews' Sunday Night Sermon," *ST*, Nov. 19, 1907, 9; *"Eddyism" "Eddyites" "so-called" "exaggerated and false"*: "Matthews Hits Theological Slummers," *ST*, Oct. 11, 1909, 11; *"declared that Christianity is strong and masculine" "done so much to blacken society" "branded by the speaker as blasphemous" "every fundamental principle" "Hold to your Bible"*: "8,000 Hear Revival Crusade Concluded," *ST*, Nov. 10, 1913, 18.

[180] *"as a last resort" "The Pharisees"*: "Christian Scientist Defend His Belief," *ST*, Nov. 17, 1913, 10.

[181] *"Great Unity Revival Series"*: *ST*, Mar. 30, 1914, 13; *"acknowledged to be the foremost"*: "Happy Christian Leads in Singing," *ST*, Mar. 31, 1914, 14; *"a monster choir"*: "Revival Service Begins Tonight," *ST*, Mar. 30, 1914, 13; *"The beginning of the series"*: John Evans, "Church Strong Only if Divine Spirit Be Kept," *ST*, Mar. 31, 1914, 14; "Pastors to Keep Up Their Revival Additional Week," *ST*, Apr. 5, 1914, 5; "Noon Meetings Held at Orpheum Theater," *ST*, Apr. 7, 1914, 10.

[182] *"a considerable improvement"*: John Evans, "1,000 Inspired By Sermon of Dr. C. H. Jones," *ST*, Apr. 1, 1914, 12; *"awakened rudely" "his eye searching accusingly" "You are expected to go back"*: "Smug Christians Rudely Shaken Up," *ST*, Apr. 2, 1914, 14.

[183] "Noon Meetings Held at Orpheum Theatre," *ST*, Apr. 7, 1914, 10; *"The very atmosphere seemed surcharged"*: "Crucified Christ Rouses Audience," *ST*, Apr. 7, 1914, 10.

[184] *"the Adversary, Satan"*: Pastor Russell, "Falling Into Infidelity In the Evil Day," *SS*, Jan 25, 1915, 2; *"The growth of Christian Science"*: Pastor Russell, "Christian Science: Is It Reasonable?" *SS*, Apr. 26, 1915, 3; Pastor Russell, "Christian Science: Is It Scriptural?" *SS*, May 3, 1915, 2.

[185] *"leader of that cult"*: "Says Woman Healer Visited Man at 2AM; Wife Away," *SS*, Apr. 2, 1915, 1.

[186] *"attacked by pulpit and press"*: "From the Boston Globe," *CSS*, Apr. 6, 1899; *"Be patient towards persecution"*: "Dedicatory Address of Rev. Mary Baker G. Eddy," *CSS*, Apr. 6, 1899; Eddy, *Miscellany*, 191.

[187] *Hippodrome*: "Faith Heals, Says Professor Herring," *ST*, Apr. 20, 1914, 10; *Yellowstone*: Margaret Pitcairn Strachan, "Early-Day Mansions: No. 8 — Judge James T. Ronald," *ST*, Oct. 22, 1944, 34; *Vestryman*: "Episcopalian Year is Prosperous," *ST*, Apr. 21, 1908, 7; *St. Mark's*: "History," Saint Mark's Episcopal Cathedral website. (saintmarks.org/events-2/history) accessed March 7, 2018; *"For many years"*: "The Lectures: Seattle, Wash." *CSS*, Sept. 12, 1914.

[188] *"celebrated anti-Christian Science"*: "Baptists Denounce Christian Science," *ST*, Apr. 28, 1909, 14; "Boston Lawyer to Lecture," *ST*, Oct. 12, 1909, 18; "Peabody to Deliver Lecture," *ST*, Oct. 20, 1909, 23; *"scathing denunciation"*: "Peabody of Boston Denounces Mrs. Eddy," *ST*, Oct. 14, 1909, 13; *"The whole discourse"*: "The Lectures: Seattle, Wash." *CSS*, Sept. 12, 1914.

The Peabody lecture was held at the YMCA Building, introduced by Rev. M.A. Matthews and Rev. W.H.W. Rees. A similar lecture was given a week later at First Presbyterian Church where Matthews was pastor.

[189] *Virginia, Harry John, and Orison Marshal Dutton at Principia School*: "Society," *ST*, June 9, 1917, 4; "Society," *ST*, Dec. 14, 1918; "Society," *ST*, June 8, 1919; "Personal Mention," *ST*, Dec. 23, 1925, 10.

[190] *"a sermon that will please nobody" "I have tried to rid my mind" "It is a spiritual idealism"*: "Preacher Finds Good in Christian Science," *ST*, Sept. 22, 1911, 19; partially reprinted in "Selected Articles," *CSS*, Dec. 9, 1911.

[191] "Buy Church Site," *SS*, July 22, 1914, 3; *"illustrative of the activity"*: "Apartment Houses Show City's Growth: Whitworth Home Sold for $60,000," *ST*, Aug. 30, 1914, 12.

[192] *1,500*: "History of Fourth Church of Christ, Scientist, Seattle, Washington," undated [est. 1932], 2. MBEL (04ChSea) Box 40737 Folder 165635; "Historical Sketch Read at the Dedication Services of Fourth Church of Christ, Scientist, Seattle, Held August 1, 1937," MBEL (04ChSea) Box 40737 Folder 165635; *"Madison Square Garden of Seattle"*: "Carnival and Electrical Exposition This Week," *ST*, Mar. 2, 1913, 58.

[193] *"a few students of Christian Science" "known as the old"*: E. Nora Yoder, "Letters To Our Leader," *CSS*, Sept. 26, 1908.

[194] "Among the Churches," *CSS*, May 10, 1941; *Weed Building*: US Dept. of Interior National Park Service, National Register of Historic Places, Columbia City Historic District, King County, WA. OMB No. 1024-0018; *Music teacher*: US Census 1910, Seattle Ward 7, King, WA; Roll: 7624_1660; P 4B; ED 0123; FHL 1375673.

[195] Notes for special meeting, Feb. 26, 1915, 8. 01ChSea. The author of this document is almost certainly Allen H. Armstrong.

[196] *"marks an epoch in our history" "While each has drawn"*: Charles A. Griffith, Report of the Board of Directors, Dec. 8, 1914. 01ChSea; *West Seattle society*: "Among the Churches," *CSS*, Oct. 17, 1942.

[197] *"Beloved Brethren"*: Eddy, *MW*, 154.

[198] *Armstrong as board chair: Minute Book June 27, 1911 to December 11th, 1914 and also includes report of the Annual meeting of December 11, 1914*, 303. 01ChSea.

[199] *"surprises" "every liability and asset"*: Notes for special meeting, Feb. 26, 1915, 8. 01ChSea.

[200] *"unswerving obedience and trust"*: "Support," *CSS*, Feb. 6, 1915.

[201] *Armstrong's speech*: Notes for special meeting, Feb. 26, 1915, 2. 01ChSea; "*Giving does not impoverish*": Eddy, *S&H*, 79-80.

[202] "*Wireless*": Allen H. Armstrong, "Present Salvation," *CSJ*, Aug 1905.

[203] "*Thus, you see*" "*If we had only ourselves*" "*Resolved that the members of this church*" "*The battle is on*": Notes for special meeting, Feb. 26, 1915. 01ChSea.

[204] Board Minutes, University District Christian Science Society. 03ChSea.

[205] *UW YWCA history*: Archives West, "Young Women's Christian Association (University of Washington) records, 1903-1982: Historical Note," Orbis Cascade Alliance. archiveswest.orbiscascade.org/ark:/80444/xv26006 [accessed May 4, 2017].

YWCA-CS relationship: A YWCA sign is visible in a historical photo of the Seattle Theater building, which was across the street from the earliest location of the first Christian Science church and reading room, and was the location for the first Christian Science lectures. Allen H. Armstrong was among the financial contributors in 1911 when the downtown YWCA needed a new home, see "YWCA Campaign Quarters Removed," *ST*, May 20, 1911, 7.

[206] Safronoff, Cindy Peyser. *Crossing Swords: Mary Baker Eddy vs. Victoria Claflin Woodhull and the Battle for the Soul of Marriage* (This One Thing: Seattle. 2015), 232.

[207] Of the 42 charter members, 33 were women, 9 men. Throughout the first decade of the University District Christian Science Society / Third Church of Christ, Scientist, Seattle, the gender ratio of each group of new members, admitted twice each year, ranged between 60% and 100% women. Nearly all the men joined with their wives.

[208] "*peculiarly woman's religion*": Denver (Col.) Republican, *CSS*, Jan. 21, 1911; "The statement is often made": W.S.W. "A Woman's Religion," *CSS*, Sept. 1901.

[209] "Official List of Church Preferences of Students in the University of Washington, Fall 1925," University YMCA collection, UW SC, 2126-003, Box 1, Folder 1.

For church preference, 89 men and 329 women selected Christian Science, out of a total of 9867 counted. Christian Science was the fifth most popular choice for women, with only Catholic, Episcopal, Methodist, and Presbyterian more popular. For men, Christian Science was eighth place. Men were more likely than women to select "no preference."

[210] "*A letter from a student*": Eddy, *Miscellany*, 355.

[211] *950*: BC minutes, Apr. 12, 1920. 03ChSea; Byron Haviland to Board, Mar. 20, 1920. 03ChSea.

[212] "*scholarly manner*" "*If all doctrinarians*": Hanford (Cal.) Sentinel, *CSS*, Apr. 18, 1908; Editor, "Bicknell Young to Return," *CSS*, Mar. 8, 1913; "*Mr. Young indulges neither fervor*": Toledo (Ohio) Press, *CSS*, July 20, 1907.

[213] "Whole Edition Sold," *CSS*, Nov. 12, 1904; *Norwegian*: "From the Publishing Society," *CSS*, July 31, 1915.

214 *"a man of striking" "a rich, musical voice"*: Kinter, George H, "Words of Appreciation," *CSS*, July 30, 1904; Concord Patriot, "The Lectures: Concord, NH," *CSS*, Oct. 29, 1904; *Messiah*: Tacoma Festival Chorus ad, *ST*, Dec. 21, 1896, 7; "The Lectures: Concord, NH," *CSS*, Oct. 29, 1904.

215 *"One might have thought"*: Glasgow Herald, "The Lectures: Glasgow, Scotland," *CSS*, Feb 10, 1906; *Personal background*: Beth Stafford, untitled paper, June, 16, 2016, Ancestry.com; Wikipedia articles, "Joseph Young," "Seymour B. Young," "Mormon Pioneers"; *Normal Class Notes of 1937 as taught by Bicknell Young*, The Bookmark: Santa Clarita, CA, 2003.

216 *Eddy in Chicago*: Lithgow, Webster. "A Westward Wind: Christian Science Teaching Goes West, Part 1: Chicago," *Longyear Museum Report to Members*, Fall/Winter 2017; Eddy, *Miscellany*, 182; Stafford, 4.

217 "Dedication of the Chicago Church," *CSJ*, Dec. 1897; *"if wisdom lengthens"*: Eddy, *Miscellany*, 177.

218 *"The statement in my letter"*: Eddy, *Miscellany*, 146.

219 *"even in small degree"*: Eddy, *S&H*, 492. Also, 126, 223, 348; "There is no more age": *Normal Class Notes of 1937 as taught by Bicknell Young*, The Bookmark: Santa Clarita, CA, 2003, 49.

220 *"remarkable vitality" "Aside from a slight deafness"*: "Aged Tacoma Woman to be Buried in Utah," *ST*, Jan. 13, 1913, 3.

Jane Bicknell Young's passing was also noted in the Jan. 21, 1913, *Norwich Bulletin*, Hartford, CT, which called her "widow of Joseph Young, brother of Brigham Young" and "a prominent Christian Science leader."

221 *Concord dedication address*: Eddy, *Miscellany*, 159-163; *"finely read" "musical voice"*: "Dedication of the Church in Concord," *CSS*, July 23, 1904; *"musical voice"*: "Words of Appreciation," *CSS*, July 30, 1904. "Board of Lectureship," *CSS*, July 25, 1903; *"while listening to"*: Raddatz, C.L., testimony, *CSS*, Apr. 7, 1906.

222 *950*: BC minutes, Apr. 12, 1920. 03ChSea; Byron Haviland to Board, Mar. 20, 1920. 03ChSea.

223 *"The members knew"*: Gormley, Eileen. "Historical Sketch of Third Church of Christ, Scientist, Seattle, Washington," July 21, 1934, 3. 03ChSea.

At the University Bank Building they also had a lecture by Paul Stark Seeley. "Man Must Think His Way Into Heaven," *ST*, Jan. 10, 1917.

224 The Fourth Church building committee chair during this period is uncertain because not all internal records of Fourth Church Seattle were available at the time of research for this project. Unfortunately, few internal records relating to the First Unit building project were available. The transcript for the building committee chair's Aug. 29, 1915, talk provide no name of authorship. William K. Sheldon is specifically mentioned in newspaper articles on the building project as chair. "New Church on Downtown Site," *Seattle P-I*, July 7, 1916. "Church Edifice to be Elaborate," *ST*, July 8, 1916, p. 5. Sheldon is found in building committee records in the

early months of the Second Unit building project prior to his resignation from the committee.

225 *Vermont, Vital Records, 1720-1908* [database on-line]. Provo, UT, USA: Ancestry.com Operations, Inc., 2013; US Census *1880, Rutland, Rutland, Vermont*; Roll: *1348, 400C,* ED: *192;* 1900 US Census, Westfield, Hampden, Massachusetts, *17,* ED *0608,* FHL microfilm *1240653;* Carleton, Hiram, *Genealogical and Family History of the State of Vermont: A Record of the Achievements of her People and the Founding of a Nation, Vol. 2,* 1903, New York and Chicago: The Lewis Publishing Company, 656; BC Minutes, 50. 01ChSea; Membership minutes, June 1, 1906, 36. 01ChSea.

After William K. Sheldon joined his father's stone company it was renamed Sheldon & Sons. But William's life may have taken its dramatic turn when he managed a stone quarry in Massachusetts around 1900. It is possible he had some significant experience with Christian Science there. When he moved to Seattle and joined First Church in 1906, he did so "by letter," which meant he had previously been a member of another Christian Science branch church. He was soon elected First Reader. The church was large and already had many Christian Science practitioners and teachers in membership, therefore he must may have been perceived as having outstanding understanding of Christian Science or a closer connection to Mary Baker Eddy than any other candidate.

226 *"with characteristic enterprise"*: "F. S. Sylvester, retired. . ." *ST,* July 7, 1920, 11; "Fred Sylvester Dies on Island," *SS,* July 7, 1920, 15; "Members of Fourth Church of Christ, Scientist, Seattle, Washington," MBEL Box 40737 Folder 165635; George Foote Dunham to F. S. Sylvester, Dec. 11, 1915. MBEL (04ChSea) Box 41326 Folder 482905.

227 *"a place of worship that will reflect love"*: Building and Finance Committee Chair to congregation, Aug. 29, 1915, 4. MBEL (04ChSea) Box 41326 Folder 482905.

228 *"In [Christian Science] we cannot stand still" "This statement is made"*: Building and Finance Committee Chair to congregation, Aug. 29, 1915. MBEL (04ChSea) Box 41326 Folder 482905; *"universal and impartial in its adaptation"*: Eddy, *S&H,* 13.

229 DeCoster, Dotty. "Town Hall Seattle," HistoryLink.org essay 10109. May 28, 2012; Untitled, undated, unsigned, handwritten note. THS; Prof. Reichert, R.G.B, "Architectural Historiology: Fourth Church of Christ, Scientist, Seattle, Wash.", July 10, 1979. THS.

According to documents in the historical files at Town Hall Seattle, drawings by Dunham for Fourth Church Seattle edifice were begun in 1910.

230 "Among the Churches," *CSS,* Apr. 22, 1916; *Capacity of 2,500:* "Scientists Plan $250,000 Church," *ST,* Jan. 20, 1916, 20; "Among the Churches," *CSS,* Mar. 18, 1916.

231 *"valiantly"*: "History of Fourth Church of Christ, Scientist, Seattle, Washington," (1932), 3. MBEL (04ChSea) Box 40737 Folder 165635; *Unanimous:* untitled, undated document of motions No. 1 & 2. MBEL (04ChSea) Box 41326 Folder 482905; *Payments made:* "History of Fourth Church of Christ, Scientist, Seattle, Washington," (1932). MBEL (04ChSea) Box 40737 Folder 165635.

232 "Noted Scientist to Lecture here Sunday," Sept. 7, 1916, *ST*, 11; "Christian Scientist to Lecture Tomorrow," Sept. 9, 1916, *ST*, 8; "The Lectures: Seattle, Wash." *CSS*, Nov. 18, 1916.

233 "Contributions to Jewish Fund Growing," Feb. 20, 1916, *ST*, 23.

234 *"at such time"*: Minutes of University District Christian Science Society, 65. 03ChSea.

235 "Christian Scientists Form Another Society," *ST*, Nov. 28, 1914, 5.

236 *"Hell's stores were opened"*: *Christian Science War Time Activities: A Report to the Board of Directors of The Mother Church by The Christian Science War Relief Committee*, Boston: Christian Science Publishing Society, 1922, 249.

237 *"Mrs. Mary Baker Eddy, founder"*: "Christian Science Chief Indorsed and Argued for Preparedness for Defense," *ST*, Feb. 26, 1916, 3.

238 *"a very suitable way of telling the people"*: "War Declaration Told By Times Whistle," *ST*, Apr. 6, 1917, 5.

239 *"The United States today is at war"*: "Fly the Flag!", *ST*, Apr. 6, 1917, 6; *"The time for action has arrived"*: "The Duties of Citizenship," *ST*, Apr. 6, 1917, 6.

240 *"The need of the hour"*: "Annual Meeting of The Mother Church," *CSS*, June 9, 1917.

241 *"Even to a group so accustomed"*: *Christian Science War Time Activities*, 15.

242 *"a cordial welcome and an atmosphere"*: *Christian Science War Time Activities*, 115.

243 "Scientists to Open Service Men's Clubs," *SS*, Oct. 5, 1918, 9.

244 *Dutton membership*: Member Minutes, p 6. 03ChSea. "Episcopalian Year is Prosperous," *ST*, Apr. 21, 1908, 7.

245 *"new meaning" "Seattle's celebration" "pledged their allegiance"*: "July 4 To See New Meaning in This Year's Fete," *ST*, July 1, 1917, 11.

246 "Minute Men Busy Enrolling Men In Reserve," *ST*, Mar. 29, 1918, 8.

247 *Dutton reads*: Member Minutes, Sept. 17, 1918. 03ChSea; *"Pray for the prosperity of our country"*: Eddy, "Prayer for Country and Church," *Pan.*, 14.

248 *Orison J.C. Dutton*: "Build Broadway Club," *ST*, Mar. 25, 1902, 7; "To Raise $60,000 For Boy Scouts," *ST*, Sept. 12, 1918, 10; "O.J.C. Dutton Funeral Will Be Tomorrow," *ST*, June 15, 1944, 19; *Clifford H. Anderson*: 1914 *Polk's Seattle City Directory*, 328; 1910 US Census, Seattle Ward 10, King County, Washington, Roll: T624_1661, 4A, ED 0182, FHL microfilm 1375674; 1920 US Census, Seattle, King County, Washington, Roll: T625_1925, 3B, ED 65; *John J. Cavender*: 1910 US Census, Seattle Ward 3, King County, Washington, Roll: T624_1659, 2B, ED 0153, FHL microfilm 1375672; 1920 US Census, Seattle, King County, Washington, Roll: T625_1926, 11A, ED 124; *Monthly meetings (suspended)*: Board Minutes, Apr. 2, 1918, 60. 03ChSea; *"impersonal, unselfish, and untiring"*: Member Minutes, Mar. 12, 1918, 27. 03ChSea.

[249] "Historical Sketch of Christian Science Organization at the University of Washington," Dec. 1970. (33-page document with no attribution). UW CSO; *Priest as advisor*: Woodward, Harriett, Mary Meloy, Marshall Dutton, and Rose Kipper, Historical Committee. "Historical Sketch of Christian Science Organization at the University of Washington," Feb. 15, 1934. UW CSO. Hereafter referred to as Woodward.

[250] *Dean of Men*: "The Lectures," *CSS*, July 1, 1916; UW Tyee yearbooks, various years 1903 to 1919; *First Reader*: March 1917 *CSJ Directory*; *Priest home*: (4709 16th Ave NE) Board of Directors, First Church of Christ, Scientist, Seattle, to its members living in the University District, Oct. 19, 1914. 03ChSea.

[251] *Willa Trent's practice*: March 1917 *CSJ* Directory.

Herbert T. Condon who later became Dean of Men is perhaps best known today for giving the names "Loyalty," "Industry," "Faith," and "Efficiency" (LIFE) to four ionic roman column remnants of the original downtown university building which were moved to Sylvan Grove Theater.

[252] *Charter members and elections*: Woodward, 1. UW CSO; "U. of W. Girl to See Service in France," *ST*, Mar. 23, 1918, 2; *"It appealed to me instantly"*: Leonard, Eleanor Hoppock, testimony, *CSS*, Sept. 21, 1929; *"When Christian Science"*: Mills, Adele Hoppock, testimony, *CSJ*, Nov. 1931.

[253] *"Error tried to tell her "*: Leonard, Eleanor Hoppock, "Obedience" *CSJ*, April 1920.

[254] *"Obedience to Truth"*: Eddy, *S&H*, 183.

[255] Woodward, 1. UW CSO.

[256] *Maud W. Condon's membership*: Membership minutes, Dec. 29, 1920, 81. 03ChSea.

[257] David Wilma, "World War 1 in Washington," HistoryLink.org; "33 of University Teaching Staff in Service," *ST*, May 26, 1918, 18; "Do You Know?" 1918 *Tyee*, 18; "Our Fighting Faculty" 1919 *Tyee*, 51. "The Home Guard," 1918 *Tyee*, 22. University of Washington, Seattle.

[258] "Obituaries: Arthur Priest Dies in Ohio," *ST*, Dec. 14, 1937, 27; "Dean Priest Going to France to Be Father to Washington Men," *ST*, Feb. 3, 1918, 8; "Farewell To Dean Priest," 1918 *Tyee*, 131. UW, Seattle.

[259] "U. of W. Girl to See Service in France," *ST*, Mar. 23, 1918, 2; "'Good-Bye, U. of W.; Hello, France,'" *Tacoma Times*, March 18, 1918, 4; "I was protected": Mills, Adele Hoppock, tesimony, *CSJ*, Nov. 1931; *"petticoated soldiers"*: "Seattle Girls in Army Show Valor Under Fire," *ST*, Dec. 15, 1918, 12; *"such high standing"*: "Girl Home From War," *ST*, Sept. 22, 1919, 2; "Local Girls See Furious Fighting," *SS*, Nov. 1, 1918, 3; "What Our Women Did," 1919 *Tyee* yearbook, 58. University of Washington, Seattle. Ancesstry.com; *"divine Love went with me"*: Eleanor Hoppock Leonard, testimony, *CSS*, Sept. 21, 1929; "Girl Home From War," *ST*, Sept. 22, 1919, 2; "Will Marry in East," *SS*, Oct. 24, 1919, 8; "Marriage of Seattle Couple," *ST*, Nov. 9, 1919.

[260] "On To France," 1918 *Tyee*, 181; *"Washington Militant"*: 1918 *Tyee*, 28. UW, Seattle.

[261] *Building project meetings suspended*: Board Minutes, Apr. 2, 1918, 60. 03ChSea.

²⁶² *"influencing or being influenced erroneously"*: Eddy, *Man.*, 40; *"mean not to catch or pass on"*: Horace C. Jenkins, "Influence," *CSS*, Aug. 9, 1919.

²⁶³ "Unknown Disease Spreads in Spain," *ST*, May 28, 1918, 15; John Caldbick, "Flu in Washington: The 1918 'Spanish Flu' Pandemic," HistoryLink.org Essay 20300, Mar. 23, 2017.

²⁶⁴ *"one of the most distinguished members of his profession"*: "Eminent Doctor Reaches Seattle," *ST*, June 16, 1915, 2; "Michigan Deans to Be Given Banquet," *ST*, Apr. 10, 1910, 4.

²⁶⁵ *"If the epidemic continues its mathematical rate"* *"The saddest part of my life"* *"compelled him to question his very faith"*: "Biography: Victor Vaughan," PBS.org, undated. Accessed May 2, 2020; Walter L Bierring, M.D., "Biography of Victor C. Vaughan, Sixty-sixth President of the A.M.A." in *A history of the American Medical Association 1847 to 1947* by Morris Fishbein, M.D., Vaughan.org; "Victor C. Vaughan," Wikipedia.org, accessed May 2, 2020.

Katie Vloet notes the irony that Victor C. Vaughan wrote only a few paragraphs on the 1918 influenza pandemic in his 500-page memoir. Attributing the omission to emotional scars and haunting memories, Vloet quotes Gina Kolata, author of *Flu: The Story of the Influenza Pandemic of 1918 and the Search for the Virus that Caused It*, (2001): "If anyone might be expected to write about the epidemic, it was Vaughan. He was an epidemiologist, one whose professional life centered on understanding the causes and courses of disease, and a medical professional who had been a witness to one of the worst epidemics ever to strike the face of the earth," Kolata wrote. "But instead of dealing with the plague, he seemed almost compelled to quickly give a nod to it and then move on to something easier to talk about." Katie Vloet, "'This Infection, Like War, Kills the Young,'" Medicine at Michigan, medicineatmichigan.org, Fall 2018 (accessed May 21, 2020).

²⁶⁶ *"At a time of contagious disease"*: Eddy, *My.*, 116. This is the beginning of her article "Personal Contagion," *CSS*, July 7, 1906, later republished in *The First Church of Christ, Scientist, and Miscellany.*

²⁶⁷ *"If only the people would believe"*: Eddy, "Contagion," *MW*, 229.

²⁶⁸ *9 years*, and *"incomparably better"*: "Selected Articles," Henry Dickinson, *CSS*, Nov. 21, 1931; *"mental factor in disease"* *"a mental origin"* *"Christian Science does not depend on any power"*: "Electrical Transcription No. 2: Interview with Walton Hubbard, M.D.," a 1933 pamphlet reprinted in *CSS*, Oct. 1, 2013; *"cases which were hopelessly incurable"*: "The Lectures: Spokane, Wash.," *CSS*, July 31, 1915.

²⁶⁹ Seattle-area lectures by Dr. Walton Hubbard, C.S.B. included The Ray Theater in Olympia on Sept. 5, 1918 and Princess Theatre in Ballard in Seattle, Sept. 12, 1916; Ad, *Washington Standard* (Olympia, WA), Aug. 30, 1918, 8; Ad, *ST*, Sept. 11, 1916, 20; *"The statement that 'the germ theory'"*: "Selected Articles," Robert G. Steel, *CSS*, Dec. 28, 1918; John B. Fraser's experiments were also mentioned in "Signs of the Times," *CSS*, Aug. 9, 1919. From *Rocky Mountain News*, Denver, Colorado.

²⁷⁰ *"it is interesting to note that Dr. F. L. Kelly"*: "Selected Articles," Peter V. Ross, *CSS*, Mar. 29, 1919.

DEDICATION

271 "Signs of the Times," *CSS*, Apr. 12, 1919. From *Oakland Enquirer*.

272 *Plain Dealer*: "Signs of the Times," *CSS*, July 12, 1919; *NY Herald*: "Signs of the Times," *CSS*, Mar. 15, 1919; See also "How did Christian Scientists respond to the 1918-1919 Spanish flu?" MBEL blog post, Apr. 9, 2020.

273 *"an iron, health-minded fist"*: Nicholas Deshais, "When the Pandemic Came to Spokane – 102 Years Ago," NWNewsNetwork.org; *Spokane context*: "Spokane, Washington," *Influenza Encyclopedia: The American Influenza Epidemic of 1918-1918*, InfluenzaArchive.org; *Dr. Fluno lecture*: "The Lectures: A Spokane Wash.," *CSS*, June 29, 1899; *Dr. Sulcer lecture*: "The Lectures: At Spokane, Wash.," *CSS*, May 23, 1901; *"engaged in the healing of the sick"* and *"could not consider the character or purpose"*: "One Death, 53 New 'Flu' Cases," *Spokesman Review*, Oct. 17, 1918; "Lion Hotel Will House Patients With Influenza," *Spokesman Review*, Oct. 16, 1918; Richard Mather, "Spirituality: The Weapon that Never Fails," *CSJ*, Jan 2002; *"an appeal was made to the Christian Scientists"* and *"scrubbing floors and doing any work"*: "Christian Science Lecture by Dr. Walton Hubbard, C.S.B." *Gross Pointe* [MI] *News*, November 4, 1948; *"for the splendid aid rendered"*: *Christian Science War Time Activities*, Christian Science Publishing Society, 1922, 362.

274 *Great Lakes*: "Selected Articles," Robert G. Steel, *CSS*, Dec. 28, 1918; *Christian Science War Time Activities*, CSPS, 1922, 151; *4200 cases, 50 tents*: "Extracts from Reports Relative to Influenza, Pneumonia, and Respiratory Diseases," V1. Camp Mills Base Hospital Report, U.S. Army Medical Dept., Office of Medical History, Army.mil, accessed May 7, 2020; testimony, Zona M. Carruthers, *CSS*, May 12, 1923.

275 *"I helped to nurse five"*: testimony, Myra Atkinson, *CSJ*, Apr. 1920; testimony, Miss Mary E. Moser, *CSS*, Sept. 23, 1922.

276 *"great mass of evidence accumulated" "One of the things"*: *Christian Science War Time Activities*, CSPS, 1922, 331.

277 *"Upon reporting to the Commandant"*: *Christian Science War Time Activities*, CSPS, 1922, 152-3.

278 *"The utterly helpless attitude of the health authorities"*: "From the Press," *CSS*, Oct. 26, 1918.

279 *"Fear is the most prolific source of all evil"*: "A Mad World," *Washington Herald*, Oct. 19, 1918, 5. Reprinted from *CSM*, Oct. 8, 1918, 16. This editorial was widely republished. This *Washington Herald* version included comment from Avery Coonley, Christian Science Committee on Publication.

280 *"Surely it was a wise man" "It is hoped that by recalling"*: "A Mad World," *Washington Herald*, Oct. 19, 1918, 5.

281 *"Rarely is one allowed the doubtful privilege"*: "Selected Articles," Robert G. Steel, *CSS*, Dec. 28, 1918.

282 *"If the Bible is true"*: "Selected Articles," John M. Dean, *CSS*, Dec. 7, 1918.

283 *"the only thing we have to fear is fear itself"*: Franklin D. Roosevelt, First Inaugural Address, Mar. 4, 1933; *Witte*: 1919 Des Moines *Polk City Directory*, 1329; "Many peo-

ple have thought themselves into their graves": "Campaign Against Fear is Advocated," *CSM*, Oct. 22, 1918, 6; "Fear Causes 'Flu,' Fighters Declare," *Washington Times*, Oct. 30, 1918, 3; Judge Clifford P Smith, *CSS*, March 8, 1919.

284 *"that newspapers prepare editorials" "was endorsed by the committee"*: "Signs of the Times," *CSS*, Dec. 14, 1918; "Fear Responsible for Spread of Influenza," *Washington Herald*, Oct. 30, 1918, 3; *Byers*: 1921 Des Moines *Polk City Directory*, 237; *1920 US Census: Webster, Polk, Iowa*; Roll: *T625_507*; Pg: *16A*; ED: *187*.

285 "Many a hopeless case of disease is induced": Eddy, *S&H*, 196-7; "Looking over the newspapers of the day": Eddy, *MW*, 7; "We should master fear": Eddy, *S&H*, 197.

286 "Fear Responsible for Spread of Influenza," *Washington Herald*, Oct. 30, 1918, 3; "Anti Fear Campaign Urged by [Christian] Scientists," *East Oregonian*, Nov. 1, 1918, 4; "Quit Thinking about Influenza," *Exira* (Iowa), Oct. 24, 1918; "Fear Causes 'Flu,' Fighters Declare," *Washington Times*, Oct. 30, 1918, 3; "Princeton Churches, Etc. Closed," *Princeton Union*, Oct. 31, 1918, 4; "Christian Scientists and the Influenza," *Colville Examiner*, Nov. 9, 1918, 8; "Newspapers Requested to Oppose Fear," *Daily Alaskan*, Nov. 19, 1918, 2; "Campaign Against Fear is Advocated," *Lincoln County Times*, Nov. 21, 1918, 1; *"At the very moment when the churches should be"*: "Has the World Gone Mad?" (Ad), *Daily East Oregonian*, Oct. 31, 1918, 6.

287 *"disease . . . being so industriously promoted"*: "Resolution, addressed to City Council, Los Angeles, written by First Church of Christ, Scientist," Oct. 11, 1918; *"The efficacy of Christian Science to prevent and heal disease"*: "Petition Sent to Mayor George L. Baker by Committee Representing All the Christian Science Churches and Society in Portland, Oregon," 1. *George Luis Baker Subject Files*, 1918. Both previous sources are from *Influenza Encyclopedia*. Published: Ann Arbor, Michigan: Michigan Publishing, University Library, University of Michigan, (influenzaarchive.org).

Other cities where Christian Science churches petitioned city councils include Spokane, Washington, (as mentioned earlier in this article) and Melbourne, Australia, according to Paul Jones, of Burwood, Australia in a letter in *CSJ*, Apr. 2002.

288 When First Church of Christ, Scientist, Los Angeles held opening services in 1901 it was the first Christian Science church edifice in the "the southern metropolis of the golden state." Dr. Fluno and Dr. Sulcer sat on the platform and participated in conducting the service, during which it was emphasized that the grand edifice was quickly built through the gratitude of people healed of "all manner of diseases. . . who for the most part were hopeless cases of the regular medical practitioner, were restored to pristine health and morals through Christian Science," as recounted in "Opening of First Church of Christ, Scientist, of Los Angeles, Cal," *CSJ*, Dec. 1901.

289 *"I want it distinctly understood"*: "Must Follow Health Rule Says Mayor," *Los Angeles Evening Herald*, Nov. 2, 1918, 3.

[290] I did not find a conclusive source on how the Ninth Church of Christ, Scientist, Los Angeles, legal case was ultimately resolved. My description is based on these articles:

Dec. 28, 1918, *SS*: "Judge White decided the law was unconstitutional."

May 31, 1919, *CSS*: "That such action is well taken is shown in a widely published dispatch from Los Angeles, California, where a closing order issued against the churches by the board of health was recently declared by the court to be unreasonable, invalid, and unconstitutional."

June 21, 1919, *CSS*: "A day or two before the matter was to be finally disposed of, the judge having the case under advisement indicated in a newspaper interview that he would hold the closing order invalid. On the day set for the hearing, the judge was prevented from holding court, but the authorities promptly rescinded the closing order. The intimation evidently was sufficient."

[291] *"travelling in a slow stream"*: "Defy 'Flu' Rule; Arrested," *Los Angeles Times*, Nov. 4, 1918, 1; "Church Heads May Carry 'Flu' Fight to Highest Court," *Los Angeles Evening Herald*, Nov. 5, 1918, 7; *"technically arrested"*: "U.S. May Hear Church Fight on 'Flu Law,'" *Los Angeles Herald*, Nov. 5, 1918, 3; *$5 bail*: news clipping from InfluenzaEncyclopedia.com "Goes to Jail to Test 'Flu' Closing" labeled as (but unable to verify) *Los Angeles Evening Herald*, Nov. 4, 1918, 3; "Christian Scientists Arrested as They Attempt Service," *SS*, Nov. 4, 1918, 5; "Christian Scientists Arrested for Violating Influenza Ban," *ST*, Nov. 4, 1918, 7; "Flu Costs Million A Day in the U.S.," *SS*, Dec. 28, 1918, 2; "Selected Articles," Robert G. Steel, *CSS*, May 31, 1919; "Selected Articles," Robert G. Steel, *CSS*, June 21, 1919.

[292] "to test the legality of the restriction" and "Christian Scientists . . . are not without sympathy": Ernest C. Moses, *CSS*, Apr. 26, 1919.

[293] "Signs of the Times," *CSS*, Nov. 30, 1918. (From *Public Ledger*, Philadelphia, PA); "Held Church While 'Flu' Ban Was On; Is Fined in Court," *SS*, Jan. 13, 1919, 12.

[294] "When the order came that, on account of an epidemic" "In great gladness of heart": Maude M. Greene, "A Personal Experience," *CSS*, Mar. 22, 1919.

[295] *"The outstanding feature of the discussion"*: John Caldbick, "Flu in Washington: The 1918 'Spanish Flu' Pandemic," HistoryLink.org Essay 20300, Mar. 23, 2017. Caldbick cites as source *State of Washington Twelfth Biennial Report of the State Board of Health* (Olympia: Frank M. Lamborn, Public Printer, 1919), 23, available at InfluenzaEncyclopedia.org accessed Mar. 22, 2017; "Seattle and a Past Pandemic," WSU Press, Mar. 13, 2020, from *Eccentric Seattle*, J. Kingston Pierce, 2003.

[296] *"the army of men working in the shipyards"* *"patriotic duty"* *"intelligent and conscientious"*: "Seattle to Make Fight on Disease," *ST*, Oct. 5, 1918, 1, 3.

[297] *"Influenza Squad"*: "Influenza Squad" is widely quoted in articles about the 1918 pandemic in Seattle, but its source is not widely cited. The term came to my attention from Knute Berger, "Before Coronavirus: How Seattle Handled the Spanish Flu," Crosscut.com, Mar. 4, 2020. "Seattle, Washington," InfluenzaEncyclopedia.org, cites "Three deaths from Influenza," *Seattle P-I*, Oct. 9, 1918, 1; *"Seattle*

churches unhesitatingly will obey" "expressed their intention to comply cheerfully" "Christian Scientists are, first of all, obedient": "Churches to Conduct Services in Open Air," *ST*, Oct. 6, 1918, 12.

298 "*great patriotic-religious gathering*": "Churches to Conduct Services in Open Air," *ST*, Oct. 6, 1918, 12; "*rather small*": "Open-Air Services Held By Churches," *ST*, Oct. 7, 1918, 7; "*common thought*" "*was that more severe scourges*" "*attendance ran from a couple of hundred*": "Churches Meet Quarantine Order: Mass Celebrated in Open Because of Epidemic," *Catholic Northwest Progress* (Seattle, WA), Oct. 11, 1918, 1.

299 "*the clergy did not want to keep the members standing*": "Open-Air Services Held By Churches," *ST*, Oct. 7, 1918, 7; "*Scores of clergymen*": "Total of 1,921 Flu Cases in Seattle Now" (under subhead "Churches Closed"), *SS*, Oct. 12, 1918, 2.

300 "*take charge of the Camp Welfare Work*": Board minutes, 03ChSea, July 2, 1918, 74; *More Homes Bureau*: "Want Lot Owners Registered," *ST*, Aug 23, 1918, 16; "Attack Housing Job With Full Authority," *ST*, Sept. 25, 1918, 13; "*present to Christian Scientists and their friends*": Ad, *SS*, Sept. 28, 1918, 2; *Independent*: "Church Not Financing Club," *ST*, Oct. 17, 1918, 10; "*unoccupied for some time*": "Unidentified Men Fire at Officials," *ST*, Oct. 7, 1918. 11; "Scientists to Open Service Men's Club," *SS*, Oct. 5, 1918, 9; "*night-and-day operation*": "Club Ends Labor," *ST*, Mar. 30, 1919, 15; "*a simple, plain, comfortable place*": "Christian Scientists Plan Clubhouse for Soldiers," *ST*, Sept. 30, 1918, 20; "The Soldiers' and Sailors' Hospitality Club," Ad, *ST*, Nov. 3, 1918, 7.

301 "*fired pointblank*" "*passed about a foot above the heads*": "Unidentified Men Fire at Officials," *ST*, Oct. 7, 1918, 11; *18 weeks, statistics*: "Club Ends Labor," *ST*, Mar. 30, 1919, 15.

302 "*offering at this time the healing*": Ad, *ST*, Nov. 12, 1918, 18.

303 *About 200 testimonies*: Determined by searching a digital edition of the Christian Science periodicals (JSH-Online) for relevant terms, including Spanish, influenza, flu, epidemic, 1918, and 1919.

304 "*I had seen several of my comrades walk out of rank*": testimony, Marven L. Scranton, *CSS*, Jan. 4, 1919; testimony, Edna Saint, *CSS*, May 10, 1930.

305 "*sense of having been close to the shadow of death*" "*My wife tells me*": testimony, Harry Rix, *CSS*, July 12, 1919; "*Upon the arrival of the practitioner*": testimony, Blanche McCulloch, *CSS*, Apr. 19, 1919; "*an illusion*": Eddy, *S&H*, 584 (definition of "Death").

306 "*We knew little of Christian Science in 1918*": testimony, Eunice and Martin Verheul, *CSS*, Dec. 3, 1960.

307 *12 hours*: testimony, Louise Beemer Holeman, *CSS*, Jan. 10, 1920; "*severe attack of influenza*" "*I am absolutely convinced*": testimony, E.R. Cose, *CSS*, Mar. 4, 1922.

308 "*From that time I felt no further effects*": testimony, Louis J. Scherz, *CSJ*, May 1923.

[309] *"was a discourtesy to the health authorities" "During the recent epidemic in this city alone"*: "Selected Articles," Ernest C. Moses, CSS, May 17, 1919. Reprinted from *The Christian Century.*

[310] *"morbidity . . . and mortality among Christian Scientists"*: "Selected Articles," Aaron E. Brandt, CSS, May 3, 1919. Quote from *The Dispatch*, Pittsburgh, PA;*"Because the methods employed by Christian Science"*: "Selected Articles," A. O. Freel, CSS, June 26, 1920.

[311] *"gratuitous fling at Christian Scientists" "Careful investigation in the city of Rochester"*: "Selected Articles," Albert F. Gilmore, CSS, Apr. 5, 1919.

[312] *"[S]tatistics in Wisconsin show"*: "Selected Articles," Hugh S. Hughes, Jr., CSS, Aug 28, 1920.

[313] John Randall Dunn, "Claim Man's Immunity from Epidemics!" CSS, Jan. 18, 1947.

[314] *"The quarantine and mask questions"*: "Signs of the Times," "From Biennial Report, State Board of Health, Nevada," CSS, Apr. 12, 1919.

[315] *"The epidemic of fear, spoken of as the 'flu,'"*: "Among the Churches: Current Notes: Colorado," CSS, June 21, 1919.

[316] *"Beloved Christian Scientists"*: Eddy, "What Our Leader Says," *My.,* 210. First appeared in Feb. 9, 1899, CSS.

[317] *"We may always rejoice"*: Horace C. Jenkins, "Influence," CSS, Aug. 9, 1919.

[318] *"The evening following the issuance"*: "Signs of the Times," CSS, Nov. 30, 1918.

[319] *Quick/mysterious disappearance*: "The worldwide epidemic lasts for about a year, killing an estimated 20 million persons, then vanishes as strangely as it had appeared": "1918: A fateful Ending," The History Place: World War I, historyplace.com/worldhistory/firstworldwar /index-1918.html (accessed May 21, 2020); "Then, to Vaughan's relief, influenza seemed to slip away as mysteriously as it had arrived": "Biography: Victor Vaughan," American Experience, PBS.org (accessed May 21, 2020); "Yet almost as quickly and mysteriously as it raced around the continents, the flu pandemic subsided in 1919 and officially ended in 1920": Katie Vloet, "'This Infection, Like War, Kills the Young,'" Medicine at Michigan, MedicineAtMichigan.org (accessed May 21, 2020); "The Spanish Flu disappeared almost as quickly as it appeared and has yet to reappear with such intensity": "Influenza Pandemic," University of Washington Libraries website, lib.washington.edu.

[320] *"attended by an assemblage" "occasion for rejoicing among the local Christian Scientists"*: "Among the Churches," CSS, June 21, 1919.

[321] *"By a sort of spontaneous combustion" "There never was anything like it" "Seattle beat him to it"*: "Seattle in Ecstasy of Joy at Ending of World's Worst War," ST, Nov. 11, 1918, 1; *"spectacular climax"*: "Times Will Celebrate Peace Declaration With Big Fireworks Display," ST, Nov. 11, 1918, 1; *"mark the end of the biggest"*: Lovering, Paul H., "World Now Faces Labors of Peace," ST, Nov. 11, 1918, 1.

322 *"read in bunks and hospital beds"*: Christian Science War Time Activities, 188-189; *"Christian Scientist have sometimes been charged"*: Christian Science War Time Activities, 364-365.

323 "Club Ends Labor," *ST*, Mar. 30, 1919. 15; *"all discharged soldiers, sailors and marines"*: "Doughnuts for Discharged Men: Salvation Army to Open Club," *ST*, Apr. 2, 1919, 11; *"It has occurred to me"*: Christian Science War Time Activities, 369.

324 Board minutes, Jan. 20, Feb. 4, Mar. 11, Mar. 25, Apr. 1, May 1, May 6, 1919. 03ChSea; Eddy, *My*, 278.

Mrs. R. Ella Hensley rented rooms 1 and 2 of the University [State/National] Bank Building and the Christian Science Reading Room was in rooms 8 and 9. Second Church of Christ, Scientist, Seattle, also rented space for church and reading room in a building that had a practitioner office 1918 to 1920. Mrs. Alice S. McCarty's office was in room 4 of the Scandinavian American Bank Building at Ballard Avenue NW and NW Vernon Place, and the church in room 6.

325 *"There shall be"*: Eddy, *Manual*, 102. (Article XXXIV Sect. 1)

326 "Christian Science Leaders in Fight," *ST*, Mar. 27, 1919, 21; "Sue Mother Church," *ST*, Mar. 29, 1920, 7.

327 *Dutton resigns*: Board min, May 6, 1919, 117. 03ChSea; "Society," *ST*, June 9, 1917, 4; "Society," *ST*, Dec. 14, 1918; "Society," *ST*, June 8, 1919; "Society," *ST*, July 9, 1919; "Society," *ST*, July 18, 1919; "Society," *ST*, July 20, 1919; *"awful. . . muddy"*: "Franklin Scores Big Victory: Sweeps Reliability Contest," *ST*, Oct. 26, 1919, 10; "Activities in Seattle Society," *ST*, Dec. 23, 1925, 10; *"to tell its story in a new and vivid way"*: Leonard, Edwin S., Jr. As the Sowing: The First Fifty Years of the Principia. St Louis: The Principia, 1980. 64, 109.

Cross country driving was still something of a novelty at the time of the Dutton's road trip. Thier arrival coincided with a car reliability contest by the Automobile Club of St. Louis, and O.J.C.'s involvement won Dutton Seattle publicity even in his absence from Seattle's civic scene.

To become a Christian Science Teacher, Mary Kimball Morgan took Normal Class with Edward A. Kimball in 1899, the same year as Allen H. Armstrong.

328 BC minutes, May 6, 1919. 03ChSea.

329 *Membership Roll (Register #1)*, 38. 01ChSea; "Obituaries: Mrs. Harvey B. Densmore," *ST*, Jan. 5, 1940, 26; Marriage to Harvey B. Densmore on August 1, 1917. Washington State Archives, Olympia, Washington. Washington Marriage Records, 1854-2013, Ref. # kingcoarchmc59082; Ancestry.com. *U.S. Consular Registration Certificate, 1907-1918* [database on-line]. Provo, UT, USA: Ancestry.com Operations, Inc., 2013; *Passenger Lists of Vessels Arriving at New York, New York, 1820-1897*. Microfilm Publication M237, 675 rolls. NAI: 6256867. Records of the US Customs Service, Record Group 36. National Archives at Washington, D.C. (Ancestry.com. *New York, Passenger Lists, 1820-1957* [database on-line], Provo, UT, USA; Albert, Sarah Traux. "Our Heritage from Cecil Rhodes," *ST*, July 31, 1955, 110;

"Harvey Densmore, Former U.W. Professor, Dies," *ST*, Jan. 24, 1977, E4; 1910 *Tyee*, 63, 197, 204, 221, 253, 325. 1911 *Tyee*, 161, 185. UW, Seattle.

Prof. Harvey B. Densmore would one day name a scholarship after his wife, Ruth (Fisk Anderson), at UW Mortar Board Alumni/Tolo Foundation. See untitled article on Mortar Board's 45th anniversary banquet: *ST*, Apr. 24, 1955, 69.

[330] *Membership Roll (Register #1)*, 118. 01ChSea; 1910 *Tyee*, 22. 1911 *Tyee*, 94, 177, 218, 325. 1912 *Tyee*, 161, 300, 343. UW, Seattle; 1913 *Polk's Seattle City Directory*, 1381; 1914 Polk *Seattle City Directory*, p. 1465; 1915 *Polk's Seattle City Directory*, 1339; "Daily Statistics: Marriage Licenses," *ST*, Apr. 3, 1916, 8; "Big Reception To Be Given By Alumnae Association," *ST*, May 25, 1919, 6; "U. of W. Alumnae Entertained With Fine Program at President's Home," *ST*, Oct. 12, 1919; "Old Graduates Will Give Dinner for Judge Lantz," *ST*, Oct. 30, 1932, 7; "Death Calls Harvey Lantz, Law Professor," *ST*, Feb. 2, 1993, 1, 3; "Obituary: Hiram B. Ross," *ST*, Nov. 2, 1939, 31.

Mrs. Helen R. Lantz's maiden name was Miss Helen M. Ross.

[331] *University District Christian Science Society Membership Minutes, 1914 to 1916*, 68. 03ChSea; "H.P. Chapman, Prominent in Port Work, Dies," *ST*, Oct. 13, 1950, 16; "H.P. Chapman Enters Race for Port Commission," *ST*, Jan. 24, 1933, 9; "Nile Temple Nobles Announce Pilgrimage," *ST*, June 1, 1913, 10; "State Millers Banquet," *ST*, Feb. 29, 1919, 21; "Over Confidence Handicaps Scouts," *ST*, June 13, 1919, 10; "University Church Names Its Officers," *ST*, Jan. 13, 1912, 7.

[332] *Minutes of Membership Meetings, March 17, 1917, to Dec. 17, 1925*, 33. 03ChSea; *Membership Roll, (Register #1)*, 158, 160. 01ChSea; 1900 US Census, Hanover, Jackson, Michigan, 6, ED 0005. NARA, 1900. T623, 1854 rolls; 1920 US Census, Seattle, King County, Washington, Roll: T625_1926, 12A, ED 124; *"orthodox religions"*: Haviland, Byron B., tesimony, *CSS*, Aug. 2, 1969; Haviland, George K., testimony, *CSJ*, Oct. 1916; "George K. Haviland," *ST*, Sept. 4, 1956, 37; "Mrs. Byron Haviland," *ST*, Apr. 5, 1960, 41; *Polk's Seattle City Directories*: 1916, 801. 1917, 824. 1918, 900. 1919, 889, 1941. 1918 *CSJ Directory*; *Haviland as Second Reader*: Deduced from several sources: Hazel A. Firth, Corresponding Secretary, Christian Science Board of Directors to Eulalie L. Ketner, Clerk, Third Church Seattle, Aug. 27, 1937, regarding the issue of Bryon Haviland having served a full term as a reader in Victoria prior to his election to First Reader at Third Church. *CSJ* listings for Victoria have only women First Readers listed around 1910 when Haviland would have been there; *Havilands charter members*: "First Church of Christ, Scientist, Victoria, B.C.: A Centenary, 1902-2002," First Church of Christ, Scientist Centenary Committee, 2002, 5.

Byron B. Haviland's brother George had no interest in Christian Science until seven years later when faced with a serious health condition that seemed to require an operation. He too tried Christian Science. He testified that he was healed of that condition and that when his automobile skidded off a viaduct and crashed twenty-five feet below, he was healed of serious accident injuries with the help of a Christian Science practitioner. In George's testimony in the Oct 1917 *CSJ* he also told of being quickly healed of a severe cough and the need to wear glasses.

333 *Minutes of Membership Meetings, March 17, 1917 to Dec. 17, 1925*, 12. Third Church of Christ, Scientist, Seattle files; 1885 Iowa State Census. Ancestry.com. *Iowa, State Census Collection, 1836-1925* [database on-line]. Provo, UT, USA: Ancestry.com Operations, Inc., 2007; 1910 *Lincoln City Directory*, 150, 764; 1910 US Census, NARA microfilm T624; 1920 US Census, Medina, King County, Washington, Roll: T625_1924, 13B, ED 11; *Polk's Seattle City Directories*: 1910, 483; 1911, 424; 1912, 405; 1919, 632; JRSherrard, "Seattle Now & Then: Two Marches (On 4th Avenue)" Paul Dorpat.com, undated, accessed March 10, 2018; Robert A. DeCou to Miss Evangeline Fox, July 12, 1912. 01ChSea; "The Lectures," *CSS*, Feb. 15, 1913; Marriage Certificate no. 15262, Pierce County, WA. Filed Sept. 2, 1913; *CSJ* Directories 1914 to 1916.

Robert A. DeCou may have gotten involved in the Christian Science church in Ballard soon after arriving in Seattle. By 1912 he was serving as Secretary of the first Joint Lecture Committee. In 1913 he introduced Christian Science lecturer Virgil O. Strickler at a lecture at the Ballard train station. He married his wife Stella Hoyt in the summer of 1913, the newlyweds moved to Phinney Ridge, then Robert was elected First Reader for the Ballard church.

334 *"well-balanced"*: Board of Directors, Third Church of Christ, Scientist, Seattle, to Herschel P. Nunn, Oct. 1, 1926; BC minutes, May 6, 1919. 03ChSea; *"certain fundamental principles"*: Chairman [Robert DeCou], "Report of the Building Committee of Third Church of Christ, Scientist, May 6, 1919 to March 1, 1923." 03ChSea.

335 *"an immediate end to the undesirable"*: BC to Board, May 15, 1919; *"putting an end"*: BC minutes, May 6, 1919. 03ChSea; "rather detailed reports": BC report to members, June 17, 1919. 03ChSea; "Build New Church," *SS*, May 1, 1919, 11.

336 *"a number of books dealing with plans"*: BC to Judson T. Jennings, Seattle Public Library, July 16, 1919. 03ChSea.

337 *"impressed the committee" "a Christian Scientist"*: BC report to members, June 17, 1919. 03ChSea; In a letter to the Building Committee, George Dunham mentioned attending his [Christian Science] Association meeting in California.

338 *"carefully considered all sides" "that the church continue its plans"*: BC report to members, June 17, 1919. 03ChSea; *"maximum seating capacity" "to work with"*: George Dunham to BC, July 3, 1919. 03ChSea; *"an unusual sense of freedom" "splendid"*: George Dunham to BC, July 3, 1919. 03ChSea.

339 Mitchel, Donald J., "Annual Report of the Christian Science Literature Distribution Committee," 1919. Nimms, Nina F., "Report of Joint Committee of The Christian Science Monitor, Covering Period from April 1st 1912 to Dec. 31, 1912." Spense, Mary W., "Christian Science Monitor Co-Operative Committee: Annual Report for 1917." 01ChSea; 1919 *Polk's Seattle City Directory*, 1941; 1919 *CSJ Directory*, xciv.

340 *"did not carry with it"*: BC minutes, Nov. 25, 1919. 03ChSea; "Divine Love always has met": Eddy, *S&H*, 494.

341 *"The work on the first part"*: BC minutes, Dec. 23, 1919. 03ChSea.

[342] "Master to Make Report," *ST*, Mar. 2, 1920, 10; "Christian Science Suit Won by Publishing Company," *SS*, Mar. 6, 1920, 8; "Christian Science Workers Quit Jobs," *SS*, Mar. 17, 1920, 13; "Temporary Editors Named," *ST*, Mar. 27, 1920, 5; "Barred From Entering Suit," *ST*, Mar. 30, 1920, 5.

[343] *"purely metaphysical work"*: BC minutes, Apr. 27, 1920. 03ChSea.

[344] *"final step in our demonstration"*: Clerk, Seventh Church of Christ Scientist to Board of Directors, The First Church of Christ, Scientist, Boston, Mass., Apr. 6, 1920, (Copy). 07ChSea.

[345] *"according to calendar time" "The united thought"*: Clerk, Seventh Church of Christ Scientist to Board of Directors, The First Church of Christ, Scientist, Boston, Mass., Apr. 6, 1920, (Copy), 2. 07ChSea.

[346] *"some opposition developed"*: C.A. Griffith, "Early History and Dedication," 1932, 1. 07ChSea; *"relieve the conditions"*: Norman C. Wilson, Clerk, First Church of Christ, Scientist, Seattle, to the Petitioners, Oct. 28, 1919. From "Minutes of a Meeting Preliminary to the Formation of Seventh Church of Christ, Scientist, in Seattle Held Nov. 7, 1919, at Reddings Hall." 07ChSea; *"hearty approval" "loving cooperation"*: Miss Florence Lewis, Secretary, Fourth Church of Christ, Scientist, Seattle, to the Christian Science Petitioners of Queen Anne Hill, Nov. 4, 1919. From "Minutes of a Meeting Preliminary to the Formation of Seventh Church of Christ, Scientist, in Seattle Held Nov. 7, 1919, at Reddings Hall." 07ChSea.

[347] *"Thanking you"*: "Minutes of a Meeting Preliminary to the Formation of Seventh Church of Christ, Scientist, in Seattle Held Nov. 7, 1919, at Reddings Hall," 5. 07ChSea.

Queen Anne Hall was originally called Reddings Hall.

[348] *"just a simple little notice"*: Membership minutes, Dec. 23, 1919. 07ChSea; *"the latest addition to the number"*: "'Seventh' Church Services," *SS*, Jan. 3, 1920, 9.

[349] *"appropriate and inspiring" "The unselfish contributions"*: Board minutes, Jan 4, 1920. 07ChSea.

[350] *"for the purpose of considering"*: Special meeting of the board, Mar. 29, 1920. 07ChSea.

[351] *"neither animosity nor mere personal attachment"*: Eddy, *Manual*, 40; *"considered at some length"*: Special meetings of the members, Apr. 14, 1920. 07ChSea.

[352] *"these ambiguous, cryptic and insinuating letters"*: Board minutes, May 3, 1920. 07ChSea; *"had enlarged its activities far beyond"*: Board minutes, May 17, 1920. 07ChSea.

[353] *"unified consideration"*: Board minutes, Apr. 19, 1920. 07ChSea.

[354] *"[T]he Building Committee"*: BC minutes, May 11, 1920. 03ChSea.

[355] *"Dear Friends"*: BC minutes, June 1, 1920. 03ChSea.

[356] *"unified support for constructing" "devote its entire effort"*: BC minutes, June 1, 1920. 03ChSea; BC to members, May 29, 1920. 03ChSea; W.L. Moodie to Jean K. Cole,

Aug. 10, 1920. 03ChSea; Bertha E. Fay to Board, June 23, 1920. 03ChSea; Florence Lewis to Board, July 28, 1920. 03ChSea; John R. Edwards to Board, July 7, 1920. 03ChSea; Rubena V. Griffith to Board, Aug. 21, 1920. 03ChSea.

357 *"protective work"*: BC minutes, July 19, 1920. 03ChSea.

358 "Will Dedicate Church," Nov. 20, 1920, *ST*, 5; "Dedicate Science Church on Sunday," *SS*, Nov. 20, 1920, 12.

359 *"a structure worthy of the city"*: Allen H. Armstrong, "Among the Churches: Progress at Seattle, Wash.," *CSS*, Feb. 1901; *"little band of beginners"*: "Progress of Christian Science," *CSJ*, Dec. 1912; *"one of the finest"*: "Science Church to be Dedicated," Nov. 20, 1920, *SS*, 5.

In the 1919 *CSJ* directory, there were 98 listed in Seattle as practitioners. The number of practitioners was consistently increasing during this period. Because of the bycott of the Christian Science Publishing Society, it is impossible to know the exact number of practitioners in Seattle in 1920 from locally available sources. The *CSJ* listing for 1920 is incomplete. *Polk's Seattle City Directory* for 1920 lists 76 practitioners, also an incomplete list.

360 BC to Board, June 2, 1908, BC minutes, 39. 01ChSea.

361 *$80,000*: "Among the Churches, *CSS*, Sept. 12, 1914; "Scientist Church Will Open on June 7," *ST*, June 7, 1914, 8; *"missionary work" at $3400/year*: "The Lectures: Seattle, Wash.," *CSS*, July 29, 1911.

362 *"packed to capacity" "In humble gratitude"*: Playter, 11. 01ChSea. Taken from "Scientist Church Dedicated Simply" article transcript, attributed to the *Seattle P-I*; "New Science Church is Dedicated Simply," Nov. 22, 1920, *SS*.

363 *"The people of this church"*: "The Lectures: Seattle, Wash." *CSS*, Jan. 23, 1909.

364 *"the work of the committee"*: BC minutes, Nov. 22, 1920. 03ChSea.

365 *"unsightly condition"*: BC minutes, Sept. 27, 1920. 03ChSea.

366 *"shall not be dissolved"*: Eddy, *Manual*, 102; *"the feeling of the members"*: BC minutes, Nov. 22, 1920. 03ChSea.

367 *"Faithfully they hammered away"*: Violet Webster Dunham, "Gratitude and Unfoldment," *CSS*, Aug. 3, 1918.

368 *"read understandingly"*: Eddy, *Manual*, 32; *"devote a suitable portion"*: Eddy, *Manual*, 31.

369 "Mrs. George Cole Dies," *ST*, Apr. 23, 1948, 15; "George S. Cole, Attorney, Dies," *ST*, June 26, 1939, 8; *Polk's Seattle City Directories*: 1915, 531. 1916, p. 526. 1917, 537. 1920, 1960; *Membership Roll (Register #1)*, 126. 01ChSea; University District Christian Science Society Membership Minutes, 68. 03ChSea.

370 *"unanimous opinion"*: BC minutes, Jan. 3, 1921. 03ChSea; *"All is well at headquarters"*: Eddy, "To Students," *MW*, 156; *"There is to-day danger"*: Eddy, *S&H*, 135.

[371] *"no doubt must"*: "A Word to the Wise," Eddy, *MW*, 319; "A Word to the Wise," *CSJ*, Dec. 1893.

[372] *"We have had numerous inquiries"*: BC minutes, Mar. 7, 1921. 03ChSea.

[373] *"helpful and inspiring"*: Minutes of Membership Meetings, Mar. 17, 1917 to Dec. 17, 1929, 86. 03ChSea.

[374] *"Actual building"*: Minutes of Board Meetings, Jan. 1917 to July 23, 1922, 254. 03ChSea.

[375] *Joint building fund meeting*: Membership Minutes, 87. 03ChSea.

[376] *"because of a better understanding"*: Membership minutes, Dec. 2, 1919. See also BC minutes, Nov. 25, 1919. 03ChSea.

[377] *"institutions friendly"*: BC minutes, July 6, 1921. 03ChSea.

[378] *"seemingly impossible conditions"*: BC minutes, July 6, 1921. 03ChSea.

[379] *"earnest wish"*: Lantz, Helen Ross to Board of Directors, Third Church of Christ, Scientist, Seattle, July 11, 1921. 03ChSea; *"to avoid curiosity seekers"*: Bell, Laura C. Untitled historical sketch. Feb. 19, 1967. 03ChSea.

[380] *"No large gathering"*: Eddy, *Manual*, 60.

[381] *"Even Nature's voices"*: Gormley, Eileen. "Historical Sketch of Third Church of Christ, Scientist, Seattle, Washington," July 21, 1934, 5-6. 03ChSea.

[382] *"Thy kingdom come"*: Eddy, *Manual*, 41.

[383] *"Our Father which art in heaven"*: Eddy, *S&H*, 16.

[384] *"When the benediction"*: Gormley, Eileen. "Historical Sketch of Third Church of Christ, Scientist, Seattle, Washington," July 21, 1934, 5-6. 03ChSea.

[385] *"how the financial obligations"*: Minutes of Membership Meetings, Mar. 17, 1917 to Dec. 17, 1929, 89. 03ChSea.

[386] *"The ideal church"*: Gormley, Eileen. "Historical Sketch of Third Church of Christ, Scientist, Seattle, Washington," July 21, 1934, 3-4. 03ChSea; Building Committee report to members, June 17, 1919. 03ChSea.

[387] *"The women sold jewelry"*: "History of Third Church of Christ, Scientist, Seattle, Washington," undated, unattributed. 03ChSea.

This historical sketch may have been written in response to the 1932 call for branch church histories by TMC.

[388] *"the women came each night"*: Board notes from interview with Byron Haviland on October 10, 1966. 03ChSea; Membership minutes, July 26, 1922. 03ChSea; BC minutes, July 5, 1921, July 10 and 20, 1922. 03ChSea.

Night watch: The records in the minutes are not clear how long the watch lasted or how it was managed. An untiled historical sketch, dated Feb. 19, 1967, in the files (03ChSea) attributed to Laura C. Bell, using information received from Byron B. Haviland and Mrs. Primm, simply states, "While the church was in process of building, the members took turns sitting in the structure each night, to see that no vandals took any of the building material." Special watch was done on Halloween. BC minutes, Oct. 30, 1922. 03ChSea.

389 *"unsatisfactory"*: Board of Directors to Nunn, Oct. 10, 1926. Third Church of Christ, Scientist, Seattle files; *"inadequate to handle"*: "Edifice Cost $100,000," *ST*, Nov. 11, 1922, 8; *"looking earnestly for Principle"*: BC minutes, Jan. 31, 1922. 03ChSea.

390 *"read understandingly"*: Eddy, *Manual*, 32.

391 *"I soon came to the conclusion"*: Forbes, Ralph E., testimony, *CSJ*, July 1925.

392 Louis E. Scholl, "The Christian Science Controversy," *SS*, Feb. 3, 1922, 6.

393 1922 *Polk's Seattle City Directory*, 736, 1266; "not possible to market these bonds": Board of Directors to Nunn, Oct. 10, 1926. 03ChSea; Desk announcement: Minutes of Membership Meetings, Mar. 17, 1917 to Dec. 17, 1929, 93. 03ChSea.

At least once the sale of bonds for Fifth Church was announced at services at Third Church, as mentioned in BC minutes, Sept. 26, 1921, but for reasons not explained, this prompted objections.

394 *"extremely indefinite"* *"only vague, evasive replies"*: BC minutes, Aug. 12, 1921. 03ChSea; *"a serious error"*: BC minutes, Aug. 22, 1921. 03ChSea; *"numerous unforeseen expenses"*: BC minutes, June 15, 1922. 03ChSea.

395 *"Those of the Committee"*: BC minutes, Aug. 22, 1921. 03ChSea.

396 *"was inclined to take advice"* *"in other hands"*: BC minutes, Nov. 1, 1921. 03ChSea; BC to Dunham, May 21, 1922. 03ChSea.

397 *"the time had come"*: BC minutes, May 18, 1922. 03ChSea.

398 *"sense of burden"* *"were errors which had arisen"*: BC minutes, May 18, 1922. 03ChSea.

399 *"cement construction, finished in brick veneer"*: "Science Church to Open Sunday," *SS*, Nov. 11, 1922, 2; "Edifice Cost $100,000," *ST*, Nov. 11, 1922, 8.

400 "Edifice Cost $100,000," *ST*, Nov. 11, 1922, 8; "Science Church to Open Sunday," *SS*, Nov. 11, 1922, 2; *"The day before the opening"*: BC minutes, Nov. 11, 1922. 03ChSea.

401 *"the spiritual modesty"*: Eddy, *Miscellany*, 356-7.

402 *"the study in detail"* *"required especially careful"* *"removed many"* *"eloquent testimony"*: Chairman [Robert A. DeCou], "Report of the Building Committee of Third Church of Christ, Scientist, May 6, 1919 to March 1, 1923." 03ChSea; *"many problems and trying experiences"*: Board of Directors to Nunn, Oct. 10, 1926. 03ChSea.

403 *"One is greeted"* *"majestic and yet pure"*: Gormley, Eileen. "Historical Sketch of Third Church of Christ, Scientist, Seattle, Washington," July 21, 1934, 7-8. 03ChSea; *"sunshiny interior"*: George Dunham to Helen Ross Lantz, Mar. 15, 1922. 03ChSea; *"shade up gradually"* *"Greek Motif"* *"simplicity and purity"*: Violet Dunham to Helen

Ross Lantz, May 26, 1922. 03ChSea; *"beautifully shaded" "sunshine and soft, fleecy clouds"*: BC minutes, May 18, 1922. 03ChSea.

404 *"not be possible to build"*: Gormley, Eileen. "Historical Sketch of Third Church of Christ, Scientist, Seattle, Washington," July 21, 1934, 4. 03ChSea.

405 *"From the beginning"*: BC minutes, "Final Report of the Building Committee presented by the chairman at Semiannual meeting, June 1923." 03ChSea.

406 *"possibilities"*: BC minutes, June 19, 1923. 03ChSea; *"more than an hour's recital"* and *"truly beautiful and satisfying"*: Building Committee to Board, July 27, 1923. 03ChSea.

Prior to the decision on organ manufacturer, the Third Church building committee heard the organs at the Neptune Theater in the University District, and in Tacoma at the Scottish Rite Temple, a Methodist church, and the Holy Rosary. Apparently not all the members at Third Church were initially pleased with the sound of the new organ, but in this letter from the Building Committee to the Board they suggested W.H. Donley had proved that the problem was the skill of the organist, not the instrument itself.

407 *"Dear Little Wildflower"*: Clerk to George Foote Dunham, May 5, 1922. MBEL (04ChSea) Box 41326 Folder 482905.

Paul J. Jensen was both BC Secretary and Fourth Church Board Clerk.

408 *"get busy"*: Building Committee to George F. Dunham, Oct. 18, 1921. MBEL (04ChSea) Box 41326 Folder 482905; *"a swabbing of hot asphalt"*: Powell, Archibald O, to George Foote Dunham, Jan 4, 1917, 1. MBEL (04ChSea) Box 40739 Folder 172477. Page 2 and 3 of this letter is in MBEL (04ChSea) Box 41326 Folder 482905; William K. Sheldon to Robert A. DeCou, Dec. 7, 1921. 03ChSea.

409 *"all dust and had no paint" "rough-and-ready citizens"*: McDonald, Lucile, "Lawyer on Horseback," *ST*, Feb. 19, 1950, 8; *Roosevelt visit*: "To Meet the President," *Columbia Courier*, May 22, 1903, 5; "Hutson Will Be Deputy Under Sullivan," *ST*, July 8, 1906, 5; "CT Hutson Attorney Dies at 82", *ST*, Dec. 9, 1957, 41; "Mrs. Hutson Succumbs to Lingering Illness," *ST*, Jan. 18, 1914, 12; *daughters*: US Census 1910, Seattle Ward 3, King County, Washington, Roll: T624_1659, 3A. ED 0155, FHL microfilm 1375672.

410 *Hutson's introduction*: "Light of Truth is Lecturer's Topic," *ST*, Sept. 11, 1916, 17; *"Happiness, however interpreted" "For hundreds of years"*: "The Lectures: Seattle, Wash." *CSS*, Nov. 18, 1916.

411 *Roy*: "Roy J. Hutson," *ST*, Nov. 13, 1947, 27; *Polk's Seattle City Directory*, 1918, 979; 1922, 780; *Charles T Hutson, First Reader*: Board minutes, March 21, 1932. MBEL (04ChSea) Box B40738 F166017; *Convention chair*: "They Ignore M'Bride," *ST*, Aug. 21, 1902, 4.

412 Building Committee to Members, Mar. 31, 1922. MBEL (04ChSea) Box 41326 Folder 166432; BC minutes, Aug. 8, 1922. MBEL (04ChSea) Box 40737 Folder 165635; "Motions Affecting the Building Committee As Made At The Quarterly Meeting, Apr. 4, 1922." MBEL (04ChSea) Box 41326 Folder 482905; *Mrs. Clara Jen-*

sen: "Members of Fourth Church of Christ, Scientist, Seattle, Washington," MBEL (04ChSea) Box 40737 Folder 165635; *Secretary: Polk's Seattle City Directory*, 1917, 918. 1922, 908; "Restaurant Men Form State Body," *ST*, July 30, 1920, 12; "Hiram K. Ball," *ST*, Mar. 28, 1951, 38; "Fred Brubaker," *ST*, Apr. 2, 1947, 14; "Ben S. Booth is Dead," *ST*, May 2, 1924, 21.

The Fourth Church Building Committee minutes did not list attendees or typically mention member names. Because of not having access to Board minutes prior to 1923, the exact make-up of the Building Committee for Fourth Church throughout the building project could not be precisely determined from available documents. The documents cited above were the best lists of Fourth Church Building Committee members available at the time of this research.

413 *"unity expressed" "progress harmoniously"*: Violet W. Dunham to Paul J. Jensen, June 15, 1922. MBEL (04ChSea) Box 41326 Folder 482905; *"beautiful edifice is to be"*: Violet W. Dunham to Wm. K. Sheldon, Oct. 20, 1921. MBEL (04ChSea) Box 41326 Folder 482905; "Portrait Profile," *Orlando Sentinel*, Oct. 23, 1966, 143; *"chronic stomach and bowel trouble" "lifelong throat trouble"*: Violet Webster Dunham, *CSS*, May 3, 1924; *"stubborn physical ailment" "steady, persistent effort"*: Dunham, Violet Webster, "Gratitude and Unfoldment," *CSS*, Aug. 3, 1918; *Second Reader at Sixth Church Portland*: George Dunham to Helen Ross Lantz, Feb. 9, 1921. 03ChSea; *"boundless energy" "the original go-girl" "infectious enthusiasm"*: Smith, Ruth. "Profiles: She's Original Go-Girl!" *Orlando Sentinel*, Feb. 11, 1959, A-8.

414 *"joyfully on its way" "to proceed with full speed ahead"*: Building Committee Secretary to Violet W. Dunham, June 14, 1922. MBEL (04ChSea) Box 41326 Folder 482905; BC minutes, June 14, 1922. MBEL (04ChSea) Box 40737 Folder 165635.

415 *"Please hurry plans"*: Paul J. Jensen to George Foot Dunham, June 28, 1922. MBEL (04ChSea) Box 41326 Folder 482905; Violet W. Dunham to Paul J. Jensen, July 3, 1922. MBEL (04ChSea) Box 41326 Folder 482905; *"Am doing all I can"*: Violet W. Dunham to Paul J. Jensen, July 7, 1922. MBEL (04ChSea) Box 41326 Folder 482905.

416 *"a modern motion picture palace" "a blaze of electric lights"*: "Take Lease on Wilkes," *ST*, Apr. 10, 1921, 3; "Seattle Now & Then: The Wilkes Theatre," May 26, 2012, JRSHERRARD, PaulDorpat.com; *"Pending work on its New Church Edifice . . ."*: advertisement, *ST*, July 15, 1922, 9; Fourth Church lecture ad, *ST*, Aug. 2, 1922, 11.

417 *"asked for his version" "every one is satisfied" "Leave it to me"*: BC minutes, July 18, 1922. MBEL (04ChSea) Box 40737 Folder 165635.

418 *"We feel that the work is progressing"*: Violet W. Dunham to Paul J. Jensen, July 17, 1922. MBEL (04ChSea) Box 41326 Folder 482905.

419 *"Where is my little friend George Foot" "unofficially"*: BC to Violet W. Dunham. July 14, 1922. MBEL (04ChSea) Box 41326 Folder 482905.

420 *"He has been detained"*: Violet W. Dunham to Paul J. Jensen, July 26, 1922. MBEL (04ChSea) Box 41326 Folder 482905.

421 Chas. R. Case to Mr. R. W. Van Liew, Aug. 12, 1918. MBEL (04ChSea) Box 41326 Folder 169544.

[422] BC minutes, July 31, 1922. MBEL (04ChSea) Box 40737 Folder 165635; BC minutes, Aug. 7, 1922. MBEL (04ChSea) Box 40737 Folder 165635; "*this will eventually be THE*": BC Secretary to George Foot Dunham, Aug. 7, 1922. MBEL (04ChSea) Box 41326 Folder 482905.

[423] Stein, Alan J. "Interurban Train Service Between Seattle and Tacoma Ends on December 30, 1928," HistoryLink.org Essay 2671, posted Sept. 19, 2000; "*machines*": BC minutes, Aug. 8, 1922. MBEL (04ChSea) Box 40737 Folder 165635.

The party of 10 was Mrs. Hawkins, Mrs. Pratt, Miss Estep, Mr. Russell, Mr. Hutson, Mr. Jensen, Mr. Brubaker, Miss Shriver, Mrs. Goodenough, and Mr. Booth.

[424] BC minutes, Apr. 13, 1921. 03ChSea; McDonald to Dunham, Jan. 3, 1922. MBEL (04ChSea) Box 41326 Folder 482905; BC minutes, May 29, 1922. MBEL (04ChSea) Box 40737 Folder 165635; BC minutes, June 12, 1922. MBEL (04ChSea) Box 40737 Folder 165635; *$150K*: "Hotel Leads New Work," *ST*, Sept. 3, 1922, 12.

[425] "Green River Valley Clay Becomes Architectural Terra Cotta: Meade Pottery and the Northern Clay Company, 1905 to 1927," *White River Journal*, July 1996.

[426] "*the delicate coloring effect*" "*a shade most pleasing to the eye*": BC minutes, Aug. 8, 1922, MBEL (04ChSea) Box 40737 Folder 165635.

[427] Neil McDonald to Charles Hutson, Oct. 30, 1922. MBEL (04ChSea) Box 41326 Folder 482905; BC minutes, Oct. 23, 1922. MBEL (04ChSea) Box 40737 Folder 165635.

[428] "*unostentatious service*": "Cornerstone Is Laid for Science Church," *SS*, Oct 30, 1922.

[429] "*reinstate primitive Christianity*": Eddy, *Manual*, 17. Eddy, *Miscellany*, 46; "*Here I stand*": Eddy, *S&H*, 268.

[430] "*reinstate primitive Christianity*": Eddy, *Manual*, 17; "*The 2nd Century was the great Christian healing era*": Reichert, R.G.C, "Architectural Historiology: Fourth Church of Christ, Scientist, Seattle, Wash.," July 10, 1979. THS; Washington State Department of Archaeology & Historic Preservation (DAHP), "Robert G. Reichert, 1922-1996," dahp.wa.gov/bio-for-robert-g-reichert; Michael C. Houser, "Reichert, Robert G. (1921-1996)," docomomo-wewa.org (Documentation and Conservation of the Modern Movement in Western Washington).

[431] "*cap pulled so low*" "*tough and cool*" "*Marlon Brando's sidekick*": Lacitis, Erik, "'Architecture is just frozen music,'" *ST*, June 8, 1979, A-15; "*Reichert believed that the creation of architecture*": Nicole Demers-Changelo, "Modern Queen Anne," Queen Anne Historical Society (qahistory.org), Aug. 20, 2016; "*independent visionary*" "*I paid for it*": Jennifer Bjorhus, "Robert Reichert's Stark Home Designs Broke All the Rules," *ST*, Jan. 30, 1996, B-3.

[432] "*I religiously don't believe in age*": Lacitis, Erik, "'Architecture is just frozen music,'" *ST*, June 8, 1979, A-15.; "*iconoclast artist*": "Modern Queen Anne," Queen Anne Historical Society (qahistory.org), Aug. 20, 2016; "*I love the orthodox church*": Eddy, *MW*, 111.

433 *Best in the west*: Violet Dunham to Jensen, July 17, 1922. MBEL (04ChSea) Box 41326 Folder 482905; *Financials*: BC minutes, Sept. 11, 1922. MBEL (04ChSea) Box 40737 Folder 165635; "*fog of doubt*": BC minutes, Sept. 18, 1922. MBEL (04ChSea) Box 40737 Folder 165635; *$200K*: "Cornerstone Is Laid for Science Church," *SS*, Oct. 30, 1922.

434 *Vacation*: BC minutes, Nov. 13, 1922. MBEL (04ChSea) Box 40737 Folder 165635; "Wilkes Theatre May Change to Business Block," *ST*, Nov. 18, 1922, 1; "Plan to Remodel Wilkes Theatre for Big Store," *ST*, Nov. 19, 1922, 23.

435 "*offered the most*": BC minutes, Dec. 18, 1922. MBEL (04ChSea) Box 40737 Folder 165635; "*Obviously, Mr. Whittaker*": BC minutes, Oct. 9, 1922. MBEL (04ChSea) Box 40737 Folder 165635; "Charles J. Whittaker," *ST*, Sept. 23, 1951, 39.

Charles J. Whittaker also sold an Austin Organ to Third Church, and was involved in redesign of its organ loft layout. BC minutes, June 5, 1922. 03ChSea

436 Violet Dunham to Jensen, June 28, 1922. MBEL (04ChSea) Box 41326 Folder 482905.

437 "*a pioneer of pioneers in glassmaking*" "*twirled and whirled*" "*As one might say*": "From Sand Bank to Stained-Glass Window," *New York Times*, May 21, 1905, 8; "Proprietors of Dannenhoffer Glass Works," *Brooklyn Eagle*, Dec. 15, 1907, 30; "*the best color producer in the world*": "Johan L. Dannenhoffer Dead," *Brooklyn Eagle*, Nov. 15, 1910, 7.

438 Walter Grutchfield, "Dannenhoffer's Opalescent," WalterGrutchfield.net, 2017; Sandra Herrera, "Bushwick's Historic Opalescent Glass Factory Gets a Rental Makeover & Teaser Site," CityRealty.com, Dec. 13, 2017; "*acceptable, artistic job*": BC minutes, Nov. 6, 1922. MBEL (04ChSea) Box 40737 Folder 165635; David L. Povey to Building Committee, Jan. 15, 1923. MBEL (04ChSea) Box 40739 Folder 172477; "*so often*" "*sometimes referred to as 'Christian Science glass'*": George Dunham to Helen Ross Lantz, Feb. 17, 1922. 03ChSea.

Povey at Third Church: Third Church received art glass bids and design concepts from five companies. Bids ranged from $764 to $1490, with David L. Povey being the highest bidder by far. On the decision to use Povey: "The Povey designs were so far superior to those of their competitors and the prices really lower when quality was compared that the Committee immediately agreed on the Portland firm." BC minutes, May 1, 1922. 03ChSea. When Povey brought glass samples and three designs for BC committee to consider, they wrote, "The Committee had no trouble in selecting the glass for the main field of the windows, a beautifully shaded and mottled effect in amber and opal, suggesting sunshine and soft, fleecy clouds." When Povey later presented a more elaborate design that increased the cost by another $200, for a total of $1,700, the committee immediately voted unanimously to accept it. BC minutes, May 18, 1922. 03ChSea. However, one BC member "warned them of the necessity of keeping after Mr. Povey to insure completion of the job in time." Later George F. Dunham reported "slow progress at Povey plant." BC minutes, Aug. 29, 1922, Sept. 15, 1922. 03ChSea.

[439] *Belknap*: BC minutes, Feb. 5, 1923. MBEL (04ChSea) Box 40737 Folder 165635; Povey Bros. Glass Company contract with Fourth Church, 1923. MBEL (04ChSea) Box 40739 Folder 172477; "*Amber Flesh and Opal*": George F. Dunham to Dannenhoffer Glass Works, Feb. 19, 1923. MBEL (04ChSea) Box 41326 Folder 482905.

[440] *Driving*: George F. Dunham to Paul J. Jensen, Apr. 21, 1923. MBEL (04ChSea) Box 41326 Folder 482905; *56,000*: *Orlando Sentinel*, Nov. 4, 1928, 25; "*proper proportions of raw umber*": George Foote Dunham to Paul J. Jensen, Feb. 22, 1923. MBEL (04ChSea) Box 41326 Folder 482905.

When Violet W. Dunham came with George from Portland to Seattle, they sometimes made the trip in their new Hupmobile sedan. In just a few years time, they would log more than 56,000 miles in their Hupmobile, criss-crossing the continent for George's architecture work.

[441] Dannenhoffer Glass to Povey Bros. Glass Works, May 4, 1923. MBEL (04ChSea) Box 40739 Folder 172477; George F. Dunham to Charles T. Hutson, June 1, 1923. MBEL (04ChSea) Box 41326 Folder 482905; Chuck Holmgren, "the Panama Canal," University of Virginia, American Studies Program, 2002; George F. Dunham to Paul J. Jensen, June 11, 1923. MBEL (04ChSea) Box 41326 Folder 482905; George F. Dunham to Paul J. Jensen, June 18, 1923. MBEL (04ChSea) Box 41326 Folder 482905; Portland City Directory, 1921, 1031; George F. Dunham to Charles T. Hutson, June 23, 1923. MBEL (04ChSea) Box 41326 Folder 482905.

[442] "*cold, drizzling rain*": "Roses Decorate Transport When President Sails," *ST*, July 5, 1923, 1; "*driving, heavy rain*": "Tacoma Crowd Thrills Harding," *ST*, July 6, 1923, 4; "President Harding the Cadillac He Used in Tacoma," *ST*, July 8, 1923, 35.

[443] "Ships Given Positions," *ST*, July 24, 1923, 4.

[444] "*The Wonder City*": The Exchange Club of Seattle ad, *ST*, July 27, 1923, 6; "*Seattle Town, Seattle Town*": "The Story of 'Seattle Town'—and its Author," *ST*, July 29, 1923, 69; Jonathan Shipley, "Celebrating Harold Weeks with Some Ragtime Ditties," Town Crier: The Town Hall Seattle Blog, Nov. 15, 2018; Membership Roll, 236. 01ChSea; "School Leaders Here," *ST*, July 24, 1923, 13; "'Seattle Spirt' Is 50 Years Old: Slogan Has Been City's Creed," *ST*, July 1, 1923, 2; "*the loveliest city*": C.B. Blethen, "Seattle: Loveliest Place in the Whole World in Which to Live," *ST*, July 1, 1923, 1; "*city's growing supremacy*": *ST*, July 1, 1923, 1.

[445] Board minutes, Aug. 7, 1923. MBEL (04ChSea) Box 40737 Folder 164854; Board minutes, Aug. 6, 1923. 03ChSea; Board minutes, Aug. 8, 1923. 07ChSea; "*shared in the nation's sorrow*": "Seattle Churches Hold Services," *ST*, Aug. 10, 1923, 1, 4; *Order of services*: "Memorial Service," *CSJ*, Oct. 1901; Also Eddy, *Miscellany*, 290; "Seattle Halts Five Minutes in Harding's Honor," *ST*, Aug. 10, 1923, 1;"*from sea to sea*": "Last Rites Are Given Dead Chief At Marion," *ST*, Aug. 10, 1923, 1.

[446] BC minutes, Aug. 14, 1923. MBEL (04ChSea) Box 40737 Folder 165635; *2025 ½ feet*: Contract for Church Furniture, Feb. 26, 1923. MBEL (04ChSea) Box 40739 Folder 172477; *Concerns*: George F. Dunham to Paul J. Jensen, July 15, 1923. MBEL (04ChSea) Box 41326 Folder 482905; *Expedite*: BC Secretary to Frederick & Nelsons, July 6, 1923. MBEL (04ChSea) Box 41326 Folder 169847; *Pew problems*: BC to George

F. Dunham, Sept. 8, 1923. MBEL (04ChSea) Box 41326 Folder 482905; *Misread blue prints*: George F. Dunham to Paul J. Jensen, Oct. 1, 1923. MBEL (04ChSea) Box 41326 Folder 482905; *Opening*: BC Secretary to George F. Dunham, Aug. 15, 1923. MBEL (04ChSea) Box 41326 Folder 482905.

447 "Fourth Church Ready," *ST*, Sept. 22, 1923, 5; Charles I. Ohrenstein lecture ad, *ST*, Sept. 27, 1923, 6; *30 lectures*: Board minutes, May 15, 1923. MBEL (04ChSea) Box 40737 Folder 164854.

The Christian Science lectures during opening week at Fourth Church of Christ, Scientist, Seattle, were two of the six downtown lectures that Fourth Church sponsored that year. In total, thirty were held in Seattle in 1923. The Capitol Hill branch was scheduled to host ten downtown lectures in addition to the eight lectures that all the Seattle churches were sponsoring jointly that year.

448 *Sheild lectures*: Jacob S. Shield lecture ad, *SS*, Mar. 20, 1915, 3; "Capacity Crowd Expected," *SS*, Mar. 20, 1915, 7; "Christian Science Speaker's Theme," *ST*, Mar. 22, 1915, 8; *Ohrenstein lectures*: "The Lectures," CSS, Apr. 13, 1918; ad, *SS*, Nov. 1, 1917, 6; ad, *ST*, Sept. 27, 1923, 8; "*Christian Science is no more for one*": Jacob S. Shield, "Christian Science and the Jewish People," *CSJ*, Feb. 1902; C. I. Ohrenstein, "A Plea For Fair Judgement," *CSS*, Apr. 16, 1904; *10% Jewish*: Rolf Swensen, "'Israel's Return to Zion': Jewish Christian Scientists in the United States, 1888-1925," *Journal of Religion & Society*, Vol. 15, 2013, 8; Anna Friendlich, "Israel's Return to Zion," *CSJ*, Feb. 1905; "Contributions to Jewish Fund Growing," Feb. 20, 1916, *ST*, 23.

449 "*a humdinger of a success*": BC Secretary to George Foot Dunham, Sept. 26, 1923. MBEL (04ChSea) Box 41326 Folder 482905; "*the source of endless praise*": BC Secretary to Povey Bros., Sept. 26, 1923. MBEL (04ChSea) Box 40739 Folder 172477.

450 "*Using a Biblical term*": BC Secretary to Neil McDonald, Oct. 4, 1923. MBEL (04ChSea) Box 41326 Folder 482905.

451 "*It is our pleasure to say*": BC Secretary to George F. Dunham, Oct. 5, 1923. MBEL (04ChSea) Box 41326 Folder 482905.

452 "*I am most grateful for your words*": George F. Dunham to Paul J. Jensen, Oct. 12, 1923. MBEL (04ChSea) Box 41326 Folder 482905.

453 *$300,000*: "Fourth Church Ready," *ST*, Sept. 22, 1923, 5.

454 "Minutes of First Meeting of Special Committee to Report on Finances etc," Nov. 21, 1923. 07ChSea; Finance Committee to Board of Seventh Church of Christ, Scientist, Seattle, Nov. 30, 1923, 4. 07ChSea; "*Giving does not impoverish*": Eddy, *S&H*, 79.

455 "*to manifest the progress befitting*" "*unjust*" "*the expense involved*": Finance Committee to Board of Seventh Church of Christ, Scientist, Seattle, Nov. 30, 1923. 07ChSea.

Example reader salaries, monthly: 1908 1CCS Seattle First $100, Second $75 (Financial ledger, 195. 01ChSea). 1922 3CCS Seattle First $60, Second $40 (Board minutes, Dec. 4, 1922. 03ChSea).

[456] *"earnest and intensive work" "repeated appeals for money" "a plan that encourages"*: John Gibson, BC Chair to Board, Dec. 10, 1923. 07ChSea.

[457] *"the walls of salvation"*: Anna Friendlich, "Church Building in Christian Science," *CSS*, Apr. 29, 1922; *"rise above the temporal, mortal viewpoint"*: Ella W. Hoag, "Church Building," *CSS*, Sept. 23, 1922; *"The question, Are we ready to build?"*: Mildred Spring Case, "Church Building," *CSS*, Nov. 3, 1923.

[458] US Census 1920, Seattle, King County, Washington. Roll: T625_192T, 4A, ED 144; US Census 1910, Seattle Ward 9, King County, Washington. Roll: T624_1661, 1B, ED 0163. FHL microfilm 1375674. *Polk's Seattle City Directory*, 1915, 728, 729. 1917, 740. 1919, 793. 1922, 1573; *"I knew that God's child"*: Anna O. Gibson and John S. Gibson, testimony, *CSJ*, Sept. 1914.

[459] *"Are you as individuals ready"*: John Gibson, Chair BC, Jan. 9, 1924. 07ChSea.

[460] *Meeting minutes, Board and Membership 6/21/20 to 4/21/26, Membership Meetings 5/12/26 to 6/10/41*, 91, 92, 104-108, 110, 119. *Purchase of lot*: Seventh Church Treasurer to L.C. Downing, Dec. 4, 1922. 07ChSea; Charles A. Griffith, "Early History and Dedication," 1932, 3. 07ChSea; *Meeting minutes, Board and Membership 6/21/20 to 4/21/26 Membership Meetings 5/12/26 to 6/10/41*, 110, 112. 07ChSea.

[461] *"overwhelming sentiment" "time for thoughtful deliberation" "a growing conservatism" "it has come to our attention"*: John Gibson, BC Chairman, to President, [undated, est. Oct. 13, 1922]. 07ChSea.

[462] *Bungalow to seat 430*: List of motions from membership meetings, hand-dated 1922. 07ChSea; Gibson to President, Aug. 16, 1922. 07ChSea; *Membership*: Member Roll (Register #1), 228. 01ChSea. Admitted Dec. 9, 1921; *Approval: Meeting minutes, Board and Membership 6/21/20 to 4/21/26, Membership Meetings 5/12/26 to 6/10/41*, 124, 129. 07ChSea; *Sketches*: John Gibson to President, Aug. 16, 1922. 07ChSea.

[463] *"afford simple and suitable"*: John Gibson to president, [undated, est. Oct. 13, 1922]. 07ChSea.

[464] Meeting minutes, Board and Membership 6/21/20 to 4/21/26, Membership Meetings 5/12/26 to 6/10/41, 142. 07ChSea; Edith Lent, Building Committee Clerk to Members, Dec. 12, 1922. 07ChSea.

[465] *"earthquake, tidal wave, and fire"*: "Annual Meeting of The Mother Church," CSS, June 7, 1924; *"contributing very generously"*: Members meeting minutes, Nov. 14, 1923, Meeting minutes, Board and Membership 6/21/20 to 4/21/26, Membership Meetings 5/12/26 to 6/10/41, 175. 07ChSea.

[466] *"Are you as individuals ready"*: John Gibson, Chair BC, Jan. 9, 1924. 07ChSea.

[467] *"prominent and slightly corner" "It is a very undesirable corner" "church surroundings"*: BC to Board, May 31, 1924. 07ChSea.

[468] *"Your Building Committee"*: BC to Board, June 2, 1924. 07ChSea.

[469] Membership meeting, Sept. 22, 1924. 07ChSea. Minutes, 202; BC to Board, Dec. 5, 1925. 07ChSea.

470 *"that church members give prayerful consideration"*: Minutes, 215. 07ChSea.

471 *"helpful remarks"* *"lovingly presented"*: Minutes, Jan. 19, 1925, 221. 07ChSea.

472 Member minutes, Mar. 12, 1925, 229, 230. 07ChSea.

473 Member minutes, Apr. 30, 1925, 240. 07ChSea.

474 Member minutes, Dec. 28, 1925, 285. Oct. 16, 1925, 258. Nov 16, 1925, 259. 07ChSea; *$5700*: Griffith, "Early History and Dedication," 1932, 6.

475 *"It is with deep gratitude"*: Minutes, Jan. 27, 1926, 273. 07ChSea.

476 *BC Chair*: Board minutes, Jan. 13, 1926, 271. 07ChSea; Clerk to Oscar Marcus Kulien, Jan. 14, 1926. 07ChSea; Ad, *ST*, Mar. 29, 1926, 24; "Group of Brick Homes in Course of Erection," *ST*, May 2, 1926, 81; Ad, *ST*, Nov. 30, 1927, 2; "Triangle of Avenues Will Be Illuminated," *ST*, Feb. 28, 1929, 31; "Kulien Warehouse Fully Rented by John Davis," *ST*, Oct. 20, 1929, 36; "Site Purchased For Five-Story Kulien Project," *ST*, May 11, 1930, 32.

477 *Church Extension*: Minutes, Dec. 30, 1925, 268. 07ChSea; *Camp Lewis*: Minutes, Sept. 21, 1925, 250. 07ChSea; *Asst Supt SS*: Minutes, Dec. 11, 1925, 262. 07ChSea; *Board chair*: Minutes, Apr. 22, 1925, 234. 07ChSea; *Handled sale*: Minutes, May 4, 1925, 235. 07ChSea; *BC since 1924*: Clerk to William H. Somers, Apr. 2, 1924. 07ChSea.

478 *Design criteria*: Minutes, Mar. 4, 1926, 280, 281. 07ChSea; *Approval*: Minutes, Mar. 25, 1926, 283. Minutes, Apr. 5, 1926, 290. 07ChSea; *Revisit architect*: Minutes, Jan. 7, 1926, 287. 07ChSea.

479 "Seattle Gets Beauty Touches: City Architect Plans With Care," *ST*, July 13, 1919, 15; Daniel Riggs Huntington, Sr., testimony, *CSS*, Mar. 11, 1961; Minutes, 1920 to 1926, 273, 274, 278, 281. 07ChSea.

480 *"after lengthy discussions"*: BC to board, Mar. 31, 1926. 07ChSea; John Gibson, BC Chair, to President, [undated. Estimated Oct. 13, 1922], 07ChSea; *Thomas selection*: BC to Board, Mar. 31, 1926. 07ChSea.

Although first names were not used in records, the candidate architects may have been Frank Allen, Louis Baeder, Frank H. Fowler, and Peirce Horrocks.

481 *AIA*: Ochsner, ed. *Shaping Seattle Architecture: A Historical Guide to the Architects*, 129; Walt Crowley, "Pike Place Market (Seattle) – Thumbnail History," July 29, 1999. HistoryLink.org Essay 1602; "A World of Watercolor: Architect, 81, Exhibits Art," *ST*, Aug. 2, 1951, 45; "European Art Works Will Be Shown," *ST*, Dec. 2, 1923, 35; Mike Dillon, "Architect Profile: Harlan Thomas," *City Living Seattle* (online), Feb. 21, 2012.

482 *"the origins of ecclesiastic design"*: Jeff Williams (great-grandson of Harlan and Edith Thomas), email to Cindy Safronoff, Nov. 20, 2018; *Studying since 1916*: Dorothy Thomas Williams, testimony, *CSS*, Aug. 22, 1936; *Joined 1920*: Mabel W. Randall to members, May 4, 1920. 07ChSea; Member register, 35. 07ChSea.

DEDICATION

[483] R.G.C. Reichert, "Architectural Historiology: Fourth Church of Christ, Scientist, Seattle, Wash." July 10, 1979 (unpublished), 4. THS; "*Early Christian Revival*": Sally B. Woodbridge and Roger Montgomery, *A Guide to Architecture in Washington State: An Environmental Perspective*, (University of Washington Press: Seattle and London), 200; "Give Me 5 – FiveFaves," *ST*, Feb. 10, 2008, S4; Charles Griffith, "Early History and Dedication," 1932, 4, 5. 07ChSea.

[484] *5 bids*: Preliminary Report of Building Committee of Seventh Church of Christ, Scientist, Seattle, July 28, 1926. 07ChSea; "C. W. Carkeek Dies Suddenly At Home," *ST*, Dec. 13, 1928, 4; "Carkeek Dedication To Be Held Aug. 24," *ST*, Aug. 14, 1929, 4.

[485] *Slides*: Minutes, May 17, 1926, 296. 07ChSea; "Christian Scientists Start New Church," *ST*, Aug. 22, 1926, 56; "*seating capacity was taxed to the utmost*": Charles Griffith, "Early History and Dedication," 1932, 4. 07ChSea; "*great numbers were turned away*": Minutes, approved June 12, 1928, 13. 07ChSea.

[486] *$2000 overrun*: Jan. 10, 1927 statement, 07ChSea; $55,000: Minutes, Dec. 14, 1926, approved June 14, 1927, 6. 07ChSea.

[487] "*an amount that would have staggered*": Charles Griffith, "Early History and Dedication," 1932, 6. 07ChSea.

[488] *First Reader*: Minutes, Dec. 11, 1928, 17. 07ChSea.

[489] The historical sketch referred to as Playter gave an unusual level of description about Armstrong, recounting that in San Jose, he healed a woman dying of consumption who was brought to him on a stretcher. She quickly recovered, took class instruction immediately, and became a Christian Science practitioner.

[490] "Memorial Service Held For Scientist Teacher," *ST*, Feb. 5, 1929, 3. "Armstrong Funeral Set For Sunday Afternoon," *ST*, Feb. 1, 1929; *Polk's Seattle City Directory*, 1926, 237. 1922, 287; 1920 US Census, Seattle, King, Washington, Roll T625_1930, 4B, ED 297.

[491] *Ronald Station*: Frederick Bird, "29 Miles over 29 Years: The Seattle-Everett Interurban Railway, 1910-1939," Snohomish County History Series, May 2000, 3.

[492] *Seattle churches*: Polk's Seattle City Directory, 1929, 1999-2002; "*Instead of damning it*": Louis E. Scholl, *CSS*, Sept. 25, 1920; "People's Church is Formed Here," *ST*, Sept. 27, 1919, 5.

[493] "*imposing skyscraper*": "Shafer Building Boosts District," *ST*, July 6, 1924,14; "Shafer Building is Attractive Addition," *ST*, July 26, 1925, 31.

[494] *Wells bldg. RR*: "Church History," Oct. 23, 1967, 1, 2. 07ChSea.

[495] "Structures in New District Rise Fast," *ST*, Apr. 27, 1913, 28.

[496] *Oct. 1928*, "*frequented principally*": Playter, 16; *Maynard RR staff*: Board minutes, Apr. 13, 1932, and Dec. 5, 1932. 03ChSea.

In 1932, the Maynard Building Reading Room Committee appointed Mr. O. W. Parsons of First Church as Assistant Librarian, Mr. Geo Reams of Third Church as

First Assistant Substitute, and Mr. H. Armstrong of Fifth Church as Second Asst. Substitute; Later that year Mrs. Mary Lewis was appointed a Substitute.

[497] *Cities with joint CSRRs in 1929*: Chicago, Denver, Detroit, Kansas City, Los Angeles, London, Minneapolis, Oakland, Philadelphia, Portland, San Francisco, and Saint Louis.

[498] "Society: Mrs. McGilvra Gives Box Party," *ST*, Dec. 27, 1908, 2; "Society," *ST*, Dec. 23, 1908, 11; "Grand Opera Season," *ST*, Apr. 4, 1913, 27; "Fashionable Audience Fills Theatre Final Night of Grand Opera," *ST*, Apr. 6, 1913, 31; "Society," *ST*, June 9, 1914, 12; Robert C. Nesbit, *"He Built Seattle": A Biography of Judge Thomas Burke*. University of Washington Press, Seattle, 1961, 55, 192, 407; *"Seattle's First Citizen"*: "Historian Lauds Judge Burke," *ST*, Dec. 5, 1925, 3; "Builders Finish Foundation for 20-Ton Statue," *ST*, Nov. 17, 1929, 9.

[499] "Memorial Service Held For Scientist Teacher," *ST*, Feb. 5, 1929, 3. "Armstrong Funeral Set For Sunday Afternoon," *ST*, Feb. 1, 1929.

Index

Made in the USA
Monee, IL
05 November 2020